VICTOR FELDBRILL

To Mr Argue,

VICTOR FELDBRILL

Canadian Conductor
Extraordinaire

With thanks for your support n the "Friends

WALTER PITMAN

Walter Pitman

DUNDURN PRESS
TORONTO

Editor: Allison Hirst
Design: Courtney Horner
Printer: Transcontinental

Library and Archives Canada Cataloguing in Publication

Pitman, Walter
    Victor Feldbrill : Canadian conductor extraordinaire / by Walter Pitman.

Includes index.
Issued also in an electronic format.
ISBN 978-1-55488-768-2

    1. Feldbrill, Victor, 1924-. 2. Conductors (Music)--Canada--Biography.
I. Title.

ML422.F312P68 2010   784.2092   C2010-902447-8

1   2   3   4   5   14   13   12   11   10

We acknowledge the support of the **Canada Council for the Arts** and the **Ontario Arts Council** for our publishing program. We also acknowledge the financial support of the **Government of Canada** through the **Canada Book Fund** and **The Association for the Export of Canadian Books**, and the **Government of Ontario** through the **Ontario Book Publishers Tax Credit program**, and the **Ontario Media Development Corporation**.

Care has been taken to trace the ownership of copyright material used in this book. The author and the publisher welcome any information enabling them to rectify any references or credits in subsequent editions.

J. Kirk Howard, President

Printed and bound in Canada.
www.dundurn.com

Dundurn Press
3 Church Street, Suite 500
Toronto, Ontario, Canada
M5E 1M2

Gazelle Book Services Limited
White Cross Mills
High Town, Lancaster, England
LA1 4XS

Dundurn Press
2250 Military Road
Tonawanda, NY
U.S.A. 14150

To my wife, Ida, my partner for over half a century

CONTENTS

Preface   9

Acknowledgements   13

Chapter 1   Beginnings   16

Chapter 2   The Harbord Collegiate Experience   34

Chapter 3   *The Navy Show*   57

Chapter 4   Abroad   73

Chapter 5   The Last Hurrah   89

Chapter 6   The War and Zelda Mann   109

Chapter 7   Transition   129

Chapter 8   Becoming a Conductor — A Work in Progress   145

Chapter 9   Building a Reputation   165

Chapter 10   The Road to Winnipeg   182

Chapter 11   The Halcyon Years   197

Chapter 12   "I Should Have Left!"   221

Chapter 13   Louis Riel and the World of Opera   245

Chapter 14   Inspiring the Young   267

Chapter 15   Toronto — A Return   285

Chapter 16   Have Baton, Will Travel   309

Chapter 17   An Invitation to Japan   327

Chapter 18   The Far East   340

Chapter 19   Assisting Canadian Orchestras   355

Chapter 20   Celebration, Despair, and Retrospection   381

                Notes   405

                Index   423

PREFACE

Victor Feldbrill has spent some sixty years on the orchestral conducting podiums of virtually every concert hall across Canada, as well as several in the United Kingdom, Europe, and Asia. He has led all of the major and many of the minor symphony orchestras of his native land and built a formidable reputation in Japan, the United Kingdom, the Philippines, the former Soviet Union, the Czech Republic, and China.

His career has been marked by honours bestowed by his country (Officer of the Order of Canada), by the province in which he was born and where he worked over many decades (Order of Ontario), and by the most significant orchestral performance venue in the city of Toronto, where he has lived most of his life (Roy Thomson Hall Award). In his mind the most prestigious honour he has received is the Canadian League of Composers' Award, which was presented to him in 1967. It was given in recognition of his promotion of Canadian music — the only such recognition ever presented to an orchestral conductor. The fact that the latter award came from his composer colleagues and friends in appreciation of his intense commissioning and performing of contemporary Canadian works made it particularly welcome and appropriate as well as unique.

Victor Feldbrill grew up in "The Ward," the late-nineteenth-century Jewish ghetto community in the centre of Toronto. His parents were poor and sacrificed much to provide him with at least a modicum of preparation as a violinist. The fact that this local Canadian boy rose from a humble home to become an orchestral conductor, and even more so that he achieved this rank from a membership in the string section of the Toronto Symphony Orchestra (TSO) — which he was to lead and devote some six decades of service to — is quite striking. This is because, normally, the tradition in symphony orchestras is that players do not move up in an orderly fashion even to assume sectional leadership within symphonic ensembles — replacement of leadership is more likely to be sought and found in other orchestras. Thus it is a rare event, indeed, for a player to be appointed a conductor in an ensemble in which he or she has performed.

Victor's career as a conductor was fashioned during the years when being a prominent Canadian citizen and seeking a leadership role in the entertainment industry could be perceived as virtually unprecedented. Canada in the mid-twentieth century still reflected the lack of confidence displayed by a colonial society in which leadership in the professions and business was rarely offered to any but members of the motherland's elite or to pre-eminent figures from other European countries. This assured that the aspirant was born and trained outside the colony and had gained pre-eminence in the most prominent centres from which classical music had emerged in past centuries.

Victor Feldbrill's determination to present a large number of newly composed Canadian works was considered strange behaviour indeed at the time. Yet it means that today there remains an incredible history of composition available on compact disc and vinyl and remembered by thankful composers and appreciative audiences. This collection is a national treasure that will inspire the increasing numbers of composers determined to create a body of "serious" or contemporary classical music, compositions that reveal what it means to be simultaneously a Canadian and a world citizen.

New generations of music lovers are recognizing how important it is for any country aspiring to sovereignty and a role in the world to produce music that heralds its existence and celebrates its strengths and its values. Feldbrill's legacy will be continuously enhanced as both scholars and performers take advantage of a rich, vast spectrum of composition that now exists and continues to grow.

Feldbrill developed an interest in performing and teaching beyond Canada's borders later in life, He spent a large part of his mature years in the 1980s in Japan, and on tour in the former Soviet Union, the Czech Republic, China, and the Philippines. As a result of the work of this extraordinary figure, Canadian musical creativity was recognized abroad. Music critics and artists in these countries had never realized that in the mid-twentieth century there was a cultural revolution taking place in a land occupying the upper half of the North American continent. A host of composers, including Harry Somers, Harry Freedman, and R. Murray Schafer, inspired by the example and influence of John Weinzweig, were producing splendid music that deserved the attention of the world of orchestral and choral music-making.[1]

Yet Victor never aspired to become an international figure with the intensity necessary to achieve such a role. He was frankly unwilling to be "marketed" in such a way that his values would be diminished and his personal and professional relationships damaged. He wanted to perform in his native land, play music composed by its own citizens, and inspire future generations to listen to and perform that music.

Further, it could be said that Victor's commitment to the promotion of great musical performance for the specific benefit of children and youth, both in Toronto and Winnipeg, over many decades, was a particular gift to the future well-being of new listeners who would become mature audiences. As well, his commitment to the training of young ensemble musicians ensured that many would become the occupants of chairs in the Canadian orchestras he continued to serve as guest conductor. Feldbrill realized the need to nurture young people on the best music of the past if new contemporary Canadian music was to be composed, performed, and appreciated. He emphasized throughout his life the fact that contemporary music had to be both composed and performed as an essential element of any healthy and mature culture.

Even for classical music enthusiasts, contemporary composition was not a popular cause to espouse. The sounds did not arouse familiarity, expected harmony, or tuneful expression. Victor Feldbrill understood that without the continuous outreach by the purveyors of "serious" music, the tendency toward triviality and titillation of a "pop" culture would bury the glory of past and present Canadian musical presentation. The classical forms of music that expressed the full richness of the nation's cultural expression must be treasured. For that insight and commitment, every Canadian music lover should be introduced to Victor Feldbrill and his work. That is the purpose of this book.

Victor Feldbrill's career did not follow the pattern of most symphonic conductors. Normally an aspirant to the podium of a symphony orchestra spends decades in preparation for such an elevation. The tendency is for conductors to reach this mountaintop as the climax of their careers and then retire decades later as conductor emeriti amidst spasms of recognition and adoration from all sides. That is the expectation placed upon the career patterns of the European and American symphonic conductors by media and colleagues. But Victor was a Canadian and his career pattern was in sharp contrast to these norms.[2] He achieved that perceived height of orchestral leadership as a conductor of a major ensemble at a very young age but became convinced that there were other goals he wished to pursue. These related to the creation and strengthening of a Canadian symphonic repertoire and an increased Canadian-born and trained participation in the orchestral life of his country, as well as the need for developing new and younger audiences and widening the reach of the symphonic orchestra in every community he touched. Without some success in achieving these outcomes he believed that the musical heritage of his beloved Canada was at risk. These were the goals to which Victor wished to focus his attention, and he did so for the rest of his long career. In making this extraordinary commitment to music, its makers, and the young people, he would ensure its future.

Victor had a capable and devoted companion who became his wife, his support, his mentor, his confidante, his ever-present colleague, and the mother of his children … Zelda Mann. No account of Victor's career could be complete without the recognition of her central role in his success.

ACKNOWLEDGEMENTS

In the research that accompanies such a volume, there are a host of people who have made a considerable contribution.

First, my wife and children have contributed their wisdom and caring to this project. Ida has read every word several times over as has my daughter, Anne. Both Wade and Mark have ensured that disasters in the technological mysteries of the computer have been avoided. In the latter stages, I was assisted by my grandson, an Ottawa University student, Jared Davidson, who provided valuable guidance in manuscript editing.

Once again, I must thank those at the York University Archives who have not stinted in their efforts to secure Victor Feldbrill's papers and organize them to my timetable. Suzanne Dubeau has been my main contact over these years but the entire staff deserves my deepest appreciation. In preparing this volume I was also dependent on the records of the Toronto Symphony Orchestra and it was the volunteer archivist, John Dunn, who assisted me beyond all I could have expected. Thank you also to the TSO's director of artistic administration, Loie Fallis, who ensured that I had access.

As always, my experiences throughout the publication process of this book have been made pleasant by the professionalism of those at Dundurn Press, from the office of the CEO, Kirk Howard, and his colleague, Beth Bruder, to those who have contributed so much to its production, especially publicist Marta Warner, editors Shannon Whibbs and Allison Hirst, and designer Courtney Horner.

Throughout the entire process, Victor has given countless hours to being interviewed, as has the Feldbrill family, his present companion Mae Bernstein, daughters Debbi and Aviva, sister Eileen, along with others whose knowledge of these events was essential.

Then there were the sixty or seventy individuals who were contacted by email, by telephone, and in some cases, in person. All gave their time and perceptions without restraint. Listing them in a paragraph so inadequately displays their contribution, but appropriate introductions would fill another volume.

The individuals listed below were major contributors but there were others whose comments were invaluable but have been necessarily omitted: Andrea Alexander, Trish Baldwin, Douglas Bairstow, John Beckwith, Elizabeth Bihl, Ruth Budd, Howard Cable, Joseph Caron, Lawrence Cherney, Esther Cole, Robert Cooper, Johnny Cowell, Lori Davies, Victor Davies, Peggy Dettweiler, Takani Egami, James Ehnes, Angela Elster, Glyn Evans, Mary Lou Fallis, Carol Fitzpatrick, Ann Cooper Gay, Errol Gay, Jerrold Gerbrecht, Evelyn Greenberg, Klemi Hambourg, Joanne Harada, Rosemary Hazelton, Harcus Hennigar, Walter Homburger, Harry Hurwitz, Morry Kernerman, William Krehm, Patricia Kreuger, John Lawson, Leon Major, James Manishen, Christmann Mieke, Mary Morrison, Ken Murphy, Nancy Nelson, Kazushi Ono, Ron Polinski, Jackie Poplack, John Reeves, William Richardson, Roxalana Roslak, Val Saunders, Ezra Schabas, Robert Sirman, Stanley Solomon, James Spragge,

Steven Staryk, Leonard Stone, Janet Stubbs, Stella Sung, Gwen Thompson, Patricia Wardrop, Joan Watson, John Weinzweig, Nancy Westaway, Lee Willingham, and Kenneth Winters.

Not included in this list are the dozens, yea, hundreds of casual conversations with individuals who were members of Victor's audiences, mainly in Toronto, but as well in many other Canadian cities. Their insight was essential in weighing the role this individual played over so many decades.

In spite of all this assistance, there will be errors and omissions which will be regarded as unforgivable. I take all responsibility for them and express my sorrow in advance.

CHAPTER 1

Beginnings

The surge of cultured, energetic, and artistically inclined Jewish immigrants that took place in the first years of the twentieth century changed the city of Toronto, the province of Ontario, and the Canadian nation forever.

York, as the municipality was first called in late-eighteenth-century British North America, bore the sudden arrival of immigrants from other less amenable areas of the world throughout its history. Indeed, thousands of Irish arrived to escape the poverty and destitution of their homeland in the first half of the nineteenth century as a result of the Irish Potato Famine. That event certainly changed the demography of Upper Canada, later Ontario, which had up to that point revealed a dominant presence of Loyalists from the thirteen colonies, who, after suffering the indignities foisted upon them by their revolutionary neighbours, found a happier life on the north shores of the St. Lawrence. At the time, the area was largely occupied by the French-speaking inhabitants, members of the old French Empire that remained after the Seven Years' War of the mid 1800s. As a result, many of these colonists, anxious to serve a British king, had travelled west to occupy lands on the north shore of Lake Ontario, an area already settled by a sprinkling of French-speaking former soldiers and their families. This was the start of the town that would become known as York, and later Toronto. By the end of the twentieth century, Toronto, with its two and a half million people, had the miraculous reputation of being the most multicultural municipality in the world — a matter of distinct pride in a country that in the nineteenth and twentieth centuries had opened its doors to people from every corner of the planet.

The population continued to increase in Toronto during the nineteenth century, with most coming from the United Kingdom, largely Scots and English settlers. By the last years of that century, the Czarist Russian Empire was proceeding through a period of increased demand for complete loyalty, an expectation that was in conflict with the Chosen People status celebrated by the large Jewish population of the eastern reaches of a country seeking to be born — Poland. Many of these reluctant citizens of a dying empire left before the calamity of the First World War made most departures impossible — and thousands more departed as soon as possible after the Treaty of Versailles failed to either satisfy the defeated or to protect those who were obviously at risk in the tensions of post-war eastern Europe. Subsequently, in the first years of the twentieth century, the Jewish population in Toronto exploded, doubling, and doubling again. These families and individuals in turn became hosts to those who continued to arrive throughout the century, particularly after the Second World War.

There had always been a cost for following the religious practices of an unfamiliar religious tradition such as Judaism in the Russian Empire. At any time a focused attack on a particular minority could be unleashed. Homes and businesses would be confiscated, and the very lives of the faithful would be at risk. One can find the roots of the Holocaust that was to follow in 1945 in the many centuries of European anti-Semitism.

In twentieth-century Toronto, the influx of Jewish immigrants before and after the Second World War found a haven in which religious tension was being largely played out between Protestants and Catholics. Torontonians were largely Protestant, with members of the establishment Church of England dominating the political life of the city. However, Methodism was gaining in popularity, and by the mid-1920s a union of Presbyterians, Congregationalists, and Methodists was to form the United Church of Canada, which became the largest Protestant denomination in the country.

The most honoured day of the year in Toronto during that time was July 12, when the Loyal Orange Lodge put on a huge parade. The spectacle was accentuated by the sounds of fife and drum, led by a man on a white horse dressed as "King Billy," or William of Orange, who had landed on England's shores in the seventeenth century to assure a Protestant succession which would banish the Stuart royal line and its predilection for Roman Catholicism.

Toronto, best known for its numerous church spires, became the home of numerous synagogues in the early years of the twentieth century, adding to the architectural diversity of the city. Men in strange black clothing, sporting fedoras and unusual hairstyles, began to make their way, with wife and children in tow, to these places of worship. It was apparent on Friday evenings in the mid-century that a quiet and friendly invasion had taken place. Although a small number had arrived in the nineteenth century and contributed to the life of the city, by the 1920s the increasing numbers allowed for a Jewish community that covered a large area of the west-central part of the municipality, referred to as "The Ward." This is where Jewish immigrants came, and where they were welcomed and assisted by co-religionists to begin their new life in a strange land. Eventually this pseudo-ghetto dispersed as the more affluent found their way north to what is now Forest Hill or — largely in the 1950s and '60s— to communities east and west of Bathurst Street. Thus considerable numbers found themselves on the city's northern edge, in the borough of North York. By the end of the twentieth century, Jewish families could be found in every corner of Toronto. Though they were dominant in very few neighbourhoods, their influence was felt far beyond, and would be key to the social and cultural future of an extraordinarily diverse city.

Those who had come first in the late 1800s in small numbers were quiet and almost invisible. However, after the turn of the twentieth century, the Jewish immigrants who arrived were from various parts of the Russian Empire, in particular from the region that would eventually be known as the country of Poland. These new Canadians were mainly urban and sophisticated and quite baffled by the efforts of the government to encourage them to settle on the land, particularly in the empty former Hudson's Bay Company tracts of the Canadian West. They soon found greater comfort in the urban centres of Montreal, Toronto, and Winnipeg, in communities that provided employment that recognized their skills and thereby produced jobs that were more conducive to supporting their well-being.

They were cosmopolitan but in the beginning largely financially bereft. Soon their numbers harboured members of every class and interest. Their past in Europe had made them intensely conscious of their Jewishness, having suffered and faced humiliation and threats of annihilation if persistent in continuing to follow their faith. They represented an enormous spectrum of behaviour from the very traditional dress and the deportment that included consistent attendance at the synagogue, to those who could be described as secular Jews — rarely to be found in the synagogue on the Sabbath but nonetheless expressing the traditional values of a community in regard to learning, to civil liberties, to the caring of the less fortunate, and to the arts of instrumental and choral music, dance, and theatre.

It was into this environment that Nathan Feldbrill and Helen Lederman, newly arrived from Poland in 1920, prepared to build a new life. Both had come from major cities in Poland. Nathan had lived in Lodz and Helen in Warsaw. In the latter decades of the twentieth century the term "community" became associated with people who cared deeply for each other and shared their sometime meager goods with those less fortunate. In the early decades of that century, "community" and the Jewish neighbourhood were synonymous.

Nathan and Helen joined a burgeoning array of relatives who had already abandoned the Russian Empire under the czars, many with little hope that a newly created Poland would be treated any more generously by the revolutionaries who had so recently banished czarist dictatorship and privilege and promised equality and justice in a brutal civil war carried on amidst the chaos of the last months of the First World War. Nathan and Helen had come in the realization that the Treaty of Versailles had failed to conceive a nation that would survive the revival of a strong Germany, and took advantage of the rush of immigration to Canada that had been interrupted by the events of 1914–18 but resumed in the 1920s, thereby opening the gates to the new world once again.

It is simple-minded to assume that immigration solved all the problems of inequality and discriminatory behaviour. Such blindness can be the result of believing the myths of the "happily-ever-after" fairy tale that hides the tragedies of family break-up — the separation, the loneliness, the pain and disillusionment — that were inevitably present for those who felt their homeland was no longer a place of peace or of prosperity and eventual contentment, and found even more challenges in the move to a new national setting.

Nathan had come to North America to find his brother, Sam, who had settled in Detroit but had found it necessary to change his name to Feldman, something less than a common designation for those who were Jewish. Two other brothers had come to Toronto, but found that they would have greater opportunity under the name "Field." Only brothers Alexander and Jack had retained the surname "Feldbrill" and the latter was operating a combined variety store and tinsmith operation on Dundas Street, a major Toronto thoroughfare that delivered people from the west end to the very centre of Toronto. Nathan, who had from the earliest years of his working life pursued the textile trade in Poland, saw his future in that same trade, becoming an employee of Tip Top Tailors, a major manufacturer of quality clothing for men.

Helen, a member of a smaller family, came to Canada without the enormous support system that had surrounded Nathan and eased his transition to a new life. Indeed, personal tragedy struck her immediately. She had arrived in Toronto expecting to be welcomed by a father who had already come intending to seek employment and a place to live. Together, she assumed, they would plan to send for their mother as soon as there were sufficient resources. Helen came unexpectedly, hoping to find her father ready and willing to include her in his life. She was shocked to discover that he had found another partner with whom to live and had no intention of sending her mother the money to join him in his new homeland. She was saddened by what she perceived to be despicable behaviour that now proclaimed the disintegration of her family unit. Happily, she soon connected with the Jewish community in her new homeland, found work, and through sheer determination was creating a new life for herself when she met Nathan. In the chaos of this abandonment, the maintenance of a strong family became her first priority in any marital union she might be part of, and, indeed, her understandable obsession. It was a lesson in fidelity that she taught her children.

The impact of all this chaotic family severance was significant. Nathan and Helen met at a Jewish Benefit Society in 1922, appropriately courted for some months, married, and together moved to a home on Leonard Street in the Dundas and Spadina area. This was the very heart of the "The Ward," which was now expanding west in the city. But they soon moved, this time to nearby Markham Street. Indeed, they became occupants of three residences on that street in the years to come. Victor was born close by, in the Western Hospital, on April 4, 1924, and remained with his parents in one or another flat in this significant enclave of Jewry until he left to join the Royal Canadian Navy (RCN) during the Second World War.

Victor was the object of his parents' pride and became a frequent visitor in the homes of an army of uncles, aunts, and cousins that made up a mélange of Nathan's extended family. Although answering to different surnames, they were a close and supportive group. In Helen's case, there were no such figures to be found in her life, though with her outgoing personality she soon added a collection of close friends who became surrogate "uncles" and "aunts" to Victor and eventually to his two younger sisters, Ruth and Eileen, who came to make up the Feldbrill family. At one point in his childhood, a complete stranger came up to Victor on the street and informed him that his grandfather had died. Victor had not realized there had been any living person in Canada or Poland who could occupy that relationship with him. Obviously it was Helen's father, but it was a shocking revelation that Victor never forgot. Family became as precious to him as it was to Helen, and this commitment moulded his life within the performing arts, one in which close personal relationships too often are forfeited in the effort to achieve success.

With all this confused history in the back of his mind, Victor never for a moment considered the prospect of changing his name. It had "old world" connotations he valued and a connection with a Jewish past he had no intention of abandoning. The reality of an immigrant beginning was etched in his memory, and the sacrifice his parents had made on his behalf was a matter of pride throughout his life. It was no surprise when, in his mid-teens, he chose a young woman who came from similar beginnings to whom he could give his love and commitment — a commitment that lasted for more than half a century. Never did he allow his career decisions to endanger their intimacy or the well-being of the family.

᭥

Nathan struggled to provide an adequate income to support Helen, Victor, and, within four years, a daughter, Ruth. It was fourteen years later, with Victor already serving in the Royal Canadian Naval Services, that the family was surprised and delighted with the arrival of a second daughter, Eileen.

Nathan, it could be said, did not have the intense, competitive nature to excel in the business world, but in 1929 he nevertheless traded in the sweatshop conditions of the textile manufacturing trade and Tip Top Tailors for a new working life. This shift resulted in a series of largely unsuccessful attempts to operate a neighbourhood retail grocery business, the first of which was located on the corner of Euclid Avenue and Dundas Street. The timing could not have been worse in terms of the economic climate. The relentless Depression of the 1930s dogged his every effort as he went from store to store in various locations in "The Ward" — streets such as Beatrice, Markham, and Harbord appear again and again.

Part of the problem was Nathan's reluctance to deny his destitute neighbours sufficient credit to buy the basic necessities to feed their children. His creditors were unable to pay their debts — or find cash to purchase food. Nathan's decency and compassion made tough response to need impossible. However, his generosity resulted in debts that inevitably led to bankruptcy. One after another the stores failed, leaving Nathan and his family even more at risk. Helen was the stronger partner, more aggressive and competitive, but she did not fend much better than her husband.

At one point, the children had to be dispersed amongst friends of the Feldbrill family until Nathan was able to find another opportunity in the grocery business. Nathan's effort to be successful in the retail business dictated the living accommodations of the family, as they invariably inhabited the apartment over the store, and, as they moved businesses, so too did they have to move house — a challenge for the Feldbrill children.

This constant relocating meant a frequent change of schools for Victor. He began his schooling at Charles G. Fraser Public School, but was transferred to Dewson Public School when Nathan took over a store on Harbord Street. Another failure and inevitable move meant that Victor then attended Clinton Street Public School, and his elementary-school career ended with two years at King Edward Public School, where he graduated with marks that put him at the top of his class.

This sort of itinerant schooling can often devastate the learning life of a student — but not Victor. He was fortunate to have teachers who gave him confidence in his abilities. Miss Springate and Miss Farquarson at Dewson Public School and an exchange teacher, a Miss Langdon at Clinton Public School, spring to his mind even to this day. Even music inspectors and consultants such as Emily Tedd and Eldon Brethour, who visited and provided advice to teachers on the classroom music programs that would most benefit students, find a respectful resonance in Victor's memories. There are no stories of neglect and disenchantment or abuse and humiliation in Victor's recollections of a satisfying elementary-school career. He had arrived at school with no competence in the English language — Yiddish was spoken in the Feldbrill household and Victor had to become instantly bilingual if he was to learn anything of the curriculum that was in the hands of Toronto's unilingual English-speaking teachers. With his interest in languages, he joined colleagues whose parents often spoke Polish, German, Russian, and other assorted languages depending on European country of origin. His capacity to communicate with orchestral players in the various countries he was invited to perform in was supported by the multi-language preparation in the Jewish neighbourhoods where he spent his entire childhood and adolescence.

Unfortunately, there was a downside to the saga of elementary-school achievement and recognition. His sister Ruth, four years behind him in grade level, had to endure the constant accolades about her older brother and, as so often happens, the circumstance aroused a resentment that spilled over beyond the classroom, particularly in the light of Nathan and Helen's apparent favouritism toward a male offspring whose accomplishments were so evident. It meant that Ruth, though bright, endured a diminished sense of competence that remained long after Victor had moved on and was no longer competing scholastically. She was not as quick as Victor either in elementary or secondary school, nor did she develop effective academic study skills. The contrast was quite apparent to her teachers and to her parents. Because Eileen was such a late arrival to the family — more than a full decade after Ruth — she did not have to experience any academic competition with her distinguished older brother. By the time the mid-1940s rolled around, Victor had joined the Armed Forces. Then, upon his return to Toronto after the war, he entered into a marriage that ensured his future absence from the Feldbrill family home forever.

These years of childhood and youth provided Victor with valuable lessons in the wisdom of restraint and practicality. The Feldbrills were poor at a time when being poor was a common condition. However, Victor was determined very early in life that poverty would not be his chosen path — this despite the fact that he had decided to seek personal satisfaction in a risky business, the performing arts, and in particular, "serious" music. He never forsook his vocational goals nor allowed deprivation or destitution to touch his own family. The state of poverty suffered by his parents in his early years never left his mind and heart. Yet throughout his career he made choices that had a lesser chance of providing economic prosperity than others. (Becoming a Canadian orchestral conductor and stressing the performance of contemporary classical music represented a vision of questionable financial security in the music industry of mid-twentieth-century Canada in particular.)

Victor never flinched as he worked through a career as a formidable musician in a place that some musicians around the world perceived to be a poverty-stricken backwater of artistic expression. However, at no time did he place the well-being of his family at risk in any of the overly optimistic schemes that abound in the world of making music. He had seen the impact of poverty and had no stomach for any path that would see his family suffer it again.

In the Feldbrill family there was no history of musical appreciation. So where did this passion for music come from? As we learn more about human mental and emotional development, the question of particular reasons why there is a surfacing of musical intelligence in a particular generation of a family still remains mysterious. Certainly there was no predilection toward making music in either Nathan or Helen's background nor was there any to be found in the interests of his siblings. Yet Victor's excitement about the source, nature, and quality of musical sound is one of the earliest memories of his life as a small child.

He remembers vividly the family excursions to Hanlan's Point on the Toronto Islands in the Lake Ontario harbour that served as the city's southern boundary. In those innocent days, swimming and playing on the beaches of the Toronto Islands were common childhood pastimes, but band concerts were also part of the island entertainment. Victor was overwhelmed by the magical sounds of a brass band and the impact it produced. On every occasion he quickly found his way to the front of the seated audience and his concentration was rewarded by a sensitive bandmaster who often invited him to sit on the stage of the bandshell. Soon he was amusing the audience by mimicking the motions of the kindly conductor, who good-naturedly found Victor's enthusiasm most engaging.

There was no piano in the Feldbrill living room as there were in so many Jewish homes, nor was there a radio that might have brought strains of music into the atmosphere of Victor's household. There was, however, a gramophone that could be wound up and on which a needle on paraffin records could bring delight. There were recordings of Jewish folk music but this was unfortunately the entire repertoire of any musical moment that might be imposed on a largely silent home environment. Nonetheless, Victor played these selections ceaselessly, gathering only approbation from the rest of the family. Most of his childhood years were spent in the gloom of the Depression and new recordings were far beyond the dreams of Nathan and Helen. Indeed, there came a time when even the luxury of the trips to Hanlan's Point on the Toronto waterfront had to be abandoned, much to Victor's disappointment.

In those years, Jewish families, even those in need, were expected to provide their young with some form of musical education. There was a pressure to be part of a Jewish culture that demanded an experience that might result in some kind of employment. Morry Kernerman, Victor's closest friend in his youth, speaks of walking down Clinton or Markham Street and hearing a succession of piano sounds, whether it be scales or the simple pieces written for beginning musicians. It was a common experience in any Jewish neighbourhood. The only relief came from the presence of the sweet tone of a violin that might emanate from occasional front doors where another instrument had been chosen, sometimes simply to replace the absence of a keyboard. In general terms, on the economic front, the textile industry might well have a Jewish monopoly of interest, but music was the Jewish art form that held the attention of community and gave Victor his start in life. Even the fragile nature of the Feldbrill household's financial well-being could not break that tradition in early-twentieth-century Toronto.

Parents had some inkling that there was a place in the artistic life of a great city for accomplished musicians. There were theatre orchestras in an age of silent film … as well as the brash and colourful world of vaudeville. The age of radio was coming into its own and music was an economical way of filling otherwise infinite time periods when the spoken word was inappropriate or too expensive to produce. It was also a time when music was central to the religious practices of most Protestant and Roman Catholic churches and the teaching of music, either within the school system or without, was a commendable form of employment. Though many would be instructed, at least a few would be chosen to play for at least modest remuneration sufficient to support themselves and possibly a family. For Victor, this penchant for music came to be seen as a possible path to the reward of future employment.

Elementary schools had a particular interest in the promotion of music. Victor remembers an occasion when he was a cast member of a kindergarten production that revolved around a railway train devoted to the teaching of personal hygiene. It was called "The Health Train" and Victor's role was — ironic in light of his eventual occupation — that of The Conductor. It was a meager part demanding that he call out "All aboard" at a specific moment early in the drama. However, being on stage gave him an opportunity to observe all that was transpiring about him. In particular, he was able to watch an older cousin, Irving, who was playing violin in an ensemble gathered to provide incidental music to support what was being presented by the actors onstage. To Victor, on the cusp of an age when an instrument might be part of his life, Irving's role seemed much more interesting as a contribution to the production than that of bellowing but two words, as important as they might be to the plot of the play.

When he was nine years old, at considerable sacrifice, a violin was purchased and Victor took his first steps toward a career as a performer of considerable repute. Thus, early in life Victor had been provided with an instrument of sorts and a music teacher of modest attainment and had joined his friends in the torture of daily practice. However, it was not to be a joyful and positive beginning to a life in music presentation.

Victor's introduction to string instruments had a number of obvious impacts. First, he realized he could pick up tunes and play them quite beautifully within a few months. Within a few weeks of his initiation he found he was being invited to social affairs at which his violin was made welcome.

Unfortunately, the teacher selected failed to ignite Victor's genius, and the young student was as outraged by his mentor's bad taste in repertoire as he was by the limitations of his instructional technique. Victor, even at an early age, had developed some sense of quality in musical expression and found the teacher's choices of pieces for him to learn uninspired and downright boring. The result was that after a few months he gave up on any serious study of the instrument, forsook the lessons and the teacher, and played only for his own delight. His parents were initially disappointed that their son would be bereft of instruction, but realized that this abandonment would benefit, in the short term, the immediate collective family fortunes.

Victor looks upon this desertion of formal studies at this early stage as a most significant event in the development of his life work. A continuing focus on string performance would likely have resulted in the creation of a child prodigy. There was no doubt he had the talent. In his view, this talent would not have carried him very far and he would have become a disappointed violin player in an orchestral string section — at best as a first chair, or possibly even a member of a string chamber music ensemble. Attention at that point in his life to virtuosity would have led him to see his role as that of a solo violinist in recital and concert with very little chance of ever climbing to the pinnacle of international prominence that very few hopeful musicians ever reach. Most important, focusing on his aptitude as a violinist would have diverted him from ever recognizing his broader capacity to give leadership in the performance of music and thus become an orchestral conductor.

He was to return to the violin after he had become obsessed with the sounds of large orchestral ensembles and did so in the context of wishing to improve his orchestral playing. That became the focus of his immediate ambition. In that context, his experiences in music seemed to compel his attention as a leader, first as a concertmaster and later, in his mid-teens, as a conductor. A continuous pursuit of solo performance might well have led him to see orchestral participation as a form of failure rather than as a path to what became an inexorable journey to the role of "maestro." In that role, he came to make a unique contribution to Canada's cultural awakening, one that changed the lives of countless people around him.

There was another advantage to Victor's rejection of violin studies at such an early age. He had developed a splendid boy soprano voice that attracted considerable attention and allowed him ample opportunity to perform at various events, particularly in the programs of the many Jewish social clubs that flourished in the community. Indeed, he soon choreographed an act that included "take-offs" on the presentations of such famous figures as Al Jolson. Thus he continued to be engaged in the drama of music performance. Soon vocal music had become yet another entrée to the excitement of the concert stage.

There was yet another form of entertainment with which Victor surprisingly became "au courant." Throughout the Depression years there was one form of theatre that became available and did much to ameliorate the sad circumstances of those who lived through those hard times — the cinema. Even access to the local emporium would have stretched the pockets of the Feldbrill family, but Nathan's brother Irving had become manager of the Duchess Theatre, located just down the street from the Feldbrills' abode. Recognizing the presence of need, Irving made it possible for Helen and Victor to be admitted free of charge, and Helen took every advantage of that opportunity, often attending three or four times a week with Victor as her companion.

Hollywood recognized that its profits depended on it raising the morale of those who were caught in the whirlpool of economic disaster that plagued the era, and films with considerable musical content graced the screens of

North America during the 1930s. Victor became caught up in the delight of these musicals, one being an adaptation of Sigmund Romberg's *The Desert Song*. Once, after an evening of visual and sound magic, Victor returned home, devised a costume that included a cap and a handkerchief that was long enough to hang down over his shoulders, and for days sang constantly every song he could remember from the popular musical. It was an introduction to the world of music theatre, an area in which he would eventually make a splendid contribution, despite the fact that the creation of music for film never attracted him. He did, however, over many years, become a familiar figure in the live broadcast studios of the Canadian Broadcast Corporation, first on CBC Radio and eventually on CBC Television, where he benefited from those teenage experiences with recorded music and drama.

It was fortunate that by the time he had reached his final elementary experience (at King Edward Public School) Victor had achieved a change of heart with regard to his violin. In spite of his boredom with the musical limitations of his first instructor, he had come to realize that the instrument could be a path to the delight of making music with other equally gifted and enthusiastic colleagues, and he was soon drawn back into formal violin studies. A woman wishing to sell a radio console to the Feldbrill family came to the home when Victor was amusing himself on his instrument. She encountered Victor and had an immediate sense of his musical talent and informed his parents that she knew a fine instructor of violin who lived not far away from their home on Markham Street. His name was Sigmund Steinberg. It led to an association beyond Victor's wildest hopes. Not only was Steinberg a fine violinist himself, playing in the TSO and the Promenade Orchestra series in Varsity Arena every summer, he was a part of the enormous web of musicians playing in a variety of ensembles in Canada. He was not only a gifted teacher and performer but was able to reveal to Victor the importance of attending both rehearsals and concerts of orchestras as a learning experience. He revealed to Victor how he might find and open the doors that would allow his entrance to the venues of music-making for the rest of his life.

An immediate opportunity to broaden his reach presented itself to Victor in the guise of a Toronto Board of Education gala concert in the city's major performance venue, Massey Hall, in which a spectrum of choirs and instrumental groups were gathered to dispense an evening of musical entertainment to parents and school officials. Not surprisingly, Victor was a member of the All-Toronto Public School Choir. As a member of the audience as well as a participant, he discovered to his delight that there were other public schools that had instrumental ensembles able to conquer at least the simplest of melodies on their stringed instruments. It was a revelation, and when Victor returned to school the following morning he accosted the King Edward School principal with the question, "If these schools can have an orchestra, then why not us?"

The principal's reaction was both positive and challenging: "Why not indeed! Are you prepared to organize and rehearse such a group?" It was a fair question that forced Victor to take action. He found schoolmates who were similarly talented on an instrument and prepared to give time and focus to the enterprise of creating a school orchestra. For the first time, the sounds of strings filled a classroom and the nearby halls of King Edward School, both before and after regular school hours.

Within a few weeks, this collection of string players found themselves entered into an appropriate category of contestants at the local annual music festival sponsored by the Board of Education that produced a massive gathering of young musicians. It was a precursor of the prestigious Kiwanis Music Festival that was to attain a considerable presence in Toronto, involving music students of all ages and ability. Included in the process were the very school orchestras that Victor had observed on stage just a few months before. It would have served the drama of the occasion if King Edward Public School and its motley band of beginner string players had swept aside the competition to capture first place, but in the demanding context of string performance it was not to be. However, one judge in this category of musical performance was distinguished musician Eli Spivak, concertmaster of the Toronto Symphony Orchestra (TSO). In his judge's comments accompanying the evaluation of the contestants, he referred directly to the leadership displayed by "that musician" from King Edward Public School. That young musician was Victor Feldbrill, a young man who would become Spivak's TSO colleague later in his life.

The accolade did not go unnoticed. An inspector of music in the Toronto schools, Harvey Perrin, driving Victor home from the competition, considered carefully an unusual invitation he wanted to offer this youngster who had caught the attention not only of the judge but other members of the small audience gathered to witness the competition. Perrin, along with Eldon Brethour, was an avid promoter of music performance in elementary and secondary schools. The two had organized an ensemble of elite instrumentalists from several downtown secondary schools. Perrin decided that this Feldbrill boy from King Edward, though still in elementary school, could be an asset in the orchestra, which had been formed to challenge secondary-school students who were prepared to address a repertoire and achieve an orchestral sound and level of achievement that would be impossible in any single institution. The invitation went out formally from Brethour, the conductor, and was accepted by Victor with intense enthusiasm.

The rehearsals of this ensemble took place at Jarvis Collegiate, the historic secondary school named after the north–south Toronto thoroughfare on which it was built. It was downtown, not far distant from Victor's neighbourhood, perhaps a couple of kilometres at most. However, it was east of Yonge Street, the major north–south divide that was used as a starting point to establish the whereabouts of every Torontonian. Victor had never before ventured alone as far away from his home.

Not knowing how long the journey would take, Victor arrived at his first rehearsal shortly after its scheduled hour. The collegiate was an imposing structure but he had no problem following the instructions he had been given. Clutching his violin under his arm, he entered the formidable front doors and soon found the room in which the student musicians were gathered. However, before entering the rehearsal venue, Victor was transfixed by the sound of the music that emanated from the room and filled the hallway. It was the first time he had heard the sound of a full, live symphonic orchestral ensemble, and it was indeed a defining moment — it was then that he realized he wanted to be part of making that kind of sound for the rest of his life. He joined the players. Among them were also sprinkled a few teachers, one of whom, Margaret Williams, shared Victor's music stand and took him under her wing. He soon felt quite at home, even though he was much younger than the secondary-school players with whom he would rehearse and eventually perform.

Very soon after his introduction as a string player he experienced the same magnificent sound of a symphony orchestra in full flight — this time that of a professional ensemble of some repute. Once again, it took his breath away. He had been taking art lessons at the Ontario College of Art (now the Ontario College of Art and Design), a short distance from his neighbourhood. His instructor was Arthur Lismer, who was to achieve renown as a member of the Group of Seven, artists who became famous for the landscape paintings that defined Canadian visual art for decades.

During a Saturday morning session, Lismer announced that he had a few tickets to an orchestral program being presented by the Detroit Symphony Orchestra at Eaton Auditorium, a space on the top floor of a newly built addition to the Eaton's retail empire farther north on Yonge Street. The orchestra was playing a Wagnerian repertoire. Victor jumped at the chance.

In the comparatively modest dimensions of the auditorium, the glorious sound of the composer's works were massive and impressive, convincing Victor that making music like this was indeed his ultimate goal, one to which his constant practise and enthusiastic ensemble participation should be directed.[1] In essence, his commitment to the sound of the orchestra and the music it played had been solidified before Victor had even reached secondary school.

His attraction to the orchestra completely baffled his closest boyhood friend, Morry Kernerman. Having been involved in these same school experiences, Kernerman was determined to be a violin soloist and had worked strenuously during years that Victor had abandoned regular lessons. He saw the symphony orchestra as a necessary presence at a concert, there to accompany the solo violin in one of the great concertos of Mendelssohn, Bruch, Mozart, Beethoven, or Tchaikovsky that graced the repertoire of the normal orchestral concert season.[2] For Victor, being part of an orchestra and experiencing what could happen to one while associated with it was the main motivation in his playing a violin. Inevitably, this perception would lead him to seek a leadership role in the world of orchestral performance. He was not alone among his schoolmates in making that role his focus. His generation not only produced Kernerman, an outstanding string player in several ensembles, but Gerald Geldblum and Harvey Siegel, as well, both members of the illustrious Boston Symphony Orchestra strings.

Toronto, already with a reputation for musical performance, was now set on the course of producing an army of competent musicians, both instrumental and vocal, that by the end of the century would be a distinctive aspect of its desire to be a more cosmopolitan city. Victor was swiftly becoming a member of the vast array of talent and genius that would transform Toronto, making it an exciting and distinguished centre for the study and performance of music as the twentieth century came to an end.

CHAPTER 2

The Harbord Collegiate Experience

For Victor, the transition from King Edward Public School to Harbord Collegiate Institute in the fall of 1937 could scarcely have been easier. He was among friends and had already achieved some prominence as a musician at King Edward Public School, which he could carry with him into this new setting. It was in the halls of the distinguished secondary school that his future was to be decided.

His academic record to that point was quite remarkable. He had arrived at elementary school totally unfamiliar with the English language. Yet he had graduated at the top of his class with marks that brought pride to his doting parents. It was a time in the pre-Second World War Ontario school system when graduation from elementary school was considered a scholastic achievement. Many students simply dropped out at this point in their education to seek some kind of employment. Nathan and Helen were determined that, in spite of the continuing difficult economic circumstances, Victor would continue his studies at all costs and possibly be the first member of the Feldbrill family to attend university.

However, a major shift had taken place in their son's interests; particularly in his final year at King Edward, music had become everything. All else, including academic pursuits, were now taking second place to the thrills he experienced playing his violin with other students and giving leadership to the development of ensembles that brought some distinction to his school. He became something of a sensation well before entering the halls and classrooms of Harbord Collegiate, the secondary school that graced his neighbourhood.

Indeed, he had now become a member of the Toronto Secondary School Symphony Orchestra and had rehearsed with that ensemble at Jarvis Collegiate for some months before his graduation from elementary school. As a result, he had come to know a bevy of older students from the city's secondary schools across the entire city. However, he had noticed that a sizable number, particularly in the string sections, came from this institution on Harbord Street that was now to be his academic home until the early 1940s. These were dramatic times that were to see an end to the Great Depression and a new prosperity based on a global conflict of monumental proportions.

He had also become aware of the fact that Harbord's student population was mostly Jewish. Indeed, as one of the oldest secondary institutions in Toronto, it was, until the 1960s and '70s, known throughout the city as "the Jewish high school." (That designation has disappeared in the 1980s and '90s as mounting numbers of students from families emigrating from the Caribbean and the Asian subcontinent replaced the predominantly Jewish population, who had by this time migrated northward.) Thankfully, the school kept and still keeps a splendid record of the contribution of its Jewish alumnae to the worlds of business, law, medicine, and politics, and that community's presence is recorded and remembered by the school with understandable pride.

One of the greatest motivating factors in Victor's education in those early years was his sense of connection with that community and his delight in all that Harbord Collegiate had to offer. It had, by far, the most distinguished music program in Ontario, one that included playing in a splendid orchestra and singing in fine choirs, and all participating in an annual operetta performance — the crowning musical achievement of both the institution's teachers and students.

The predominance of Jewish students attending Harbord Collegiate fuelled a misconception Victor carried in his mind that he was a member of the majority ethnic group inhabiting the city, and he was surprised to discover statistics in his teens that confirmed he belonged to just another of Toronto's minorities. His daily experience in his own family, in his contacts with neighbours, in his travels along the commercial strips of Harbord Street, and in his schooling and musical activities had led to him to believe otherwise. This demographic revelation came as a distinct surprise.

The negative impact of this status revealed itself on occasion, mirroring the events that were already souring civic life in Central Europe in the 1930s. Perhaps the most obvious example of racial confrontation took place a few blocks north of Victor's home. A large park on Bloor Street, the city's major east–west artery, contained multiple baseball diamonds that were a host to competing teams from across the city. "Christie Pits" was an inviting venue for amateur softball leagues, with teams that tended to be distinguished by the dominant ethnic group that formed its roster of players. Crowds were drawn by the fact that the admission was free and the competition, though normally friendly and good-natured, was intense.

One night in the late 1930s, a nasty brawl broke out between Jewish athletes on one team and a collection of fascist-leaning players on the other who, with their sympathizers, took it upon themselves to harass and confront their enemies on the baseball field and in the stands, where devoted fans of both teams had gathered to cheer on their heroes.

The struggle became ugly, continued for hours, and spread eventually to residential streets nearby, where Jewish youth had to be organized to drive their anti-Semitic combatants away. However, it was a signal that the world was entering a new phase of anti-Semitic behaviour, one that would continue until the Holocaust became the ultimate shame of twentieth-century Europe. For Canadians, though never completely devoid of racial prejudice, this minor riot was a signal, and although the Feldbrill family were not directly targeted or involved at this stage, the implications eventually became clear, even for young Victor, and the war against that Nazi philosophy ultimately became his own battle.

⁕⁕⁕

Harbord's efforts to spur on Jewish scholars and musicians most certainly motivated Victor, both in his search for his own future in music and in his desire to excel academically. His parents believed themselves to be part of that community, though they rarely attended the synagogue and most of their devotion was consigned to the High Holidays and Passover, when a traditional feast was prepared in celebration.

Nathan and Helen had come from a part of Europe where being openly Jewish could severely restrict one's social and professional choices and even threaten one's life. Though they had avoided the worst excesses of anti-Semitism, there was no reason to take chances, even in a new land. Yet they were anxious to leave open to their children the path to a more satisfying level of religious observance.

Across the street from the first grocery store the family had owned there had been a cheder — a Jewish school that opened its doors in the late afternoon and the early evening, after classes in the regular school schedule had concluded. Not only Jewish religious faith and practice were taught, but courses in both Hebrew and Yiddish languages were available. Victor, at the age of five, was enrolled — the venue was convenient and the costs were minimal.

But the intervention was a failure. The instructor was a martinet, and though Jewish philosophy and theology were to become a favourite source of inspiration both for Victor's reading and for the interpretation of his music, his teacher seemed obsessed only with the trappings of the Jewish faith, and lectured incessantly about ritual and the garments that distinguished this choice of faith. Though quite young, Victor had anticipated a lively discussion on the sources of strength and the magnificent contributions of Judaism to the society around him, and was deeply disappointed. However, he did learn to read and write Yiddish, a capacity that served him well in the future. From that point, his mother became the instructor and purveyor of wisdom and common sense. He could not have had a more compelling teacher.

When the time came for the bar-mitzvah ceremony that would recognize his reaching manhood, his father took him to a synagogue for a number of weeks, but once the event transpired he was quite pleased when Victor announced that he was not receiving any great intellectual stimulation, and both father and son quietly retreated from this plentitude of religious observance. However fragmented and inadequate this preparation may seem, the fact is that Victor's ethical position on every issue came to be drawn from these perceptions of the Jewish faith he imbibed from both his family and his close association with the Jewish community. Though not "religious" in the narrow sense of that term, his appreciation of the traditional values of Jewish thought and practice came to pervade every area of his life, whether through the music he chose for his audiences and students or in the style of leadership he exuded on the podiums of the numerous orchestras he conducted over the next several decades.

His arrival at Harbord in the fall of 1937 was troubled when opening day had to be delayed as a result of a polio epidemic that had invaded Toronto over the summer. The tragedy had created a panic. Parents were warned to keep their children away from crowds — even avoiding the Canadian National Exhibition, at that time the largest annual exposition in the world, and one that normally took over the city's attention for two full weeks in the late summer. Young people were devastated at having to miss the midway rides — the most thrilling to be found at any such event in Canada — and the free samples of food and drink.

Students of all ages soon discovered that their holidays had been magically extended and they were to miss the first weeks of the new fall term. Parents downtown were encouraged to send their children to the clean air of the countryside or to the suburbs that surrounded the dangerous environment of the city centre. The Feldbrill parents decided to send Victor and his younger sister, Ruth, to live with their Aunt Celia, a lady whose designation as "aunt" merely indicated a level of intimacy with the family that could be counted upon to assist in such circumstances. She lived in the suburbs, presumably farther from the sources of infection. The fear of succumbing to disease and thereby paralysis was real and had to be treated seriously.

When the high schools finally opened their doors some weeks later, it was evident that the music department's major annual event, the mounting of the Gilbert and Sullivan operetta, was simply impossible to achieve in the time available.

The Harbord presentation was not only the predominant extracurricular preoccupation of the collegiate; it was a show that was famous across the city. As Edward Wodson, a music critic for Toronto newspaper *The Telegram*, pointed out, "To look and listen was to forget that the entertainers on stage were schoolboys and girls." The yearly productions engaged the orchestra and choir members in endless hours of rehearsal, but also involved a large percentage of the non-musical student body and a host of teachers — there was the task of making costumes, painting sets, and preparing the technical services to assure a smooth and exciting performance. In short, it was a yearly extravaganza that gathered an enormous spectrum of talent and energy and thereby gave a sense of significance to the school and in the lives of the hundreds of students who were involved. The struggle to stage the operetta took every minute that could be found, from Labour Day until March of the following year.

So, sadly, the loss of time in September of that year could not be compensated for, and the production was cancelled for the 1937–38 academic year.

The effect of this on Victor's role as a "new" boy in the school orchestra was considerable. The Harbord Orchestra, now freed from its commitment to the Gilbert and Sullivan production, was ready to tackle a new repertoire and had the opportunity to perform with increased vigour. Orchestra rehearsals for presentations at the twice-weekly gathering of the school population in the auditorium became the central focus of Victor's schedule.

Not surprisingly, his premature experience in the city-wide secondary school orchestra assured him of special attention, and in his first year at Harbord he was proclaimed concertmaster. At thirteen years of age, he was already taking on a leadership role, one that promised excitement and the knowledge that he would be performing for classmates who were able to forget his youth and recognize his capacity.

Harbord was noted as a unique venue for young people interested in the arts and had already established a reputation for producing individuals central to the country's cultural life. Figures such as composers John Weinzweig and Lou Applebaum emerged from the ranks and soon the school would be known for producing the most famous comics in Canada's history — Johnny Wayne and Frank Shuster.

Other high schools might celebrate their football or hockey teams — but Harbord Collegiate honoured those who exhibited academic prowess and excelled in artistic gifts. During the 1930s, the school had attracted a staff of outstanding teachers who went on to produce a veritable hotbed of artists and performers. In drama, Mr. Griffin brought attention to the staging of extraordinary theatre, and Mr. Girdler placed his energy behind the production of high-level comedy. Wayne and Shuster both came through his "oola-boola club," an extracurricular exercise in producing highly regarded humour. Music had two champions: Brian McCool, the head of the department and orchestral conductor, and his colleague, Alistair Haig, who looked after the school's choirs. Victor had dropped into a veritable paradise of musical performance opportunity. He was determined to enjoy it to the fullest.

The enhanced orchestral activity that had now replaced Gilbert and Sullivan put more pressure on Mr. McCool, already far over his head in responsibilities. Realizing the obvious gifts of his new concertmaster, he sought to share the overwhelming workload he now faced. In an early rehearsal, to Victor's surprise and initial shock, McCool handed him the baton, indicating his desire to hear the orchestra from the rear of the auditorium. It was a moment that Victor never forgot. Soon, Victor was taking over the conducting of repertoire selections that were seemingly straight forward. Thus he had the opportunity of rehearsing the piece first with his orchestral colleagues, during which time he could also discover the appropriate tempo and dynamics that McCool was seeking to achieve. The "handing over of the baton" was McCool's vote of confidence in Victor's capacity to secure the respect of his colleagues and provide the leadership that was essential.[1]

One year later, a second "golden moment" moved Victor, who then occupied the first chair in the Harbord Orchestra. Alumnae John Weinzweig, later to be designated Canada's dean of composers, had been at Harbord just a few years before Victor's arrival. He, too, had played in McCool's orchestra and had been given leave to conduct it on occasion. In his determination to become a twentieth-century composer he had attended the Eastman Conservatory in Rochester, New York. Eastman was the foremost destination for students seeking to create sounds that would serve composers dedicated to inspiring and empowering listeners for the rest of the century. As the single modernist on the roster of the Faculty of the Music Department of the University of Toronto, Weinzweig had already launched students wishing to follow his example. Simultaneously, he had outraged the rest of the music faculty, who were largely devoted to the German and Russian music of the nineteenth century and had some willingness to concede the value of twentieth-century British composers like Elgar, Vaughan Williams, Walton, and later, Benjamin Britten.

In 1939, Weinzweig appeared at Harbord one afternoon to chat with his colleague, Brian McCool. He had with him a manuscript copy of the orchestral score for the recently composed "Enchanted Hill." Victor had never seen such a document before. Nor had he ever met a real composer. When McCool introduced him to Weinzweig, Victor was speechless.

Realizing the impact his presence was having, John sat Victor down at a keyboard and proceeded to take him through a version of his orchestral score, pointing out the significance of various markings and indicating his expectations of any conductor confronting the work.[2] Victor never forgot the kindness and caring Weinzweig showed him as a high-school student with a curious interest in music. Victor was fascinated by the nature and complexity of the orchestral score, and over the next decade he made it his objective to acquire and study as many scores as he could afford — or carry away. His ability to interpret the expectations of living composers from the manuscript scores at the moment of first performance became a hallmark of his career.

⋙

The development of Victor's understanding of music performance was transpiring simultaneously with Adolf Hitler's inexorable conquest of the continent of Europe. The circumstances that were unfolding an ocean away made it imperative for Canada to join the conflict and play a central role in supporting her former mother country, not as a colony, but as a fully independent nation.

The event that most impacted Victor at that time was the loss of Brian McCool, who joined the Armed Forces in 1940. He went on to become a hero at Dieppe, was wounded several times, and spent the last years of the war in a German prison camp.

Meanwhile, rehearsals for the annual Gilbert and Sullivan production, in this case *The Gondoliers*, were underway in the fall of 1939. Efforts were made to see that education was not compromised by the absence of the many young men and women who had left their teaching posts in order to serve their country. At Harbord, it was left to Alistair Haig to keep the instrumental and choral programs together, as well as to prepare and conduct the annual operetta. Realizing his inadequacy and inexperience in the repertoire of orchestral music — along with his lack of comfort with conducting instrumental forces — he took Victor aside and made it clear to him that he would have to share the responsibility and the workload. "You are going to have to give me a hand with the orchestra," was his simple plea. The impact of the Second World War was now obvious — Victor would have to be more than just a concertmaster if there was to be an orchestra at Harbord Collegiate.[3]

The Gondoliers was a Gilbert and Sullivan favourite but nevertheless demanding offering of the prolific British masters of music theatre. Victor began taking rehearsals regularly as Haig often could not be present. As well, Victor began rehearsing the solo selections and the elements of the score that involved the entire Harbord choral community. All went well, and in recognition of this extraordinary contribution, Haig insisted that Victor conduct the overture at each evening performance before taking his place as concertmaster.

Upon assuming this role night after night, Victor had every right to expect that he would be on the podium for the entire run. He waited until he felt comfortable as a conductor before inviting his parents, various relatives, and friends to be present at what should have been his triumphant appearance as an orchestral "maestro." In his mind, and to their astonishment, he would mount the podium and take on the role of conductor, leading the orchestra with aplomb and confidence, repeating his performance of previous evenings. Unfortunately, Victor had not realized the extent to which, in the performing arts, which depend so much on the attention that is cultivated by its participants, the need for notice increases rather than decreases as performers mature. Victor found, to his horror and deep disappointment, that the evening of triumph he had planned before family and friends was precisely the occasion selected by Major Brian McCool to return to Harbord for a "royal" visit before going overseas. To mark the occasion, the major would mount the podium and conduct the overture to that evening's performance of *The Gondoliers*.

Victor could not contain himself. He was devastated. Even pleas to McCool from his teaching colleagues at Harbord could not divert the major from carrying out his return in full uniform and "in style." In his mind it was a matter of staking his claim to a podium he coveted in his future and to do so by appearing on that podium on that specific evening. It was Victor's first experience with the heartbreak and disillusionment that, along with the joy of achievement, inevitably accompany artistic performers — but it would not be the last.

In contrast to the sorrow of his displacement as a conductor that evening, an event took place in 1939 that turned out to be the most important and positive of his young life. As part of his recreational activity within the Jewish community, his Saturday evenings often involved attending one of the myriad parties and dances sponsored by the many local Jewish charitable organizations. There he could meet other young people his own age. In particular, for a shy teenager, it was an opportunity to meet and dance with girls in a non-threatening environment.

The event on this particular evening, however, was not typical, as it was being held in the space normally occupied by a Jewish school, and the charitable cause was, not unexpectedly, the continuing financial health of the host educational enterprise.

As he entered the building, Victor was confronted with an extremely attractive young girl sitting at a table, taking tickets. She was slightly younger than he, but obviously had acquired a grace and easy articulation that immediately struck his fancy. Indeed, Victor was entranced with this enticing young woman, who was slim, with abundant soft dark hair and a glorious smile that seemed to put everyone at ease. She was the image of a perfect hostess, prepared to welcome every person but also determined to secure the admission price that would benefit the institution that Victor would soon discover was her father's. Indeed, it was her parents who had organized the event.

He was totally smitten. In fact, he never got past the table but remained at her side throughout the entire evening as she carried out her essential role. When there was a pause in the business at hand, he asked her to dance, but she was too shy to accept the invitation. No matter — Victor was content simply to be in her presence and talk to her when she could break away from her important duties. Once the dance ended and she had counted the proceeds, Victor insisted on walking her home. For days, he could think of nothing but making this intelligent, lovely girl his companion. More than sixty years later, he was still as much in love with Zelda as he was at that first meeting — an anniversary they were to celebrate every fall for their entire courtship and married life.

She was certainly an astounding "find" for a serious young man determined to have a career in music. She was also a student at Harbord Collegiate and was starting her second-level studies while Victor was confidently ensconced in third form. They had passed each other in the halls but had never really met.

Zelda Mann was, as were so many Harbord students, the daughter of a Jewish couple, Esther and Morris Menachovsky. She had been born in the city of Brestlitovsk. Her parents had been forced to leave Europe, in this case the area then known as "White Russia." They were both Jewish intellectuals engaged in educational endeavours, espousing socialist, leftist, and Zionist politics in a land where state communism had triumphed and the democratic socialism her parents embraced was the enemy. They had taken part in demonstrations against the policies of a Russian Empire that promised repression of any who were in opposition. They soon came to realize their Jewish roots and their progressive politics put them at risk as assuredly as they had previously been under czarist rule.

Arriving in Canada, they settled first in Winnipeg — an appropriate place, then and now the very centre of reform and progressive politics in Canada. However, the surge of Jewish immigrants to Toronto led them to believe that their commitment to learning could best prosper in that city, so they moved east and established a parochial school for Jewish youth devoted to learning and enhancing their knowledge of Hebrew and Yiddish as well as providing interpretations of the Jewish faith. Zelda and her sister, Brina, imbibed their perception of a full life from a father they loved and respected and a strong mother who supported him.

Ironically, with all the commitment to the Jewish faith and tradition, Zelda's father had changed her name formally and legally to that of "Mann" in the realization that even in Canada it might be risky to emphasize a Jewish lineage. In Zelda, Victor encountered an intellectual commitment and a philosophy of life he could seek to capture, as well as a physical charm that he found intoxicating. She was a woman who would not be content merely to accompany a distinguished husband through the years, but would seek her own contribution in a profession that stressed its caring for people and their well-being. Without her support, Victor could not have achieved his goals in a professional role that in twentieth-century Canada made such demands and presented such challenges.

Thus this teenage encounter became much more than a mere meeting of adolescents whose bubbling hormones demanded such liaisons that would see them through those difficult years. It was the beginning of a friendship that played out through a common love of literature, of great music, and of empowering ideas. Zelda's parents recognized the importance of their relationship and accepted Victor as the son they had failed to conceive. He found inspiration in that family setting that could expand his understanding of the world far beyond what his parents, from their humble station, could conceive.

For Zelda, it was a perfect link with a young man who had already achieved a degree of distinction. He was a prominent figure in the school orchestra, indeed, on occasion, its conductor. As with Victor, physical attraction was an important feature of their relationship. Victor was a tall, strapping youth with a face whose most presentable innocence seemed beyond belief. There was a tendency toward chubbiness that Zelda soon determined to keep under control. In short, he was a handsome teenager, one whose attractiveness never disappeared with time. Mary Lou Fallis is a fine Canadian soprano whose total honesty is contained in her capacity to see the humour in every situation. At the 2007 celebration of John Weinzweig's life and music, she introduced Victor as "the conductor from central casting." Even in retirement, and in his eighth decade, he is a splendid figure of a man by all standards of male magnetism. In 1939, at only fourteen and fifteen years of age, Zelda and Victor were a stunning couple, and were to remain so throughout a long courtship, marriage, the birth of their two daughters, and right up until 1995, when Zelda tragically passed away, to Victor's intense distress.

A review of the Harbord years is quintessential to any understanding of Victor's life work. They were busy years for both of them. Zelda helped her parents with their school and its mission, and developed her writing skills, serving as an editor of the Harbord yearbook.

There were some things that they could do together, and one had long-term implications. The Women's Committee of the TSO led the way in the building of future audiences by sponsoring the presentation of orchestral concerts especially designed for young people. In order to secure the best advice on appropriate repertoire, as well as in the promotion and sale of tickets in schools, a committee made up of students and music teachers from each school was formed. Victor was the obvious choice as Harbord's representative and eventually came to chair the entire committee. Zelda became Harbord's second representative and as such accompanied him to all committee meetings.

Victor's musical experience was valued, but Zelda's charm and organizational skills from years of association with Jewish youth groups turned out to be an obvious asset, as well. (Indeed, a couple of years later, after Victor had graduated, she was pressed to remain on the committee, which had come to appreciate her intelligence and imagination.) They were a formidable pair, and soon came to the attention of Sir Ernest MacMillan, dean of the university's Faculty of Music and, more importantly, the conductor of the TSO and Mendelssohn Choir, as well as to Ettore Mazzoleni, associate conductor of the TSO and the principal of the Conservatory of Music. These were connections that had an enormous impact on Victor's career.

Besides fully participating in his school orchestra, Victor had taken on solo roles. A local periodical, *The Jewish Review*, of November 1939, recorded that he was playing in a concert at the Royal York Hotel, sponsored by the Daughters of Israel Charity Society, (in this case, to support the decoration of a recreation room for the Irish Regiment at Camp Borden, a major military training centre in northeastern Ontario). Victor continued to play in the Toronto Secondary School Orchestra, where Eldon Brethour also "handed over the baton" on occasion.

Within a short time at Harbord, he also added a membership in the All-Ontario Secondary School Orchestra. This was a major gathering of gifted instrumentalists from across the province, normally conducted by outstanding teachers of music, one being Leslie Bell of Parkdale Collegiate, a prominent choral conductor who was to create his own "singers," an ensemble of female school graduates who performed weekly on CBC Radio.

On one occasion, Sir Ernest MacMillan was invited to conduct a single selection at a concert of this prestigious orchestra. Haydn's *Serenade for Strings* had been chosen as an appropriate offering to be presented under the baton of the great conductor. However, with all his responsibilities, it was not possible for Sir Ernest to rehearse the orchestra and Victor was chosen to carry out this task. When the time for the performance arrived, Victor had worked assiduously to ensure that the preparation of the composition was fully accomplished.

Sir Ernest was highly impressed at the level of performance under the young man's baton, and Victor's role was duly recognized. Upon hearing of Sir Ernest's appreciation of the orchestra's splendid state of preparedness, Victor seized the opportunity to appear uninvited and unannounced at MacMillan's office at the Toronto Conservatory (soon to become the "Royal" Conservatory of Music). The secretary, guarding the principal's privacy, tried to put Victor off to another day, but Sir Ernest, hearing the voice of his All-Ontario Secondary School Orchestra rehearsal assistant, called out, "Send him in." Victor explained that his ultimate goal was to become an orchestral conductor, to which Sir Ernest replied, "there are not enough orchestras for the number of would-be conductors, but if you're serious, go and see Ettore Mazzoleni," the man many believed to be Canada's most able orchestral leader and at that time the sole instructor of conductors for such ensembles.

These moments were to be the beginning of many Feldbrill interactions with the mighty Sir Ernest MacMillan and his TSO assistant conductor, Ettore Mazzoleni. Victor not only met the two TSO conductors at parties he and Zelda attended with the Women's Committee (where they were able to share the delicious pots of chili made by Elsie MacMillan), but a year or so later, Sir Ernest offered him a unique opportunity.

At a student concert, he was invited to conduct the TSO in the Johann Strauss Waltz, *Artists' Life*. Victor commented to Mazzoleni on this occasion that he would have preferred to lead the TSO in a more serious, extended work — to which his mentor replied, "How wonderful to be so young. You have no idea how difficult a Strauss waltz can be for a seasoned conductor." In the light of the fact that the "pop" concert included light fare such as Weber's *Oberon Overture*, a soprano's *Waltz Song* from Gounod's *Romeo and Juliet* sung by Evelyn Gold, and fragments of concertos played by a young violinist, Elsie Babiak, and pianist Molly Levinter (along with the Tchaikovsky Symphony no. 4, led by Sir Ernest), Victor's contribution seemed quite appropriate and was enthusiastically received, even by seasoned and amused TSO players.

In the midst of all this interaction, Victor was wise enough to secure, from both Sir Ernest and Ettore Mazzoleni, letters of commendation appropriate to be presented to any musical figures who might be familiar with the TSO's conductor and his associate. These documents were eventually to be placed before illustrious conductors abroad, and particularly in Britain, where they had a dramatic impact — Sir Ernest's capture and incarceration in the Ruhleben prison camp during the First World War, his success in raising the morale of his fellow prisoners, and his simultaneous earning of a degree in music from Oxford University, had made him a celebrity throughout the British Commonwealth, as well as earned him a title.

"Sir" Adrian Boult, Victor's most helpful future contact in Britain, had been Mazzoleni's instructor in the art of conducting before his arrival in Toronto. Victor would come to realize how fortunate he was to have these letters. They had the power to open doors to every rehearsal or concert hall that Victor wished to enter, at a time when, as a violinist for *The Navy Show*, he found himself ensconced in the cities of the United Kingdom and Europe, sometimes for weeks at a time.

During his high-school years, Victor played in every ensemble he could find, in addition to organizing his Harbord colleagues into quartets and trios that would examine, study, and perform the chamber music that the large orchestra was forced to ignore. When he discovered out-of-school instrumental groups he joined every one he encountered, securing the experience even when the repertoire and the level of performance did not thrill him.

He discovered there were "perks" to joining some of these outside groups. For example, he found that as a member of the Harmony Symphony Orchestra, a community amateur ensemble, he would be under the baton of his hero of that time, Ettore Mazzoleni. Through that contact he eventually became a member of the Conservatory Symphony Orchestra under the maestro's direction. Mazzoleni, realizing Victor's humble circumstances, placed him in a harmony course even though he knew that conducting was his passion, as there he could secure for him a considerable discount on his fees. Victor applied, found another colleague whose presence would further reduce the cost of instruction, and both were accepted and signed up for lessons.

Victor also encountered other teachers of considerable talent. One was a very young Lou Applebaum, working at the local Jewish Boy's Club and soon to be on his way to compose for the National Film Board. He was to become Canada's most prolific and accomplished composer of incidental music for theatre and for radio and film programming of all kinds. And, of course, the aforementioned John Weinzweig, with whom Victor studied for a short while, ravenous for every speck of information he could discover and never ceasing in his efforts to learn all he could about orchestral music, composition, and performance.

After the Weinzweig visit to Harbord and his individual lesson in reading scores, Victor had organized a strategy to broaden the range of his familiarity with the orchestral repertoire. As well as visiting the Toronto Public Library's music section, he set out to create his personal collection:

> I am going to buy a new score every week and study each one closely and thereby make for myself a complete repertoire of great symphonies. This will come in handy in case I do get the chance to conduct a decent orchestra.[3]

There were extraordinary opportunities to learn the rudiments of conducting beyond the walls of the collegiate. In particular, CBC Radio became familiar to him, as he was hired as a violinist for a special "gigs," often playing background music for drama or public affairs programs. But on one occasion Victor found himself replacing Howard Cable, who would become one of Canada's most prolific composers, arrangers, and conductors. On this occasion, Victor had the opportunity to lead an ensemble that included the incomparable Ellis McClintock on trumpet — a musician who was soon to have his own famous dance band. Another time the bass player in the orchestra was an aspiring young composer called Godfrey Ridout — a figure whose music Victor would come to champion.

Success in the world of orchestral performance is about securing the confidence of a host of instrumentalists, and Victor seized every such opportunity with intensity and focus. These "gigs" during his teen years were essential. Victor was to be wrenched from the familiar Toronto scene for war service just a few months after his graduation from Harbord, but he found that he was able to return to the musical life of the Toronto community with considerable comfort in 1946 as a familiar figure from the past.

⋙

While still at Harbord, and even before his TSO debut, Victor was presented with an extraordinary proposal. A few blocks east of his school, the University of Toronto was faced with a problem that plagued all institutions at this time — instructors, graduates, and even senior students were leaving for military service, including those who might have given leadership in any number of areas of music performance. There was — in existence since founder John Weinzweig's attendance in the mid-1930s as an undergraduate — a University of Toronto Symphony Orchestra (UTSO), at this time unconnected to the Toronto Conservatory or the Faculty of Music. Rather, it was sponsored by the Student Administrative Council (SAC) as an ensemble that could have members from both institutions, but was essentially a recreational activity for the enjoyment of any members of the university who simply wanted to play good music with others of similar talent and commitment. By the early 1940s, with no adequate conductor available, the SAC was driven to invite a soon-to-graduate Harbord student, Victor Feldbrill, to guest conduct. This meant that the young conductor would have the honour of being on the podium immediately before the city's major symphony orchestra, the TSO, took the stage.

In a few months he had made a considerable difference in the sound and performance standards of the UTSO. When interviewed by an unnamed *Toronto Telegram* journalist, Victor was asked why he had planned such a difficult concert program — one that included a Mozart symphony as well as a challenging *Overture to La Gazza Ladra* (*The Thieving Magpie*) by Rossini. His response was quite perceptive, drawn now from some years of experience: "amateurs resent things too easy for them."

The impact of this introduction as the conductor of a university ensemble of some prestige can be assessed by a headline from the February 26 *Varsity* newspaper, which read, in bold letters that could be seen from a considerable distance, "Youth Takes Over." The article in the university paper also provided an exciting account of Victor's background, and stated that "a sense of polished musicianship was the most striking feature" of the concert. The assessment continued:

> All the performers played with a confidence which was surprising. Victor Feldbrill is an exceptionally fine conductor. At all times he kept a facile control over the orchestra, never striving unduly for extreme effects and leading with an easy self assurance which was imparted to the orchestra.[4]

One might ignore the generous ruminations of the student press, but the reviews of the music critics of Toronto's major newspapers were even more adulatory. Augustus Bridle wrote:

> Victor Feldbrill conducted. In a few weeks this young student has given a youth impetus to a band of players [fifty], few of whom had been under the same baton before. There is a zippy zest in the orchestra which only young players bring…. The orchestra's best number was *The Thieving Magpie Overture* by Rossini, not heard here before: splendid, vital vivacity and evident tonal ecstasy.[5]

The *Toronto Globe*'s headline creator mirrored the *Varsity*'s preoccupation: "Youth Scores Musically at the University of Toronto Orchestra Recital." Victor was described as giving "capable and enthusiastic direction" that produced a "startlingly good performance," and the review went on to comment and predict that Victor "has already learned how to get the most co-operation from his orchestra and undoubtedly has a great future ahead of him."[6]

The success of the teenage Feldbrill became legendary. Sir Ernest MacMillan turned up at a UTSO concert and raved about Victor's performance before these university instrumentalists. Indeed, Jack Elton, the manager of the TSO, had telephoned Victor to tell him that the maestro was delighted with his performance. After Victor had joined the Armed Forces, one of the university's SAC employees, Frances Ireland, maintained a correspondence, flattering him with her perceptions of his strength in the conductor's role and encouraging him to plan a return once the war was over.

In a letter in the fall of 1943, when Victor, as a leading bandsman, was playing across Canada, she wrote how, in his absence, the UTSO had fallen into desperate circumstances. Though there were a "lot of good first year men with orchestral experience … they were prone to ask who the conductor will be and when I say that has not been decided yet, everyone has looked gloomy and sad." The experienced orchestral members' response was, "Too bad Victor can't come back."

"Don't think you are forgotten!" was her comforting comment. "I feel personally that you have built the orchestra into such a valuable organization with such splendid sound that we risk undoing your work by entrusting it to anyone who might be incompetent."[7]

It is astounding to realize that this reputation had been established by a young man still involved in his high-school studies and later occupied with a job seating the audience members in a movie theatre as he prepared to join the Royal Canadian Navy (RCN) as a leading bandsman (as a violinist, the designation seemed bizarre, but there was no other category available).

This recognition of his work reminded him that, while playing somewhat unrewarding music in a pit band, he had proven himself on the podium, before orchestras like the TSO and the UTSO, organizations made up of often unrestrained, critical, and callous colleagues, all older than him and most considerably more experienced.

With all this activity throughout the school year, one might have thought that the summer holidays would have brought some relief from the pressures of continuing performance, both in and out of school. But Victor's determination and persistence in matters musical knew no bounds. He was sure that every moment either practising on his violin or playing in an ensemble would pay off with a career in music. He was relentless in this belief. Nothing could deter him. Part of the problem for Victor was the fact that Zelda was invariably taken away to a cottage for most of the summer months. Without her, he was lonely. His solution was to immerse himself in music. Along with his friend Morry Kernerman, he haunted the rehearsals of the Toronto Promenade Symphony at Varsity Arena, conducted by Reginald Stewart, until the conductor tired of their constant presence and forbade their attendance. Only an appeal to Ernest Johnson, the manager of the Prom Concerts, assured their entry.[8]

However, not even Johnson could direct Victor's opinion of the quality of what was being heard. The terms "lousy" and "pretty smelly" were typical description of the rehearsal efforts of the Promenade Orchestra.[9] Nevertheless, it did not prevent him from making every effort to join that ensemble as a step toward the height of professionalism he sought to attain — he had set his sights on reaching the ranks of the TSO. He managed to achieve a short-term presence in the Promenade Symphony Orchestra's second violin section. He reported to Zelda that his teacher, Sigmund Steinberg, told him that if he "worked hard enough next year, he [could] arrange for [him] to have an audition with Sir Ernest to get in the Symphony."[10] The timing would have been perfectly synchronized with Victor's graduation.

It was a year later that he approached Ernest Johnson with a plan to engage new audiences. "Had the Proms ever advertised in the schools in the city?" was the question Victor posed. The reply — No — indicated that there had not been the slightest interest in attracting that particular potential audience. Otherwise, the interview went well. Johnson had prepared himself for the interaction and had questioned Brian McCool about Victor's conducting of the Harbord Orchestra as well as his work with the TSO Women's Committee. Johnson had come away from his meeting with Victor impressed by the young man's knowledge and leadership qualities.

Victor also questioned Johnson about the Promenade program repertoire and even suggested that a student guest conductor might increase the attention paid by students to Prom summer concerts. He offered to be the subject of such an experiment, but nothing came of the suggestion. However, his initiative had certainly caught Johnson's attention and a year later he was playing in the string section of the Prom orchestra. It was starting to come together.

From his seat amongst the strings of the Promenade Orchestra, Victor could, once again, observe the one figure who was becoming his hero as a conductor — Ettore Mazzoleni. He reported to Zelda that "the rehearsals were marvelous," and that at Prom concert program "he was in top form. You just can't catch your breath it is so magnificent."[11]

Victor's success in performing in the Promenade Orchestra (largely comprised of TSO players) represented another step toward the career in music he coveted. It was obviously too soon to make his move toward what was already his ultimate goal, that of becoming a conductor — but he was learning what it was like to be part of a professional orchestra. As well, summer was a time when he could play and conduct in the Conservatory Orchestra that Principal Mazzoleni had revived, uncomfortable as it was in the airless rehearsal hall during one of the hottest summers on record in the city. These experiences may not have been artistic highpoints but they were all a part of building relationships within the close-knit musical community of 1940s Toronto.

In the spring of 1943, Victor graduated from Harbord Collegiate Institute. His final results on the provincial examinations were not outstanding and did not represent his intelligence or the extent of his understanding. The reality was that music had diverted him from the academic achievement that had been promised by his elementary schooling. Music had become his obsession — only Zelda's constant encouragement had prevented him from failing to secure the marks that would allow for further educational opportunities when the time came. Indeed, without her intervention it is possible he would not have graduated from Harbord at all.

However, it was time to reassess his future direction. Zelda, his parents, and, indeed, her parents wanted him to pursue a university degree. Yet his examination results gave no hope of scholarship support. He needed a year away from academic pursuits, time to think over his future direction — and time to save some money. With so many men now caught up in military service, finding a job was quite easy. That, and carrying on his music studies, particularly on the violin with Steinberg, would also be possible. He found afternoon and evening employment at a local movie house, the Uptown Cinema, which worked perfectly as it left the rest of his daytime free for practising his violin and other musical activities.

This organization of his year also solved another problem. By the following spring, Zelda, too, would graduate from Harbord. They could then proceed together to the next level of their educational expectations. Even the separation of grade level at secondary and post-secondary would disappear. However, the RCN had other plans for the future of this talented young violinist.

By 1943, the war in Europe, North America, and the Far East had taken a turn for the better. After many months of disaster upon disaster, Rommel had been stopped in North Africa and the Allied powers were now poised to invade Europe — first from the southeast, then ultimately from Sicily and the Italian peninsula. Hitler's greatest error had been that of attacking Russia before defeating the United Kingdom, and that mistake was to be fatal.

However, it was plain that there would be no peace for some time. As early as 1942, Stalin and his generals were appealing to Churchill and Roosevelt for a second front — an invasion of the French coast that would relieve the pressure on Russia. It was, at first, an unreasonable expectation at a time when the Allies had neither the forces nor equipment to mount such a massive frontal attack against considerable fortifications and concentrations of troops guarding the continent's beaches. Canada had played a major role in a small invasion of Dieppe on the French coast. It did not go well and an unsupportable number of Canadian were killed, wounded, or taken prisoner. It was apparent that an attack on mainland western Europe from the sea would be an incredibly complex and costly affair demanding enormous air and sea power along with masses of troops who must be thoroughly trained. It would take time and could not be considered until 1944. Even with successful campaigns in Sicily and then Italy, Russia could not be satisfied until the sacrifices of the Allied powers through the European invasion indicated that unconditional surrender was truly the goal of Allied military strategy.

By that year, it was obvious that another wave of Canadian youth would be required to complete the country's commitment to the cause of stamping out Nazism. Included was a need for naval strength to maintain a British presence in the war and to support the will to continue the inexorable defence of the sea routes to the islands of the United Kingdom. For the fighting troops, whether on land, sea, or in the air, there was a need to provide a lift to morale. Many had been involved in fierce fighting on the Mediterranean front; others had now impatiently spent three long years waiting in Britain to participate in an invasion of Europe. All were in need of moments of entertainment, of visual and musical delight; they needed to laugh and forget their fear of possible death and disability, even for a few moments. Victor Feldbrill, though scarcely out of secondary school, was to find his life very much challenged and changed by these imperatives, which he quickly came to appreciate. He was to be part of a cause to which he could bring his talent and give his time and energy.

CHAPTER 3

The Navy Show

While Victor had been conducting and pursuing his musical activities during the months following his graduation from Harbord Collegiate and simultaneously seeking to make some money tending to the needs of patrons at Toronto's Uptown Theatre, the conflict with Germany (and, by December 1941, the Japanese Empire) had spread to every continent but the Americas, Australasia, and Antarctica. Even so, it seemed to have little relevance to a Jewish lad whose world was largely contained within the familiar neighbourhoods that were close by his home in Toronto. In Victor's case, his closest family members still spoke and read only Yiddish, and the impact of the war on the recently arrived co-religionists who were his extended family was very limited. Their preoccupation was very much that of getting settled and "getting on" in a new homeland. This could be said of thousands of others who had come to Canada after the First World War, and even those fleeing the rise of the Nazi scourge.

Certainly Canadian interest in the Second World War went far beyond just the former inhabitants of the British motherland who had been so overwhelmingly prominent in the country's Armed Forces in the early years of the First World War. In this conflict, the struggle had little to do with the mysteries of imperial rivalry, the complexities of an arms race, or the subtle balancing of power in Europe. The cause was much clearer — a dictator fuelled by an ideology of master race domination had decided it was the right time to crush all opposition to Nazi plans for expansion no matter what the cost. Germany's grievances flowing from the Treaty of Versailles were certainly a factor, but only one of many issues that could be used to arouse the pride of the German people.

In the late 1930s and early 1940s, there was an aspect of this conflict that most certainly aroused the concern of those in Europe whose allegiance to the Jewish faith made them anathema to Adolf Hitler and his colleagues in the Nazi Party. They were blamed for everything that had gone wrong since the First World War and were openly identified as the enemy of a strong and vibrant Germany. But the full extent of his plan was not totally revealed until the early 1940s, and the institutional arrangements and methodologies for the destruction of the Jewish community were not wholly in play until after 1942. Even when the details of the concentration camps began to spill out of Europe, the Feldbrill family, like many others, could cope only through a strategy of denial. The letters from the family back in Poland had ceased, particularly from relatives in Warsaw and Nathan's brother and his daughters in Lodz, but they, like other Jewish Canadians, could not bring themselves to believe that an evil force of such intensity could have been unleashed in the civilized Western world of the twentieth century.

⚊⚊⚊

In spite of Victor's greater experience as a result of his reaching out to musical ensembles beyond his Harbord Collegiate Orchestra, he was of little help to his family, who assumed him to be a musical genius with interests focused beyond the family but having little relevance to its day-to-day needs. That fact enabled Victor, now approaching his twenties, to be largely unaffected by the events that were creating headlines in English-speaking newspapers. It seems that the gravity of the situation had yet to resonate in the behaviour of a young man rapidly reaching the age when conscription into the Armed Forces of his country promised to bring about a profound change in his way of life.

Indeed, he was insufficiently aware of the impact of the war to realize that he might well be called up for military duty. He was in good health and had no direct dependants. He was not enrolled in a university — a status that would have protected him for some years after his high-school graduation. In the frantic rush of job, rehearsals, musical studies, and gigs with numerous musical ensembles, he was surprised when he was informed that he should present himself at the local recruiting office as a candidate for service to his country. He had reached the age of eighteen and was now considered capable of the task of defending King and Country; however that might be identified and determined.

By the summer of 1943, the pressure on England and America to mount a second front was both a military and diplomatic necessity. Hitler had moved too soon in his desire to crush the communists, who, along with Jews, were enemies of the Fatherland. He launched the attack on Russia before his rearmament program had provided the necessary abundance of tanks, submarines, warships, and airplanes (both bombers and fighter air-craft), and had not assured his access to the oil that would allow the success-ful execution of a two-front war. In these circumstances, the Canadian navy had special pressures to offset. Nearly four years of supplying Britain with food and other essentials across a submarine-infested Atlantic Ocean had been successful — but they had sustained major losses of ships and person-nel, particularly those associated with the merchant navy.

It was obvious that the war could not be won without an invasion of the European continent, and this strategy would demand a command of the northeastern Atlantic and in particular the English Channel. As well, the massing of troops and equipment in the British Isles would take many months. This provisioning would place special pressures on the navy as they worked to keep the flow of food and fuel coming from North America. Yet it was realized that the launching of an invasion was the ultimate necessity in any strategy to defeat Hitler. A shorter-term goal was that of supporting the Russian forces, who were suffering horrendous losses. But that, too, would demand the defence of sea routes to the U.S.S.R. Stalin was impatient, realizing that only an assault on the beaches of France and the Netherlands would alleviate the pressure on the Soviet Union. He became increasingly convinced that Britain and the United States were allowing them to bear the brunt of the war — perhaps as a cynical strategy to ensure a weak Soviet Union once hostilities ended. This perceived strategy corresponded to a theory that the capitalist states would ultimately use the war to weaken and destroy the cause of the socialist revolution.

If these doubts could not be overcome, was it possible that the Soviet Union might make a separate peace? Anything could happen in the volatile relationship of communist and capitalist nations joined as allies only by their need for an immediate defeat of a common enemy.

By 1943, the war had reached a point where invention and new technologies of warfare could make a dramatic difference. For the Canadian navy, the dangers were significant. German admiral Karl Doenitz promised that with two hundred improved electro submarines armed with radar and acoustically guided torpedoes, he could completely blockade the British Isles, thereby undermining the very base from which any invasion on the European western coast could be launched.

Doenitz was one of the few who had Hitler's ear. That possibility, plus the plan to use unmanned rockets on English cities — the much feared V-1s and V-2s, which could not be intercepted effectively — demanded a more intense Allied response to the requests for increased forces on land, air, and sea. These considerations, along with the rumours of a Nazi atomic bomb in the early stages of development, ensured that Victor and many other young men would have to be recruited. Without a major increase in personnel along with new weapons in massive quantities, there was every chance that there could be a German Empire ruling Europe and seeking to dominate the globe — if not for "a thousand years," at least for a few decades.

As well as provisioning the greatest invasion force in history, there was the need to find the means of transporting these fighting troops by sea and air to the shores of the European continent. Only the presence of strong naval forces that could carry an invading army those few miles across the English Channel and protect them until the beaches of Normandy were successfully occupied could guarantee success. France, Belgium, and the Netherlands would be immediate destinations for liberation and use as bases in order to establish a foothold for what would now become a European front. Victor, who as a secondary school student had been virtually psychologically and emotionally uninvolved, now had to make a decision. How could he make a meaningful contribution to this enormous enterprise?

The autumn and winter months away from Harbord had thrown him more into the world. He was moving, no longer with school chums, but more often with adults. He was becoming aware that this war did, in fact, affect him. He began to understand that an evil philosophy might already have exterminated members of his own family along with millions of other members of his faith community. In spite of Nathan and Helen's unwillingness to talk about the family "back home," he realized that these far-off relatives had likely been the victims of what would come to be known as The Holocaust.

Those processing new recruits were looking for a broad range of skills. It was not just about numbers of men and women who had to be put in uniform to add to the fighting forces in the field or at sea. There was the reality of addressing the quality of morale and resulting determination of those who had already given years of their lives to the cause. The war had waged for four years and there were those who had fought in North Africa and Sicily and were engaged in working their way up the Italian boot. Now on leave, they needed relaxation and entertainment that could revive their spirits and remind them of why they were risking their lives in a war that for Canadians was thousands of miles distant. There were other servicemen and women, both in Canada and in the United Kingdom, who had endured the frustration of waiting … and waiting … and waiting, for the invasion that all knew was inevitable but which never seemed to come about.

In each of the fighting forces — army, navy, and air force — there was a need for an expansion of all the strategies for maintaining and raising the spirits and enhancing the desire to achieve total victory. In the RCN, one such strategy was the creation of a theatrical presentation that was highly entertaining, but could, through laughter and song, remind naval personnel (as well as civilians and members of other armed forces who might become audiences) that this cause was worth fighting and dying for. It would require a sophisticated production, one that came with first-class performers — singers, dancers, choristers, and comedians — but also script writers, choreographers, songwriters, and technicians. Most important was the need for musicians — not those connected with a traditional military or naval forces band, but a group of instrumentalists who could be part of any professional ensemble, one that could play the wide range of music that any fine variety show orchestra encounters.

Once again, an important figure in Victor's life intervened. It was Sigmund Steinberg, Victor's violin teacher. He was one person who had connections with the instrumental music community on a number of levels across Canada. Through his associates he had heard that the RCN was looking for musicians who would join what was already being referred to as *The Navy Show*, or, more precisely, *Meet the Navy*. He saw in that ensemble an immediate opportunity to find a place for Victor, now a fine violinist with a broad spectrum of experience, one that would provide him with a valuable new opportunity for musical growth and simultaneously allow him to carry out an effective role in the service of his country. Thus, in the spring and summer of 1943, Victor, whose only experience with ships had been excursions to the Toronto Islands on a passenger barge, became a seaman with a rank of Leading Bandsman. The fact was that *Meet the Navy* would be almost entirely land-based, visiting the concentrations of servicemen across Canada. Indeed in 1943 and 1944 it crossed the entire country twice, eventually reaching the United Kingdom and a liberated Europe by 1945. Although enlisted men and women were the designated audience, it became clear that there were civilians who also needed the lift in morale that accompanied the show's appearance wherever it went. Canadian servicemen and women were dying in the air over Britain and Germany and had participated in North Africa and on the Italian front. With a special mission role overseas, Canadians had faced considerable casualties during the invasion at Dieppe; however, compared to the experiences of citizens of the United Kingdom or the conquered countries of Europe, the war had not affected the daily lives of most Canadians. If continued support for the war and the sacrifices that lay ahead was to be achieved, some intervention at home must be launched from coast to coast. As seemingly trivial and inconsequential as it might seem, *Meet the Navy* would play a significant role in that effort to rouse a nation and its Armed Forces.

It turned out to be a superb show that, through dance, songs, skits, and choral presentations, magically reminded audiences what the essence of the conflict was — the defeat of an evil force that threatened the entire development of democratic institutions and could undermine the moral basis of a decent, humane society. Victor had indeed found his place in this world-shattering event, one that he was to learn even more about as he attended the first rehearsals for *The Navy Show* and began his basic training in Toronto.

⤬⤬⤬

Victor was sitting at the second stand directly behind the concertmaster just below the baton of Eric Wild, the conductor who would become a major figure in Canadian music in the decades after the war. For a young Victor, still a teenager, it was a surprising position of leadership. When Eric Wild was absent, the regular concertmaster took over the baton and Victor took his place in the first chair. That *Meet the Navy* was successful is beyond dispute. It ravished the senses of audiences that swarmed to see and hear an extraordinary array of talented singers and expert comics supported by a cadre of splendid instrumentalists in a first-class pit orchestra. It was understandably compared with Irving Berlin's *U.S. Army Show* and declared imminently superior in every category of presentation. It became a production to which major political and military figures were invited, including Canada's then prime minister, Mackenzie King. The ultimate moment came later in the war, while *Meet the Navy* was stationed in England, and Britain's royal family attended a performance. On every occasion superlatives described the quality of the show. All were unanimous — it was a triumph!

There were many "stars" who went on to careers in show business after the war, including the Lunds, Alan and Blanche, who as dancers and choreographers captivated audiences on stage and in film for decades. Perhaps the most famous on-stage comic figure was John Pratt, who sang "You'll Get Used to It," the selection that became the hit of the show. He left comedy for politics and was, in the 1950s and '60s, a prominent figure in the municipal politics of Quebec. He later became a leading member of John Diefenbaker's Conservative government. But it was not "stars" that ensured the quality of performance, it was the team effort of dozens of Canadians, most of whom had never before been on the stage, but who were well-rehearsed and eager to make the show work. Victor was one of them.

In short, *Meet the Navy* was an achievement of no small measure that benefited all the Armed Forces, so much so that it became a continuing phenomenon after hostilities in Europe ended in June 1945. In fact, its success became a major problem for most of its participants, who by this time just wanted to go home — and Victor was one of the most anxious to do so. *The Navy Show* even became the basis for a British feature film, a process that further extended the service of participants as rehearsals for new actors, singers, and instrumentalists had to be arranged. The filming of *Meet the Navy* went on for weeks, time that the participants resented now that the enemy had been defeated and their futures lay back in Canada.

⚒

Before all the clapping and cheering of a theatrical production, however, the seemingly mindless process of transforming these players into seamen and women had to be accomplished. Victor's basic training as a member of the RCN took place in Toronto, on the familiar campus of its university. The initiation process included physical exercise — unthinkable for this group of performers — and endless marching, along with an education in a wide range of naval matters. Victor found many aspects of his training fascinating, but soon discovered that the worst aspect of the navy experience would be the long periods of separation from his beloved Zelda and his supportive family.

As soon as rehearsals of *The Navy Show* began, it was apparent that there would be no challenge demanding the acquisition of new skills as a violinist. However, the pit orchestra initiation was a different world for Victor, even though he had played the same score for several nights in the runs of Gilbert and Sullivan at his collegiate. But this same score for *Meet the Navy,* with minor alterations, would be his sole focus for more than two years. Obviously, Victor would have to find ways to keep his technique at its height as well as constantly refurbishing his sight-reading if *The Navy Show* was not to have a negative effect on his preparation for a peacetime career as a professional musician. As one might expect, it eventually became a "hell on wheels" — the mere mention of *Meet the Navy* half a century later occasions a grimace and a muttered deprecatory comment from a famously "cool and collected" Maestro Victor Feldbrill.

The Navy Show was under pressure to conclude rehearsals and be on its way across Canada by early September of 1943. Although the first performance took place in Toronto to great accolades, a trip to nearby Brantford for a virtual dress rehearsal for the touring pressures of the production indicated whether *Meet the Navy* was ready. The Brantford audience responded marvellously. By mid-September, *The Navy Show* was given a further trial by fire at a gala in Ottawa with Canada's prime minister, Mackenzie King, and numerous politicians from the House of Commons and Senate present. "The Show was a terrific hit with everyone and the applause was deafening to say the least," was Victor's observation in a letter to Zelda.

Victor sought to find *Navy Show* venues at which he could arrange to see Zelda, but the early performance spaces were some distance from Toronto. Alas, in the one opportunity in Peterborough where she could have appeared for a pre-production liaison, the show's performance was cancelled. This was merely the beginning of two years of both short (a few weeks) and long (a year and a half) separations that would bedevil their efforts to remain a loving couple.

It was not an easy task to accommodate the first stage of a national tour — it was a complex production and there were not many well-endowed theatres with lighting and sound equipment equal to the task of dealing with *Meet the Navy*, particularly in communities that were conveniently close to naval bases, army camps, and air force training centres. The first major stop was, appropriate for any navy show, Halifax, Nova Scotia, and *Meet the Navy* formally opened there on September 28, 1943.

By late October, it became obvious that the constant movement and continuing performance would be exciting but exhausting. On the twelfth it was Annapolis Royal and H.M.C.S. *Cornwallis*, on the thirteenth it was Kemptville and a performance for an army base nearby. By mid-October, it was back east to Truro, Nova Scotia, Moncton for three days, and Quebec City for four days. The end of October had special significance for Victor — he had met Zelda in that month back in 1939. Now she was also graduating from Harbord and a ceremony at the end of the month would recognize that achievement. As a prominent and gifted student, she would be expected to attend not just the convocation but the graduation dance in mid-November, as well. It seemed it would all take place without Victor, whose schedule would take him back to Ottawa and then on to the Niagara Peninsula, with stops at St. Catharines, Welland, and Niagara Falls. Zelda was devastated by her lover's absence, though the atmosphere cleared when Victor informed her that conductor Eric Wild had given him leave to escort her at least to the Harbord Graduation Dance.

By December 1943, the show was creating a storm of enthusiasm with New York producers wishing to create an American tour. But that fantasy soon disappeared and late November saw instead appearances in London (Ontario), Sarnia, Windsor, Stratford, Kitchener, Guelph, Galt, Oshawa, and finally Peterborough. By the end of 1943, all the major centres in eastern Canada had been visited. The next stage would be a western tour that would consume some several months and complete the mission of reaching seemingly every targeted Canadian serviceman and woman in the country, to say nothing of a large number of civilians.

During these months Victor came to realize he was faced with a serious decision. He had taken on a commitment to place his talent and energy behind an element of the war effort that he now had the training and capacity to perform. However, this work in the RCN could not only end his hopes for becoming a professional musician — one who could hold his own in any respectable ensemble, large or small, upon his return to civilian life — but even more likely, divert him from achieving his ultimate goal, that of becoming an orchestral conductor. He wanted to play his part in a just struggle against an evil enemy, but did the cost have to be so great? It was not only the limited and diminishing function of playing a rather simple score night after night (with an additional matinee on certain days), it was the schedule that left him bored while awaiting each performance, hours that were filled with scenic travel by bus or rail that gave some relief but little inspiration.

He had a choice. He could spend his time gambling on cards, playing darts, engaging in casual conversation, discovering the drinking establishments at every stop — a lifestyle that would allow him to forget the utter boredom he found so debilitating. Or he could choose another solution. He could set a regimen for himself whereby he could improve his technique as a violinist through hours of practising, and, in anticipation of being a conductor, work on the basics of harmony and orchestration and find unfamiliar repertoire he could study — all those essentials that would determine the quality of his future career making music. Fortunately, he decided on the second course.

It was well that he was not entirely alone in his misery. There were other colleagues who were faced with the same dilemma. Once the initial rehearsals of the score of *Meet the Navy* ended and instrumentalists knew the notes by heart, some of his colleagues in the orchestra pit came to look to Victor for leadership in finding some form of self-fulfillment in professional development. It was significant that these older, and in most cases more experienced, instrumentalists came to look to this young man as the one to form small orchestral ensembles to play an extended chamber music repertoire and to organizing duets, trios, and quartets that allowed the addressing of the great classics of those chamber music genres. It was all in the process of finding opportunities to play good music and to seize some measure of relief from being totally jaded by the unyielding schedule of performing the same score night after night, month after month, accompanying the singing and dancing and providing the linkages from skit to skit as each segment inexorably found its way on to the stage. After a few months, it had become a mindless exercise in patience and self-control.

A few weeks into the fall of 1943, Victor found an orchestral associate cellist who wanted to play duets and he, along with another violin, a violist, and bass player in the pit band then determined upon playing string music. It was often difficult to find a place to rehearse, but many of the managers of the theatres were accommodating and finally respectable levels of performance of Haydn and Mozart ensued.

During the Canadian tours, Victor was billeted with an older musician, a violist, Ross Lechow. The two had discovered a contemporary viola concerto written by British composer William Walton, which soon became a source of inspiration and a challenge to their musical virtuosity. Several years later, they found themselves sharing a place in the TSO, faced with the challenge of rehearsing the Walton concerto in anticipation of the arrival of William Primrose, who was to be the highly vaunted viola soloist. Victor informed conductor Sir Ernest MacMillan that his colleague Ross Lechow could substitute for the delayed Primrose, allowing the orchestra to achieve a more valuable rehearsal experience before his eventual arrival in Toronto. Sir Ernest and the entire ensemble were both surprised and pleased.

There were also a few unanticipated opportunities. At one point in the Maritime tour, the concertmaster was forced to replace Eric Wild as conductor. Victor was approached to work with the string players, giving him the opportunity to do some conducting. "What was it like?" asked Zelda when she heard the news. Victor's ready answer: "It was wonderful! I felt so confident." He had the sensation of knowing that his orchestral colleagues had accepted his leadership and his judgment.

He spent Christmas of 1943 back with Zelda, but in the early months of 1944, began a tour of the western provinces, with multiple performances in the larger cities (ten shows were scheduled in six days in Vancouver and nine shows in five days in Victoria). Victor was thrilled with the mountains and river valleys, forests and wildlife in British Columbia, and promised Zelda that together they would come to enjoy this area in the future. And indeed, while living in Winnipeg a couple of decades later, they were able to take their children and drive west to revel in the scenery of the Canadian Rockies and the West Coast.

While playing with *The Navy Show* in Vancouver on this second tour, Victor met with Sir Ernest MacMillan, who was conducting that city's symphony orchestra. Victor turned up at one of the maestro's rehearsals, and Sir Ernest, delighted to see him, introduced him to the Vancouver Symphony Orchestra's concertmaster as "an accomplished young violinist and a very fine conductor." There was another surprising moment when Victor could verify Sir Ernest's high opinion. Such was the maestro's reputation across the nation that there were MacMillan Clubs to be found in several communities. After his encounter with Sir Ernest, he met a Miss Agnew, who was the president of the Vancouver Sir Ernest MacMillan Club. She relayed to Victor that the maestro had commented in his remarks to the club that he had met Victor but a day before and "how wonderful a job he did with both the University of Toronto and the Toronto Symphony Orchestras … and was quite enthusiastic about it." [1]

Victor, enjoying these exhilarating moments of support from Canada's pre-eminent musical figure, had been considering the possibility of moving to Vancouver after the war, and completing his preparation at University of British Columbia, He had pointed out to Zelda that she, too, could conclude her studies for a degree in social work at the same institution. Ironically, it was the same Sir Ernest who threw cold water on that plan. "The mountains are very high between Vancouver and the musical world of Toronto," was his advice — a reminder to Victor that in the 1940s there was not the opportunity for music-making on the West Coast that was to be found in the St. Lawrence Valley. With a wrong move, Victor might find himself ensconced in a veritable cultural backwater. Nothing more was said about moving to the West Coast!

The West Coast tour also included another special treat for Victor. The Victoria Symphony Orchestra needed extra players for a performance of Beethoven's Symphony no. 5, which, ironically, in the light of the composer's ancestry, had contained in its first few bars the theme that had come to represent an Allied victory over the enemy. The Victoria Symphony rendition needed more sound and body, and three of the *Navy Show* string players were contacted for the rehearsals and concert. They would each be paid five dollars. The performance was cheered wildly, but more importantly, Victor met another coterie of instrumentalists who would be part of his life after his time in the navy had been served.

The five-dollar stipend was added to a fund that Victor and Zelda had already established as a down payment for the house they would eventually purchase once they were married. There was no doubt in either partner's mind that they would be joined, and they hoped to have a sum of one thousand dollars gathered by that time. The money was mainly from Victor's recompense, though some of Zelda's wages from part-time summer employment — either at Borden's, a Toronto-based purveyor of milk products, including ice cream, or from the varnish factory in which she worked for a short time one summer. Ominously, it was after the Victoria

Symphony concert that Victor informed Zelda that he would return for a leave in Toronto in May 1944, but that he then expected they would be parted for a year or more as *The Navy Show* went over to the United Kingdom and then possibly to Europe. The week of Victor's arrival home on leave was the very time when Zelda was both writing and preparing to write more examinations, but the few hours of bliss that were rescued from this overall disappointing schedule were warmly remembered during the months of separation that ultimately followed.

The first West Coast and western prairie tour was completed in the winter and spring of 1944, and before any overseas excursion, *The Navy Show* was back to the Maritimes. *Meet the Navy* was stationed in Sydney when a reassuring interlude came to enliven Victor's day. At a rehearsal of the resident navy band, Victor was offered an opportunity to lead the ensemble in a concert brass rendition of Schubert's Symphony no. 8 (*The Unfinished Symphony*). He knew the work from his own private study and conducted it with the aplomb and confidence that only a youth could muster under the circumstances. He gave a clearly defined beat, insisting on accuracy and clarity from the percussion. At the end of the rehearsal, the members of the percussion section approached him and reported that "it was the first time anyone has paid attention to us." They also expressed the wish that he would conduct the band again very soon. But that was not to be, as *The Navy Show* was soon on the road again, back to the West to spend several days in each of Edmonton, Calgary, and Winnipeg, where, at Zelda's insistence, he contacted friends of her parents who were still living there.

These first months in *The Navy Show* established the pattern that dominated Victor's behaviour throughout the war. To some extent it was a continuation of teenage enthusiasms that had already aroused him before the R.C.N. had become part of his life. He was able, with Zelda's encouragement, to rehearse several hours a day. He found new repertoire that he could play — shorter pieces that delighted hosts of informal meals he shared with friends and relatives. He continued to be entranced by the art of filmmaking at a time when cinema was the foremost relief for people from the more than half a decade of death and destruction they had been living through. It was the same strategy that people had developed for fighting the depression of the 1930s. Victor attended every serious film he could discover ...

providing Zelda with critical comment and encouraging her attendance at the best of his choices.

But even more than either of these alternatives, there was the solace of quality radio. These were the years of Toscanini and the NBC Symphony … but both the New York Philharmonic and Cleveland orchestras were regularly heard, as well. While Victor was still in North America, he and Zelda tried to hear performances simultaneously no matter how time zones might seek to frustrate their intent. The experience of listening to great music together even though apart, was the closest intimacy that the couple could achieve over the many weeks and months of their enforced separation. Such was the supremacy of radio broadcasting and such was the commitment that the newly created missionary CBC Radio adapted itself to serve the war-sickened country.

The major networks in the United States vied with one another, all seeking to define themselves some distance from the plethora of small local stations, by connecting to a cultural feast of great musical performance. It was part of the war effort — to sustain the best aspects of a culture that was now seen to be in threatened circumstances. It was at a time in a global war when the values and cultural achievements of Western liberal democracy were at risk. The relatively new technology of radio was pre-eminent in the struggle for the minds of the nation's citizens. Victor and Zelda felt surrounded by a host of those who believed great music could inspire and improve the world in which they wished to live out their lives.

The two Canadian tours were a revelation for Victor, a fantasy become real for a young man who had scarcely seen beyond the borders of his native city. He had now visited every region of the country and had been hosted at family dinners, as well as at parties and receptions associated with *The Navy Show*. He never lost his passion for the beauty of the land that he called his home. In future decades, invitations to occupy the podiums of orchestras in other countries beckoned, but could not capture his full attention. He wanted his daughters to be educated and to live in Canada. London, England, and Amsterdam in the Netherlands were favourite places to visit. Florida might eventually become a retreat from the cold, ice, and snow of winter, but Canada was home.

However, Victor's years with *The Navy Show* had a further impact beyond that opportunity to see at least a part of the world "out there." He experienced the thrill, no matter how debilitating it ultimately became, of being part of an artistic achievement of no mean stature. Perhaps the most adulatory comment about *Meet the Navy* came near the end of the war. The show had been given a new look and had been rehearsed more enthusiastically for a longer run in London, England. Beverley Baxter, a noted British arts critic, gave the production its greatest review, one that Victor, with some pride, passed on to Zelda in a February 25, 1945, letter. Of the orchestra, Baxter commented that "Their playing was first class." However, it was the degree of perception of the total purpose of the show that this review revealed that moved every member of the cast: "It was vital. It was attractive. It was skillful. We began to ask ourselves if this was not the best musical show we had ever seen. We were seeing the story of Canada unfolding itself to our eyes and it was not a matter of professional slickness."

Baxter was particularly moved by the singing, which he declared to be "not unworthy of the finest opera house in the world." However, it was the total impact of the production that overwhelmed him: "The audience was electrified, applause grew to cheers and the whole thing proceeded to its climax in a gale of excitement. The Canadian Navy has sailed up the Thames and London is its prisoner."[2]

Could there be any doubt that Victor's years with His Majesty's Royal Canadian Navy had been well spent?

CHAPTER 4

Abroad

Amost dramatic moment in the Second World War had taken place while *The Navy Show* was still touring Canada, awaiting its opportunity to reach Europe. The expected invasion of the continent had finally come on June 6, 1944, and Allied troops — American, British, and Canadian — were now fighting their way toward the borders of a German nation that would soon be under siege from both West and East. Germany's ally, Italy, had already surrendered. The Mediterranean, the African coast, the Middle East, and the Balkans were now in Allied hands. Even more important, Russia had beaten back the German forces and now threatened to outperform the Allied forces invading from the West. For Hitler and his

Nazi leadership it was now only a matter of time … and that time would be filled with fighting Allied troops determined to liberate a continent and end an evil régime. The Allies had no plans to end the hostilities on the basis of a hurried negotiation. None wanted any of the confusion over winners and losers that had fuelled the bitterness upon which a future German leadership could blame the nation's failure. "Unconditional Surrender" it was to be in 1945.

However, with no hope of a negotiated settlement, the Nazis could command the complete support of both the army and civilian population. The savage bombings of German cities were a warning to the Nazi leadership of what might transpire after defeat. It was apparent that the war would not necessarily end immediately upon a successful invasion of Normandy. Every inch of European soil would have to be occupied and its people set free. It would take time and an extremely complex strategy on a number of fighting fronts before an occupation of Germany could be achieved and victory assured.

Victor had realized that his May leave before embarking for Europe might be the last time he would see Zelda for many months. He had no idea that it would, in fact, be a year and a half before they could finally be together. In those many months, *The Navy Show* would be entertaining the troops still remaining in Britain as well as war-weary civilians. After Europe was freed, the production would then be expected to transfer its attention to the continent, to entertain occupation troops and the citizens of those countries who had endured horrific years of Nazi hegemony.

On leaving Canada, *The Navy Show* was booked first in Scotland, then in Ireland for a short time, before moving on to a much longer run in England and, finally, its main destination — continental Europe. Though totally committed to doing everything possible to play his full part in the show, as early as the fall of 1944 Victor was planning in some detail his own strategy to benefit from this time spent in the British Isles and Europe, of whose musical culture he knew very little. That had to change. From his arrival in Scotland, he was determined to become familiar, not only with the great musical heritage of that country, and particularly that of England, but to have some contact with those who were responsible for these musical riches. He knew that a bevy of composers had put Britain at the forefront of serious music creation in the twentieth century — Stanford, Parry, Elgar, Delius, Holst, Vaughan Williams, Walton, and Britten were all names he had encountered in his studies. Now he might meet the interpreters of their music.

Actually, Victor had prepared himself for this possibility before he left Toronto. In one of the last exchanges with Ettore Mazzoleni he had explored his conducting mentor's close relationship with British conductor Sir Adrian Boult. Thus, Victor could inform Zelda that Boult "is, shall I say, my musical grandfather. Therefore with a letter from Mazz it might mean something."[1] He could not have been more prescient.

Victor arrived fully aware that an overseas experience "could be one of the greatest things that could happen to him." He was conscious that a career in the arts normally demanded enormous preparation as well as talent, or more accurately, intelligence, but that good fortune also played a part: "All it needs is one lucky break over on the other side and a future is almost secure for there is all the opportunity in the world if I take advantage of it."[2] He realized that relationships were important in an "industry" that so often depended upon creativity and collegiality and these were best assured by face-to-face interaction of artists with similar objectives, many of whom dwelt in other countries.

The trip across the Atlantic was thankfully uneventful. The German offensive had turned into a costly retreat and even the frontline of the war at sea had been affected. Troop ships could now outrun German submarines that had not been improved through available technology, largely as a result of misplaced priorities in the mind of Adolph Hitler. *The Navy Show*, its cast, and all its sets and costumes arrived safely and were immediately transported to Glasgow, Scotland. Thus transpired an unexplainable bout of "good fortune" that was to change the course of Victor's life. He was surprised and delighted to find that he was billeted in a building near the Glasgow Academy of Music. Indeed, on the day of his arrival in early autumn, he was greeted by the sounds of the Glasgow Amateur Orchestra rehearsing only few hundred feet from his bunk.

On the following day, that ensemble had been replaced in the academy's rehearsal hall by the renowned Scottish Symphony Orchestra. Victor lost little time finding his way to the entrance of the academy and, clutching a letter of introduction from Sir Ernest MacMillan, awaited an inevitable break in the rehearsal schedule. Finding his way to the podium and the orchestra's conductor, Warwick Braithwaite, he presented him with the MacMillan letter he hoped would initiate his best chance of finding a sympathetic response. Braithwaite read the missive and was overwhelmed — he knew of Sir Ernest's experience in the German prisoner of war camp in the First World War.

Victor had miraculously placed himself on a track to a series of introductions and invitations that led eventually to a number of enormous opportunities to move his education as a musician to a new level entirely. Through Maestro Braithwaite, he linked himself to John Barbiroli in Manchester, Adrian Boult in Birmingham, and even Thomas Beecham in London. They, along with a platoon of lesser-known but nonetheless internationally recognized figures had, up to this point, been just names of compelling importance to a man wishing for a career in their ranks, but together they opened for him the full spectrum of the English musical scene. It changed his life forever.

Victor knew what he wanted. He wished to sit in on every rehearsal he could attend (when not playing in *The Navy Show*), to do so with score in hand, and if possible, secure a seat in the subsequent performance if it was an off-night for *Meet the Navy*. He wanted to view and analyze the conducting skills and the interpretive genius of the finest English-speaking (and once he left for the continent, the French and German-speaking) conductors in the musical world. The full extent of these doors and windows that were opening became apparent when, some time later, he arrived in London and reported to Zelda, "I have only been here for two days and already things are happening. I made three valuable connections in one day — one at Boosey & Hawkes Music Publishers, and two at the Royal Academy of Music."[3]

For the time being, however, the Glasgow Academy became his artistic home — he was even able to secure a room in which he could practise his violin. However, his personal time was reduced when the number of *Meet the Navy* performances increased. It was in Glasgow that the show became so popular that it had to be divided into segments that could simultaneously perform in more than one venue. This in turn put more pressure on cast and orchestra to produce the full sound and the complete repertoire of the original production even though only a fraction of the total ensemble complement was present at any one time — no mean task. Yet Victor still had time to converse with Braithwaite and other ensemble conductors at the Academy, and was in constant interaction with the professional orchestral players who came through the institution's doors. His association and friendship with violinists in the Scottish Symphony Orchestra revealed to him just how British orchestras were organized and how they were expected to behave — from the inside! Discussions of interpretation of works in rehearsal led to long debates about how, for example, Beethoven's Symphony no. 6 "could be played in a truly pastoral manner."

Victor became a fixture at rehearsals week after week, one result being that he came to realize that British orchestras were expected to play the works of British composers. Thus, the works of contemporaries could become as familiar to both instrumentalists and audience members as the often performed Beethoven and Mozart. Victor became familiar with Peter Warlock's "Capriole Suite" and, of course, Elgar's enormously popular "Enigma Variations." Although the British orchestral repertoire was still buried in the works of the German masters along with Tchaikovsky, he was able to hear, for example, the less familiar symphonies of Borodin. There was a realization for Victor at this early stage that the repertoire of an orchestra was more than just giving people what they thought they wanted to hear again and again, but that it had to be balanced with what audiences needed to hear in order to create an intelligent and satisfying music listening life.

Warwick Braithwaite did much more than merely give Victor a prominent seat at his rehearsals; he insisted upon engaging Victor in a continuing discussion of repertoire. Even more surprising, Braithwaite came to trust his judgment on compositions that were being rehearsed. There were good reasons for his confidence. On one occasion the full conductor's score of the Brahms Symphony no. 4 and Wagner's *Overture to the Flying Dutchman* was passed into Victor's hands. He studied them carefully and found two errors in a score that led Braithwaite to remark that he would have to bring them to the orchestra's attention at the subsequent rehearsal. Watching this conductor, Victor learned something of the gentle discipline that was to be his own style, indeed his trademark, over the years of conducting that were to follow.

Just as significant were Braithwaite's warm and compelling introductory letters to his musician colleagues, which could act as door-openers for Victor throughout his weeks and months in the British Isles. To Jean Peugnet, the concertmaster of the London Philharmonic, he wrote:

> A friend of mine, Victor Feldbrill, a Canadian sailor, has been attending my rehearsals here and I would like the London Philharmonic to extend the same privilege to him whenever possible either in London or elsewhere…. I would like this letter to serve as an introduction for this purpose.[4]

To John Barbiroli in Manchester, he wrote:

> Dear John,
> I would like this letter to introduce a Canadian sailor, Victor Feldbrill, who is very interested in conducting and has attended (whenever he has the time) several of my rehearsals at St. Andrew's Hall. I would like you, as a favour to me, to extend this privilege to him, when he comes to Manchester if you can do so.[5]

But it was not just invitations to the rehearsals and concerts of distinguished conductors that Victor was acquiring. It had been back at Harbord Collegiate that Victor had come to the conclusion that being a conductor demanded a capacity to interpret complex scores, and through doing so, read the mind and purpose of the music's composer. His accumulation of marked scores in his kit-bag could be traced back to that afternoon at Harbord with John Weinzweig, several years before his presence in the United Kingdom.

Victor came to realize that although he had spent the past five or six years concentrating on great serious music, he knew so very little. There were so many works in the basic symphonic orchestral repertoire he had never heard — so many scores he had never seen. Now, in the British Isles, he had a god-given opportunity to prepare himself for the day when the conductor's baton replaced the violin as his major instrument for making music. In Glasgow, he wandered into a music store and found before him on a shelf the score of William Walton's Symphony no. 1, a majestic piece of music that revealed how passionately a contemporary composer could write for a competent orchestra. It was accessible and composed in a style that followed the inspirational lights of Beethoven and Brahms, but there were flights of harmonic vitality that were obviously from the twentieth century. Here the score was displayed in a small Glasgow shop, yet he knew that it had never been played in Canada. He decided that day he wanted to be the first Canadian to master its contents. This ambition to bring the works of contemporary composers to life in his native land never escaped Victor's mind in the decades that were to follow — even when he was bereft of a particular orchestra under his baton, or at least one capable of addressing a complex new score from a contemporary classical composer.

Victor was becoming conscious that through the intimate contact with conductors, musicians, composers, and teachers, he was accessing the entire British culture through the music, which was, in this case, the "medium of the message" he coveted. He became increasingly aware that this culture was unique. In sports it might be a passion for football (a game Canadians called soccer) and cricket rather than ice hockey. In music, there was an emphasis on choral music that was not reflected in European nations to the same extent yet that this genre had been exported to North America and had been given special attention in his own native land. Although at that moment he was consumed by the desire to conquer the orchestral repertoire, and orchestras, not choirs, were where his interests lay, it is no mystery that later in life he became a source of knowledge and inspiration to choral conductors who wanted to learn the secrets of orchestral conducting as an accompaniment to their choirs' efforts.

Throughout the fall of 1944, Scotland and Glasgow continued to be the base for the operation of *The Navy Show*, and the Glasgow Academy continued to be Victor's artistic home. He was fortunate that he was able to view in the academy's amphitheatre a relatively obscure film of Arturo Toscanini conducting a performance by the NBC Symphony Orchestra and Westminster Chorus in the Verdi Requiem, one of the most demanding but also one of the most popular showpieces in the choral repertoire (more attuned to the concert hall than the cathedral). Victor was possessed by Toscanini's command of the considerable forces before him and wrote to Zelda, "his face is beautiful when he conducts, his eyes are miles away, his face set in grim determination, one hand over his heart with thumb extended, his right arm describing circles and driving his men to unbelievable heights."[6]

This was still a time when there was no doubt that Edinburgh was recognized as the cultural centre of Scotland (referred to as the "Paris of the North" in the United Kingdom). Soon after its arrival, *The Navy Show* respected that city's pre-eminence and scheduled three matinees at the Empire Theatre. Victor soon discovered the rich array of book and music stores, and his moments of discovery continued. It was in an Edinburgh music store that he found another Walton score, *Façade*, a most unusual and ironic offering that exposed the composer's lighter side. The proprietor of the store, in shock over selling such a score to a Canadian seaman, celebrated his good fortune by giving Victor a copy of the Beethoven Symphony no. 5 — no doubt honouring the symbolic status that the piece had now achieved as the source of a musical phrase presaging the Allied determination to secure absolute victory. This generosity became a habit of music stores when Victor finally reached London and visited the most famous music publisher and purveyor of scores in Britain, Boosey & Hawkes.

This discovery set Victor on a new course — one of acquiring scores, many of which were "impossible to buy in Canada." His collection came to include a "rare score" of De Falla's *El Amor Brujo* ("Love and the Magician") and one of Elgar's most popular compositions, the *Cockaigne Overture*, as well as Vaughn William's *Overture: The Wasps.* His collection grew rapidly.

However, by November 1944, Victor had decided that the informal practice of observing rehearsals and studying scores was an insufficient response to the wealth of musical learning opportunities in the British Isles. A visit to the Music Faculty of Glasgow University and to another "big name" in the creative side of music, Sydney Newman, convinced him that he must conquer the mysteries of harmony and orchestration before he could become a knowledgeable conductor.

The first steps were taken toward arranging a correspondence course on harmony that Victor could address wherever *The Navy Show* might take him; but later, when it was apparent he would spend some time stationed in

London, he saw he had an opportunity to attend a tutorial in an academic setting with an outstanding instructor. Meanwhile, a visit to Birmingham brought more visits to music stores and the scores for the Beethoven Violin Concerto, a Bach Suite in D, and the Sibelius Violin Concerto, raising his total to sixty, a number he knew would impress Zelda, the source of his inspiration and determination.[7]

Haunting music stores became a Feldbrill obsession, but the visit to Birmingham had a more important agenda. He wanted to establish a relationship with Sir Adrian Boult, the "musical father" of his mentor Ettore Mazzoleni and Victor's best hope of securing the preparation he needed to be a conductor when he arrived back in Toronto. Arriving at his office, he discovered to his disappointment that Maestro Boult was leaving the city and was already on his way to the hotel. He determined that he would intercept him. Reaching Boult as he boarded the train, he was surprised to find that the famous conductor recognized him: "You are the chap ... I'm awfully glad you found me ... here's my train. I'll get a seat and then come and talk." (Mazzoleni had obviously been in touch with Boult on Victor's behalf.)

Once in Boult's presence, all that was needed were the letters of introduction from Sir Ernest and Ettore Mazzoleni to rouse all the enthusiasm from the maestro that Victor could have hoped for. A hurried conversation was all it took for Boult to realize that Victor needed formal academic attention from a gifted teacher, and he indicated to him that he would find someone in London. With the promise of a further chat over tea in the near future, Boult was running down the platform to his now moving train car and his seat on the London–Birmingham express.

But Victor was still not finished with Birmingham. He had gained permission to attend the Birmingham Symphony Orchestra's rehearsal with "the very thorough George Weldon on the podium." The upcoming concert included the Richard Strauss tone-poem *Don Juan*, a Haydn symphony, and the Beethoven Violin Concerto, a familiar composition to which Victor needed no introduction. More important, he was fortunate to discover that Thomas Beecham and the London Philharmonic were playing in Birmingham a day or two later with a program that included a favourite selection of Victor's, Beethoven's Symphony no. 4, the score which he already had in his possession and under his arm as he made his way to the Jewish service canteen in that city and secured a ticket for the concert. It was an overwhelming experience for Victor, one that he tried bravely to describe to Zelda:

> He [Beecham] electrified everything from the orchestra to audience. And for the first time in my life I was almost moved to tears — it was all I could do to hold them back … it's this man Beecham — he's some sort of god … he's so great. His performance was so meticulously perfect — every nuance, every phrase, every rest artistically executed. There's only one Beecham.[9]

Victor had in his pocket, as always, the MacMillan letter and a Braithwaite letter of introduction to the concertmaster of the London Philharmonic, who, on this occasion, happened to share a dressing room with the maestro. While Victor was engaging a fellow violinist in a post-concert conversation, Beecham strode into the room. Once again it was Sir Ernest's well-worn letter that was exposed. Beecham was delighted: "I'm very glad to meet you my boy." A memory of his appearance in Toronto in November 1940 in the midst of a snowstorm was one that Victor could share. Beecham promised to arrange for Victor's attendance at any London Philharmonic rehearsal and concluded the interview with, "The next time we meet, we shall have a long get together, eh?"

Victor was in a trance. Assuming he had been dismissed, he walked down the corridor, but was soon surprised to find Beecham calling after him, waving the Sir Ernest letter in the air, "Don't forget this, it is of great value to you — keep it!" Victor pocketed the well-worn document, still speechless and in shock at the warmth and generous treatment he had received from a man whose reputation for savaging underlings was an international legend.[10]

The promised afternoon tea with Sir Adrian Boult resulted in a plea from the maestro: "Let me know what you have done in the past." Victor was able to present him with programs from the UTSO concerts and his famous debut with the TSO. Boult was amazed that an eighteen-year-old could have had such a "brilliant start." He then informed Victor of his plans. He would contact Herbert Howells at the Royal College of Music and arrange lessons in harmony for Victor from this recognized master teacher. Victor was staggered by Boult's willingness to act as his advocate and mentor: "He was at my disposal anytime." Victor was experiencing the thrill of meeting a truly great figure in British musical circles, one whose personal behaviour exuded an interest in other musicians' careers, even those whose future exploits might exceed his own. It was a lesson Victor never forgot as he came to meet with countless younger Canadians seeking comparable assistance.[11]

Boult followed up on his promise with a note to Howells commending Victor's "recognition that a conductor is no use unless he is also a scholar." In the meantime, for Victor, it was further *Navy Show* appearances in Bradford, Liverpool, and Sunderland in November, and in December it was on to Lincoln, Leeds, another short trip to Ireland, and, simultaneously for half the cast and orchestra, more appearances in Wales. For Victor, January 1945 brought yet another trip to Ireland, but by the end of that first month of the new year, *Meet the Navy* was once again a single unit in Nottingham. Then it was back to London, a city that Victor was coming to love.

Thankfully, there were times when performances could not be scheduled in England and the arrangements for following the troops into Europe could not be completed. In these weeks, the Royal College of Music became the centre of Victor's strategy to use this time in the Armed Forces to prepare for a future in music. Boult's initiative in contacting Howells resulted in a note from this eminent educator and composer: "You can come anytime — I would be glad to have you." Victor's response to Zelda was, "The unbelievable has happened."

It was apparent that Howells saw his work with Victor as part of his own war effort, and in spite of the fact that his instruction had to be a one-on-one transaction and though he never taught beginners, he was determined to carry out this task. Howells, to Victor's embarrassment, refused to take any payment from his sailor-pupil. Over subsequent weeks, under Howells's personal supervision, Victor became a capable and enthusiastic scholar, spending hours a day on his studies, determined to eke out every bit of knowledge he could before being sent off to Europe.

Howells began by testing Victor's knowledge base, and found it to be modest rather than negligible, as he had expected, but was astounded by his new pupil's capacity for work. It was a classic example of the argument for emphasis on adult continuing education based on the intensity of learning when student motivation drives the process with relentless determination. Howells, on his part, placed the basic text, A.O. Morris's "Foundations of Practical Harmony and Counterpoint," in Victor's hands and geared his teaching to the needs of an aspiring conductor. "You must be able to spot a harmonic mistake at a flash," was the master's admonition. All this personal attention was being given by the man Victor came to describe as "the best man in the Royal College, one of the greatest in the world." [12]

Victor never ceased in his determination to acquire and conquer orchestral scores that were central to the repertoire of any decent ensemble. Moussorskey's *Pictures at an Exhibition,* Kodaly's *Harry Janos Suite,* and Benjamin Britten's *Les Illuminations* had become part of his library, but now he could use his status as a Royal College of Music student to secure scores at the lowest price at Boosey & Hawkes. Victor became a familiar figure and, recognizing the pressure he was under as both a student and a naval violin bandsman, Mr. Erwin Stein, an executive at Boosey & Hawkes, agreed to put aside low-cost scores when they became available. Thus, Mahler's Symphony no. 1, Beethoven's Symphony nos. 6 and 7, and Britten's *Sinfonia da Requiem* were acquired at little personal expense. [13]

Victor took pains to explain to Zelda how his own personal journey through all this music was being influenced by Herbert Howells:

> His lessons have given me greater insight to my music —
> new worlds seem to open up when I look at a score now
> — phrases take on new meanings, where they should be
> accented, what notes should receive prominence etc. …
> I have never before been filled with such lust to acquire
> knowledge — I want to drink in as much as I can while
> I am here…. I want to come back to you a much wiser
> person than when I left. [14]

With new confidence, Victor began to acquire a more critical outlook on the many rehearsals and performances he was able to attend.

His assessment of Sydney Beer's conducting of the National Symphony Orchestra in Rachmaninoff's Symphony no. 3, his *Variations on a Theme of Paganini* (with Benno Moseivitch at the piano), and Debussy's *L'Après d'une Faune* was quite negative. A later rehearsal of a Beethoven concert by the same conductor he found quite incomprehensible: "His Beethoven is like the Olympics, fast and furious. He completely misses the massive beauty of the music — it was heart-rending … his elevation to the conductor's role could only be explained by the intervention of a wealthy patron who could underwrite the orchestra's costs."[15] It was not the last time he was to discover that money sometimes trumped musicality in the world of great music.

The long wait for the European tour continued through the early weeks of 1945. It was not a pleasant time to be in London. Unmanned missiles had been one of Hitler's hopes for ending the war with a German victory, and Londoners now found themselves the target of these assaults. However, fortunately for Victor, the concert halls and theatre remained open. He could visit The Palladium and see a lavish musical, *Happy and Glorious*, but was moved much more by the concert of the London Symphony with Myra Hess (now a beloved figure whose concerts at the National Gallery during the blitz of the Battle of Britain had moved an entire nation) playing Beethoven concertos. Victor had made it a practice to visit the Royal Albert Hall every Sunday morning, but on one Sunday the regular rehearsal time was to be taken up by Handel's *Messiah*. For once, Victor decided to miss this occasion. He was horrified to discover that the bus stop shelter which he used in his trip to the hall had been blown up by an enemy missile, with great loss of life, on that particular Sunday morning. Indeed some of his colleagues presented him with a piece of shrapnel with an admonition, "this was for you," as a remembrance of his avoidance of an early demise.

The long wait continued as *The Navy Show* rehearsed and refurbished itself for the European experience. There were trips out to smaller communities but most were close to London, which remained the show's home base. These interruptions did not deflect him from visiting the Abbey Road recording studio of the His Master's Voice label, where he met Sir Thomas Beecham, who commented, "I see that our sailor friend is back," but took the trouble to introduce his "friend" to his patient wife during an intermission of his recording session.[16]

It was at this debilitating time in Britain that the film *Henry V* was released — an extraordinary manipulation of historical record geared to the giving of confidence to the British people in this time of trial. Part of its success was due to William Walton's splendid composition of the background music. This viewing, in the midst of the tension created by the last throes of the Nazi war machine, was an introduction to great filmmaking, and demonstrated what a quality musical score could produce when added to the visual excitement of the realistic portrayal that film allowed. It was a valuable lesson that Victor was to learn for the hours he would spend with CBC microphones placed before his conductor's music stand in post-war Canada, when television became to be so important for the transmission of music of all genres.

Even as they awaited their transportation to the continent, Victor and his colleagues began to realize that their lives in the Armed Forces might be coming to an end. Indeed, there was considerable tension around the future of *Meet the Navy*. Musicians and cast members felt considerable apprehension that the very popularity of the show might delay their return home to Canada and civilian status. Indeed there was consternation over the fact that the naval officers in charge of the show were rather enjoying this foray into show business and the receptions and parties that animated the opening and closing of each run. For them, returning to civilian life held no great attraction, but continued performances of *Meet the Navy* held the promise of ongoing excitement.

In the midst of this crisis in morale, the result of total collective boredom on the part of both performers and musicians, Victor was approached by his string colleagues to give leadership to a weekly process of confronting new music that might result in honing their sight-reading skills. His continuing contact with Herbert Howells was invaluable. Howells suggested that addressing new repertoire after repeating the *Meet the Navy* score for all those months would be a suitable shift of application. He advised Victor to secure the score for Gustav Holst's *St. Paul's Suite* as a beginning step, to be followed by the much more demanding Bela Bartok Divertimento for Strings. It went well. It also occasioned a remarkable moment in Victor's cultural awareness.

Howells took Victor to the nearby St. Paul's School and showed him the very room containing the very desk at which the *St. Paul's Suite* had been composed by Holst for the young ladies in his school orchestra. Howells went on to reminisce about the happier days in the past when he, Gustav Holst, and Ralph Vaughan Williams had premiered the latter's latest symphony on the piano in that very same room. Indeed, in a drawer were to be found the original manuscripts of the Vaughan Williams's efforts at symphonic orchestra output.

Howells had advice for the young musician with such high ambitions. He warned Victor that too often fine musicians are seduced into jobs associated with the music industry but not involved with the direct making of music. He recounted how he had rejected a very prestigious, high-paying job at the BBC administering the presentation of classical music in the realization that he would lose all contact with the creative figures, like Holst and Vaughan Williams, and the thrill of making or teaching others to make music. These moments of revelation were crowned with Howells's evaluation of Victor's accomplishments: "You have got off to a wonderful start in the conquest of the intricacies of harmony and counterpoint." Howells concluded with the observation that Victor's most valuable asset was an endearing personality that would attract the most recalcitrant musician. He had been astounded to hear about Beecham's warm reception of this virtual schoolboy musician, commenting that there was scarcely an instrumentalist in Britain who had not been scolded and humiliated by the imperious maestro. Victor's feet scarcely touched the ground as he made his way back to his bunk and the opportunity to share these moments through letters to his beloved Zelda.[17]

These interchanges with major figures in the British music scene led Victor to a realization of how much the strength of that nation's cultural presence and quality was dependent on the continued association of these individual creative forces. He recognized how significant it was that there existed this continuity between those engaged in composition and those committed to performance. There was a strong linkage between those who were in the public eye associated with the highly publicized concerts and festivals and those who sought to ensure that cultural institutions like orchestras and opera companies were kept strong and vibrant. The fact that all this activity had survived, indeed thrived, amidst a war for the continued existence of the country, indicated the bonds of common support that could be developed for a culture that was inclusive rather than exclusive. That meant the celebration of the presence of the young and uninitiated in the making of music. To these insights Victor was to give his life.

CHAPTER 5

The Last Hurrah

After June 6, 1944, with the end of the war in Europe, the termination of Victor's service in the RCN was a matter of timing. He had already made efforts to discover how he might advance his learning through special post-war opportunities to advance formal education that were now being offered to veterans. He had contacted the appropriate officer in the RCN for information on levels of support available after his demobilization and through Zelda's enquiries to Ettore Mazzoleni had discovered that his education through the degree studies at the University of Toronto's Faculty of Music would be subsidized by an allowance from the Government of Canada. Ironically, courses in harmony and counterpoint were eligible for such support — but conducting as offered as a part of the diploma program was not! However, he could add on such training on his own time (and at his own expense). The important thing was that he could now get married. Through the veterans' subsidization of eighty dollars a month, and additional money from "gigs" with various musical ensembles, he could also support Zelda in her efforts to finish her first degree in social work and even assist in her goal to work toward completion of her graduate studies at the master's level.

The Navy Show stationed in the United Kingdom was awaiting the opportunity to play to troops in Europe who had borne the brunt of the invasion and now found themselves members of an occupying force in a foreign country. These were men and women who deserved the very best entertainment the show could provide. There were now thousands of Canadians stationed in France, Germany, Belgium, and the Netherlands who had endured the might of the enemy, facing dismemberment and death. They wanted more than anything to return home. They were understandably restless. There were those in positions of command who remembered the First World War, when, after the armistice had been signed, a series of riots had shaken the expected quiet of the conquering army camps and, in some cases, burned them to the ground. It had been the mistaken belief that the fighting troops would be patient in their discomfort and separation from loved ones now that their life and physical well-being was no longer at risk. It had turned out that the delay in returning home had induced an even greater discontent than the dangers of the battlefield. It was determined that these feelings of frustration in the months of separation from loved ones in Canada could be just as toxic in 1945 as in they had been in 1918.

There were many reasons for this postponement in returning veteran servicemen and women home to Canada. It was part of the overall Allied strategy that Germany be occupied in order that the entire population could be confronted with the reality of defeat. Indeed, Nazi troops were not transported by air, rail, or bus, but were made to march back to their homes, dirty and dishevelled, through German cities and towns as a visual indication that conquest, humiliation, and despair were the outcome of the Nazi aggression that had shaken Europe for most of a decade. There was to be no room for questioning in the years ahead about the basis of the war's ending.

As indicated earlier, "unconditional surrender" by the Nazi regime had to be the foundation of peace on the continent.

Sections of the German Fatherland, including the capital, Berlin, were divided and directly governed by the Allied powers — particularly the Soviet Union and the United States. It meant that Canadian troops, along with those of the major powers, would have to assist in pulling together a capacity to feed and care for large numbers of people who were now, in some cases, destitute, homeless, and starving.

Not only in Germany, but even more in the countries that had been conquered for some years, there had to be some restoration of the basic governmental institutions, allowing the transition to peacetime normalcy to commence. It was important that as far as possible, prominent Nazis and their collaborators be exempt from participation in the long process of restoration that was being initiated. It was a difficult time as the pictures of the atrocities of the death camps flooded the world's media and further outraged those who could only depart for home when justice was meted out to those at the pinnacles of power both in Germany and in the conquered countries of Europe. The Nuremburg Trials in 1946 would be a unique step toward internationally legitimized punishment for those responsible for the crimes against humanity that were perceived to have been committed by individuals commanding the forces of the defeated enemy.

Victor, though he had not shared in the horrors of the battlefield, most certainly came to understand the significance of the Allied victory. Perhaps his most depressing moments came when he saw the newsreels of the Allied troops liberating the death camps and thus viewed on screen the remains of his co-religionists. His sensibilities were shattered. He was not a supporter of vengeance and retaliation. He had no desire to view the plight of Germans, in some cases hungry and disabled amidst the ruins of their cities, but he found it difficult not to support every effort to punish the individuals responsible for such despicable, inhumane behaviour.

Victor could not fail to recognize a significant trait that made the Nazi ideology real in his mind. By the time he reached German soil on the European tour, he had developed a habit of buying candies and dispensing them to children who, in their innocence, gathered about foreigners in uniform hoping for goodies as a gesture of their goodwill. He found that when he gave a handful of candies to Dutch children, they shared their good fortune with their friends, including all the friends they could in this moment of good fortune. However, in Germany, he encountered a different reaction. The children grabbed as many candies as their hands could hold and ran away as fast as possible, if necessary, fighting off their companions in their determination to enjoy all the fruits of their fortunate encounter. Victor considered this contrast of reaction was symbolic of what the war was about. In this selfishness and greed, Victor saw the traits that had been fashioned by the ideology of fascism that celebrated individual well-being over community that had led ultimately to the death camps of Belsen and Auschwitz. Zelda's response to his account was predictable. These children were simply responding to the environment which valued and rewarded such behaviour. It supported the very theories of human development her university studies were identifying.

In conquered countries, Victor found that there were complicated issues to be faced. In some cases, there was a complete vacuum of civil government to be filled by some form of temporary authority in the hands of "loyal" citizens. In other places, municipal or regional government appeared to remain in the hands of individuals who were perceived as traitors, those who, to their own benefit, had advanced themselves by following the orders emanating from officialdom in Berlin. Some had obviously served reluctantly and others indeed had used their positions in the New Order to defend their countrymen and women from the worst horrors that might descend from above. In some situations, it was difficult to differentiate and there were those who were unfairly punished by the rough justice that followed liberation.

Then, of course, there were the thousands of men and women who had fought in the underground and who had risked their lives every day, engaging in activities that would weaken the hold of their conquerors. Understandably, there were those who saw in the interregnum an opportunity to settle old scores before the formal justice system came into place. There were instances of severe punishment meted out based on revenge for real or perceived abuses during occupation. In some instances, the occupying Allied troops found that restraining their courageous friends and supporters was as challenging as discovering and arresting the most blatant offenders. Through his and Zelda's determination to understand the fallout from such a war, Victor's months in Europe in 1945 were an intense learning experience.

Victor realized that none of these functions had been perceived as a part of the job description of enlisted men and women who found themselves members of an occupying army — but they had to be addressed. The role of peacemaker and purveyor of humane and decent administration to devastated communities filled with broken people began in the streets and public spaces of occupied Europe. These pressures were part of the argument for bringing to the liberated civilians even one evening of relief in the presence of song and dance that both entertained and inspired.

For his part, Victor remained involved in full-time service with *The Navy Show* in those months on the continent, but found that his spare time gave opportunity to forge relationships and observe a period in history that could never be replicated in his lifetime. It did something to relieve the boredom that he and his companion musicians were experiencing. A few cast members sought ways of returning home — one even secured a discharge and an immediate return to Canada by assaulting an officer. Special arrangements were made, for example, that meant that dancers and choreographers Blanche and Alan Lund were no longer part of the troupe when it reached Europe.

In the frustration of his continuing service, Victor wisely remained focused on his music and the observation of a world he had never seen but resolved would be an aspect of his future. These months of revelation affected him deeply. He had experienced a life spent in the company of decent and civilized human beings, and *The Navy Show*, for all its limitations, was reminding those who had experienced the "killing fields" that the war had been fought in defence of democracies that celebrated the virtues of co-operation and tolerance.

Nevertheless, there were occasions when he had to put the violin down and compose himself in order to deflect his impulse to scream out loud his outrage over being forced to play the same notes, listen to the repetition of the same clever text, all blurring into meaningless noise. There were examples of collective breakdown and on one occasion the entire cast performed a slapstick takedown of *Meet the Navy* to the amusement of a baffled audience. Fortunately, for Victor there were instances of welcome interludes, one including a stint with Canadian Robert Farnon's army ensemble that needed some augmentation to improve the orchestral sound for broadcast purposes. It was a welcome experience. He admired Farnon, who went on to an illustrious career in more popular genres of music, not in his native Canada, but in the British music scene. However, Victor was soon back in the familiar orchestra pit of *The Navy Show*.

Fortunately, he realized he had been granted the gift of time in a potentially rich cultural environment, now energized by the euphoria of victory. The citizens of these conquered jurisdictions were anxious to reinvigorate the arts institutions that had in past years reminded them of what they might achieve in the peacetime to come. It was, for example, no accident that the British Council for the Arts, an agency specifically created to provide public support to performing and visual arts, had been introduced in the midst of the wartime period, when the very continued existence of the United Kingdom was in some doubt. It was to become the model for the Canada Council for the Arts, with comparable goals that emerged in post-war Canada by the mid-1950s, along with a string of arts councils in provincial jurisdictions across the country all having similar outcomes in mind. These were institutions to which Victor was to give his allegiance throughout his long career. The irony of the enormous positive impact that can emerge from the battlefield was a blessing that Victor came to cherish.

It was fortunate that Victor had experienced such a productive time in London shortly after arriving, and as he awaited the European tour, was able to add to his collection of scores, which, before he completed his overseas stint numbered over a hundred — an amazing collection for a young musician scarcely out of his teenage years. After immediate study, they were shipped back to Zelda to form part of an extensive library she was determined to create and have ready to move into their home on his return. As a particular asset while in London, his friendship with personnel from the music distributors Boosey & Hawkes allowed him to borrow scores of lesser-known composers, those of John Ireland being particularly appreciated.

During these years, Victor was becoming increasingly dependent on Zelda's broad learning experience in her undergraduate years at the University of Toronto. She was studying psychology and her letters revealed a sophisticated exploration that impressed him. He considered his future hopes of giving leadership as a conductor to be closely related to insights gained through Zelda's studies. She soon had him reading Albert Walton's *Fundamentals of Industrial Psychology* and the more narrowly relevant Percy S. Buck, *Psychology for Musicians*. These, along with his own discoveries of Cecil Forsythe's volume on orchestration and Sir Adrian Boult's *Handbook of Conducting* kept his mind focused on the journey toward orchestral leadership.

This continuing presence in London in 1944 and 1945 also allowed Victor the opportunity of keeping in contact with the professional musicians he encountered at the rehearsals he attended day after day. These were men (very few women were engaged by symphony orchestras in the first half of the twentieth century) who were playing in world-class ensembles who he found did not consider him a mere student but a colleague. They sought out his opinion about things musical and listened to his responses to their questions.[1]

Finally a date came down from above — *The Navy Show* would begin its European tour in Paris on June 15, 1945. There was now some pattern of activity around which he could plan his future and his ultimate return home. It was a time for farewells — Victor was not sure whether the show would return to Britain before returning to Canada and there were those who had made efforts on his behalf. His greatest debt was to Herbert Howells, who had given his time freely for all these months. Victor made at least the gesture of appreciation that was possible, realizing that he could never repay his volunteer instructor for all his contribution to his understanding of music. At a time of severe restrictions on the availability of "sweets" in Britain, he was able to secure chocolates for Howells's wife and daughters, as well as tickets for a London evening performance of *Meet the Navy*. For both, Herbert Howells was signally grateful.

The Navy Show opened in Paris and not only the military "brass" were on hand but so were a bevy of entertainers who were simultaneously bringing joy to American troops similarly involved in the occupation of Europe. Of particular interest to Victor was his meeting with American comedian Jack Benny. His form of humour included a well-worn but hilarious take-off on the performance of a concert violinist whose only repertoire appeared to be a rendition of the sentimental tune, "Love in Bloom." It was an act guaranteed to bring down the house on every occasion. In the 1970s, he was to remind Benny of their previous meeting when the comedian played a TSO benefit concert with Victor on the podium. It was an evening program of musical merriment that entertained an overflow audience in Massey Hall, much benefiting the TSO Pension Fund for retiring players.

A tour of Belgium gave Victor and his colleagues an opportunity to visit the incomparable beauty of Bruges — "the Venice of Northern Europe." But the glory of the landscape had less impact than his confrontation with the severe distress of the citizens and their children, obviously starving in the streets of the towns he visited. The show then made its way to Amsterdam, a city in which the troupe was to be stationed for a number of weeks in July of 1945. His stay in that city led to an experience that was the highlight of his time in Europe and established relationships with Dutch citizens that lasted throughout the century.

Victor had arrived in Amsterdam in the midst of a heat wave. It was 2:00 a.m. and, though ensconced in luxurious surroundings, Victor could not sleep. He arose, made his way past sleeping colleagues to the open window of the hotel that had been assigned as a barracks for the orchestra, cast, and backstage technicians of the show. Suddenly, Victor heard a familiar tune being whistled by a passerby in the street below. It was a theme from J.S. Bach's Concerto for Two Violins and Orchestra, a masterpiece that Victor had played many times. As the whistler, a visual artist by the name of Sjert Kuit, tired of his informal performing, Victor took up the tune and whistled back the remaining bars of the Bach theme into the night air of the great city. The individual peered up through the darkness of the summer night to see the person who had been his audience and now had become his musical colleague. Victor, sitting on the window ledge, accepted the invitation to descend to the street in order to meet and chat in a more intimate setting.

The ensuing interchange opened the door to a series of friendships that gave delight and meaning to Victor's European experience. It was revealed that this Dutch citizen and Amsterdam inhabitant was a visual artist and a member of a gathering of young people, though slightly older than Victor, who were sharing a common apartment and seeking to survive the horrific events that had brought an end to the Nazi domination of their country. There was little food to be found and they were dividing what they could find, but much more, were keeping their love of music, of great literature, and of great visual arts alive in their minds and hearts under the difficult circumstances they now had to bear. It was a collection of like-minded Dutch nationals determined to endure after suffering through a war that threatened everything they valued, and they were now confronting a peace that was at that moment providing little hope for the future.

A quiet conversation in the cloying heat of the Amsterdam night ensued, resulting in an invitation to visit the Kuit studio, one that Victor accepted with delight and expectation the following day. The directions were easily understood — the studio, shared by a handful of colleagues, was over a spice store just a few blocks away. It was momentous good luck. In the next few days, Victor was to find himself welcomed to the home of not only Kuit but of several of his cohabitants, one being a young man by the name of Wim Boost, another visual artist and cartoonist, who along with his fiancée, Puck, became special lifelong friends. These attractive and vital young people were to become Victor's window on the world of post-war Europe. He came to treasure his liaison with these Dutch citizens as much as they were to delight in his occasional presence. Years later he would visit Amsterdam and find them all gathered at the airport to celebrate his return. However, at this point, this handful of young Dutch citizens were intent upon not just surviving physically, but nurturing the beauty and meaning of the arts that were the expression of a humanity that had almost disappeared from their lives.

These unusual young men and women described to Victor the wartime experiences they had suffered that were beyond his imagination. The Netherlands had tried to avoid the confrontations that nationalism had perpetrated among the countries that made up a continent now virtually in ruins. Holland had remained neutral in the First World War and had hoped for a similar status with Hitler's Germany in the 1930s as a second conflict developed. The most perceptive and most at-risk European citizens in those years had been the members of the Jewish community in that Germany. Many had read *Mein Kampf* and had realized their days were numbered as normal citizens of their homeland if Hitler and his followers took power. Jewish citizens who had the resources and opportunity left that country and chose to live, understandably, in the most tolerant country nearby — Holland — a country that had been generous and welcoming to this minority who, down through the centuries had attracted the hatred and violence of Christian bigots in most European countries. For this reason, Holland had a higher proportion of Jews in its population than any other European state. For Hitler, it was a reason to attack without warning and without any normal diplomatic exercises devoted to the avoidance of conflict. The Dutch were an impediment to the domination of the European continent and, more importantly, the effective defence of the continent's shoreline.

Throughout the Nazi occupation of Holland, the Jewish citizens had been under continued threat — the most compelling and poignant account of the horror of war on the life of an individual victim was that left by Anne Frank, who lived, of course, in Amsterdam, the very city in which Victor was now resident. Her personal struggle to survive continues to move people over half a century later.

Through this exciting group of students with whom Victor now regularly conversed and debated, he became aware of the trials they had faced. Also, in their company he listened to great recorded and broadcast music and sought meaning in the wretched circumstances of the immediate postwar period that now so unfairly followed these years of occupation, deprivation, and terror. All these experiences became a part of his awareness of the depravity that human behaviour could reach and the evil it could impose on the lives of innocent people. It was particularly incomprehensible for the Dutch, who considered themselves "honorary Germans" in a war supposedly being fought to establish suzerainty over non-Aryans. Hitler's early promises of special treatment for the Netherlands came to mean nothing; indeed, there seemed to be a special brutality meted out to those countries whose citizens failed to appreciate the meaning of the New Order.

The large population of Jews in Holland were particularly resented in the light of the fact that many of them were obviously refugees from the German Third Reich. The landscape offered no opportunities for hiding — there were no mountain retreats and the cities were open and accessible to intense policing. Soon there had been resistance to German occupation, beginning in Amsterdam. A general strike was organized to protest the treatment of the Jews who had soon lost all the status they had achieved and had become the objects of continuing programs that promised either work camps for the strong and healthy or death camps for those whose capacity to labour on Germany's behalf was insubstantial.

Victor, whose experience of the war was from the relatively safe venue of *The Navy Show*'s orchestra pit, and who was viewing for the first time the total inhumanity of people consumed by an evil ideology and a willingness to circumvent the basic tenets of acceptable human behaviour, was shocked beyond measure. Through this coterie of young people, still clutching a love of music, of gracefully phrased text, of overwhelming beauty of form and colour, he was able to view the ultimate heights of human courage and decency. Some of these youths, particularly Wim Boost, he visited whenever he found himself in Britain or Europe after the war. On occasion, Wim and Puck came to North America to share Victor's artistic triumphs as well as quiet contemplative moments with their conductor friend, his wife, Zelda, and their lovely children.

However, at that moment the very survival of the people in the Netherlands was in question. The defeated Nazi forces, in their efforts to hold their conquered countries, had cared little for the well-being of civilians. Victor viewed the result — young and old literally dying in the streets in full view of their neighbours, who had no food or medicine to share with them. Others were simply expiring in their homes, to be found by friends and relatives days or weeks after taking their final breath.

Victor, a member of a new occupying force, became a godsend to these young people, bringing food and candies and even cigarettes. He brought packages that promised not only a further moment of life and health but a touch of magical delight. Even more extraordinary, informing Zelda of their plight resulted in package after package arriving from Canada. Indeed, his beloved in Canada became a close friend, *in absentia*, whose presence was celebrated years after, when, finally, she could retrace some of the travels that Victor had described in his wartime letters and meet the individuals whose names she now knew by heart.

Victor, though a non-smoker, was aware of the pride of those he had come to respect and developed the practice of lighting a cigarette and passing on the object of desire to those around him. It was years later that his masquerade of being a confirmed smoker was revealed as a ruse to maintain the recipient's need for self-respect. Victor, in the midst of these interactions, truly came to understand what victory in the Second World War truly meant. *The Navy Show* was following the heroic efforts of Canadian troops to liberate the Netherlands. In early May 1945, a few days before V-E Day, the Netherland liberation was celebrated as a special occasion. The revelations of his newly minted Dutch friends made it possible for Victor to view in retrospect the significance of all those hours in performances of the show, the playing of the same tunes and waiting through the same inevitable interludes of spoken text and moments of unsuppressed audience laughter; there had been a noble purpose behind it after all.

The time spent with good friends and great music from old phonograph records and a static-oppressed radio made less acute the days of separation from Zelda. It also relieved her tension over the pressure of loneliness that both were suffering. Inevitably, his friends soon learned of his intense love and desire for union with Zelda and this even more than the packages of provisions was her entry to their circle of intimacy and caring. It was an overseas collective relationship that was transformed beyond these days of deprivation to a lifetime of continued contact and occasional visitation back and forth from continent to continent.

Victor, through these interactions, also came to understand the terrible reality of the rough justice meted out to those who, in some cases in ignorance or in support of family, had seen an advantage to collaboration with the enemy. There were those who simply wanted to be left in peace, and quiet co-operation seemed the wisest course. There were inevitable reprisals, in some cases simply the settling of old scores. For those who were simply seeking survival of their innocent children from ruthless extermination it seemed particularly cruel to be judged and punished by one's fellow citizens. Victor was viewing the complexity of human relationships in the midst of conflict. It became a common thread of recorded conversation that led Zelda to realize that her future husband was experiencing what she was learning through her study and research.

Viewing the severing of relationships even within families became another influence on Victor, making him even more determined to place his family at the peak of his values in spite of his presence in a world of performance art, where precepts of success demand absence from the family home. Victor came to live, in some years, what some would call the peripatetic life as a musician with responsibilities that stretched across Canada and extended to countries in Europe and Asia. In the light of all the pledges never to be apart, Victor's life, in some decades, became a series of absences from Zelda and the children, once again relieved by the commitment to letters that bridged the intense loneliness of complete separation. These absences affected his religious life, though his family carried on the traditional rites and remained in the circle of synagogue intimacy that ultimately strengthened both parents. Victor and Zelda never lost sight of their Jewish family celebrations. Even after Zelda's death, he returned home from considerable distances to be at family marriages and bar mitzvahs, often at some expense and significant discomfort.

Victor had very early realized that Amsterdam could be the venue of his most dramatic confrontation with the visual arts. He was introduced by his Dutch associates to the glory of a Rembrandt exhibition. Victor's reaction was immediate: "It was unbelievable ... he gets into the very soul of the people he portrayed."[2] Then it was a Van Gogh exhibition and Victor was now on his way to becoming a contemporary art collector. He purchased prints of the particular paintings that caught his eye and mailed them back to Zelda for the walls of their first home. Eventually he was to become an art collector of fine contemporary visual artists, and the Feldbrill home became a gallery containing colourful paintings that he and Zelda cherished.

Amsterdam was also the site of what was perhaps the most dramatic event he was to witness in his lifetime. *The Navy Show* had arrived in the city on July 8 — exactly two months after the formal liberation celebration. Yet, even through these weeks of exaltation, the city's major orchestra, one of the leading ensembles in the world, the Concertgebouw Orchestra, was rent with controversy over its role during the Nazi occupation. Victor was determined to hear this great orchestra, and its first post-war concert was scheduled while the show was stationed in Amsterdam. The Concertgebouw had not performed for some months and the loyalty of the ensemble was under some suspicion. The conductor, Maestro Mengelberg, was perceived by some to have collaborated with the Nazis. The orchestra had, for example, obeyed the edict that it was not to play the music of Germany's enemies — particularly the Russian repertoire. The citizenry believed itself "Tchaikovsky-starved." Even more despicable, the music of all Jewish composers, whatever their nationality, had been banned. At the rehearsals Victor attended, he had been moved by the determined commitment of the orchestra members, some obviously emaciated through lack of food, to revive the performance fortunes of their magnificent orchestra.

Fortunately, the major battle over leadership had been settled well before the concert and Victor soon became a colleague of the new Concertgebouw conductor, Eduard Van Beinum. Victor was enormously impressed by him, sitting spellbound as the orchestra rehearsed Tchaikovsky's dramatic Symphony no. 5: "The sound filled the room. It was indeed colossal. Van Beinam gave a heart breaking interpretation that was meticulous — nothing passed unnoticed."[3]

A day later, Victor met Van Beinum, and as a result of a discussion with him about Gustav Mahler, came away with the score of the master's monumental Symphony no. 2, (*The Resurrection Symphony*). Victor was unfamiliar with the work, but Van Beinum's words kindled an immediate enthusiasm for this moving masterpiece. Mahler's music would receive considerable attention from this young conducting aspirant in the days ahead.

Victor had tickets to the Sunday concert. (Thankfully there was no *Meet the Navy* performance that afternoon.) It was the first exposure of the controversy-ridden orchestra before an aroused audience, some 2,500 strong, crowding the Amsterdam Concert Hall in anticipation. No one knew what to expect. What had these months of musical inactivity done to the fine-tuning of this complex instrument? Would the intense politicization of the orchestra affect its musicality? For example, officialdom had decreed that in the wake of all the controversy over loyalty, it would not be allowed to commence the concert season with the national anthem. It was to be a symbolic gesture of dissatisfaction with what seemed at best a lack of national pride in the orchestra and at worst indication of positive evidence of collaboration with the enemy on the part of the orchestra's leadership.

The audience would have none of it — this was their orchestra and there were no hesitations in its collective response. As Van Beinum mounted the podium and raised his baton to begin the concert, the audience took matters into their own hands. To Zelda, Victor wrote:

> Rising from their seats, the audience suddenly burst forward with the Dutch National Anthem — gratefully, determinedly they sang and my spine played tricks on me. How much I wish you could have been with me to hear it.[4]

Transfixed, Victor was in an orchestral paradise. It was, in Victor's words, "one of the finest concerts I have ever heard. The Tchaikovsky was played with such virility and strength." The audience reacted: "They shouted, they stamped, they cheered ... it left me breathless."

Victor became close to Van Beinum and a number of his orchestral colleagues. A member of the first violin section lent him a copy of Bruchner's Symphony no. 8, another composer whose deep spirituality would resonate with Victor. Indeed, members of the Concertgebouw referred to him as their "third conductor." After the disgraced Mengelberg and the heroic Van Beinum, came Victor. When it was time to leave Amsterdam, the orchestra members presented Victor with a sketch of a hand reaching in from outside the frame holding a carton of cigarettes — obviously a veiled reference to the fact that Victor had brought considerable joy to the cigarette-addicted Van Beinum. With no thought of recompense, Victor had brought cigarettes day after day to the beleaguered conductor he admired so totally. Years later, on Maestro Van Beinum's first visit to Toronto, Victor encountered the distinguished conductor, who exclaimed with joyous recognition, "Ah yes, the cigarette seaman."

From Amsterdam, the show went on to Germany, with Oldenburg the first stop. Victor informed Zelda that as far as he was concerned there would be no fraternization with the people of that country, who had, after all, elected Hitler. The contrasts he experienced were palpable. He had spent the last night with his friends in Amsterdam, listening to recordings of Beethoven's Symphony no. 4, a Stokowski transcription of a Bach Choral Prelude and a Schumann Violin Sonata played by Yehudi and Hepsibah Menuhin. It had been an evening that celebrated the power of the great masters. Hours later, Victor was in Oldenberg, confronted with "sad, sullen and dejected faces." Yet he came to an awareness that these hungry and desperate people were also victims. Initially he could not forget the images of the death camps, but then he viewed the results of Allied bombing of the magnificent cities, such as Bremen. Soon he found himself sympathizing with the terrible plight of the German people.

Once again, he reacted emotionally to the suffering he saw around him. He was surprised to find that, though the stores were empty, Germans were, on the whole well-dressed, unlike the Netherlands people he found in tatters. He could only conclude that the "'loot of Europe' had been gathered by the Nazis, thereby allowing the German population to avoid the sacrifices that Hitler's regime had imposed on the citizens of Europe's conquered countries. "They must be taught a lesson," had been his initial conclusion, but eventually his sympathy went out to the German children and future generations who would have to bear the cost of restoration. He had found neighbourhoods "all in ruins, rubble wherever you look … just shells of what was truly magnificent."[5]

In the midst of all this horror, Victor had not lost his appreciation of the absurd: "Can you imagine anything more ironical. Here am I, a Jew, eating wurst sandwiches in Germany." Obviously this was not his regular diet because he could report to Zelda in the same letter that his weight had fallen from 191 to 176 pounds.[6]

On August 7, Victor became aware that, in truth, a new era had arrived. The report of the dropping of the atomic bomb on Hiroshima and later on Nagasaki convinced him that music would now serve a more dangerous world. It was the end of the war in the Pacific, ending all rumour that *The Navy Show* might be sent on yet another tour of Canada and the Pacific Rim upon its return from Europe. However, Victor's world would now be dominated by the Cold War and the constant threat of a nuclear holocaust. Significantly, it was a confrontation that could be softened by the presence of shared music. As a musician, a conductor, a music instructor, Victor was to play his part in the process of finding in the making of music a speck of common ground that would be sufficiently substantial to make more possible the negotiation of political and economic conflicts that had to be avoided or contained.

Now it was time to go home. But not before another hurdle was to be leaped. On September 24, 1945, *The Navy Show* returned to London, not for immediate transport to Canada, but for a three-week leave, followed by some weeks on the set of a film about the production. As Victor put it, by the end of September, *Meet the Navy* no longer existed … it was just a film in the making." Victor could only express his appreciation with two heartfelt words: "Thank God!"

Victor faced London in a state of anticipation laced with a streak of apprehension. He had told Zelda that he had every expectation of being back in Canada by Christmas. She had been left with arranging all the details of the wedding that Victor was determined should take place immediately upon his arrival in Toronto. That decision had assured that the celebration of their union would be a small, private affair, with family and only a few friends invited to the ceremony and reception and meal to follow. It was left to Zelda to inform her mother-in law-to-be that the TSO would not be playing at her son's wedding as she had dreamed.

During his weeks of leave in London, Victor took on two projects — a return to his music studies and a trip to parts of London that had borne the brunt of the German bombers and missiles. Victor was also back to the study of his scores, in particular the Beethoven Symphony no. 4 he had borrowed from music publishers and distributors Boosey & Hawkes. "Each note seems to live, have its own character yet all together they make up one beautiful pattern," was his response to the latest reading.[7] As for the devastation of London, Victor had now witnessed the horror of blocks of destroyed buildings in Germany. Now he was determined to see what havoc had been endured by Londoners. As he walked through the wreckage of what were the delightful neighbourhoods of the great city he had come to admire, he was astounded to discover how many a ruined storefront had the names of Jewish proprietors prominently displayed amidst the rubble. Even in London, his companions in the faith had suffered disproportionately.

In the limited time available, Victor wanted to do more than simply resume his music studies with Herbert Howells. He was anxious that while still in the service and assisting with the *Navy Show* film, he would find a way to forward his skill level and gain greater experience in the role of becoming a conductor. Once again, good fortune shined. Sir Adrian Boult was in rehearsal at the Royal College of Music. An immediate audience with him revealed that there was an orchestral conductor's course being offered at the Royal Academy of Music. A call from Maestro Boult was all that was needed. There was no entry to such a course in the last months of the year, but in Victor's case, with his experience with the UTSO and the TSO, an exception could be made. Victor, still in naval uniform, was welcomed by the distinguished instructor, Ernest Read. In his class, he would study conducting technique, the reading of scores, but more important, would spend much of his time actually conducting the Royal Academy Orchestra, made up of young musicians, highly capable but largely amateur, studying in the academy and honing their instrumental technique.

Victor could scarcely believe his good luck. He was also conducting both the London Junior and Senior Symphony orchestras. Although work with Howells at the Royal Conservatory in London would not be abandoned, it was plain that Victor's focus would now also be on the practical techniques that would forward his ambition to become an orchestral conductor.[8] It meant serious and intense study of this art as well as continuing with his plan to experience every great conductor he could in the great concert halls of London. Soon after he reached this decision, Sir Thomas Beecham arrived in the capital to conduct the London Philharmonic in a program of Richard Strauss, Sibelius, and Wagner. It was, in Victor's words to Zelda, "stupendous" to say the least.

At another concert, his mentor Sir Adrian Boult conducted the BBC Symphony. The guest artist was the now middle-aged Pablo Casals, who, Victor observed, "plays with all the fire of youth," resulting in "a masterful solo and artistic string playing in the Dvorak Cello Concerto."

However, Victor, realizing that in a few more weeks he would be bound for Canada, spent every moment he could find in the presence of Ernest Read and the Royal Academy of Music Orchestra that was assigned to provide an opportunity for would-be conductors to engage in a concert experience. Read quickly realized that though this was an intermediate class, this young Canadian seaman had more experience and talent than any of the rest of his classmates. He was aware that Victor had only a few weeks in October, November, and a few days in December, and ensured that every moment counted.

In the very first session, Read had Victor take over the conducting of the Royal Academy Orchestra, made up of "almost-professional players," through Mozart's *Overture to Don Giovanni*. It went well and Victor received a warm ovation from orchestra. This single reading of the composition led to Read's comment, "You have them in your hands, do as you will with them."[9]

Then came the real test. Read pulled out of his briefcase the score of the first movement of Borodin's Symphony no. 2. It was a difficult piece, because, as Victor put it, "the time changes every other bar." He had never conducted the composition — indeed, had only heard it on radio a couple of times. The orchestra responded to the young sailor who obviously "knew his stuff." There was only one slip at an awkward page turn when there was indeed a missed beat. However, Victor, stopping the orchestra and with a request for a repeat of those bars "for my benefit," endeared himself to the musicians with his sensitivity in not shifting the blame to their shoulders. At the conclusion of the movement, Read expressed his enthusiasm for his student's performance — he had revealed the clearest beat among the aspirants — and the use of his left hand to encourage an interpretation of the score's meaning had been inspired. Victor was thrilled. He had felt secure and confident and Ernest Read's acclamation had been deserved.

Too soon Victor was coming to the final moments with Ernest Read. Once again, Peter Warlock's *Capriole Suite* was on the podium music stand and Victor took charge of the ensemble before him, in this case members of the London Junior Symphony Orchestra. Read was impressed. "He admired how I could keep the music alive through the more difficult passages — usually the players bury their heads in the music and everything becomes forced and stodgy. My beat had given them confidence."[10]

A day later, members of the London Senior Symphony Orchestra occupied the Royal Academy stage and Victor, once again on the podium, animated a recently arrived Russian instrumentalist to ruminate that he had been the "first conductor who had broken through the cold English exterior of the players and made them put their soul into the playing."[11]

On December 10, he went to the Royal Academy for the last time. Read asked him to conduct the entire rehearsal. As the music concluded, Read announced to the class that, as he was returning to Canada, this would be Victor's last session. He then "made one of the most touching and flattering speeches I've ever heard," claimed Victor. Reporting this interchange with Zelda, he informed her that this would be the last letter she would receive and that his next contact would be by telephone from Halifax.[12]

By late November, even though making the soundtrack for the *Meet the Navy* film had soon crowded out the frequency of his attendance at Royal Academy classes, his evenings were mainly free. He sought out every concert he could find. A performance of Elgar's Symphony no. 1 by the London Symphony under George Weldon moved him even though he noted a certain "lack of integrity" and a "shaky intonation." However, it was, once again, Sir Thomas Beecham who introduced Victor to a repertoire he would conduct in future decades to come — excerpts from Benjamin Britten's new opera, *Peter Grimes*.

Before departing from Britain, there was one concert that overwhelmed him. The Paris Conservatory Orchestra came to London to play an evening of French music. It was Ravel and Debussy who were celebrated. Victor was thrilled and his account to Zelda vibrated with emotion:

> God, what a concert. I've always wanted to hear a French orchestra play French music and they far surpassed anything I expected. The way they played Ravel and Debussy was one of those things that words cannot describe. I was completely carried away. Dearest, oh how I wish you could have heard it.[13]

Victor's final London concert experience was appropriately that of Sir Thomas Beecham conducting the Paris Conservatory Orchestra he enjoyed so thoroughly two nights before. This time it was German and Russian music, Beethoven's Symphony no. 2 and Tchaikovsky's Symphony no. 6. Once again he bombarded Zelda with his enthusiasm. At the end of the performance of the mighty sixth, "The audience went wild." How better to bring his overseas listening experience to a conclusion. "What a performance! He seems to find things in the music that no one else seems to dream of."[14]

By December, Victor's attendance at the concert hall had become infrequent. By this time it was decided that although the *Navy Show* orchestra augmented by London radio studio professionals would provide the sound, the players would be off-screen. Indeed the whole production entered the fantasy land of Hollywood-like filmmaking, adding another hundred army and air force personnel for one "gigantic production number." Of course Victor was fed up with *Meet the Navy* live, but being part of a film version, though entertaining at times, was even more debilitating. The only moment of delight came when there was no one available to conduct parts of the Russian segment of the show and Victor was dragooned into service — to lead the orchestra off-screen. Even the film ordeal had conspired to make his final days memorable.

However, by mid-December, the ordeal finally came to a conclusion and *Meet the Navy* was no longer a part of his life.

CHAPTER 6

The War and Zelda Mann

War is about killing and maiming people and incredibly in the twentieth century it became increasingly about killing and maiming women and children. Most certainly, modern war is about the destruction of countless lives of innocent people through the infliction of violence and mayhem. It is also about the separation of loved ones leading to feelings of loneliness and a sense of abandonment. On the scale of the pain and unhappiness we see each day transmitted by our television sets from war zones wherever they may be, the saga of Victor and Zelda's relationship during the last years of the Second World War does not seem to count for much on any recognizable scale of human tragedy. Indeed one senses through their war years a period of personal growth, both emotional and intellectual, that eventually came to enhance their lives together. Zelda was a schoolgirl when Victor was called up and chosen to be part of *The Navy Show*. When he returned at the end of 1945, though she was but twenty years old, she was a mature, highly intelligent woman, well on the way to a university degree and with plans to take post-graduate studies to prepare herself for a role in a profession that was coming into its own in the twentieth century — that of social work.

The more than two years of war separation most certainly led to an impatience and misery that was palpable for the couple. Certainly, Victor and Zelda were unprepared for the extended months of parting that war brought. Except for the summer holidays, they had maintained a daily contact through their years together at Harbord Collegiate. They had walked back and forth to school, had been side by side in the halls, and had sat together in the cafeteria. They had arrived hand in hand at the TSO Women's Committee meetings and had gone together to parties and dances sponsored by Jewish organizations, particularly those for whom Zelda was the initial contact. As well, Victor had spent countless hours at Zelda's home, warmly received by her parents who had the highest regard for him, and Zelda was always a welcome visitor to the Feldbrill household.

Between 1939 and 1943, years that had included separations lasting several weeks in the summer, they had discovered that their loneliness for each other's company could be relieved by writing frequently; indeed, when apart, they wrote letters to each other every day. These were long and intense missives that not only provided news of each others' activities but explored the emotions they were both experiencing at the time. From the summer of 1940, these letters reveal the growing intimacy and caring that was developing as they expressed their affection for each other.

One might expect a boy and girl in their mid-teens to expose a rather simplistic yearning, but for Victor Feldbrill and Zelda Mann these letters are a monumental account of two deeply committed young people maturing in their loss of each other's presence and determined to maintain the deep love that they shared. For example, in the summer of 1941, they agreed to spend a few moments simultaneously thinking about the other each day: "At 11a.m., 3 p.m., and 11 p.m., we will spend 10 minutes thinking of us — and to relieve the tension … we will go for a walk each evening."[1]

Early one summer, Victor had made the trip to Zelda's cottage, then had left for Toronto. His sudden departure had occasioned a written eruption of emotional fervor:

> I feel I am going to burst. O why did you have to leave? Why? I want to have you close to me, your lips pressing close to mine. O, I would be in Heaven, I am crying now enough to drown a nation and I want you near me. Oh, Vickie, I love you so much, I can't go on without you … tears blind me....[2]

As the years went by they came to realize how much music could be a bond, and although Zelda expressed her need "to have you near me, to hold me tightly, to tell me you love me, to ask me to marry you," and to assure her lover that "I miss you every minute of the day," they discovered there was comfort in their mutual delight in hearing the sounds of great music. It was agreed they would listen at particular times to the recordings of great music that they could experience "together though apart," music that expressed the depths of their feeling for each other. Tchaikovsky's *Overture to Romeo and Juliet* and Schubert's "Unfinished" Symphony no. 8, both conducted by Leopold Stokowski and played by the Philadelphia Orchestra, became love songs filled with deep emotion. Zelda, though not as musically knowledgeable as Victor, soon developed a sophisticated ear for the sounds of great artists, great orchestras, and magnificent musical expression. Later, the César Franck Symphony in D Minor and the Tchaikovsky Symphony no. 4 in F Minor took on the role of a bridge that the two lovers could employ to strengthen their sense of sharing a moment of deep caring.

On the other hand, Zelda also found comfort in the classics of English literature, the description of the depths of despair to be found in the lives of parted lovers. When apart during the Second World War, she also advised Victor to read Tolstoy's *War and Peace* and the descriptions of human breakdown in the Napoleonic campaigns depicted in that great novel. As she became more conscious of social problems besetting modern society, she convinced him that he should read the works of Upton Sinclair. She also commended Aldous Huxley's *Brave New World* to Victor as essential reading for any understanding of the possible future once hostilities ended.[3]

Though Victor graduated in the spring of 1943, their love for each other had not diminished despite the fact that Zelda now had ambitions to pursue a professional life even as she was completing her days at Harbord Collegiate. She had continued to excel academically in her final year, while providing stellar leadership in producing the school's yearbook and continuing to give advice to the TSO on the programming for its student concerts — a role she took on with confidence despite Victor's absence. (Even after she left Harbord, she volunteered to be on the makeup squad for the school's production of *The Gondoliers*.) Most important of all, she had decided that she would go on to university and take the arts courses that would lead her to qualify for a specific program in social work. Even though she was an "A" student, Zelda had one handicap — a traumatic fear of examinations. To her they represented a devastating personal trial every time she faced them, but with Victor's support she developed the determination to persist and overcome these irrational fears of failure and humiliation.

As soon as Victor's basic training was completed in Toronto, *The Navy Show*'s perambulations back and forth across Canada ensured that letters and an occasional telephone call would be the method of communication for the couple. The postal service was not particularly reliable as a form of daily contact. The show was continually on the move, with Victor stationed for only a few days in most communities, and mail delivery was sporadic. The frustration of virtual "silence" for days at a time, particularly after Victor went overseas in 1944, was enormous. Then there would be a deluge as letters arrived in batches, six or seven at a time, the lapses causing considerable consternation. However, both remained committed to a future together and letters were simply the only way to keep in constant contact.

Both Zelda and Victor had come from strong Jewish family backgrounds and shared many of the same values. Zelda, year after year, demanded that Victor carry out his duties in celebrating family birthdays and anniversaries and recognizing the times of religious observance with cards and gifts — no matter how difficult procuring these objects of remembrance might be when he was constantly "on the road." They shared a caring about an extended community of friends and relatives, and Victor was constantly reminded of the people he should contact or arrange to share a meal with as he travelled with the show through Winnipeg, Vancouver, or Detroit.

Without any formal decisions having been made at the outset, their commitment to each other remained strong, though not without tensions and questions, thus sustaining their understandable physical attraction and giving it a wider meaning and purpose. Even now that Victor was absent from Toronto, Zelda was at the cusp of Victor's ambitions as a musician and a conductor. As she was completing her final year at Harbord, Zelda enrolled in courses in the liberal arts at the University of Toronto, a Social and Philosophical Studies program that included modern languages. At the same time, Victor was enduring his initiation as a recruit with the RCN.

Her highest ambition for Victor was that he not only develop his professional skills as an instrumentalist, but that his interests range more broadly across a cultural plain that included great literature, theatre, film, and a knowledge of profound philosophic expressions, particularly those associated with the Jewish faith. She felt this could give an enriched background to everything they did together. For example, she insisted that Victor should read a history of Yiddish literature. Victor had once been an avid reader and connecting him to great literature was a part of her strategy to see that *The Navy Show* did not turn him into a mindless practitioner in a musical comedy. Particularly after she reached her undergraduate years at the University of Toronto, she became a dynamo of personal intellectual energy and focus and she wanted a man and a husband who would challenge her with his mind and spirit. She was encountering the monumental concepts upon which Western civilization had been built and, in her mind, represented the very reason for Victor's presence in the Canadian navy and she was determined that he realize that these values were an essential part of their love for each other.

With all her caring and admiration, Zelda could see that simply living with a Victor playing gig after gig, night after night, was not going to be a satisfying future as far as she was concerned (although she insisted that he practise his violin rather than going off to see just another film or spending time amusing himself in mindless conversation with his colleagues in the *Navy Show* orchestra). Victor tried to convince her that his choice of films was a part of his personal preparation. He managed to see the film adaptation of the play *Of Mice and Men*, with a score by Aaron Copland, as well as *Tomorrow the World*, a production that included the background music of his friend Louis Applebaum. However, though Zelda conceded the value of this cultural genre of film, she wanted the stimulation of intense interchange of debate and discussion that could be shared with others of like direction. Along with a mutual delight in music, intellectual intervention must also be a means of bringing insight to things of the mind and spirit.

She was aware that she would be the initiator of this expectation and that her drive and determination contained risks. Victor loved his shy but lively and lovely high-school sweetheart, but to place pressure on a serviceman disconnected from all the things he knew and valued in the form of a constant challenge to scale the heights of intellectual discourse, was taking a real chance in the process of retaining a relationship that was so precious. But Zelda never relented. She saw an even greater danger — that Victor and she would become two totally different people, moulded by years of coping with contrasting lifestyles leading to an inevitable disruption of their intimacy.

She was adamant that no person in any relationship had the right to impose ideas on the other, but she was watching relationships breaking down as returning young men who had been engaged in military service soon found they had nothing in common with the girl they had left behind and with whom they were hoping to resume a relationship. Hence, Victor was bombarded with books he must read and ideas that demanded his attention, whether it was in terms of appropriate human personal behaviour or the maintaining of intimacy in the conflicting cut and thrust of the political ideas that were abroad in a world at war that contained opposing ideologies. Indeed, even Victor's personal hygienic habits were addressed as well as his tendency in the direction of becoming overweight. Victor, on his side, was not the least diplomatic in pointing out to Zelda her many spelling mistakes, a failing that was particularly disconcerting for a writer of her quality. It was the one fault that her lover felt he could comment on without restraint or reservation.

There is no doubt that of the two, Victor was the most apprehensive about the impact his time in the service would have on their relationship. Zelda had left the Harbord context that he knew well and was on a university campus he had never experienced but had heard much about. There would be all kinds of bright young men vying for the attentions of his beautiful beloved. There would be parties and receptions, some associated with athletic events, all part of the normal experience of an undergraduate and all filled with the possibility of an intervention that would terminate his special place in her life. It was happening all around him as marriages of his fellow musicians were collapsing and he witnessed the disintegration of commitments his colleagues had undertaken to wives and sweethearts back home. In fact, one of his colleagues was actually engaged to two girls in a single hometown. Victor was frantic to assure himself that his Zelda would be there when this sojourn in the services was completed. It meant that he came to resent any news that indicated she was enjoying an active social life, one that Zelda had every right to expect as part of her life, not just as a university student but as a mature adult.

Victor came to believe that the only way to strengthen his chances of keeping this intelligent and physically enticing young woman was to secure her in matrimony at the first chance he could arrange. From 1943, it became a constant plea in his letters and a source of friction between them. Zelda, however, was not willing to become an estranged bride, living with either of their parents and enduring the same loneliness that her status as a single woman had brought her. She wanted a real marriage that would change her life and bring Victor to her side in their own home — not just a sham joining that satisfied their occasional sexual needs and made a public statement about their relationship that contributed neither comfort nor meaningful intimacy. She made it clear that she would not "run off with another man," but she wanted to live a full life in a university setting that promised rich experiences that had nothing to do with love, marriage, or commitment. Zelda never lost sight of the promises she had made. On his part, Victor used his remuneration as a musician to buy war bonds that would represent a fund to purchase their home on his return. At least this was agreed upon and represented their mutual expectations of a future together.

It could be said that the lifestyle imposed by *Meet the Navy* represented both salvation and perdition. On the one hand, there was no question that Victor was using his greatest skill to enhance the war effort. This was a matter of enormous pride to his family and close friends. However, there had been no motivation behind all the marching, physical exercise, and information gathering about the naval arm of the fighting forces that formed the content of his initiation. Within a few weeks in the fall of 1943, he realized his total role was that of playing in a variety show pit orchestra. He was not grounded either at a naval base or on a vessel in His Majesty's Service. There was not the daily drama of chasing enemy submarines or guarding the approaches to convoys carrying life-giving food and other necessities to the people of Britain Nor had he any hope of a change of function as a result of any elevation to higher officer status. He had been recruited as a bandsman and like his orchestra comrades would remain as such throughout the war.

The Navy Show was essentially a touring ensemble, rehearsed and ready to provide a couple of hours of quality entertainment (and, for some, a soupçon of inspiration). The repertoire never changed. The music was composed and arranged to accompany actors, singers, choristers, and dancers through a series of presentations that were aesthetically pleasing but more likely humorous and irreverent. The show did not develop or improve, though the dialogue and song lyrics were updated, and some transformation was necessary before the show was presented to British and European audiences and eventually revised for filming. But essentially, once the production was prepared and rehearsed, its musical score and spoken text remained sacrosanct. There was no pressure to learn new music, no expectation of higher standards of performance. Whenever there was no matinee performance, Victor's time was his own. He had lots of opportunity to practise, to listen to music, and to informally join with his colleagues in making music for their own pleasure — and lots of time to worry about losing Zelda. Indeed, a paramount concern for Victor was the fact that on so many days there was no news with which he could fill letters to Zelda and there was a terrible disappointment if the long missive she invariably wrote each day, filled with the description of exciting events in Canada and stirring concepts, failed to arrive.

On the campus of the University of Toronto, Zelda was going through the frantic schedule of a first-year student along with other responsibilities associated with family and worthy causes. Very quickly, she was becoming a self-assured young woman on whom the implications of the changing roles of women in wartime were not being lost. It was clear that soon after Victor's departure from Toronto she assumed a more confident stance. She wrote of her desire to participate in "a marriage of equals" and to take her place in "a model modern home" in which their children would "have a sense of independence." These were worrying signs of a new woman that Victor now had to deal with from a distance. At the same time she expressed pride that she had baked the cookies that she sent him and assured her loved one that she was learning to cook.[4]

While Victor was pleading for an early marriage, Zelda was ensuring that he realized what kind of marriage she envisioned. She was taking courses in psychology and philosophy that challenged the ancient orthodoxy of male dominance and was determined to see that her future would be affected by what she was imbibing from her scholarly reading and classroom debate. For example, she was determined that after marriage they could not live in the Feldbrill home where the definitions of comfort and order were in some opposition to her own. She made sure during Victor's absence that she regularly visited his mother, father, and sisters, often sharing a meal with them. However, she also made it clear that she was not going to be as family-obsessed as she felt her mother-in-law-to-be certainly was! She was aware that she was viewing the Feldbrill household in difficult years. A pregnancy, a full decade later than one might expect, had resulted in the birth of Eileen, a baby now disrupting a home inhabited by a teenage daughter and abandoned by an even older son.

The bedrock of stability for Victor in these years of absence was Zelda's close connection within the Jewish community. However, differences within families of faith can be as divisive and tension-filled as those between peoples of altogether differing commitments. Though in sophistication and social status Zelda's family was certainly a level above the Feldbrill clan, there was a close rapport in the matter of faith from the outset of the young couple's courtship. It was based on mutual respect and much more. Zelda's father, as an educational leader and scholar as well as a leading figure in the radical wing of Judaism, was also an icon for Victor seeking a male figure to emulate. His future father-in-law's reputation in the Jewish community was such that even in the midst of the war and the Holocaust he could give a public lecture on "Why Jews hate Jews."

For Zelda, her father was a hero who had defied the authorities in the old Europe and had courageously brought his family to a new home, a model of the kind of man with whom she wished to spend her life. On one occasion, she used her daily letter to reprimand Victor for spending too much time watching silly movies with the admonition that he should be reading good books, or practising his violin. "I don't want you to be just a musician," she wrote, reminding him that he would be shifting from "a violin to a baton at the right moment."[5] Zelda was confronted by the dichotomy of wishing for a husband who was a mirror image of her father while at the same time insisting on a relationship that recognized the equality of the partners in that marriage.

Zelda, as the months passed, began to make her presence felt on the university campus, yet even there she consistently associated herself with Jewish causes and interests. After much discourse about the foolishness of such membership, she joined IOTA Alpha Pi, a sorority whose fees were the lowest and that welcomed Jewish students. She provided leadership to young people in the Jewish Youth Association (JYA) and played a major role in setting up the Jewish Student Fellowship on campus. In short, she reconstructed the leadership status at the University of Toronto she had enjoyed at Harbord Collegiate.

Zelda was constantly attracted to events that were related to her faith — attending a Labour Youth Conference (following in the steps of her radical father), one that considered the unfair position of young people seeking to enter the labour market but rejected because of their lack of experience. Attendance at a lecture by Ted Corbett, the founder of the Canadian Association for Adult Education, had an enormous impact on her attitude to the importance of Victor's use of time. On numerous occasions when Victor was in London or Paris, Zelda would advise him to forego the touristy attractions and visit the slums, take pictures and notes, and learn to appreciate the conditions that real people had to face. In 1945, Zelda attended a lecture by Rabbi Sachs on the Balfour Declaration, the post–world war document that had sought to provide a solution to the Jewish need for a nation state in the Middle East. She reported to Victor proudly that she had also attended a lecture offered by A.J. Binder, the author of a book *The Jew and His Music*. Her delight was revealed in a letter to Victor:

> I am so happy about the Jewish music. I know more than
> ever that you are Jewish … obviously it is more than just
> belonging to a group — it is taking an active interest in it.
> It is so important.[6]

Two months later she expanded on that theme: "It will mean so much to our children to be born into a Jewish home … and not an assimilated one. My parents were very pleased with my choice."[7]

Zelda could even find within her university studies an advantage in preparing herself for a family experience — more evidence of her desire to bring Victor happiness. In October 1944, she began to participate in a practicum focused on those moving more directly into social work. She reported that she would be devoting many hours to a course called Wartime Day Nursery. "I'll be learning to be a good mother," Zelda assured Victor, along with an observation that each of them had the responsibility "to share knowledge with each other." At the time she was reading the *Grapes of Wrath*, a novel that was considered so outrageously critical of capitalist society that it was for a time banned from the shelves of the Toronto Public Libraries. Zelda recommended the book to Victor as a revelation of social injustice that brought into question the moral superiority of the Allied fight against fascism in the light of the treatment of the dispossessed and impoverished in the 1930s.[8]

Perhaps the most predictable of Zelda's behaviours was the attention she gave to the well-being of the UTSO, the ensemble that Victor had conducted before joining the navy. Victor's friend Hans Gruber now occupied the podium, but Zelda assured Victor that although the orchestra was "not together," she had enjoyed the concert, which was well attended. For the sake of the ensemble, though, it was apparent to Zelda that Victor must return home to the role of conductor as soon as possible.

The most consistent commitment for Zelda was her continuing concern about the Feldbrill family. She visited frequently. However, there was an element of tragedy in the role that Zelda felt she had to play during Victor's time away from home. Her extraordinary learning and experiential social work skills were at work as soon as she realized that things were not going well. She expressed the considered assessment that Eileen, Victor's newborn sister, was very bright. However, she also realized that her mother was unable, at her advanced age, to provide all the sensitive caring that a new child needed. As a teenager, Zelda became almost a surrogate mother to the child, a position she would fill until Eileen herself was a teenager, responding with extraordinary sensitivity to her (by then) sister-in-law's learning and emotional needs.

The dysfunctional nature of the Feldbrill family had an even greater impact on Victor's sister, Ruth. Zelda intervened directly as a mentor and an instructor, helping Ruth with her school work and attempting to improve her study habits. Her intervention was an invitation to disaster. Ruth, who had understandably resented Victor's pre-eminence within the Feldbrill family, now perceived Zelda as an unwanted new family acquisition who was imposing herself as a teacher and who displayed a perceptible preference for her younger sister. She was unaware that Zelda was critical of Eileen in that she thought she was a "beautiful and clever kid" but that she was "jealous of any affection shown by the family to others rather than herself." When Zelda tried to warn Ruth's mother of the impending confrontations, she unfortunately added to the unhappy situation by encouraging her future mother-in-law to openly express her disappointment that her older daughter had been unable to attract a boyfriend. In the old world view of the survival of the female offspring, courtship by and marriage to a man of commendable station was the most hoped-for culmination of a school career. The failure of a daughter to focus on this necessity could mean a life of poverty and unhappiness. Zelda, in full flight away from such a perception of female prospects, was horrified but unable to make any headway in dealing with the crisis.

Zelda was particularly prescient about Ruth's unfortunate position in the family. Invariably, she found, Ruth was being blamed for Eileen's mischief and was not given the self-confidence she craved at home:

> Seldom does she get the praise that you, Victor, or Eileen, or even I get. Instead she is always blamed — even unduly. Not only that — she is made to take care of Eileen much too much. And what I really find horrible: they keep reminding her that she hasn't a boyfriend. All in all, the kid is quite miserable and it could mark her for life.[9]

In spite of Zelda's close involvement with the life of his family, Victor still remained anxious about his relationship with the young woman whose letters spoke of dances and receptions, of friends and acquaintances (some male) — normal occurrences on a university campus. He was concerned about who Zelda was meeting, how she was being escorted to sorority affairs (and by whom), and, in short, about all the ways in which Zelda's affections might be captured by an interloper who was on site. Zelda assured Victor constantly that there was no other man in her life — yet she still refused to go through a marriage ceremony, even a secret one, feeling that it would be meaningless in terms of greater closeness and the delights of co-habitation and would simultaneously bring pain to both sets of parents. By her second year, she was at the top of her class, even though the inevitable examinations brought on hysterical trauma of no mean proportions. Invariably, when the results were posted, she had excelled even in economics, a subject for which she had no great enthusiasm. In languages and the social sciences, she had outstanding results. There was no dispute — she had chosen demanding courses and had met all their challenges with distinction. But in Victor's eyes this made her an even greater prize for the discerning classmates who would revere her intelligence as well as being swept away by her beauty.

Victor's letter written in the winter of 1944 revealed more of his insecurity about the strength of their relationship. He was obsessed by the "dangerous" implications of her dating and in a series of missives told her so without reservation. Zelda was furious. Admonitions that advised, "I wish you wouldn't be so supersensitive," became angry questions, such as "How can you write such biting letters?" and demands that Victor "suppress [his] moments of anger." Zelda pointed out that while Victor was touring the country, "doing his bit," but also enjoying the sights and sounds of exciting places, she was apparently expected to sit at home. "What about me?" she asked with some impact.[10] However, Victor's intense love had come through even the most acid comments and by the spring of 1944, though not prepared to marry, Zelda was prepared to be publicly engaged. On his last leave in May, Victor gave her a ring, and in a paroxysm of happiness, she was able to show it to her working associates at Borden's, her summer workplace. The office was "in an uproar," was Zelda's report to Victor.

Ironically, Victor was not impressed with his new status. Even though formally engaged, Zelda remained a magnificent trophy for the attentions of the many young men with whom she was associating daily. Indeed, it was in June and July of 1944 that his seeming lack of trust hurt her deeply and brought forth an angry reply: "You haven't got rid of that horrible habit of flying off the handle and saying nasty things. You must get out of that habit. — it is not good for any marriage. Be careful."[11]

An admonished Victor was quick to mend fences but the incident galvanized Zelda's determination to engage Victor in a most astonishing way around the issues of loyalty and liberation. She had, by this time, been writing very scholarly papers for her courses on the topic of human sexuality. The concept of virginity had been one of her topics. She was reading books that challenged the standard morality that she and Victor had grown to accept, in particular, a tendency toward judgmental responses toward other peoples' private behaviour. For Zelda, the recent engagement, an open commitment to marriage, meant that there was "no excuse for jealous rages." She insisted that this symbol of their expectation did not mean that she would "throw away all her friends." Her ultimatum: "I can't live that way." Victor was seeing the great cities across Canada and soon would be visiting Britain and Europe. She fully expected him to go out and enjoy himself. But she, too, had a right to an active social life.

The spring and summer of 1945 brought even greater tension, now that he was even farther away — both geographically and intellectually. Victor's letters were laden with jealous commentary and Zelda's displeasure reached a climax. He was making her "upset and miserable." In her mind, jealousy had no place in their marriage and that "must be one of the first commandments." She warned Victor, "I have my own ideas." When his letters became even more "vicious, so nasty, so miserably mean," Zelda lashed out: "Grow up and be a man for a change — I won't stand for it and that's definite." To emphasize the seriousness of her threats she pointed out that she recognized that Victor might well meet other women while he was in Paris.

The altercation continued when Zelda took a position that shocked Victor to the core. Preparing him with all that she had learned about sexual behaviour, she made her point clear:

I wouldn't mind in the least if you made a pass at another woman … it depends on how intense it is. Being away from sexual release for so long is pretty tough — I know. I would know it was only a release and nothing more. I'm serious.[12]

It was a bad time for Zelda on many fronts. She was enmeshed with the tensions in the Feldbrill family, and she had left her summer job at Borden's (a manufacturer of confections — packaging Mello Rolls had been her first task) when she decided she could make more money and would have better hours at a varnish factory. She soon realized she had made a disastrous move, and returned to Borden's. Unfortunately, when an over-stocking of certain products demanded a smaller workforce, she was the first to go.

In the fall of 1945 Zelda was back at university, where she now felt comfortable, and she was well aware that Victor would soon be coming home. He had been assured that in spite of the rumour of a victory tour in Canada, *The Navy Show* would be back before Christmas and he would be home with Zelda.

Once again, Victor saw the foolishness of his position and the recriminations ended. It was time to plan their union rather than focus on their discontent. Zelda was ecstatic about the opportunity that the war had provided for Victor to meet influential people — including Boult, Beecham, and a host of others — and she saw that he was taking every opportunity to advance his career. Most important, Victor promised Zelda that he would take her back to all the romantic sites in London, Paris, and Amsterdam, and that she would get a chance to meet all those with whom he had become friends.

The healing had begun and music continued to play its part. They told each other about the works that they had heard on radio. Zelda could report that she had heard both Beethoven's Symphony no. 9 and the Shostakovich Symphony no. 1 for the first time, and Victor kept her up-to-date on the concerts he attended, as well as the broadcasts he heard and the scores he had found. Zelda discovered that her capacity to listen with a critical ear had developed, and she informed Victor that she had listened carefully to a contemporary composition of which she complained, "there was a lack of fire in the third movement." But most of all they found solace in music they both loved and Zelda relayed her joy in hearing Eric Leinsdorf and the Cleveland Orchestra playing a Tchaikovsky program that included his glorious Violin Concerto.

There was another source of agreement that brought satisfaction in these months of separation and was a part of the growing realization that nothing could destroy the love that Victor and Zelda had for each other. Zelda had identified herself in a first year essay, "Who Am I and Why Did I Come to University," as "an introvert," and having been brought up in "the serenity of a home environment that resulted in a very uneventful youth."[13]

The university experience and her enforced separation from Victor had banished that wonderfully naïve and innocent person. Her reading and writing had exposed the radical roots of her upbringing. She wanted to believe the war would forge a new kind of democratic society more devoted to equality and the humanitarian causes that surrounded her. During the last years of the war, there was a surge of idealism on both the North American and the European continents, as liberal democratic nations sought to renew their governments through the electoral process and choose parties that espoused more egalitarian and socially progressive policies. Victor, isolated in the travelling show, was, at first, little involved. But he soon became aware of the socially conscious and politically astute partner he had chosen as Zelda described her expectations of the world they would together inhabit after the war had come to a conclusion. She saw faults in the existing order that demanded change. It was an exciting time. She wished to participate in the progressive movement she saw developing.

The Co-operative Commonwealth Federation, or CCF, was a democratic socialist political party in Canada that emerged from the economic horror of the Depression. Public opinion polls in the mid-1940s indicated an acceptance of CCF policies on a scale that had not been seen since its formation in Regina in the early 1930s. People who had endured both economic disruption to their lives, followed by the demanding sacrifices of a global war, were determined to see a government that would support their desire for old age pensions, health insurance, and support in periods of unemployment and in the case of disability — all the elements of social progress that it was believed a welfare state could provide. During the early 1940s, Saskatchewan had elected Tommy Douglas and the CCF. The effect had been the creation of a progressive government that brought reform and development where just years before economic disaster had threatened the very survival of the province.

When George Drew called an election in Ontario on June 4, 1945, there seemed a chance that a new opportunity had opened for a repeat of the Saskatchewan experience in Central Canada. Zelda was anxious to engage in political activity. Her work in economics, sociology, and anthropology had produced a very socially sophisticated young woman, one who had built upon the values and precepts that had been learned at her father's knee. She was very much "au courant" with the swirl of political philosophy that filled the air in countries now looking to a post-war world and determined that the disintegration of democratic societies that had given rise to the fascism should not be repeated. Zelda wanted to be part of this movement. The role of the Soviet Union as a prime ally lowered the level of terror over the possible triumph of communism that had been part of the fascist strength in Italy and Germany.[14]

By early May 1945, Zelda had joined the head of her sociology department and had become a worker for the CCF, folding leaflets and distributing them in the Cumberland–Yorkville constituency in the centre of Toronto. She could see that the CCF had support, even though it had initially only prospered in rural Saskatchewan. Then, suddenly, an issue arose in the campaign that diverted the campaign away from social issues. A daring attack was launched by Ontario CCF Leader Ted Jolliffe on Premier George Drew, charging that as premier, Drew was using a secret unit within the provincial police to spy on progressive agencies, including trade unions and indeed, the CCF itself. Referring to this activity as "Gestapo" tactics, and in particular pointing out the incredibly despicable Conservative strategy of linking the CCF to the communist party, Jolliffe charged Drew with making reports from this internal group available to all the anti-CCF propagandists engaged in a muckraking campaign to wipe the party off the Canadian political scene. Apparently, the success of the Douglas Government in Saskatchewan had aroused the more virulent forces of capitalist enthusiasm in Canada and "dirty tricks" had entered the electoral strategy of the ruling party in Ontario.

George Drew faced the charges head on. He appointed a commission to investigate and promised to resign if the charges were proven true after his election victory. Zelda experienced a visible cooling toward the CCF as election day in June approached. The results were devastating, with the CCF receiving 6 percent lower approval by the voters than they had received in 1943. It was an important election. The CCF returned to the position of being a small third party in the Ontario Legislature and so it would remain for most of the twentieth century.[15]

Zelda, with all her idealistic expectations, was disappointed at a time when her private affairs seemed lacking in resolution. The summer of 1945 was a time when she felt particularly abandoned, especially when servicemen and women were returning and couples she knew seemed to be building their lives together. There were moments, particularly at an event enjoyed by both Sir Ernest and Lady MacMillan, when she bitterly asked herself "why not us?"

Indeed these were expressions of despair she passed on to Victor. She felt that they were "poor, ineffectual souls trying to work against greater forces." Yet she never lost faith in the possibility of progress in both their relationship and in the world they would face together. She kept Victor informed of her political activities, without attempting to influence his vote.

Zelda then turned to the electoral system, which had distorted the results of the voting pattern through the "first past the post" system of voting in every constituency, ignoring all the votes received by other parties and bringing victory to George Drew's Conservative Party, even though a minority of citizens had actually voted for their candidates. It meant that Drew's government gained a majority even though "more people voted against Drew and his Government." It was an issue that was to remain dormant in Ontario until well into a new century. At the same time she was criticizing the electoral system, she observed with clear vision, "I'm afraid too many have become rich during the war and are afraid of a socialized program."[16]

Within a short time, a federal election took place and, once again, the voters refused to take a chance on the CCF, expressing a preference for the promised social reforms of the Liberal Party of Mackenzie King (who described the CCF members as "Liberals in a hurry") and re-electing them for another term. It was a second disappointment for both Victor and Zelda in their initiation to active involvement in the political life of the country.

Just a few weeks later, Zelda was thrilled to see the British Labour Party under Clement Attlee win the election in Britain, defeating the man who had led the nation successfully through the war, Winston Churchill. Zelda's August 2 letter to Victor revealed her excitement. "How do you like the election in England. Isn't it wonderful … Here's hoping the Labour Party can live up to the expectations of the people."

After delays around the making of the film about *The Navy Show*, it became official: the entire company would be sent back to Canada and demobilized before the end of the year. Victor returned on a large vessel carrying troops from all sectors of the Canadian Armed Forces.

The conclusion of Victor and Zelda's long and eventful courtship almost ended in farce. They decided that, after an intimate sojourn together in Montreal, they would at once have a small wedding in Toronto for their immediate family and closest friends. It was to be held on the next to last day of 1945. However, during the journey across the Atlantic in rough seas, Victor suffered a serious fall and badly injured his shoulder. When he arrived in Montreal to met Zelda he was almost immobilized in a plaster cast that encased him from his shoulder to his hip. It must have been quite a shock for her, who perhaps envisioned her triumphantly returning future husband running off the ship and into her loving arms. A decision that allowed the couple to have a day alone together before being overwhelmed by family and friends was welcome. The next day the bridegroom arrived in Toronto with his bride-to-be on his one intact arm, looking as though he had suffered war wounds that might well undermine his future plans — married or not.

It was a thrilled Victor who soon realized what a magnificent companion he had — very different from the young girl he had loved and left just years before. She remained a woman of striking beauty but had become one of strong will and intelligence. The war, during the two years they had been separated, had matured both of them in countless ways that would be revealed in the decades ahead. Most of all it had transformed a withdrawn young girl into a woman who would not just be supportive of his ambitions, but would be a source of strength and wisdom as Victor faced the prospect of transforming himself into what was then a rare phenomenon in musical circles — a Canadian-born and largely Canadian-educated orchestral conductor.

Without Zelda, it is unlikely that Victor Feldbrill would have risen to the level he did in his distinguished career. They were a couple whose commitment to each other was never in question; indeed, their loving relationship was the envy of musicians and Canadian music lovers from coast to coast.

CHAPTER 7

Transition

The Toronto to which Victor returned was in some contrast to the city he had left just two years before. For Canada the war had been unofficially over for some months and in place of a war economy there was a frantic rush to shift to one that emphasized, indeed celebrated, the manufacture and sale of consumer goods. It was time to replace the stoves, refrigerators, cars, and trucks that had been nursed through the years of the Depression and wartime restraint. For the first time, many Canadians had money in their pockets that allowed their participation in such an economy. Victor and Zelda Feldbrill had carefully saved a considerable sum of money, some one thousand dollars, during the war — but their attention had to be on the fact they would have years of preparation to fulfill their ambitions as students and scholars before they could become wage-earners able to establish a home and begin a family.

Though consumerism reigned supreme, the arts had suddenly taken on a new significance. Thousands of Canadians had discovered that great music, theatre, visual arts, and film had not just made the war bearable but their survival was a justification for all the sacrifices that winning had demanded. Indeed, a sizeable number of men and women had decided that they would spend their lives making music, either performing or composing it. The Toronto Conservatory (soon to be crowned the "Royal") and the University of Toronto's Faculty of Music were overwhelmed by the number of enrollees and even more by the quality of their commitment. Mostly they were veterans, male and female, with experience and maturity that staggered their professors, who were used to instructing less intense adolescents straight from the high-school classroom. These adult learners also seemed to have a vision — the transformation of the frontier-like nature of their Canadian society to include the expression of its cultural essence through sound, speech, colour, form, and movement.

Shortly after his return to Toronto, Victor and Zelda were married on December 30, 1945, much to the delight of parents, siblings, and close friends. A place to live was at once provided by Zelda's parents — a flat on the second floor in a house the Menachovsky family had acquired at 202 Glenholme Road, northwest of the central Toronto neighbourhood Victor and Zelda knew so well. It was to be their home for the five years they spent as students and part-time employees, up until the time they were ready to start a family.

For Zelda it was an opportunity to complete her Bachelor of Social Work and turn her attention to a Master's Degree. She had been an outstanding student and scholar and her professors encouraged her to continue. A second degree was becoming a necessary qualification if she wanted to address the more complex implications of human behaviour that had excited her in her undergraduate reading, research, and study. She was to use these years to complete her studies and join the staff of a Jewish social service agency, one that was providing assistance to Holocaust survivors who had miraculously reached Toronto but were continuing to experience

the trauma caused by their experiences during the Holocaust. Like survivors around the world, these victims were faced with horrendous questions. How could a Chosen People have been destroyed in this way with no
intervention from a loving Jehovah? Why did I survive when everyone else
in my family perished? How do I banish the nightmares of the torture and
dehumanization I witnessed? How do I go on living a normal life after such
an experience? There could not have been a more sympathetic and sensitive
mentor, one whose studies had produced a nonjudgmental and thoughtful counsellor. As a professional social worker, Zelda thrived, drawing the
attention of her colleagues and the appreciation of her clients.

For Victor, the journey was a little more complicated. First, he had
arrived at the Conservatory in the middle of the academic year — January
1946. Second, he was a professional musician and had engaged in a massive
effort to educate himself through his work at both the Royal Academy of
Music and the Royal College of Music in London, England. How could the
names of his formal and informal mentors — Boult, Howells, and Beecham
— not impress the admissions officer in any music faculty or school in
Canada? In spite of the limited formal secondary-school qualifications,
there was no question of his eligibility. Both Sir Ernest and Ettore Mazzoleni
could attest to his suitability in the diploma program. After all those weeks
in the rehearsal and concert audience, among conductors and musicians of
the London Symphony and Philharmonic Orchestras, the Scottish National
Orchestra, the Paris Conservatory, and the Concertgebouw in Amsterdam,
how could he reduce his expectations and conform to the limitations of an
undergraduate music institution? Would there be sufficient challenge for
him in a program designed for academically oriented students with little
professional musical experience and having had no contact whatsoever with
the musical culture of other countries?

In the midst of all this confusion, Victor found some refuge in playing his violin, in particular, addressing the delights of chamber music. It
was his salvation, both physically and spiritually. First he had to recuper-
ate from his accident, an obvious necessity for an active violinist. As it
turned out, playing the violin helped to a greater degree than the physio-
therapy that was suggested by his medical advisers. Indeed, within a few
weeks he was playing in the pit band for the "Ice Capades," a professional

skating presentation mounted annually in Toronto. It proved a good way to exercise a very painful arm, indeed more effective than any prescribed medical intervention. As well, the very act of performing music regularly restored his soul.

For the final few years of the 1940s, Victor seemed to be involved with music everywhere! He played violin in duos, string trios, and quartets, in chamber ensembles and in orchestras of varying quality and accomplishment. He soon became a familiar figure among the coterie of musicians who were responsible for the scores of live performances in a city not yet noted for its cultural strength, but just beginning to reveal its enormous potential.

Most disconcerting during these years was the frustration that he could pursue and could prosper from a career as a fine violinist — either as a soloist or a member of a small ensemble — and, with a modicum of teaching and adjudicating, could thereby support a family in modest but acceptable circumstances. However, Victor had developed an addiction to the role of conducting at a time when there were few such positions to be had. Toronto supported few orchestras, and it seemed that most if not all of its podiums were occupied by individuals whose tenure seemed everlasting and relatively secure. The UTSO had replaced Victor with fellow conductor and friend Hans Gruber, who had no intention of handing the baton back to a returning Maestro Feldbrill. The TSO was at a pinnacle of its post-war calibre, solidly led by the incomparable Sir Ernest MacMillan and was totally beyond Victor's ambitions. The Toronto Conservatory Orchestra was appropriately in the hands of the institution's principal, Ettore Mazzoleni. The newly established Conservatory Opera School now had its own ensemble but the recently acquired Nicholas Goldschmidt was solidly in place. There were also several other musicians who aspired to the conducting role, patiently waiting in the wings like Victor was, all attempting to position themselves as possible successors to one or another of the incumbents.

Even Victor's expectations for further study on his conducting technique with Ettore Mazzoleni were frustrated by changing circumstances. "Mazz," in becoming principal of the Conservatory, did not have the time or the inclination to offer courses in conducting. The only alternative offered in the Senior School was that of studying with Nicholas Goldschmidt, a fine singer and singing coach who was on the cusp of becoming, within a few years, Canada's most celebrated arts entrepreneur. Unfortunately, he did not have the instruction of orchestral conductors as his first interest. To reach the levels of conducting instruction expertise Victor had in mind, he felt that he would have to travel abroad. Thus, his most valuable time was spent outside Canada's borders — in the United States and Europe — in order to achieve what he believed were international standards in conducting. It was the worst of all times to be travelling abroad — Victor's stipend from the Department of Veterans' Affairs each week (along with the few dollars he might command from small gigs as a violinist participating in some ensemble performance) did not go far in keeping Zelda and himself alive and well. Indeed, any efforts to add to that part-time income automatically reduced his Veteran's Allowance. At one point only the intervention of a helpful civil servant who discovered a legal but more advantageous way of filling in his income-tax form enabled Victor to keep a few more dollars from the recompense he received from performances and, for the Feldbrills, that made remaining debt-free possible.

By the end of the 1940s, Zelda had completed her Master of Social Work (MSW) and had begun working, thereby adding to the sparse cash available each month. She knew that social work for all its recently discovered importance was not a fast track to a high salary. But helping others was her passion. It was a tough time for both of them, but being together balanced the books psychologically and the later years of the 1940s were ones of frantic activity, filled with the joy of finally being together.

Victor's formal admission was to the Conservatory and its diploma program and was as a musician — more accurately, as a student of the violin. It was also one engaged in all facets of musical performance, including its history, the mysteries of harmony and counterpoint, the process of its composition, and the elements of orchestration. It was obvious in terms of enhancing his violin performance that Victor could not return to his old teacher, Sigmund Steinberg. It was time for him to move on. He chose to enroll in the studio class of Kathleen Parlow, a legend as a solo violinist, but even more in terms of her knowledge of chamber music performance and particularly the repertoire of the string quartet.

Victor was faced with a grim reality: he needed to become an effective wage-earner. His preference by far was that of becoming an orchestral conductor. At the same time, he realized that he had, through all his efforts during the *Navy Show* years, become a very good violin player. It was a view that was supported by his new instructor, Kathleen Parlow, who thought so highly of his full-bodied tone and his extraordinary virtuosity that she saw him either as a potential solo performer or even more likely as the mainstay of a fine string quartet. She was determined to see him in one of these roles.

Victor, for his part, could not directly oppose Parlow's intentions. He realized that the string quartet was at the very core of great orchestral preparation — both as a performer and as a path to conducting pre-eminence. There was purity and transparency in such music preparation that could be transferred to the performance of the full symphonic orchestra. There was also both the simplicity and complexity in the presentation of such music that was relevant to his goal. He wanted to know the workings of such a musical entity "from the inside." Here was his chance, and being led by a towering mentor like Parlow, the opportunities were made manifest.

The string quartet provided the thrill of observing the lines of musical development in the transparency and intimacy of limited instrumental sound. The patterns of repetition that enhanced the enjoyment of both the players and the listeners were obvious. There was also an element that reflected Victor's personality — the reduction of the individual ego in the direction of collegial rather than dominant behaviour on the part of a leading figure. He found the enhancement of musical performance by a diminution of solo extravagance most seductive. It also gave him the opportunity to master the viola, the instrument he enthusiastically adopted in the first sessions of his program with Kathleen Parlow. Once again, it was an opportunity to extend his experience with a new instrument and explore its strengths in tone and flexibility.

During the rest of the 1940s, chamber music became Victor's major commitment — alas, as well, the practical realization that there was more remunerated work to be had with a violin or viola rather than with a baton in his hand. Nevertheless, with all these pressures and opportunities, conducting the symphony orchestra in performance remained the pinnacle of his ambition.

The central element of Victor's attachment to the violin can be assessed in terms of its pathway to the conducting role. His complete lack of keyboard experience was, in some peoples' view, a major disadvantage for anyone seeking to be a conductor. For Torontonians, even today, the memory of two of the most successful TSO conductors, Sir Ernest MacMillan and Sir Andrew Davis, is that both were outstanding on the piano and the pipe organ. The belief is that conductors and concert pianists or organists display comparable breathtaking virtuosity with that expected of conductors, and that for those who attend concerts to be hypnotized by the gyrations of the man or woman on the podium, the keyboard is surely an appropriate pathway to that position. Victor, by contrast, came from the midst of the full symphony orchestra, or more recently, the string ensemble, in terms of his preparation to provide orchestral leadership. The core challenge of Victor's career at that point was of playing stellar violin performances, both solo and in small ensembles, while still reminding people in the music world that he was now a partially trained conductor and wished to follow this course to its proper conclusion as an artistic director of a major symphony orchestra.

However, Victor was dealing with a Kathleen Parlow who was relentless. As soon as he had found his place in her studio, she saw that he was soon connected with other Conservatory chamber music students, both in her own studio and those of her colleagues. Within a little more than four months, he was playing in recital with Earl Moss on piano and Mary Oxley on strings, the Mendelssohn Trio in C Minor, a substantial challenge to the finest of musicians. Within another year, Victor had become an established member of the Conservatory's Senior School String Quartet and by the middle of that second year the quartet was playing its first full recital in the Conservatory's concert hall at College Street and University Avenue. The Parlow Studio students — John Mair, Victor, and his old friend from school days, Morry Kernerman — were joined by James Hunter from Isaac Mamot's studio. Together, with Victor surprisingly accomplished on viola as a part of his strategy to understand the string quartet "from the inside," they played a program that included Mozart's popular melodic Quartet in B-flat Major (*The Hunt*) and the demanding Ravel Quartet in F Major, in which Victor played the first violin part. A mere week later, in June 1947, the Conservatory Senior School String Quartet, with only a replacement of James Hunter by Donald Whitton on cello, played in a recital with other Parlow students in the same concert hall. Victor played the Andante: Allegro movements from the Lalo Violin Concerto. But the above were only the formal occasions organized by the institution within which he was enrolled. Other occasions in the community increased exponentially his commitment to his instrument..

Upon arriving in the summer of 1947 at the Berkshire Festival in Tanglewood, just west of Boston, Victor found himself playing his violin before the prestigious attendees of that famous event. A Norwegian composer, Knut Nystedt, needing a talented violin performer to present his Sonata for Violin and Piano, Opus 10, during a spontaneous recital of contemporary music, drew on Victor's willingness to play. It was a triumph made possible by Victor's virtuosity and even more by his extraordinary sight reading skill and his familiarity with the idiom of modern compositional techniques.

In the winter of 1948, the Conservatory Senior School String Quartet played a recital at the Art Gallery of Ontario. Now Victor was back on his more familiar violin and along with his colleagues was playing the Mozart Quartet in C Major and the Dohnanyi Quartet in D-flat major, repeating the program a few days later at a concert sponsored by the London Chamber Music Society.

At the closing concert of the year, presented by the now Royal Conservatory of Music, in May 1948, the ensemble played the Mozart-Dohnanyi quartets, but now the ensemble was designated as the RCM Senior School String Quartet. The emphasis of the evening concert was on the performance of Department of Veterans' Affairs' students now graduating from the Conservatory and Harry Somers, soon to become recognized as a major Canadian composer, played his own piano sonata, *Testament to Youth*.

It was an important engagement and an early moment of collaboration with a Canadian composer. Indeed those years at the Conservatory were unique in the close relationships that developed between composers and performers, like Harry Somers and Victor, never to be replicated by any institution throughout the rest of the century. Many years later, Victor was being courted by an American orchestra but turned down the offer of an appointment for a number of reasons, one being that he did not want to lose the close friendships he had developed with Canadian composers like John Weinzweig, Harry Somers, and Harry Freedman, all colleagues in music creation during these post-war years at the Conservatory.

The closing concert of the Royal Conservatory was an event that drew guests far beyond the institution's students and professors. Even major Toronto newspaper music critics arrived to hear performances by the potential music-makers they would be reviewing in the years to come. Journalist Rose Macdonald recognized the "fine performers" of that evening, "who presented the program with discernment, with universal finesse and the fine presentations of tone colour a constant joy." Augustus Bridle praised the quartet in particular for its "soft thematic passages that were tonally expressive," providing "a rendition of the Dohnanyi that was really outstanding."[1]

Early in 1949, The RCM Senior School Quartet presented a Hart House Evening Concert. It was a part of a musical series that commanded major attention from music lovers, not only on the University of Toronto campus but across the entire city. Along with the familiar Ravel work the quartet had mastered, the members played the Schubert Quartet in D Major (*Death and the Maiden*). Critic Douglas Valleau was most impressed:

> It has the makings of an entirely first-rate quartet. The precision of attack, the sense of rhythm were quite phenomenal. As well, they presented an intelligent grasp and expression of the structural unities of the music. Passages occurred every once in a while when nothing further could be desired.[2]

Within a few months, the Royal Conservatory of Music presented a violin recital at which Victor played sonatas by Handel and John Ireland along with a Mozart's Concerto no. 4 in D Major. It was in a way Victor's farewell concert as a violin soloist and chamber music performer. By 1949 he had been selected as a member of the TSO at an audition attended by Hyman Goodman, the TSO concertmaster, and with Sir Ernest himself presiding. Victor came through handsomely. He now had a full-time appointment as a regular and valued member of the first violin section of the TSO and that would be his first responsibility throughout the concert season for the next few years. His time as a Department of Veterans Affairs student had come to an end. He was now a graduate of the Conservatory Program but more important he was now recognized in his hometown as a musician of professional stature. With his sensitivity to the repertoire and style of chamber music, he would be in demand as a conductor by smaller ensembles across the country. As well, with his new role at the TSO would come opportunities in the early 1950s to conduct that orchestra more frequently, particularly in concerts for children and young people, as well as at pop concerts for those wishing a lighter and more popular fare. Most important, he was slowly but surely making the successful transition from performing string player to orchestral conductor.

However, the TSO was not only interested in Victor's presence as a member of the string section or as a conductor of concerts that encouraged a less demanding repertoire. As the 1940s ended, there was a realization, especially among the younger members of the TSO Women's Committee, that the survival of symphony orchestras depended on attracting more youth to the delights of classical music. These were strong, vocal, and determined women who in some cases had children whose musical futures were high on their agendas. Outreach to children and youth had been a challenge to these women for some time, particularly under the Sir Ernest MacMillan régime. Indeed, Victor himself had participated in those early programs when he and Zelda had been at Harbord Collegiate. He had never forgotten the meetings of the advisory committee of teenagers and the social affairs hosted by Sir Ernest and Lady MacMillan. It had led to his first conducting experience with the TSO and a relationship with Sir Ernest that had opened doors wherever he was posted with *The Navy Show*.

Victor's inclusion as a string player was a vote of confidence in his musicianship, but there was also another agenda being played out. There was now an expectation that Victor would lead the forces of commitment to outreach at a time when the wartime thrust of enthusiasm for serious music might wane. If children and young people were to be reached it would take TSO resources and energy, and having a figure like Victor associated with the orchestra would be central.

Now he could feel that his reputation as a conductor had finally been recognized by a major symphony orchestra. More important than learning about conducting in a classroom, there was the actual satisfaction of leading fine musicians in the process of regularly exciting and inspiring an audience of people who had been gathered for just such a noble purpose.

There was a downside to this recognition as the TSO's "conductor in residence" for pops and student concerts. In a strange way it came to severely undermine his future in Toronto. He could never shake off that role as the TSO's reliable and very popular purveyor of music to the young and unsophisticated when, in fact, he had mastered a wider and more profound repertoire — one he began conducting outside Toronto and overseas. Also, having played a role as a member of the TSO's string complement made it even worse, as his instrumental colleagues, though respecting his skill, training, and experience, saw him as "one of us," making more difficult the task of maintaining some measure of discipline in orchestral ranks. And for an orchestral administration seeking to establish order and place in the institution's formal employment and remuneration decisions, Victor was seen as being in both camps.

In actuality, the shift to conducting had been hesitatingly taking place during all those chamber music years from 1946 to 1950. The trips to the Berkshires and Maine (to be described in a later chapter) were based on his determination to see his career as a conductor prosper. He knew that only through constant performance could both his ability be recognized and his potential realized. In December 1946, Victor accepted his first conducting challenge — that of assistant conductor to Nicholas Goldschmidt of the Conservatory Orchestra. Goldschmidt was busy with countless other tasks, thus Victor was asked to replace him on the podium at the Opera School presentations at Hart House on the University of Toronto campus. That wintry night he was faced with a small orchestra gathered to support the stellar vocal forces preparing to take their places on the operatic stages in Canada — Mary Morrison, Elizabeth Benson Guy, Andrew MacMillan, and Louise Roy. These performers were a part of that first post-war flight of voices that came to give quality and leadership to the early years of that exciting genre as it appeared in Toronto and ultimately emerged as the Canadian Opera Company. For Victor, it was the beginning of a career that resulted in the command of a restrained conducting style in a pit ensemble that soloists, both vocal and instrumental, came to appreciate, and one that gave support while avoiding overwhelming volumes of sound that could bury the solo performer.

Within a few months, another conducting opportunity presented itself during rehearsals for Smetana's *The Bartered Bride*, presented by the Opera School in Eaton Auditorium — an acoustically more appropriate venue than the Hart House Theatre with its low ceiling and compromised sightlines. Though in this particular performance he was the concertmaster, in reality he was sharing the rehearsals with colleagues George Crum, Clermont Pépin, and George Hurst. Later he played a similar role in the Opera School's presentation of Humperdink's *Hansel and Gretel* and in the 1948 and 1949 productions of Mozart's *Marriage of Figaro* and Puccini's *La Bohême* respectively. He was learning about the mechanics of the "pit" orchestra, once again, "from the inside." As for the solo concerto repertoire, in 1949 it was instructor Boris Berlin who called on Victor to provide the instrumental accompaniment as a conductor of a small ensemble at a recital of piano students that included a movement from a Beethoven concerto as well as the contribution of other short selections.

During these years, Victor's conducting opportunities ranged from formal invitations to "come by chance" affairs. For example, when the Toronto Musicians Protective Association found work for its members by providing a concert for a youthful audience at Humberside Collegiate in Toronto's west end in a program that included Bach, Brahms, Schubert, and a twentieth-century composer, Benjamin Britten, Victor was chosen to conduct. From this experience, Victor began the debate in his own mind whether it was better to take orchestral forces into the school or to bring youth to the concert hall. He eventually came down on the latter course — young people needed the experience of the concert hall, and though Humberside had a fine auditorium, many modern educational structures had nothing but a gymnasium or a cafetorium with little acoustical quality. Victor, unlike his good friend and colleague, the incomparable pianist Glenn Gould, never gave up on the inspirational potential of bringing people together in a common space to be collectively moved by great music, well-performed and intelligently interpreted.

By the late 1940s, whenever there was a need for a small orchestra to accompany student recitals, Victor was there to ensure the chairs were filled with competent musicians that were rehearsed to provide adequate support to his Conservatory colleagues. It was a time of enormous élan and synergy among more mature veterans playing in the Conservatory Concert Hall, an ancient building in central Toronto at the corner of University and College Streets that would soon be destroyed to make room for a glass and steel monster structure to house Ontario Hydro's administration.

It was in the closing concert in 1948 that Victor conducted the Conservatory Symphony Orchestra at Massey Hall in the opening of the evening's musical proceedings. As principal, Ettore Mazzoleni was the regular conductor, and once again, Victor had taken over the role of concertmaster and assistant conductor. As with Goldschmidt and the Opera School Orchestra, Mazzoleni had many duties, and rehearsing the orchestra was often an impossible burden. Also, it was a time of waning hopes for one who many would say was Canada's finest conductor, with his career now stalled in Conservatory administration and his brother-in-law, Sir Ernest, still in place as the TSO's permanent, unchallengeable maestro. Perhaps as a result, his manner on the podium came to be particularly negative. As well as being brilliant and helpful, he could harass and humiliate. Players came to resent his barbs and cruel comments.

Whenever Victor appeared as a replacement, a different atmosphere prevailed. Klemi Hamburg, a fine violinist from a family that in the early years of the twentieth century had dominated music education in Toronto, remembers that Victor's time on the Conservatory Orchestra's podium was warmly welcomed by the entire ensemble.

Victor never lost his temper, rather he tried to make his time as rehearsal conductor as enjoyable as the circumstances would allow. At a concert that was to have enormous consequences for Victor, at Mazzoleni's insistence, he took over the orchestra for the opening selection, Beethoven's *Egmont Overture*. The members of the Royal Conservatory Symphony Orchestra were determined to play well for him. Critic Augustus Bridle reported the results of this collaboration:

> Victor Feldbrill had a great opportunity to express himself as an orchestral conductor in the "Egmont." The number has contrasts in plenty and his players responded generously to his well defined beat. They were never self-

assertive and his left hand said things of a right helpful sort. His personality is genial and his intuitions quick — right or wrong. This is surely a beginning full of promise.[3]

In the summer of the same year, Victor's help was requested once again, this time to conduct the Royal Conservatory Summer School Orchestra. On July 27, after weeks of rehearsal, the ensemble was ready to give its first concert. Victor had prepared an ambitious program which concluded with the familiar but challenging Beethoven Symphony no. 5 but he also premiered a Canadian work, Godfey Ridout's Dirge for Orchestra. Even more twentieth-century composers were included: Eric Coates's arrangement of Purcell's Suite for Strings and a Britten work filled out the program. It was clear that these amateur musicians were to be stretched to the limit technically, but also were to become familiar with contemporary compositional techniques. Rose Macdonald, the *Toronto Telegram*'s music critic, commented that, "Victor Feldbrill had his work well in hand and a clear-cut way of communicating his wishes to the big ensemble before him."[4]

By July of the following year, he was back in front of the Royal Conservatory of Music's Summer School Orchestra in the Conservatory Concert Hall with another challenging program, which included Mozart's *Overture to Don Giovanni*, Beethoven's Concerto no. 3 in C Minor (with Gordon Kushner at the piano), Bartok's *Rumanian Dances*, and concluded with Mendelssohn's Symphony no. 4 (*The Italian*). Strangely, for Victor, there was no Canadian composer represented. There was an overflow audience and an unidentified reviewer asserted that "Feldbrill's command over the group is sure, precise and his manner is friendly and musicianly. He is in a position to make a first-rate contribution to music in Toronto."[5]

Soon, another orchestra had taken notice of this young man who was still in his mid-twenties yet conducting the city's more able orchestras — the Toronto CBC Orchestra, formed in 1952. It was a time when Canada's national broadcaster, the CBC, believed that its mandate was that of being a source of unity and understanding in the entire country. As such, it was expected to intervene in the making of music by commissioning works from contemporary Canadian composers from across the nation and ensuring their music was heard in prime time. It also meant the enlisting of fine musicians who would form ensembles to play this music. With the best musicians available, excellent orchestras were created in every major region of the country. The Toronto CBC Symphony, made up largely of TSO players, was considered by many the best in the land. Victor Feldbrill's memory of this significant development was conveyed in an email that caught the author's attention:

> In 1948 CBC started a special Wednesday Night series and even had a small orchestra under contract. Terence Gibbs, a producer at the BBC was brought over by the CBC to be the chief producer of music programmes for that series. People who wanted to perform were invited to audition for him.
>
> That was fine for instrumental groups and singers but useless for conductors. Fortunately, in the spring of '49, my graduating year from the U of T Senior School, I was asked by Mazzoleni to conduct the opening work on the final concert of the Conservatory Orchestra of which I was concertmaster. I conducted Beethoven's *Egmont Overture*. Here at last was an opportunity for an audition, so I invited Gibbs to the concert.
>
> He came and immediately followed through with an upcoming CBC Wednesday slot. The programme included Wm. Boyce's First Symphony, Elgar's *Serenade for Strings* and Mozart's Symphony no. 29. This was an important beginning because it was followed by more broadcasts and a long association with the CBC Symphony Orchestra as a guest conductor on numerous occasions.[6]

Gibbs was also a great admirer of Sir Thomas Beecham and thought there was a theme he could exploit on *CBC Wednesday Night*. Beecham had just turned seventy and in Feldbrill he had a youthful conductor who had met and been influenced by him. Why not feature both of these conductors? After playing a recording of a Mozart symphony by the famous septuagenarian, he introduced Victor as "a very young Canadian fired by ambition on the veritable threshold of his career. One of his assets is his single-mindedness as far as conducting is concerned. In short, he simply must conduct." And conduct Victor did. The performance of the *CBC Wednesday Night* orchestra of both the Mozart and the Elgar were declared to have been outstanding by listeners, performers, and CBC management figures.

That same year Victor was back in front of the TSO but now as a member of the orchestra's string section. Though popular, it was a substantial program, beginning with the Sibelius *Finlandia* — often a hackneyed though strangely moving composition, but on this occasion, as one critic commented, "its performance emerged a gripping thing." William Krehm, a perceptive reviewer, reviewed the program, which also included the Mendelssohn Violin Concerto played by another Canadian of impressive status, Betty-Jean Hagen. Of Victor's final selection, he observed:

> Mr. Feldbrill has cherubic stage presence that is largely deceptive. Despite his youth he has devoted years of earnest study to conducting and today is in possession of a terse purposeful vocabulary that gives him an amazing command of orchestras. This skill is coupled with a sure musicianship that strikes a happy balance between temperament and design ... the orchestra sang the lovely music of Schubert's Unfinished Symphony ... not a phrase was lost.... [7]

As the 1940s came to an end, so did one of the most difficult decades of Victor's life. However, he had successfully shifted his musical life from the violin to the baton. He was prepared for the challenges of the 1950s and was now recognized for his leadership qualities in addition to his musical attributes. He would still have to prove himself in every concert — that is the struggle that every performing artist must accept, but in Victor's case he would indeed prove it with great confidence and skill.

Young Victor Feldbrill poses confidently with his violin, 1935.

Victor Feldbrill on the day of his bar mitzvah, 1937.

Victor Feldbrill, a teenage conductor in company with his closest companion, Morry Kernerman, a splendid violinist, 1948.

Harbord Collegiate Reunion. In the middle is teacher Charles Girdler. To his right is Sam Shopowitz (seated) and entertainer Frank Shuster, and on his left, Victor and entertainer Johnny Wayne.

The *Navy Show* orchestra. Victor is in the front row, second from the left.

Victor Feldbrill in uniform, enjoying the victory parade in Paris celebrating the end of the Second World War.

German composer and influential musical educator Carl Orff (right) with Victor Feldbrill, in 1950. The two found a common bond in their fondness for children and the desire to instill a love of music in them from a young age.

Victor with Zelda at her convocation
at University of Toronto, 1947.

The Winnipeg Symphony Orchestra at debut concert under Victor Feldbrill's leadership.

Victor and Zelda Feldbrill at debut concert with WSO president Ernie Brown and his wife, Hazel, 1958.

Canadian composers (from left) John Weinzweig, Harry Somers, and Harry Freedman, with Victor at their favourite conductor's sixtieth birthday party, 1984.

Victor with Aaron Copland in Banff, 1976.

(Left to right) Harry Somers, Phil Nimmons, Victor Feldbrill, John Weinzweig, R.Murray Schafer, and John Beckwith at John Weinzweig's eightieth birthday party, 1995.

Victor Feldbrill with internationally renowned conductor Sergiu Celidibache after a Tokyo Geidai concert, 1985.

Victor Feldbrill receiving an honorary degree from Brock University chancellor, the Honourable Robert Welch, 1991.

Victor Feldbrill on the occasion in 1997 of his receiving of the Roy Thomson Hall Award, with Jean Ashworth Bartle and Oscar Peterson, both previous recipients.

Victor Feldbrill with Norman Symonds at debut rehearsal of N.S. Concerto Grosso for the Jazz Quintet and CBC Symphony Orchestra in January, 1957.

A meeting of the minds during rehearsal for Godfrey Ridout's TV opera, *The Lost Child*. (Left to right) Victor Feldbrill, Godfrey Ridout, John Reid, Mario Prizek.

Victor and Zelda Feldbrill with Sir Ernest MacMillan, Canada's first Canadian conductor of the Toronto Symphony Orchestra, 1956.

Victor Feldbrill with mentor, conductor Pierre Monteux, 1950.

CHAPTER 8

Becoming a Conductor — A Work in Progress

Exposing the ultimate truth and beauty of musical composition through the process of moulding the efforts of splendid musicians gathered as an instrumental ensemble was Victor's highest ambition. However, it had been evident that in the 1940s adequate instruction was not available in his hometown of Toronto. There were limited opportunities to test his leadership qualities as a guest conductor with student orchestras, but that, and the infrequent opportunities to lead CBC ensembles and the TSO, was the sum total of Toronto's capacity to satisfy Victor's learning needs as a conductor.

It was not enough. Victor's wartime experience in Europe observing some of the great conductors of the era in Britain, France, Germany, and the Netherlands had opened his eyes to the experiences that eluded him in Toronto's musical scene. He decided he must travel to wherever he could learn more, where good conductors and their potential conducting colleagues gathered in usually festive settings. That was where the next generation of conductors would be identified by their presence and their strengths recognized by the experts. He wanted to see these "giants" like Koussevitzky, Monteux, and von Beinum, hear what they had to say and how they went about inspiring the members of their orchestras.

He realized that reaching his goals of becoming a conductor would entail a difficult journey from sitting before a music stand in the string section of the TSO. There were few Canadians to refer to as models of success in making that transition. Certainly there were Sir Ernest MacMillan and Ettore Mazzoleni, but few other Canadians had succeeded in their goal of reaching the conducting role. He was aware that many parts of the world celebrated the shift from instrumentalist to conductor, but usually the elevation came as a distinguished shift from a solo performing background.

He also had no interest in the reprehensible tendency to see the orchestral conductor, not as a music-maker, but rather as an exciting and bizarre phenomenon, one with a reputation for living an outlandish lifestyle. Such a figure, with considerable media "hype," could attract an audience of great numbers to a performance of serious music. Victor wanted no part of that game. He simply wanted to be recognized as an effective orchestral conductor with an exemplary style and technique, with an acknowledged interpretive capacity, and with a commitment to and a knowledge of the orchestral repertoire sufficient to inspire an ensemble, and through it, an audience. He wanted the composer's message to be the focus of his role as conductor.

There was also the example of the dictator-conductor that entranced some musicians and potential audience members. One would hope in a perfect world that the conductor, considered as first among equals, would be able to establish a relationship with his orchestral colleagues in a synergy that assures the production of pleasing sound as a communal effort. The role of the "powerhouse" conductor, often conductor-composer, had many precedents, but it was mainly the nineteenth century and, some would say, an extension of the influence of Felix Mendelssohn that eventually led to acceptance of the respected position of non-instrument-playing orchestral leader. Unfortunately, this development had also led to the emergence of the power-mad autocrat by the late nineteenth and early twentieth century.

It is not a perfect world and too often the dictator-conductor is the image pervading the context of classical music in many circumstances (though the perception of conductor as first among equals has never been totally abandoned). With all the tension around the role and behaviour of conductors, the wonder is that great music is satisfyingly produced at all. It was not a stereotype, whether false or in some cases accurate, that Victor wished to emulate.

In a perfect world, one would hope to find a sizeable coterie of music lovers who would fill every concert hall in any community. They would come as a result of the admonitions of the great philosophers who have commented on the importance of music as a strategy for listening to the sounds of the universe and the truths so acquired, thereby supporting in a practical way the desire to make good music an element of every culture. The symphony orchestra, as an instrument capable of extending itself in sound quality and variety, is without doubt the most exciting and challenging source of musical expression. Thus, it could be assumed such an instrument would surely have no financial difficulties associated with its efforts. In that world, there would be no need for lavish promotion, and thus no need for flogging the personality and photogenic power of "The Conductor" as if he were a Hollywood movie star.

Unfortunately, in this imperfect world, the symphony orchestra has become but one of many elements in a broad spectrum of an entertainment industry seeking to make a noticeable commercial impact. That is the ultimate aim — survival in a sea of performing activities mounted to make, in the case of more popular forms of musical activity, considerable profit for its purveyors, both artists themselves and the commercial interests promoting them. For the symphony orchestra, survival in a largely uncaring environment has to be the over-riding preoccupation of managers, musicians, and conductors, even in the twenty-first century.

Victor, during these early years, became the victim of this perception of dictator as conductor, partly the result of the contrast with his restrained behaviour and his pleasant personality. It was plain that he was not interested in the bizarre, the immodest, or the crudely picturesque, which in a world dominated by popular culture draws crowds of curious and easily titillated audiences. He was obviously determined to be a serious musician dedicated to the expression of music composed by creative artists as a way of understanding oneself and the world.

His private life would reflect a childhood, youth, and now an adulthood with a set of values emanating from a warm and supportive family, a cultural experience of a faith tradition that he found sufficiently profound and satisfying, and a relationship with a woman of like mind with whom the creation of a stable home life and its nurturing was of the highest priority.

Victor had come from a poor family. He had no rich relatives nor had he any wealthy friends and associates who might have provided a social status more appropriate for one hoping to become a conductor of a major orchestra. And while it was manifestly clear that Zelda was an enormous support, she had not come from the social world of the wealthy or upper-middle-class community leadership in cultural affairs upon which arts organizations were, and still are, forced to rely. Most important, though, she never behaved in an aggressive or pro-active manner that one might have expected from a member of a family that had provided radical social democratic leadership in czarist Russia and now in Canada. She attended Victor's concerts and she was an imposing presence at receptions and events associated with the orchestra. Indeed, that the room "changed whenever she walked in," is the assessment of a host of admirers as well as her daughter, Debbi. But her focus was first on her family and second on her professional role as a social worker. In the beginning, with her own family and career pressures and the modest but comfortable accommodation the Feldbrill's could afford, she could not be the ever-present hostess for countless after-concert receptions. Pat Wardrop, a major figure in the volunteer life of the TSO, put it simply: "She was a dear, dear woman — completely devoted to Victor's career." But the achievement of conductor status and its recognition depended on Victor alone, as it should in any profession.

From the outset, Victor had become attracted to the aspects of making music that promised a career devoted to the civilizing nature of the creative, the inspiring, and the beautiful. Unfortunately, for those who think that the wildly entertaining, shocking, and melodramatic should be the basis for attracting people to a public performance, the concepts of competence, reliability, and collegiality were the attributes that tended to surround him. This image became a constant. His first TSO performance was that of a teenage phenomenon, a high-school student conducting his superiors in experience and instrumental virtuosity in a Strauss waltz at a youth concert. Not a bad place to start — but with no reason to see it as an auspicious beginning for a conducting career in his home city.

His second appearance as a conductor with the TSO had come some five years later in 1948 when he was a mature student at the University of Toronto. It was a secondary-school concert and the main composition on the program was a very complex and demanding work, the Ernest Bloch Concerto in A Minor for Violin and Orchestra, conducted by Sir Ernest MacMillan. The soloist was Victor's closest friend throughout his youthful years, Morry Kernerman. The focus of the media was not on Victor and Morry's musicianship but a fictitious rumour concocted by a local newspaper reporter about these two Toronto boys chumming together on a school playground who they claimed had written down and buried a pact that they would eventually perform together on a stage as conductor and soloist before a Toronto audience. Here they were carrying out their adolescent dream!

In fact, it was a tale manufactured by the fevered imagination of the interviewing reporter seeking a seductive theme for his modest article. Fortunately, the concert had gone well and the audience had been responsive, but the media response was distorted by this misleading story of schoolboy prescience.

It was three years later, at a TSO secondary-school concert, when he received his first recognition as a conductor (as opposed to a guest conductor of a single selection). Now, as a member of the string section, he was perceived as part of the TSO team available for leading youth concerts. The repertoire included the Dvorak Concerto for Violin and Orchestra and the remaining works on the program were of a popular nature but contained substantial repertoire that carried forward a view that Victor espoused throughout his life — that young people should not be "played down to," that they should be served the very best musical fare. In this case it included Enesco's *Romanian Rhapsody No. 1*, and the Beethoven *Overture to Fidelio*. In another gesture in the direction he would follow in the future, Victor included the *Etudes for String Orchestra* by Canadian contemporary composer Godfrey Ridout.

It was another six years before he conducted again, this time at a Sunday pop concert in a program that was obviously directed at an audience that had essentially come to be entertained. The soprano soloist was engaged to sing "Songs and Arias from American Lyric Theatre" — in other words, Broadway tunes. It was followed by a series of popular repertoire items. This appearance after so many years indicated that Victor's career as a conductor of professional ensembles in Toronto was on a slow track.

By 1957, it could be said that Feldbrill had become a familiar name to TSO audiences. As well as a prominent string player, he had become the assistant conductor regularly leading the TSO in its outreach concerts. Unfortunately, his presence did not include his occupying the podium for any of the major subscription series' concerts at which the mountain-top musical compositions of the ages could be expected to be performed. He was very much the orchestra's conductor for students and audiences unprepared to listen to that more serious repertoire. This concentration in the 1950s produced an image of Victor as the predictable figure to conduct with reliable and consistent excellence the "soft outreach" programs offered by Canada's major orchestra. It was an unfair label that he had to fight in his native city throughout his entire career.

Victor's solution to this image problem was predictable. He had found that he would have to extend his image by developing his craft and securing a reputation abroad. From 1947 to 1950, then again in 1956, that became his strategy. His second practical thrust in developing his career as a conductor had been that of waving his baton before every ensemble he could reach. First, as assistant conductor to Ettore Mazzoleni, he conducted the Conservatory Symphony Orchestra, and as assistant to conductor Nicholas Goldschmidt, the Opera School Orchestra. Eventually he reached the summit as a guest conductor of the splendid Toronto CBC Symphony Orchestra and for a short time he led his own Chamber Orchestra. It was quite an array of ensembles with varied repertoires and contrasted competencies. With the exception of the Chamber Orchestra, however, he was not the artistic director of any of these ensembles; he appeared as guest conductor, as assistant conductor, and as a replacement conductor on occasion — in short, in any role that brought the satisfaction of orchestral leadership.

These activities certainly kept him very busy throughout the late1940s and the early to mid-1950s. When a major Canadian orchestra began looking for a conductor for a single concert, Victor became seen as a candidate with a passion for outreach performances in the community, one comfortable with the playing of Canadian contemporary classical music, and, more important, always available, competent, and experienced in conducting the regular, well-recognized repertoire.

In these years, there is no record of a more determined Canadian musician prepared to endure the discomfort of foreign travel and to endure the humiliation of being ignored in order to learn the intricacies of the conducting craft. Yet, to be seen mainly as a violin player rooted in the string section of several ensembles, to have a reputation as a chamber music devotee in string duos, trios, and quartets, all seemed to work against the achievement of his central passion — that of concentrating on orchestral conducting.

The first foreign destination for expanding his reputation had been suggested by his mentor, Sir Adrian Boult, while he was still in Britain — the Berkshire Festival in Tanglewood, some miles west of Boston, Massachusetts. Even in the mid-1940s, the festival, under the aegis of Serge Koussevitsky and the Boston Symphony Orchestra, had achieved a position of pre-eminence. It had become the major gathering of American composers around Aaron Copland and Leonard Bernstein and was also reputed to draw the best students to its conducting program. It was Boult's letter to Koussevitzky that resulted in Victor's acceptance into that program.

Sadly, once again, without Zelda (there was no money to pay for her to accompany him), Victor arrived with two colleagues in the beautiful Berkshires, a landscape that inspired the efforts of every participant. The first activity for would-be conductors was to join a chorus to learn Randall Thomson's *Hallelujah* and to provide an audience for the festival director Koussevitzky's welcoming comments. For one who had become familiar with Beecham, Barbiroli, von Beinum, and Boult, it was disconcerting for Victor to hear Koussevitzky introduced as "the world's leading conductor."[1]

It was also disappointing to discover that in reality there were two conducting groups gathered in one place — those associated with the maestro, along with Copland, Bernstein, and their close colleagues, and those who were not. Victor was very much in the latter coterie and found himself a foot soldier, a role which included an invitation to sing in the Festival Chorus and audit lectures that were part of the presentations to all present and enrolled. Victor decided to take advantage of whatever he could access in order to learn all he could and hopefully be inspired by his experiences. Even though he had "not sung since Public School," he found it "one of the most thrilling experiences I've ever had." Ironically, it was in the choral area that he touched the paradise of his hopes for understanding and inspiration. (Little wonder that later in his life the cause of training choral conductors to deal with orchestral accompaniments became paramount in his mind.) The reason for this excitement was provided by the leadership of the choral activities, a young Robert Shaw, who, mentored by Julius Herford, had even by the 1940s taken his place as the most prestigious choral conductor in the United States. He wrote to Zelda:

> He's only about 30 and is already considered the first choral man on the continent. He prepared choruses for Toscanini, for example. I learned more about phrasing and choral direction in 1 ½ hours than I learned in a whole year at the Conservatory. He's really a good conductor and I mean that.

It was at Tanglewood that his admiration for Robert Shaw shone forth, and Victor had no difficulty terming him "a genius," responsible for "thrilling rehearsals." While attending a Shaw lecture, he was profoundly moved. In his missive to Zelda, he continued:

> He spoke of music in a highly philosophical light with great love for it: his talk was like listening to a great masterpiece of music during which more than once I had a lump in my throat. And you know how he was dressed? He had on sloppy overalls rolled up above his ankles and a sloppy drooping shirt — his hair, blond, was in his eyes. But as far as I'm concerned he is the greatest mind bar none. Zel, darling, how I wish you had heard him. His

talk should go down in musical history as one of the great talks given. And to think he is only 30 to 32.[2]

Victor's orchestral conducting classes raised his morale. One of his motivations for coming to Tanglewood had been that of assessing his skill in comparison with those of leading American colleagues. The first candidate conductor to perform was "awful." The second "could not beat time correctly." Victor was unimpressed by "what America produces in the way of conductors," and to Zelda he proclaimed, "I now know where I stand…. It's the breaks we need now, darling and that's the toughest part."[3]

There were those who caught Victor's attention and provoked a positive reaction. He met a charming Aaron Copland in a music store, bought the score of his Symphony no. 3, and had the composer autograph it. He would later bring Copland to his own podium in Canada — and he also played his music with generous regularity. Of Leonard Bernstein, he was not so impressed: "He's a conceited prick…. I'm waiting to see him conduct, maybe he'll redeem himself" And redeem himself he did:

> Bernstein then did Copland's *Appalachian Spring* … he did a fine job — blast his conceited hide! And again a few days later he conducted the Stravinsky Rite of Spring. It was excellently done — he certainly knows that score, damn him.[4]

Things began to look up early in the conducting program when its leader, Dr. Stanley Chappell, decided to create an orchestra from the auditors in the program. Very quickly Victor's qualities as a violinist became obvious. Though by this time Victor had decided he enjoyed listening in the Festival Chorus as much as he did playing in the Festival Orchestra, when Boris Goldovsky asked for volunteers for his Opera Orchestra, Victor appeared again and was made assistant concertmaster.

Victor could not stay for the gala final concert of the festival and absented himself from both the orchestras. He had a gig back in Toronto. By that time he had seen all thirty-five of his conducting colleagues and though the experience convinced him that it would take hard work and the breaks to see him through a successful career, he had gained new confidence. He had witnessed the best of young North American conductor hopefuls developing beside him and he had surpassed them in his accomplishments. Two years later he was on another similar excursion, seeking to extend further his knowledge and experience, and gaining even more confidence in his own gifts.

Pierre Monteux was one of the major figures on the podium as the twentieth century reached mid-point. As he had grown older he had decided that though he was not a composer and could leave behind no legacy of his own music that his successors could play, he could at least devote some part of his last years to the training of the next generation of conductors. His venue in Hancock, Maine, had none of the extravagant features of the Berkshire Festival with its crowds of many thousands. Nor did he invite any of the big names in American serious music to attend. It was a comparatively small, modest program in conducting for serious students prepared to work to the limit of their capacity over more than a single summer.

Only a few days in 1949 provided Victor with an appraisal of Monteux and his Hancock, Maine, enterprise. In his view the conducting students were better than those he had encountered at Tanglewood — many were drawn from professional orchestras like the New York Philharmonic, the NBC Symphony, or served opera company orchestras of the calibre of "The Met" in New York City.

There were no heroics — Gerhard Kander and Leon Fleisher were visiting students, soon to become internationally known soloists. The course included the intense study of orchestral scores. In Victor's view this was "a more simple and sincere" approach to the art of conducting than Tanglewood had provided and he thrived.[5]

Pierre Monteux's arrival had been delayed and although the program had commenced on August 1, the maestro did not turn up until the 8th. During the initial phase, in his absence, all the conductors had performed and Victor had been alone in not receiving considerable criticism. Indeed, in his presentation of the Bach's *Brandenburg Concerto no. 5,* he had not been stopped once and the course critic had exclaimed, "You have excellent baton technique, good musical taste, and you know how to go after what you want in music —bravo for you!" Even the pickup orchestra had joined in the applause. In a later session, working on the Schubert Symphony no. 5, he was told that his technique was impeccable and that his musical ideas on the work were excellent.

When finally Monteux arrived, it was apparent that high standards were expected. He had a reputation for bringing reality to pretentious students in a most harrowing fashion. One participant thought he could impress the maestro by conducting a composition without a score. Monteux listened and then informed the class that this young conductor was about to write on the blackboard, from memory, the first page of the score for the edification of the entire class. The student was aghast and informed Monteux that this was totally beyond his capacity. Monteux's response was, "Use the score! Unless you know every note of the score from memory you cannot be of help to the orchestra — and that is your role as conductor — so open the score and start again please." For Victor, it provided a solid argument for ignoring the tendency of conductors to impress orchestras and audiences by conducting without a score.

While other conducting students were criticized rather sharply, Victor could inform Zelda that "I was the only one he had a good word for," and that Monteux had told him, "You are a good conductor, with fine technique — perhaps your Mozart is a little heavy — for me it should be more joyous than virile."[6]

Monteux had adopted a rigorous process. Successful students were expected to commit themselves to return the following year — the first summer was considered introductory — and Victor did indeed come back the following year. But for the present, the maestro drew up lists of the finest candidates — after a few sessions he was down to ten from the fifty who had been in his original group. The selected few would form a special class that would be invited back another summer and if chosen again would be also eligible to conduct in the summer's final concert. On August 12, Victor was approached by another instructor, Dr. Wilbur Kris, who informed him that "you did a splendid job — really impressed the old boy. I wouldn't be surprised if you made the special class." This was an unheard of elevation for a first-year candidate and Victor remained skeptical. As it turned out, on the fifteenth of the month Victor was one of the five finalists selected — "quite an honour," as he put it to Zelda.

Even Monteux's compliments were always laced with critical commentary. Victor's assignment had been to prepare any movement of Bach's Suite no. 3 and Mozart's Symphony no. 39. Monteux's evaluation was guarded: "Perhaps you give too many cues — but better too many than too few." His assistant, Joseph Baroné, was more positive: "You talk with the baton rather than the mouth. Congratulations!"

The next day, Victor conducted the first movement of Schumann's Symphony no. 1. At the conclusion, Monteux said simply, "Joe wants to talk to you." Baroné's message for Victor was that "The Maestro has chosen you to conduct on the final night Gala. It's the first time a first-year student has been selected."

Victor's triumph had a bitter taste. He could not stay for the gala — he had to conduct a CBC broadcast. It was not a disaster. Monteux was a professional and knew how important engagements were for young conductors. An actual job always trumped a course performance. Monteux was gracious, commenting on the fact that he had received a letter from Sir Adrian Boult extolling Victor and had not been disappointed. The summer of 1949 began a long association of Feldbrill and Monteux. Victor returned to Hancock, Maine, in the summer of 1950 and again years later, and also hosted Monteux both when he came to Winnipeg and to Toronto.

Indeed, on his trip to Toronto, Monteux insisted on Victor preparing the orchestra in rehearsal before his arrival. It was in the 1950s, when Victor's mind was in some turmoil over the direction he was heading. He had reached the level of an assistant conductor but saw no likelihood of reaching the top with the TSO. Monteux sensed Victor's unrest and questioned him on the reasons behind his discontent. "I'm working hard but do not seem to be going anywhere," was Victor's reply. Monteux response seared itself in Victor's memory:

> Are you conducting to the height of excellence you are capable of? Do you know where I began my conducting career — in the pit at the Folies Bergères [A famous Parisian nightclub featuring scantily clad females]. Anything you do to perfect your métier is a leap forward.

It was a salutary comment. It led Victor to see every appointment and every concert as a single challenge and to let the future decide itself. In the shorter term Monteux's remark led him to seek out one last source of strength and inspiration outside his native land.

In the mid-1950s, Victor chose to return to Europe, in particular to a program for conductors at Hilversum in the Netherlands. For some years he had actually been named assistant conductor of the TSO but he realized there was no permanency in that role. Sir Ernest's retirement in 1955 had created a very difficult environment. In a sense his close association with the maestro meant that as Sir Ernest shook off his role as the TSO's conductor, Victor's position was less assured. As successor, Walter Susskind's style was very different from that of MacMillan — the TSO was no longer a family with great commitments to its players based on past successes and affiliations. A different set of priorities emerged that left Victor cold and feeling very much on the outside. There was no assurance that Susskind even wanted an assistant conductor. It was a disappointing time for Victor and he came to realize that Zelda had suffered from his feelings that his career was "on hold." He needed to compare his capacity now, a half-decade after the Monteux summers, with European conductors. With little encouragement in Canada, he even considered the possibility that he needed to find new opportunities to conduct and that they might well be found in Europe and Britain rather than in North America.

Victor's extended absence on another continent was a dramatic prospect for Zelda. She was now looking after two young girls. She had given up her employment to start the family both she and Victor had coveted. She was determined to give herself full time to the children in those early years, in part to make up for a peripatetic husband whose frequent absences to travel across Canada and abroad were essential to his burgeoning career. Victor realized that a trip to Europe would mean, once again, a time of loneliness for both of them. But Zelda insisted that he go.

It was in 1956 that he stopped off first in London. In the tangled situation in Toronto, he wanted to develop a relationship with the BBC and its orchestras throughout the Britain. He had developed an enthusiasm for radio conducting, first at the CBC, particularly since 1949, and he was invited to conduct the BBC Scottish Orchestra in Glasgow in

1957 — largely as a result of Sir Adrian Boult's sponsorship. The radio concert turned out well.

He wanted to meet, once again, David Cox, the head of serious music in the overseas division of the BBC and a producer who had been most amenable to his return to the BBC podium. During an informal conversation, Cox raised the topic of the Bartok *Concerto for Orchestra*, a composition that Victor had made his own with the CBC Symphony Orchestra. It was a complex work and Cox was surprised to learn that in Canada Victor had prepared the orchestra in but three sessions, a fraction of the time a BBC Orchestra had devoted to its rehearsal. In a process that measured cost of programming largely in terms of orchestral preparation, it was impressive. The result of this visit was extensive. Victor Feldbrill became an annual feature at the BBC, first in Glasgow with the BBC Scottish Orchestra but year after year through the 1950s to the early 1980s in other British broadcast centres. It was another reason to return to Europe and keep in touch with musical presentation on the continent as well as in the British Isles.

Then came an opportunity to pursue a commitment close to Victor's heart — the broadcasting of the works of Canadian contemporary composers. His friendship with Harry Somers had included an intense interest in the composer's first effort at composing a symphony. Cox was enthusiastic about having this composition prepared for a radio broadcast on July 1, Canada's birthday, along with a true orchestral classic, the Brahms *Variations on a Theme of Haydn*. It turned out to be a perfect combination and an outstanding broadcast. Once again, behind the scenes was Sir Adrian, supremely confident of his Canadian associate and determined to find openings for Victor both within the BBC and in the concert halls of London. Much to Harry Somer's delight, his symphony sounded majestic and impressive and was heard around the world on BBC International.

The European visit was dramatic in other ways. Victor had not been back for over a decade. The world had changed and the wartime friends he had been looking forward to renewing a warm relationship with might all have gone their separate ways. His hesitation proved to be wrong-headed — he arrived in Amsterdam on the way to Hilversum to find all his friends at the airport to celebrate his return. It was a glorious if tearful moment.

Hilversum was an extraordinary place in the Netherlands, being a broadcast centre that had not one but four orchestras, each with its own mandate, audience, and broadcasting responsibilities. There, Victor found himself studying with Willem van Otterloo, a conductor who had a splendid reputation in Europe.

However, the Hilversum enrollment experience was both a challenge and a delight. Victor was one of forty-eight picked from some five hundred applications representing almost every country in the world. Once again, he found that his conducting was of a quality equal to those who were now his colleagues in what was a highly competitive rather than synergetic situation.

For example, at an adjudication session, Victor was conducting Weber's *Euryanthe Overture.* He had been told not to speak to the orchestra under any circumstances. Suddenly, the orchestra slowed the pace of its playing, rather than following the beat of the baton. Victor lowered his arms and announced in an authoritative voice that indicated he knew this was a test to determine whether the conductor was leading or following the orchestra, "There is no rallentendo in my score — please follow me." The performance of the work continued according to the movement of the conductor's baton and Victor knew he had won that battle even if he had lost the war. As it turned out, everyone in the hall was aware of what had transpired and was impressed by Victor's response.

Even more important, van Otterloo had discovered he had a talented student from Canada on his hands who already knew a great deal about conducting. He was quick to take advantage of the situation. It was so patently obvious that Victor out-classed his colleagues that van Otterloo began to choose him as the first conductor for those classes devoted to giving opportunities for every student to lead the gathered ensemble. Within a day or two, the ultimate embarrassment came when, after the Feldbrill performance, the entire orchestra broke into applause. Van Otterloo saw Victor's pre-eminence becoming a factor in the disintegration of his program and sharply suggested to the orchestra members that they must desist from responding in that manner. He admitted that the performance had deserved the outburst but insisted that the orchestra must refrain from such demonstrations in the light of what it would do to the morale of the entire class![7]

One of the least capable in van Otterloo's class was a choral conductor with little experience conducting orchestras. Realizing how undeveloped his technique was, the maestro explained to him that this program was about interpretation rather than baton technique. Van Otterloo assigned the dejected student to Victor's care. Feldbrill took on the challenge and in a few days van Otterloo was astounded with the transformation, announcing before the entire class that Victor had "worked a miracle with this student's technique."

In the following week, the class had the opportunity to conduct the Netherlands Radio Philharmonic, one of the Holland's best orchestras. The repertoire to be conquered was substantial: Stravinsky's *Petrouchka* and Debussy's *La Mer*. On this occasion, Victor was not "on" first or second, but third in performance order. By the time he arrived on the podium the class was in chaos. It was the complexity of the time changes in *Petrouchka*, and Victor's solution was simple. He took the orchestral sections apart, rehearsed the difficult bars with them separately, then brought them together in a logical sequence. The players were delighted and, as one pointed out, Victor had been "the first one to exert real authority" in the program. At the subsequent concert performance, Victor's appearance on the program concluded with bravos from both the orchestra and the audience. He came away from the experience feeling he had really made his mark.[8]

Victor's program led him eventually to a Munich suburb and an interchange organized by the CBC with composer and leading authority on introducing children to the performance of great music, Carl Orff. As one who by this time had established his own reputation for bringing children to the concert hall at an early age, Victor was captivated by Orff. The discussion about technique and methodology revealed that the famous composer had an intense love for children and that shared passion was the basis of both Orff's and Victor's determination to see them well served.

Seeking to make the best use of his time and expense, Victor also enrolled in a conductor workshop program in Salzburg, one that had an emphasis on opera. After his Hilversum experience, he was outraged by the machine-like process of dealing with a class of 150 students. There appeared to be no standards being sought and no small groups in which to learn effectively. Victor found a way of entering a small workshop of conducting opera. It was in the hands of Meinhard von Zallinger of the Munich Opera, another international figure on the podium of the European orchestral and operatic circuit. Victor was outraged to discover that his acceptance into the program was dependant, once again, upon a drawing of his name from a proverbial hat. Having travelled halfway around the planet, he was not to be deterred by such an unfair admission policy. Victor took the matter into his own hands. He made it plain to von Zallinger that he had come all the way from North America. Von Zallinger was equally dismayed and Victor entered a class in opera conducting, with the playing of the last act of *The Magic Flute* being the main repertoire to be conquered. As well, he was assured that he did not have to be a pianist in order to benefit from the program, a deficiency that had haunted Victor in his ambition to establish his role as a conductor. Victor became a full member of the class and eventually was granted an apology as well as a promise that the faulty admission process would be revised.

By the end of July, Victor's opera class had only seven members. Dr. von Zallinger's main focus was on training the concert hall conductor to adapt himself to the special pressures of the opera house orchestra pit. The transfer had been, in Victor's words, "a smart move." He came to realize there was "a real art to the conducting of operas and I got a lot out of the program ... they have it down to a science here." Little did he realize that a decade later he would be conducting Canada's most acclaimed opera, composed by his friend and colleague Harry Somers.[9]

Victor found, as well, that he enjoyed conducting singers and that they enjoyed him. He made quite a hit with the choristers. Several of them proclaimed that he was the only student conductor "to show any authority" and they felt that "real leadership was coming from [his] baton." Once again, Victor had to leave before the program ended and the gala concert had been scheduled.

Vienna was a feast of great music and Victor had yet another major conductor enliven his musical consciousness. He attended a performance of *The Marriage of Figaro*. The accompaniment was played, as usual, by the Vienna Philharmonic, on this occasion conducted by Karl Böhm, who produced "moments of sheer beauty that you wanted to cry." The same conductor, in concert with the Vienna Philharmonic Orchestra a few nights later, had programmed the Schubert Symphony no. 7. It was not a composition that Victor had enjoyed, considering it "long and boring, playing or listening to." However, the Böhm "freedom of phrasing" was the key and he now knew he would "always remember it was one of the greatest performances [he] had ever heard."

Back in class, Victor's outstanding performance based on the excerpts from Mozart's *The Magic Flute* was judged to be first-rate. Yet again, he had competed with the best that Europe had to offer and had distinguished himself. It was Victor's last experience with such tests of his skill and experience. From this point he himself would become the instructor both in Canada and abroad. He had learned a great deal, both positive and negative, about the process of guiding the learning of others, lessons that he would use to enhance his own teaching techniques in the years ahead.

Once again he was under pressure to return to Toronto. There were his professional responsibilities, as always, and Dr. von Zallinger was loathe to see him go, telling Victor that, in fact "the only people not sorry to see you go were other conductors in the class." The experience turned out to have been monumental. Victor felt confident that he had "a place in the world of conductors — be it European or American." He knew he had to leave the string section of the TSO in order to be perceived as a full-time career conductor.

And there were other pressures. Zelda, normally uncomplaining, was expressing concern over her constant exhaustion. She had two young children and there were now complicating factors emerging. Just before her second birthday, it was discovered that Debbi was diabetic. For a young child lacking understanding about the seriousness of the condition, to be forced onto a special diet and to be treated as continuously sick was a shock. Her defence was predictable. She came to loathe the food to which she was limited and expressed her dissatisfaction by demanding to be fed in the family car. Month after month, Victor had done just that. Now he was not there … and Debbi needed him. Though Zelda was able to visit relatives in Montreal for a few days, it was only a pause in what was a period of trial that lasted the several months of Victor's absence in Europe.

And then there was Aviva, born in 1954. In a poignant comment that appeared in the usual daily letter, Victor admitted to himself and Zelda, "I don't even know Aviva." It was a terrible realization when his young

daughter was indicating a need for his love. Her older sister Debbi's dia-
betes had focused her parents' attention on her needs and Aviva, though
only two years old, felt the need of their presence, love, and caring. It did
come … and especially from Victor. He became her special companion
through the years of childhood and adolescence and she came to experience
a unique relationship with her adoring father.

Hilversum, Salzburg, and Vienna were the last distant sources of
Victor's search for the heights of conducting excellence. They were successful for particular reasons that had not much to do with the mandate of the
programs in which he had participated. Victor had matured too much to be
inspired by regal pomposity of either instructors or fellow students. Nor was
he overwhelmed by the historic pre-eminence of these communities. From
this point Victor felt he had a right to be considered a recognized figure in
the North American conducting community. He internalized the striking
features of Shaw and Monteux in particular, but he was now his own man
in terms of fashioning the kind of conductor he would strive to be.

By the later 1950s, Victor had conducted the CBC many times over
to audiences from coast to coast. He was interviewed in 1958 for an article
in the *CBC Times*, and was asked, "What is a conductor's job?" His answer
now came after a decade and a half of preparation and would serve his purpose for the rest of his career. Feldbrill answered the question succinctly:
"With two words — 'structure' and 'shape.' Upon the conductor's direction
depends the 'sound' of the orchestra, the nuances, the feeling or expression,
the final 'appearance' if one may use the word, of a composition."[10]

As well, he was now hearing from the people he respected most — the
composers. They were thrilled with his work. In April of 1959, Murray
Adaskin wrote of Victor's playing of his *Serenade*, "it was one of the most
beautiful performances I have ever heard of the piece." John Weinzweig,
that same year, of Victor's performance of *Edge of the World*, wrote "it
caught our ears and they were delighted ones. It was the best performance
I have heard. The tempo was just right." And Violet Archer wrote to say
how pleased she was that he was conducting her piano concerto. For a half-
century, Victor was to be the recipient of such letters from the Canadian
composers he admired, encouraged, and supported.

A very different "take" on his desire to be a conductor was provided by the landlady at a European festival residence who accosted him with her advice about the world of musical performance. "You have to have sharp elbows to get others out of the way," was her assessment of Victor's field of endeavour. His response shocked her: "If that is what music is about, I would rather dig ditches."[11]

The final trip abroad had, in some ways, come too late. Once again it allowed a measure of self measurement, but by this point Victor had reached his goal through his own efforts in Toronto and across Canada. Now all that was necessary was a podium on which he could stand before a good orchestra and make great music for a number of years before an audience with whom he could share his passion for the very best repertoire that had been composed, particularly that of his native land. The latter mission would, of course, be the real challenge, but he was now ready to take it on.

The next time he came to Britain and Europe it would not be to gauge his success as a potential conductor, but on a holiday with his beloved Zelda.

CHAPTER 9

Building a Reputation

T he 1950s provided the turning point in Victor Feldbrill's career. He was now developing his confidence in the possibility of pursuing a conducting career. The 1940s had served him well. He had now moved from his central role of a student conducting assistant with the Conservatory Symphony Orchestra to a guest conductor for its summer-school edition and from an assistant to Nicholas Goldschmidt with the Opera School Orchestra to that of a frequent conductor of pop and student concerts for Canada's major symphony orchestra, his hometown's TSO. For the first time, he was invited to conduct the Prom Concert Symphony Orchestra, made up largely of TSO players, but now performing spring and summer in a Varsity Arena on the University of Toronto campus. As well, he was still welcomed back to the former ensembles associated with the Royal Conservatory — only now as a guest conductor. Along with this concert scene came an expanding position as a respected conductor of the CBC Radio orchestras, not only in Toronto, but in other regions of Canada, as well.

Gradually, his image began to change. Though still playing in the string section of the TSO and the CBC Symphony for most of the first half of the 1950s, he was now perceived as a respected figure on the podium. He had broken through! His colleagues saw him not as just a string player with a penchant for the baton, or even as a leading participant in string trios, quartets, and quintets, or even as the director of his own chamber orchestra, but as an ambitious young musician who wished to be an orchestral conductor and was ready to travel extensively if necessary to fulfill obligations across Canada and abroad. He was operating on a different plain, following a new course, courageously abandoning any kind of established career he might have secured as a violin player. Indeed, by mid-decade he had resigned as a member of the TSO's string section, recognizing that this role was restraining him from accepting opportunities as a conductor during the TSO's regular season, which, of course, coincided with the concert season of every other Canadian orchestra.

Victor now felt he had reached a level that brought authority to his conducting performance. His work with Pierre Monteux in particular was now accorded recognition and appreciation. Worldwide, symphony orchestras were entering a new phase of competition from a myriad of entertainment features and the topic of outreach was gathering emphasis in orchestral management circles, including those associated with the TSO. To have Victor in the wings to play a special role as adviser for a thrust in the direction of more popular programming was a special advantage the TSO came to cherish.

His reputation at the CBC by the end of the 1940s could be built on with little difficulty. The Terence Gibbs introduction of Victor on *CBC Wednesday Night* had been a major leap forward, but was in essence only one of many contacts. Now other producers, like John Reeves, became interested and Victor joined older conducting colleagues like Geoffrey Waddington, Samuel Hersenhoren, and Lucio Agostini as a regular performer on radio. It was a time when the CBC was committed to the maintenance of fine ensembles for radio presentations of various kinds, as well as formal concerts of classical fare. Victor's developing talent for the articulate expression of music was particularly valuable. His efforts to reach out to young people with relevant commentary about music and the composers who wrote it were invariably welcome. On radio, performing artists are obviously invisible, but their words create mental images that audiences nurture. Over the airwaves, Victor was "cool." As well, he had avoided any reputation for attitudes and podium pyrotechnics that conductors can use to manipulate audiences in a concert hall but have no place in the studio. He became a favourite CBC conductor not only with musicians but with technicians who had no time or stomach for inappropriate theatrical gyrations.

Thus, by the 1950s, the place, style, and content of Victor's contribution to the musical life of his community had been established. Now it was only a matter of time, waiting for a break. But before that could happen, the building of a track record was essential. Only then could he attract the attention of a major Canadian symphony orchestra. That breakthrough came as the decade proceeded to change both Feldbrill and those who were watching his capacity strengthening.

As the decade began, Victor was back again at the helm of the Conservatory Summer School Symphony for the closing concert, this time performing at the University of Toronto's Convocation Hall. The orchestra's major work was Beethoven's Symphony no. 7, a favourite composition in Victor's orchestral programming. Another respected Canadian composer, John Beckwith, had contributed excerpts from *Music for Dancing*. But reviewers like Ed Palmer now more fulsomely recognized his talent. He wrote of the concert, "Mr. Feldbrill was leading an orchestra of young musicians playing for the love of music, their verve and their enthusiasm for resounding music was evident. Under the vigorous leadership of the young conductor, a bond was created between the orchestra and the listeners."[1]

The year 1951 brought performances with the TSO, again a secondary-school concert at which he repeated works he had introduced by Ridout and Enesco. However, at another such concert, for the first time he was able to tackle more complex repertoire, such as the Dvorak Concerto for Violin and Orchestra and the familiar Beethoven Symphony no. 5 and his *Fidelio Overture*.

This concert was soon followed by a CBC Radio presentation at which he played a favourite of his own — the Beethoven Symphony no. 4. Further opportunities in the spring and summer were the regular Prom concerts. His first appearance received considerable positive comment. George Kidd, who had watched the up-and-coming conductor for years, was now much taken with Victor's rendition of the Bartok *Dances*: "The various rhythms of the separate dances were brought forth with amazing clarity under Mr. Feldbrill's baton. Variety predominated and he and the orchestra responded splendidly."[2]

Leo Smith, a highly respected former cellist with the TSO, upon retirement, had become a music critic. He penned an even warmer response to a musician with whom he himself had performed:

> Mr. Feldbrill, who is perhaps the youngest of all Toronto musicians to have attracted attention as a conductor, performed his task with a sense of leadership, with a thorough knowledge of his scores, and a sense of musical values.[3]

Victor had not forgotten his learning experience at Tanglewood with Robert Shaw and was anxious to engage in all the choral performance he could find. In the winter of 1952, he collaborated with Gerald Bales, a fine musician, to present Handel's oratorio *Solomon* in St. Andrew's Church in central Toronto. The concert was graced with both a Handel and a Rhinekergn organ concerto to fill out the program. It was a choice beginning of many nights Victor would spend in front of glorious choirs. He was now recognized as an orchestral conductor who loved choral music and the people who made it.

In the summer of 1952, a portentous occasion transpired that was to have an impact of Victor's future. Eric Wild, the former conductor of *The Navy Show*, under whose baton Victor had played, was scheduled to conduct the CBC Winnipeg Orchestra. He had scheduled a much needed holiday and Victor was found to be available. Geoffrey Waddington sent Victor to Winnipeg for two weeks to cover the time for rehearsals and broadcasts. So it was off to a city he had come to know during the war, indeed a city in which he knew Zelda had lived the earliest years of her life and where friends of hers were still to be found.

He enjoyed his work with the CBC Winnipeg Orchestra enormously. More importantly, the musicians, many of whom also played in the Winnipeg Symphony Orchestra (WSO), were impressed. They found him to be knowledgeable, affable, and truly effective. That appreciation would be a paramount reason for the extraordinary response to Victor's application to be the orchestra's conductor just a few years later.

On this occasion, quite unexpectedly, there came a request for an interview by a journalist from the *Winnipeg Free Press*. Victor accepted. At a time when the role of the orchestral conductor was under discussion and vociferous debate raged whether the dictatorial approach or a congenial "first among equals" position could be validated, Feldbrill was quite outspoken, revealing a new confidence in his perception of the conductor's role:

> The day of [the] prima donna conductor is over. There must be closer co-operation between conductor and musicians. It is not only the conductor's duty to know the music, but he should also know his orchestra members.[4]

It was a strong position illustrating a philosophy of life as well as a view on the making of music. It was an orchestral players' understanding of the respect that must come from the occupant of the podium if great music was to inspire its listeners. A violinist, Janet Roy, who had known Victor from those days when he had been a student of Kathleen Parlow and she was concertmaster of the CBC Studio Orchestra, had watched Victor's career as a conductor with great interest. She states that from the outset he "had a good way of working … methodical, congenial and always observant of what needed to be done." As a violinist, she stressed his strength to be that of "knowing the ways of the bowing world."[5] Victor, the former teenage conducting prodigy was now ready to assume a new role.

It was not surprising that some four years later, when Walter Kaufman suddenly resigned from the role of artistic director and conductor of the WSO, a number of the CBC musicians and WSO board members remembered Victor's 1952 visit and invited him to apply for that position. Nor was it surprising that a number of the CBC executives who were on the board of the WSO played a role in assuring a successful search for a conductor they knew would enhance the work of the CBC in Winnipeg as well as achieve much for the WSO itself.

These were the years when Victor became notorious for his willingness to be enthusiastically positive about Canadian contemporary music. Yes, it was sometimes dissonant and unlike the melodic and comfortable music that emanated from previous centuries. Yet there was much that was dissonant about the society "out there." One could hear new sounds emanating from the instruments of orchestral players and unusual, disquieting musical forms that proved experiments were taking place as composers attempted to bring relevant messages to twentieth-century audiences. Victor's predilection for contemporary music was apparent when, a year later, he had prepared the CBC Symphony Orchestra (CBCSO) to play, "on air," Harry Somers's Symphony no. 1. Victor would be giving a world premiere to the composition. When questioned whether it was "good" music, Victor not only responded positively, but added pointedly, "I admire Harry's complete honesty and sincerity."

He now had the confidence to make his views known about Canadian contemporary composition. In a letter to the editor of a Toronto newspaper he brought down on his head the opposing voices of orchestral managers both near and far by suggesting that they "were afraid to take chances" with Canadian composers, who he felt "had a great deal to offer." It was a courageous, perhaps foolhardy stance for a young conductor who would be dependent on these individuals for recommendations for conducting commissions in the future.

Victor further complicated his future dealings with potential orchestral leadership figures by "walking the talk." He had become involved in a Conservatory concert of contemporary music with Glenn Gould that drew precious few patrons, but featured entirely modern compositions, particularly the works of Berg, Schoenberg, and Webern. Reviewer John Kraglund spoke for many who stayed home by suggesting the music was as appealing as "sounds left over from the tuning up process," but nevertheless conceded that Victor "handled very capably the task of conducting the erratic, scary score of the quartet for tenor, saxophone, violin and piano."

In January 1954, Victor made his first appearance of many at a TSO pop (later to be termed "pops") concert. The whole concept of popular concerts were about to be re-thought. It seems unbelievable that in the fifth decade of the twentieth century, the Sabbath was regarded as holy, and entertainment such as the presentation of orchestral music was considered unacceptable in Toronto, commonly described as the "city of churches." After 1960, it became acceptable for cultural events to take place on Sunday — but only as long as no admission was charged. With all this controversy it became apparent that pops concerts could be profitable, especially if the CBC paid to record them for future broadcast and capacity audiences could be encouraged to make a donation. Victor believed that capacity audiences could be predicted for concerts with more accessible repertoire and attractive solo appearances. The early elitist reluctance to having concerts for the "unwashed" disappeared. Indeed, Victor's program on one occasion included a Prokofiev march from *Love of Three Oranges,* a Strauss waltz, the *Elegy* from Elgar's *String Serenade*, and the most serious but most popular of all, César Franck's *Symphonic Variations* with the brilliant young Canadian soloist Patricia Parr at the piano.

George Kidd, in his *Telegram* review, commented on the truly difficult challenge that Victor was facing every time he mounted the podium, at least in Toronto: "To step from the ranks of the orchestra and take over the baton is no easy matter, but Mr. Feldbrill did it with a most engaging personality and good musical understanding." [6]

Reviewer John Kraglund was not so favourably impressed, pointing out that the orchestra was "too loud in soft passages," but he conceded that Victor had "got excellent responses from the orchestra that had indeed clarified certain passages." However, he concluded rather pessimistically that, "Mr. Feldbrill did not quite manage to fully integrate these pieces into a composite whole." One might argue whether Mr. Kraglund understood the purpose and the nature of the pops concert, where variety was the key and discontinuity the price.

Once again in 1954, Victor was back on the podium of the Prom concert from Varsity Arena. The programs were often unusual. In August, Victor was conducting and the guest performers were the Summer School Choir of teachers taking a Ministry of Education course at the University of Toronto campus. There was a repertoire that extended from Mozart to Debussy to Tchaikovsky and on to Stokowski (an arrangement of Bach's

Little Fugue in G Minor). Critic Hugh Thomson found the Mozart "crisp and vivacious," and John Kraglund felt that Victor "conducted with boyish charm and a slightly mechanical flair." George Kidd, commenting on Victor's Mozart, thought there was a "determined sparkle to his conducting which is frequently filled with authority," and concluded that, of the Tchaikovsky, "the conductor and the orchestra had given a splendid performance ... that included both control and vigorous excitement." This concert was promoted in the press some days before the concert by a most appealing picture of Zelda, Debbi, and Aviva (then only two months old), under the headline "Conductor's Children Stay Up for the Show." Indeed, the whole family had stayed up.

The issue of Canadian music heated up again that same year, ignited no doubt by the contemplation of the Canada Council, whose financial support would be essential, and the fact that its generosity might be tied to some level of performing Canadian composition. The *Canadian High News* of January/February 1954 contained an interview featuring a quotation from Victor Feldbrill, who was asked to comment on a special concert of Canadian music in New York's Carnegie Hall conducted by Leopold Stokowski. Under the headline "Canadian Music Has Limitless Possibilities: Nothing Can Stop It," Victor used the interview to point out that there was a wide range of works being written by Canadian composers from the conventional Healy Willan to the contemporary school of Weinzweig, Somers, and Freedman. He characterized the contemporary as revealing strong rhythm and a clear development and, recognizing the fact of a concert of Canadian music in question was in New York, the works presented were in the direction of the music of Aaron Copland and George Gershwin. He then made a statement that occasioned the wrath of the more conservative music community — that every concert in Canada should have a Canadian work included in the program. It was, by that time, as he noted, the policy of CBC Radio in its broadcast concerts and it had been welcomed by listeners.

On this point, Victor was to confront every hesitant manager who believed that scheduling Canadian contemporary music would simply empty seats in the concert hall. In Victor's view, it was time for some confidence in the ultimate creativity of Canadians writing for symphonic ensembles in the country and, even more, time for conductors to program this music thoughtfully and consistently. It was time for conductors and performers to articulate clearly their commitment to Canadian contemporary music, thus making each performance a learning opportunity for those who had previously perceived music as mere entertainment. It was an opportunity for Canadians to understand that music was a means of non-verbal communication that could say much that was valuable about the human condition and its present and future prospects. He never lost confidence in his Canadian contemporary orchestral music composers — Schafer, Archer, Beckwith, Pentland, Applebaum, Davies, Prévost, Matton, Papineau-Couture, Ridout, and Glick, as well as Somers, Freedman, Weinzweig, and a host of others who were to emerge in the final decades of the twentieth century. However, it was a position that threatened some orchestral management personnel and by so doing he placed himself at considerable risk.

By 1955 he was appearing regularly as conductor of both the TSO and the Prom Orchestra. He was also a favourite of choral conductors and appeared again and again with dance companies who appreciated his consistent beat and collegial approach to the connecting of music and movement. At a memorable concert program in August 1955, he led the Prom Orchestra in a Somers' ballet score, *Lamentation and Primeval,* and critic John Kraglund, no lover of Harry's music, suggested it should have been played for dancers alone and conceded that, as dance music it had been "highly commendable," but he had severe reservations about the relevance of the work in the concert hall. For another critic, George Kidd, though, Victor had shown "remarkable musicianship throughout the evening."

At a pop concert that fall, Kraglund's review noted that Victor had revealed "a concise conducting style, detailed without being cluttered," but he went on to say that the players as well as the conductor had been "too much taken up with the notes to give much thought to the interpretation." Victor found that his restrained conducting style often occasioned that perception. He was not prepared to play up to the audience with dramatic gestures that would openly convey what critics called "interpretation." At yet another pop concert, in the fall of 1955, reviewer Pearl McCarthy remarked that Victor had done "good work that had both lightness and unpretentiousness," and was indeed "crisp with a touch of elegance." William Krehm, speaking on a Toronto radio station, CJBC, referred to Victor Feldbrill as a "wonder child … with a 'clean beat,'" and remarked to his conducting being both "conscientious and knowledgeable." However, Krehm went on to comment on the "serious gaps." While Krehm appreciated Victor's high-voltage energy, he felt the "subtler sublimations had escaped him," that he "never explored the soft blandishments of the waltz, its teasing rubato," and that indeed his waltzes were lacking in any "voluptuous quality." (The critique was heard by Victor, who realized that in this regard he was in a rut and telephoned Krehm to thank a very surprised commentator for his helpful observations.)

In Victor's mind, at this time, it was becoming clear that playing so much popular, but perceived as trivial, classical music at pop and prom concerts was diverting audience response to the recognition of the quality of interpretation he was giving to this repertoire. Even more important, it was depriving these audiences of the depth of interpretation that Victor might have brought to the more profound offerings being presented, for example, in the TSO's regular subscription series of concerts. When he was abroad he never had to face such criticism and his interpretive skills were being recognized.

He saw that he was becoming regarded as a convenient and reliable replacement for indisposed conductors — in 1955 for Sir Ernest MacMillan and in 1956 for successor Walter Susskind. It was a godsend to have Victor around. He had a command of the broad repertoire so that changes in program demanding expensive rehearsal could be avoided. Even after he left the orchestra, in the late 1950s and '60s Victor was retained as a part of the TSO organization as its major adviser on youth and popular programs and was a welcome occupant of the TSO podium, particularly in times of crisis.

At another pop concert before the close of 1955, the repertoire not only stretched Victor's tolerance for the insubstantial, but brought to his attention once again the perception of his role as a conductor was in danger of being diluted. The headline of the review was "Stars Two TSO Violinists," the result of the presence of concertmaster Hyman Goodman as a guest artist to play the last two movements of the Bruch Violin Concerto in G Minor in the evening's program. The rest of the program, the Verdi *Grande*

March from Aida, Tchaikovsky's *Andante Cantabile*, and Bizet's *Carmen Suite*, told him something else. It was time not only to abandon the fiddle but also the time to leave Toronto. Actually, the reviews of the concert were fine. The usually supportive George Kidd stated that as Victor did more conducting, the results were becoming apparent: "He leads the orchestra in a clean and straightforward manner." On this occasion, John Kraglund was even more appreciative. Recognizing that some of his past criticisms of Victor's work were no longer valid, he wiped the slate clean: "It has been our suspicion that Feldbrill was afraid to allow sentiment its rightful place were proved quite wrong by his excellent reading of the Tchaikovsky *Andante Cantabile*. It combined reasonable lucidity with romantic charm all the time avoiding the pitfall of sentimentality."

When the December pop concerts were followed by three nights of the gaiety and delight of the TSO Christmas "box" concerts, it was again Victor who was on the podium. He was even more convinced that he had reached the end of an era. For Sir Ernest, "bubbling with mirth," these evenings were favourite opportunities to bring laughter to the sober citizens of Toronto. On this occasion, he had once again brought Victor into the picture as his assistant. Victor was of two minds. With MacMillan's departure eminent, it would be the last time such collaboration would take place and Sir Ernest's warmth and joy in making music was an element of Victor's admiration for his mentor. On the other hand, five December nights of less consequential music and accompanying levity were too much. It was time for Victor to look beyond Toronto.

In 1955, Sir Ernest had informed the board that he wished to retire as conductor of the TSO at the end of the 1955–56 concert season. For Victor it was traumatic news. He had known Sir Ernest for a decade and a half and the maestro had been his strongest supporter. He had always been there to give advice and grease the wheels of administration both at the Conservatory and the Faculty of Music. Now Sir Ernest would be gone. It was like watching the breakup of a family.

He knew that in spite of his new recognition as assistant conductor in 1955 there would be no chance of succeeding Sir Ernest. He was equally convinced that life at the TSO would be very difficult without the maestro's presence. The successor might not want him as an assistant conductor.

Whoever he might be, he would have his own ideas about with whom he wished to share the TSO podium.

Others around him realized the time had come for him to move on. CJRT critic William Krehm, attending another TSO assignment for a special entertainment feature directed at youth, this time a Children's Easter Holiday Concert, saw his future in another role somewhere else. Commenting on a poorly attended prom concert, he noted that Victor "had moved into a more subtle area of the conductor's art ... beginning to acquire spread as well as bounce." Paul Scherman, also a violinist and one who had been Victor's major competition for the role of the TSO conducting assistant's position, had already moved on. The Hilversum–Salzburg– Vienna–Munich experiences had provided an opportunity for Victor to justify his absence in the midst of the TSO interregnum. In the midst of his dissatisfaction with his TSO role and in the lack of future prospects across Canada, he knew he must look abroad. Yet he was a Canadian nationalist. Indeed, on his return from Europe in late summer of 1956, he took the trouble to write a letter to the federal government about how little was known about Canada's musical culture in Europe. His suggestion was the creation of a cultural relations office in Ottawa that would provide resources and personnel to the Canadian embassies around the world.

There was little chance of this in the early and mid-1950s! It was a tired Liberal government under Louis St. Laurent that would soon succumb to a dynamic Diefenbaker Conservative Party assault. However, in the years to come, Victor would be a familiar representative of Canada on podiums in Europe and Asia, and would play a significant role in making his country and its music better known beyond Canada's shores.

But nothing was happening with any immediacy — he was still on the TSO podium and enlarging his role with the CBC. Now that all the pop concerts were being broadcast and a series of CBC Symphony concerts for secondary schools were being relayed across the country, Victor has acquired a national presence. It had not come too soon.

He was also moving his opera conducting career ahead. It was, once again, the presence of Harry Somers in his life, a composer who had decided that of all Canada's conductors, Feldbrill was his choice to play that role in regard to a short opera he had composed, *The Fool*. It was to be presented alongside another work, Maurice Blackburn's *Une Mésure de Silence*, with both being given a world premiere on November 17, 1956. The performances were greeted enthusiastically ... the only criticism being that in places the accompaniment had been a "little loud." However, Victor had every reason to feel that his instructor, Dr. von Zallinger of the Munich Opera, would have been proud.

In spite of his impatience, Victor was making some headway. Even critic John Kraglund, in a review of yet another TSO pop concert — now well-attended on a Sunday afternoon — was giving cautious recognition to a more effective Victor Feldbrill, now ready for a new challenge:

> Victor Feldbrill demonstrated that his growing ability as a conductor extends beyond that of providing accompaniment for soloists ... and offered competent performances of music by Strauss, Saint-Saens, Bach, and Smetana....

But he could also not resist the opportunity to repeat his observations of the past: "He is still not making attempts to probe beneath the surface of the music."[7]

The fall of 1956 was filled with Sunday pop and secondary-school concerts. In one of the latter programs, Victor broke the mould. The final piece was a full rendition of the Tchaikovsky Symphony no. 5, with all the intense drama fully exploited. The audience of teenagers went wild. It supported his theory that young people wanted the best music, long or short, soft or loud.

It was at the first Sunday afternoon pop concerts of the 1957 season that Victor engaged in a bold experiment that revealed his capacity to reach across seemingly entrenched and isolated genres of music creation to find bridges of understanding. He programmed a composition that engaged performers from the world of jazz. It was a courageous enterprise even though good jazz, by the mid-1950s, had achieved a level of respectability that such an effort made some sense. It was composer Norm Symonds who conceived of writing a composition that invited such collaboration and a CBC commission that made possible Concerto Grosso for Jazz Quintet and Orchestra. It was applauded ferociously and perceived a successful experiment. Yet, unhappily, there was little mainstream continuity. Victor was prepared some years later to repeat the collaboration, but jazz and symphonic music occupied two walled camps. Certainly Victor's role was seen as valuable. Helen MacNamara, in a review, stated: "Praise is due to the conductor, Victor Feldbrill, whose enthusiasm and sympathy for new work resulted in a brilliant performance by the 65-piece orchestra."[8]

In January 1957, there was a break in Victor's Toronto schedule and he was invited to conduct a regular subscription series concert of the WSO. It was a surprising invitation. He was the first guest conductor since the WSO had been established in 1948.

The circumstances were extraordinary. Very suddenly, the founding conductor, Walter Kaufman, had resigned and gone off to the University of Indiana and a distinguished academic career in the United States. The symphony board had two challenges — to put someone on the podium as a replacement for the departed conductor and artistic director for the rest of the 1956–57 concert season, and, more importantly, to find a permanent conductor. A search committee was immediately formed to address the latter concern.

There was a realization that the WSO was a fragile instrument. It had no musicians under contract. Every concert was essentially a gathering of freelance musicians for a single performance commitment, including, of course, the rehearsals that were necessary to prepare for the event. As well, the orchestra was burdened with a dreadful performing venue, a barn of a building that held four thousand people and was a huge space that had the worst acoustics imaginable. When the orchestra toured or played in even more modest theatres and auditoriums around Manitoba, the contrast in the sound of the orchestra was dramatic.

As one could expect, a financial crisis was always on the horizon. Although Winnipeg had the only symphony orchestra in the province, there was no connection between the capital and other cities that might have provided an audience for concerts and a source of support for an expensive enterprise.

Victor was quite knowledgeable about the Winnipeg scene. He had conducted the CBC Winnipeg Orchestra back in 1952. This ensemble shared many of its musicians with the WSO and he was welcomed when he arrived at the first rehearsal in 1957 by players who had become his colleagues in 1952. As well, he had been posted there when *Meet the Navy* had stopped off on both the tours of Canada in the 1940s.

It was apparent that Victor was hoping for a call. Kenneth Winters, covering the concert for the *Winnipeg Free Press*, was not taken with Victor's Brahms, which, though it conveyed "commendable clarity of detail," did not quite plumb the depths of the work. He also felt the orchestra had been more "strident than spontaneous." Yet, in his assessment for the concert as a whole, Winters was obviously impressed: "Feldbrill knows his stuff … the orchestra under his baton sounded better than it has ever sounded. The strings especially showed new restraint and elegance."[9]

S. Roy Maley, the *Winnipeg Tribune* reviewer, was taken with Feldbrill's "quick-moving, full of energy" presentation. He had conducted with "vivid" excitement, but had "not been extravagant." In his view the concert had been a "grande success."

Victor returned to Toronto immediately after the concert to a busy schedule of TSO pop concerts through the winter and spring of 1957, assuming that he would hear from the WSO search committee. His first assignment that summer was a BBC Radio concert date in Britain that he had arranged on his trip to Hilversum. Victor realized that moving to Winnipeg would be a dramatic break in his career and he was not sure what he would do if he were offered the job of the WSO's conductor. It would end the seeming continuity of commitment to the city of his birth and its resident orchestra, the TSO.

As well, Victor realized his decision would have considerable implications for his family. For Zelda, it would certainly interrupt opportunities to return to the profession she had so recently left in order to have the children and to nurture them through the early years. There was another concern for her, which she kept in her thoughts, one related to Victor's youngest sister, Eileen. She was a mere toddler while Victor had been overseas. One of her earliest memories had been that of being dressed in her finest clothes in order to be taken to the wedding of her newly arrived brother, Victor, who was marrying the beautiful lady who in the past years had been a regular visitor to the Feldbrill home. She had been told that this Zelda was the sweetheart of a brother she longed to meet, who was over in Europe.

She was thrilled by all the attention she had received from this wonderful woman, all the hugs and kisses that had been such a part of being a baby and then a small child amidst these older members of the family. Now she would command the attention not only of Zelda, this lovely lady, but as well that of her newly discovered serviceman-brother who apparently loved her so dearly.

Indeed, for well over a two decades, Eileen had two mothers — the aged one with whom she lived and the vivacious, outgoing, energetic one who understood her moods and feelings so completely. There were days in her teens when her only solution to adolescent misgivings was to board the bus and visit Zelda in the apartment she shared with Victor some distance away. There she would be warmly welcomed and a long chat would help ensure that she could face the impending crisis at school or at home.

Or, she might just wait until Victor and Zelda visited the Feldbrill homestead and know that her sister-in-law would simply look at her, contrive to take her aside to join in some task, then ask the inevitable question, "Why are you unhappy"? As long as Victor and his beloved were in Toronto, Eileen could be assured of a sympathetic and helpful response to her sadness. But the crisis came — her brother was suddenly famous as the new conductor of a symphony orchestra many hundreds of miles away. He would take Zelda with him, along with her two nieces, and she would be left back in Toronto.

After much soul-searching, Zelda decided where her responsibility lay. Her place was at her husband's side, and as a mother to her own children she must go with him. Could they take Eileen with them to Winnipeg? No, that would divert her educational future, and she would lose all her friends, her "real" mother and father, as well as her sister Ruth.

In the midst of these supportive relationships, there was a downside to the circumstances surrounding the late arrival of Eileen Feldbrill and the miraculous connection to a surrogate mother married to a brother she was to come to adore. Older sister Ruth, feeling already diminished by the example of a brother whose exploits at school and otherwise were beyond emulation, and feeling, with some cause, unfairly imposed upon as an available babysitter by an aging mother, never felt included in the intimacy of Victor, Zelda, and Eileen's attentions for one another. There was a tragic innocence on all sides, a flood of misunderstanding that contained rather than released these tensions. The Feldbrill family was never able to build the trusting and transparent relationships that allow for the complete celebration of "family." Amidst a loving, caring extended family there was a vacuum that represented Ruth's place and a tragedy of disconnection that could not be avoided or reconciled.

As for Winnipeg, Victor was more than ready to make this dramatic change in his life. Zelda and the girls had been warned and were soon in a state of anticipation. Fortunately, Debbi was just about to enter elementary school and Aviva was still at home. Their education would not be negatively affected. For Zelda, Winnipeg was like "going home." For Victor, the leading of one of Canada's four most prestigious symphony orchestras would be an extraordinary experience and an opportunity to prepare himself for the next stage in his unique career.

CHAPTER 10

The Road to Winnipeg

Victor had every reason to believe his 1957 WSO concert had been a success, and that an invitation to become its artistic director and conductor would be immediately forthcoming. Alas, he heard nothing from the WSO search committee. He discovered that rather than succumb to a frantic move to replace the empty podium, the committee, deluged with some fifty applications from around the world, had decided to delay any immediate decision. It was thought to be a wise reaction to this wealth of interest in the position of conductor and artistic director of the WSO and that the list of applicants should be perused for names to provide guest conductors for the remaining concerts in the 1957–58 concert season. Victor came to the conclusion that his chance to become Winnipeg's appointed conductor and his opportunity to give artistic leadership to a symphony orchestra in a major Canadian city, had disappeared.

He was still the assistant conductor of the TSO but he was not sure how long the position would last in the shuffle of bringing onboard Sir Ernest's replacement, Walter Susskind. The immediate challenge was a December 1, 1957, pop concert, and in light of the recognition that he was now in the running to occupy a distant podium, reviewer Michael Olver commented that Victor had showed "his usual acute musicianship and steady control of the orchestra," and added a hope that more Torontonians were coming to share: "I wish we had more than just one or two opportunities a year to hear this talented conductor." [1]

Ironically, in light of that observation, there would be a veritable flood of such opportunities in the subsequent weeks. A particularly difficult chore was that of assisting the newly appointed conductor, Susskind, who was faced with either keeping alive a Sir Ernest tradition — the Christmas "box" concert — or finding a replacement feature for this annual orchestral treat. It was conceded that no one could replace MacMillan as host of this glorious evening of musical fun and games that normally characterized that affair's popularity as the TSO's contribution to the holiday season. However, Victor's participation with Sir Ernest in past years' Christmas "box" events had prepared him to host a concert that would be amusing if not reaching the level of hilarity that MacMillan had achieved. A week later, Victor concluded the TSO's year with a more traditional Christmas repertoire that included pianist Jane Rowland as guest artist and received John Kraglund's reluctant concession that under his baton the orchestra had "achieved good balance and clarity." [2]

But it was with the Toronto-based CBC Symphony that he was rehearsing a program of outstanding contemporary music, the very repertoire that was establishing Feldbrill's reputation as a force in the Canadian conducting world. The broadcast concert would include the Symphony no. 1 of a rising American composer, Alan Hovhaness, who would eventually establish himself as one of that country's most imposing twentieth-century creative figures. Along with that composition, Paul Hindemith's *Symphonic Dances* were to be played. Once again it was John Kraglund who, in his January 9,

1958 review, expressed his satisfaction that Feldbrill had performed well. Indeed he had

> molded both performances with an understanding of the whole and a care for detail found in his other performances…. He made an engrossing experience of the Hovhaness Symphony with its contrast of solo and full orchestra passages, and the many climaxes in the Hindemith Dances were skillfully realized.[3]

Within another month, Victor was conducting an orchestra made up of CBC and TSO players in a Toronto concert devoted to the works of Jewish composers, including Samuel Dolin and John Weinzweig, a concert made more popular by the inclusion of Felix Mendelssohn's music. By March of 1958, he was leading a string orchestra in a special concert sponsored by the Canadian Music Association and the Canadian League of Composers. John Weinzweig's Divertimento no. 1 for Flute and Strings and Harry Somers' *North Country Suite* were included along with Barabara Pentland's Concerto for Piano and Orchestra. In spite of the savage reviews the latter work received, the concert was a triumph for Canadian music and for Victor Feldbrill, who was becoming the Canadian composer's conductor of choice.

Meanwhile, in the midst of this spasm of conducting in Toronto, Victor recognized that the city of Winnipeg was considering the future of its symphony orchestra. A realization had dawned that the search was more than about finding a person to wave a baton in front of a collection of instrumentalists. It was more a question of finding a true orchestral leader, an individual with a vision of the future for this ensemble at an important crossroad of its presence in the city's musical life. As well as judging the concerts that Victor and other aspirants were conducting, the search committee requested that each of those on the short list provide a statement of their expectations of, and plans for, Winnipeg's beloved though troubled orchestra.

Victor had no difficulty complying with that requirement. He knew exactly what he would propose to do. The first priority was the condition of the orchestra and its musicians. Previous conductor Walter Kaufman had found it difficult to keep the central core of some forty musicians together year after year, concert season after concert season, with no binding commitment on either side. Beyond an expectation of performing (and, of course, being paid to rehearse) every few weeks in the fall, winter, and spring, the players had no assurance of continuing employment. With the Winnipeg CBC Orchestra gathering these same musicians for broadcast concerts, along with a little teaching and possibly informal "gigs" around town, they could make ends meet. It was essential to stabilize a continuing relationship with the basic core of the instrumentalists, some of whom were as good as could be found anywhere. Indeed, a number had made their reputations in Europe and on the occasion of the Soviet invasion of Hungary had fled their homeland. Miraculously, a sizeable contingent had found its way to Winnipeg.

Victor's plan was that of placing the nucleus of some forty-five members of the orchestra of professional quality under contract. That would ensure continuity of employment and an assurance of quality of sound from concert to concert. There would still be thirty or forty instrumentalists who were of professional quality, but had other forms of employment and would appreciate, at least at the outset, the consistent presence of reliable virtuosity at the centre of every section of the orchestra.

The impact on the commitment and morale of this nucleus would be substantiated in the years ahead. Victor, with all his background as an orchestral musician, had placed the provision of a contract at the top of his priority list. It would be a justification for a process of audition that would take place on his arrival — the only way to ensure competent performance as a norm in the orchestra's future. As well, establishing a high quality of tone and ensuring commendable technique would make it possible for Victor to take the WSO beyond the central body of nineteenth-century works that had to that point dominated, almost monopolized, the performance repertoire of the orchestra.[4]

At the same time, Victor was careful to assure the orchestral players of his confidence in their capacity. "The sight-reading, for instance, is as good as you will find anywhere," was his initial assessment. There would be no massive turnover upon his arrival as music director was his promise to those orchestral members who feared for their jobs.

When Victor's plan for the orchestra was revealed upon his appointment, it was clear just how important this step was to be. After his engagement, he wrote:

> A milestone in the history of symphonic music in Winnipeg has been reached already with the decision to put under full season [26 weeks] contract the approximately 45 musicians who make up orchestra's professional nucleus. The advantage of this situation over the old one in which the players were hired for each concert singly, is obvious and enormous.

The second point in Victor's plan for the future of the orchestra was equally essential. His vision for the WSO included a dramatic increase in the number of concerts. No orchestra could improve its performance with only the handful of concerts that had traditionally made up the WSO regular subscription series. After 1958, the number of concerts would rise exponentially. Obviously, an increase in the performances already available to the Winnipeg audience would not be sufficient to justify the addition of numerous additional concerts — new audiences must be found.

Victor knew exactly where he would find the audiences that would benefit the long-term well-being of the WSO. His Toronto experience had shown him that there were large numbers of people who loved the sound of a symphony orchestra but were, in various ways, "turned off" by a concentration of too-serious and lengthy selections of Beethoven and Brahms, or made to feel uncomfortable and unwelcome in the regular format of concert presentation. Victor proposed filling out the season with more pops and family concerts that would attract new attendees who could be drawn by a more informal approach, one which included some short introductory remarks about the compositions being performed and the lives of their composers.

There was another audience that Victor revealed he was anxious to capture and entrance — children and youth concerts were to become an essential addition to the present audiences being served. More important, they represented the audiences of the future that the WSO would be dependent upon attracting if there was to be any future at all. Upon his appointment, he insisted on scheduling special concerts for them in both the schools and the concert hall.

Victor was aware that in the middle of the twentieth century, Winnipeg had the only symphony orchestra in the entire province of Manitoba. However, the WSO played almost all its concerts in the city's Civic Auditorium and had rarely ventured outside the municipal boundaries. Out there was a musically deprived hinterland that included communities in northern and western Ontario, far beyond the reach of orchestras in the southern municipalities of that province. As well, there were huge areas of the north-central United States that were inadequately served by the fine ensembles of the eastern or western seaboards — even such splendid orchestras as the Minneapolis Symphony Orchestra, though touring extensively, rarely ventured into these sparsely populated regions. Victor saw here an opportunity to tour in such a way as to benefit financially from commissioned appearances as well as reaching appreciative audiences from whom some valuable support might be forthcoming to a WSO in a constant state of penury.

There was another Feldbrill strategy that was not revealed in the spring of 1958, but would soon become his obsession. It involved replacing the performing venue available to the WSO musicians that was the bane of an orchestra seeking to provide an exciting sound and wishing to address a more challenging repertoire. The Civic Auditorium, a huge structure, was more suited to the presentation of the boxing matches that actually did take place within its walls when the WSO was not playing. There were in that same building (thankfully) smaller halls (one holding about eight hundred people) that more intimate ensembles, one in which, for example, the nucleus of the WSO that Victor was placing under contract, could play.

Victor realized that improving the WSO's performing space was essential and he set his sights on a single-purpose orchestral concert hall. With national centenary celebrations in the wind by the mid-1960s and extra funds from the federal government assigned to the erection of such celebratory venues being planned, there was a good chance of making this happen. Having such a venue was essential for the well-being of good music in the city of Winnipeg — both for musicians and audiences — and Victor set his sights on achieving that objective.

Many cities in other provinces were already planning to build performing spaces — even in provinces that had not been created for decades after the 1867 date of the promulgation of the British North American Act that had completed the unions of Canada East and Canada West (Quebec and Ontario) and two of the Maritime provinces — New Brunswick and Nova Scotia — and made possible the larger union. Even though Victor knew his successors would be the likely beneficiaries, he was determined to make a proper orchestral hall a priority. As well there would be a special centenary celebration for Manitoba in 1971, the actual date of that province's creation and entry into union. Indeed, a couple of years later, there would be launched the centenary of the establishment of the city of Winnipeg. The time was right for a battle to establish an appropriate concert venue, an opportunity that might not return for decades.

There was great interest generated in the press and the music community across Canada upon the announcement that finally came — that Victor Feldbrill, the young Canadian, was to be the conductor of the WSO. Indeed, the entire country was informed that for the first time in twenty-five years a Canadian had been selected to be the music director of a major orchestra in the nation. The first Canadian so chosen had been Sir Ernest MacMillan, a splendid appointment, but to some extent justified by the extraordinary role that he had played as a prisoner in the First World War, resulting in the creation of a heroic figure of imperial significance. Indeed he had been eventually knighted by King George. In this case the board of the WSO was determined that no one could cast aspersions on their choice on the basis that some kind of misplaced nationalism had raised its head and that something other than musicianship and leadership qualities had prevailed.

In the words of the announcement mailed to WSO subscribers on April 17, 1958, it was made clear that "one reason alone" had led to the decision to acquire Victor Feldbrill: "He was very simply the best conductor suited to carry out the work of bringing the W.S.O. to the highest standard of musical performance, thus making the greatest contribution to the community."[5]

It was made plain that the decision had been unanimous at the board level. It was not yet a time when orchestral players were accorded any significant role in the selection of conductors, but it was revealed that an informal poll had taken place and the vast majority of the members of the WSO had been in agreement. The letter went on to provide a detailed account of Victor's work at London's Royal College of Music and its Royal Academy, along with his participation at Tanglewood and Hilversum, with special attention to his close association with Pierre Monteux and other conducting luminaries in Britain and Europe.

Victor was not reticent in placing before the Winnipeg public his plans for the future and his confidence in the existing quality of the WSO players. He had come from orchestral ranks and knew that ultimately the success of his work as conductor was in their hands. At the same time he made it clear that changes were ahead … that the status quo was not an alternative. Beginning with an audition of the players, his aim would be "to build the orchestra gradually though as quickly as possible to full professional status; to perfect it as an instrument; to make it an asset to the community."[6]

There was even expressed the dream of forming a training orchestra for young instrumentalists from which the WSO could recruit its future members — an ensemble that could be made available for young potential conductors seeking to learn their craft.

Very much involved in Victor's plans was the mind and spirit of Zelda. April 1958 became a springtime rebirth in Zelda's heart. The previous months had been very difficult — "now I can breathe again" was her way of expressing her reaction to the announcement of Victor's appointment. To Toronto journalist Peter Worthington she expressed her delight. "I'm thrilled to be going back to Winnipeg," where, after her parents had come from Europe, they had briefly settled. Zelda expressed her pride that Winnipeg had shown the courage to appoint a Canadian. However, even after all these years with Victor, she was careful not to be perceived as an expert in musical performance. "All I am is a good listener — that's all," was her modest self-assessment.

For Victor, it was an emotional time. He had actually heard of his appointment from surreptitious telephone calls from various sources like the all-knowing Geoffrey Waddington, his CBC associate, and from others. When the formal announcement came, he went immediately to the home of Sir Ernest MacMillan, the mentor who had always been at his side.

MacMillan was ecstatic — Victor was following in his footsteps. Now there would be a Canadian conductor on a podium of a major Canadian city once again. The TSO, through its manager Jack Elton, assured Torontonians that Victor would be returning to Toronto to conduct pops concerts, but now as a guest identified as the conductor of the WSO.

It soon became apparent that Winnipeg would see little of its new conductor that summer. Although Victor immediately moved to the city, leaving Zelda in Toronto to assist Debbi in finishing her school year and to clear up her own responsibilities, there came immediately an invitation to be guest conductor at the International High School Music Camp at the International Peace Gardens from July 6–13. It was important for him to be there. Not only was the camp in North Dakota, an area he had identified as a potential touring site for his WSO, but he could not resist the opportunity to work with young people, some of whom would be coming from his new home base.

Even more difficult to turn down was the invitation to conduct the now-famous Hart House Orchestra at the Brussels World Fair. The performance would be the final Brussels appearance of the orchestra created by Boyd Neel in post–Second World War Canada, and the CBC wished to include a pickup of the concert on its prestigious *CBC Wednesday Night* program, but only if Feldbrill would be available to conduct. At the pre-flight presentation in Toronto, Victor conducted the orchestra in Mozart's Divertimento for Strings, K130 and a Stravinsky concerto. It did no harm for Winnipeggers to hear the results of the efforts of its new WSO conductor on CBC Radio and to know he was welcomed and acclaimed in Europe just weeks before his inaugural concert with their city's orchestra.

The reviews of his performances in European newspapers were extraordinary — more positive than he had ever received in his homeland. The Brussels newspapers were ecstatic: "A perfect interpretation of Mozart and Stravinsky. This last was played naturally, with simplicity; no virtuoso effects."[7]

And a second Brussels paper expanded on the treatment of the repertoire and spoke of

> [Feldbrill's] magnificent mastership and musical sense.
> He directed Mozart's Divertimento to perfection and

Stravinsky Concerto with a particularly appropriate sense
of that composer's characteristic punctuation. The different themes were interpreted in such a way that this work
had total unity and seemed to be gathered in one breath.[8]

The third paper also focused on the conductor's leadership:

Victor Feldbrill was deservedly applauded for he conducts
with such sensibility and intelligence. This just balance
from which fervor was not absent gave the performances
its human character as well as its greatness."[9]

Under the headline, "Conductor Victor Feldbrill Wins 'Rave' Reviews
at Brussels' World Fair," the *Winnipeg Free Press* informed its readers of their
new conductor's success abroad.

Victor was more concerned at what he perceived to be the laissez-faire
attitudes of Canadian officials at the Canadian Pavilion that took these
responses to the performance of a Canadian ensemble and its conductor
quite unemotionally. He quoted one Belgian critic, who commented to
him, "Your Canada is a young country and we felt that you have little culture. But we had our eyes opened from the first note of the opening of the
Mozart Divertimento. You have won a new friend and ally."

It was not the first time, nor the last time that accolades came to Victor
from appearances in the British Isles and Europe more easily than from his
work on podiums in his own country. Yet, at this stage, his success would
be accompanied by what seemed to be a consistent disinterest on the part
of Canadian officials on the spot! Thankfully, that attitude changed in the
1970s, when he was concentrating his attention on the Far East.

The triumph of Brussels quickly became a memory as the planning of
the WSO's eleventh season, and Victor Feldbrill's first, loomed. Realizing
the importance of the short "honeymoon" opportunity to achieve his plans
for expanded concert appearances, Victor worked ferociously on planning
the months ahead. There was no change in the regular subscription series
of ten Thursday night concerts — it was already set in place. However, the
repertoire would, this time, include the works of five Canadian composers

— John Weinzweig, Godfrey Ridout, Harry Freedman, Murray Adaskin, and Pierre Mercure. Added to the schedule were three special concerts to be presented by what came to known as the "nucleus" of professional, under-contract WSO players who would focus on both ancient and contemporary music.

Victor had already arranged to put on concerts for secondary-school students. To secure the interest of the administrators of these institutions who were, on the whole, reluctant to upset any regular schedules, Victor asked to attend a meeting of the principals and took the opportunity to place before them his proposals for school concerts, but making it clear that he would not be able to include all the schools in the first year. Their competitive spirits were aroused and immediate concert dates were claimed. He soon had a full schedule of appropriate concerts, often as not in gymnasiums of Winnipeg high schools for the youth audiences he was anxious to serve. It was an initiative that received considerable attention from the Winnipeg media.

Victor established his availability for interview with the press and expressed his willingness to speak to any group with an interest in good music. Most appreciated was his confidence in the orchestral players. That the WSO could "come to rank with the finest professional musical groups in the country" was his belief. When questioned about which proposed developments were the most important, Victor responded that the increased children's concerts would be the "most significant undertaking of the coming season" and expressed a long-term hope that a school of music associated with the University of Manitoba would eventually be a reality.

The *CBC Times* celebrated Victor's arrival in Winnipeg under the headline, "WSO: New Era with a New Conductor." The article included references to Feldbrill's growing reputation as a conductor of the works of contemporary composers but with a comforting and sensitive comment from Victor that he would need to balance audience receptiveness and his own tastes, including a promise never to play any composition he could not respect and find convincing. He made it plain that, in every case, the works of living composers deserved to be well played after being well rehearsed. Victor made the point that his preparation as a conductor had taken place in the ranks of orchestral musicians, a fact that he believed, with some good reason, gave him a greater understanding and appreciation of the challenge that new music presented.

He made the point that in Canada, and certainly in Winnipeg, it was the symphony orchestra — not the opera company, as it was in Europe — that bore the responsibility of bringing along the audience to appreciate what contemporary composers were saying about the world around them. They shared that world with their audiences each time the members picked up their instruments.

The extensive CBC interview gave Victor the opportunity to examine and comment on the artistic director's role. He made the point that it included but was much more extensive than merely conducting the orchestra on a regular basis. Giving "shape" and "structure" to the entire performing activity of the orchestra was the essential contribution to be made, not as some "prima-donna" figure, but in a complex, synergic relationship with the membership of the ensemble. Keeping the respect, admiration, and confidence of the players was at the core of Victor's concept of orchestral leadership.

As the concert season approached, it was essential that every person in Winnipeg be made aware of the new beginning. Thus, September 13–20 became Symphony Week in the city. It was the first but not the last — it became an annual Winnipeg tradition. Not only were there some eight free noon-hour concerts in the Dominion Theatre downtown but WSO musicians were made available to appear at service clubs, schools, and various public events. Attracting even more attention was the piping of orchestral music into the streets at the corner of Portage and Main, in the very heart of the city. If one accepts that Winnipeg is the geographic centre of Canada, then that famous corner is the pivotal point in the entire nation. Feldbrill was successful in projecting his music to the ears of Winnipeg citizens "at the centre," thus preparing them for a season of great musical expression on a scale never before witnessed in that municipality. Even the CBC became involved, airing on the local television station a program, *Symphony Backstage*, a rehearsal of a work in preparation for its performance at the opening concert.

That first concert of the year set the pattern even though in this case it included no guest artist. The Berlioz *Roman Carnival Overture* was a rousing opener, thus indicating through a nineteenth-century paragon of romantic expression the strength and capacity of the renewed WSO. The second offering signalled a new commitment to Canadian creativity. Harry Freedman's *Nocturne*, a work both modern in sound and form, but also accessible to any audience that gave attention to its performance, was played beautifully. Its position on the program as the second selection, not the first, meant that it could not be easily avoided by audience members planning to arrive late!

The third item on the program was the familiar and melodic *Faithful Shepherd Suite* by a favourite baroque composer, George Frederic Handel, but arranged for full orchestra by Victor's British colleague Sir Thomas Beecham. The finale was one of the dramatic mountaintops of the orchestral repertoire, the Tchaikovsky Symphony no. 5, a work guaranteed to bring any responsive audience to its feet.

The *Winnipeg Free Press* gave it the spirited headline, "Symphony Sounds Clean, Strong, Well-Practiced." Its music reviewer, Kenneth Winters, began his column, "I think Mr. Feldbrill must be an extraordinary teacher … the details of execution and style were thoroughly thought about … complexities in the score had been investigated, decisions had been reached…. Nothing was ill-considered. The playing was clean, telling and confident."[10]

The *Winnipeg Tribune* shouted its enthusiasm to the heights under the headline "Symphony in Triumphant Opener." The audience was present in impressive numbers, only once before achieved in the orchestra's history. Reviewer S. Roy Maley put his attention to the Tchaikovsky. The WSO's new conductor had been responsible for a presentation " that built up surging climaxes with unnerving instinct and meticulous detail … spine tingling episodes in an evening which savoured of rare technical and musical finesse … a performance of irresistible vitality, excitement and drama, in particular, inner voices one rarely hears were accentuated nicely."[11]

Feldbrill was given five curtain calls. It could not have gone better.

Now the challenge was that of following up that opening concert with programs that were equally satisfying. The second concert included Mozart and Beethoven. Winters once again heralded the orchestra's prowess: "It was good to hear Mozart's miraculous G Minor Symphony so cleanly played." With the Beethoven violin concerto and Betty-Jean Hagen as soloist, Feldbrill had worked his "magic" and Winters congratulated him on a "healthy, explicit, absorbing and miraculous proportional reading of the work." He concluded that "Mr. Feldbrill and the orchestra were splendid ... altogether this was a satisfying and edifying experience."[12]

S. Roy Maley, in his critique of the concert, sought to expose the secret of Victor's success with the orchestra:

> I could sense the skill into which, as interpreter, he communicates his ideas to his musicians. He impresses himself upon the orchestra by his knowledge and sensibility, not by force of assertive dominance. He seems to know that one of the secrets of having power is not using it. He conducts more or less quietly, very modestly. He seems to converse with the orchestra through the medium of his baton.[13]

It was a shrewd description of the Feldbrill style — one in complete contrast to the bombastic, self-fulfilling, power-tripping that was sometimes perceived as the parody of real orchestral conducting, but had its devotees nonetheless. It was a style that he was not prepared to change either to impress audiences or musicians.

The month that followed brought the first children's concert, one that critic Kenneth Winters found "was a model of its kind, a credit to everyone concerned ... easily the best I have attended and well and simply presented." An advantage was the fact that the concert was in the city's Playhouse, a smaller, more intimate venue. Here Victor could introduce the orchestra and its instruments to the assembled children and they could hear in close proximity the variety of sounds that could be made. It was little wonder that Winters was so positively impressed.

Strong as it may have seemed, Victor completed his 1958 conducting not in Winnipeg but at a December TSO pop concert in Toronto. Perhaps encouraged by the seasonal time of goodwill, John Kraglund, who had been normally lukewarm to mildly critical in his assessment of Victor's efforts on the podium — or perhaps, influenced by Victor's recent accolades in other cities, both in Canada and in far-off Brussels — gave him a warmer reception than was his wont: "Mr. Feldbrill appears to have grown in stature as an accompanist. He achieved a fine balance between orchestra and soloist" (who happened to be, on this occasion, his old friend and colleague Hyman Goodman).[14]

It was only the first weeks of his time in Winnipeg, but Victor had triumphed.

He had achieved acceptance by the orchestra. He had convinced his board and the public that they should have confidence in the expansionary plans he had proposed and had thrilled them both with the music he had produced. He had reached out successfully to new audiences of children and youth and had placed the WSO at the centre of the artistic life of the city. He had also fulfilled all the expectations that had been placed upon him as a Canadian conductor of a major musical institution. These were giddy and demanding times. He had made his mark.

CHAPTER 11

The Halcyon Years

For the Feldbrill family the move to Winnipeg in 1958 was a godsend. Though daughter Debbi was initially disappointed in losing her school friends, she was to find that the years in Canada's West provided her with a most satisfying learning experience. For Aviva, the transition turned out to be relatively easy. Manitoba provided her first formal schooling and she enjoyed her new friends in her new kindergarten, although she was to return to Ontario for most of her secondary-school education. The important thing was that they both did extremely well in school. Both soon had a host of friends and enjoyed their lives in the pleasant neighbourhood that contained their comfortable home.

Most important, Victor now had well-remunerated regular employment doing what he cherished — conducting — and, surprisingly, now had more time with Zelda and his girls.

Both Debbi and Aviva were very outgoing and fully conscious that they were part of a family that was making a unique contribution to the Winnipeg community. However, they were allowed no illusions of grandeur. Victor was determined that they would grow up with no elements of the excessive behaviour for which the children of prominent performing arts parents are famous. With all the media coverage of his arrival, Victor was soon to be recognizable wherever he went and automatically received attention he found rather embarrassing. He made it clear to the girls that being the conductor of the WSO was no more deserving of special treatment than being a street cleaner or garbage collector. It was one lesson they were never allowed to forget.

As well, they were inculcated with the simple concepts of justice that Victor demanded of himself. When they were together on a playground he was adamant that every child have a turn on the slide or swings. Being bigger or being accompanied by an adult or an older sister gave Aviva not an ounce of advantage. He knew that his children's ethical behaviour, particularly their sense of fairness, was assured by an intimate knowledge of Jewish tradition. He expected programming that contained precepts of proper behaviour and he was not beyond complaining to the local television station when their Saturday morning offerings reflected the distortions that modern society celebrates in cartoons that emphasize forms of racism that demean people of colour and in so doing threatened to undermine his family values.[1]

For Zelda, the Winnipeg years, at least in the beginning, were a time of special joy. First, Victor had achieved one of his goals — he was now a full-time conductor and was thriving in the context of an obvious recognition of his learning and experience. As well, it meant that there was now a home base for the family. She knew that Victor would have to go back and forth to Toronto for guest appearances ... and to Montreal ... and to other cities ... but she hoped there would be no months-long absences away from the family. She had withdrawn from full-time employment when the first of her two girls was born in Toronto, and for the first few Winnipeg years she remained at home. But the expectations of returning to her profession of social work were never allowed to die.

Her greatest delight came in the summer of 1960 when, with the reliable care of their girls in the hands of doting grandparents, Zelda accompanied Victor for a few weeks in Europe. She joined Victor as he sought out all his old wartime haunts of London, and met the musical conducting giants who had given him so much delight in the mid-1940s. Then came the Manchester visit in order that Victor could conduct the BBC Orchestra in a soon-to-be-broadcast concert. (Victor programmed a work of Canadian composer Harry Freedman — *Tableau.*) A return to London was brief as Europe beckoned, and finally the promises that Victor had made to her when in the *Navy Show* tour and during subsequent visits to that continent became real. Zelda visited Paris, Brussels, Salzburg, Vienna, and Munich, but most important by far was the stopover in Amsterdam and her opportunity to embrace the close friends with whom Victor had never lost touch, particularly the Boosts, the young couple who had fallen in love during the war and were planning marriage when Victor had joined them while stationed in their city.

Zelda was the toast of Amsterdam, both with that family and others who had shared her generosity and caring during the starvation days after war ended. Her food packages, sent during the first terrible days of peace accompanied by excruciating hunger, were vividly remembered. A few exciting weeks in Europe and she returned to Winnipeg, to the loving welcome of her children and with a resolve to fulfill her own ambitions of the 1940s in the context of her new home.

At the time of another such trip that Victor and Zelda were to take together, Frank Rasky, then a journalist with the *Toronto Sunday Star* was to write a revealing article. After allowing Victor to express his dependence on their life partnership, he revealed the extent of her contribution:

> I've always counted on Zel being backstage with me at concerts since we were married … she's my greatest fan and toughest critic…. She's seen me through my ups and downs. Thank God, she's got patience and a sense of humour. You need both to be the wife of a symphony conductor.[2]

Zelda added her own insight into the causes of her success as a conductor's wife. She expressed her dependence on having "a career of [her] own." She explained: "It doesn't bother me not being in the limelight, but I have an ego, too. I'd probably be a drag if I didn't fulfill myself in my other jobs — as mother, wife, and social worker."[3]

For Zelda, a university education was more than training for a job, but now she was determined to make the best use of the preparation she had received at the University of Toronto. Within a couple of years of her arrival in Winnipeg she was anxious to make a direct commitment to the development of another social work faculty in another institution. Soon the University of Manitoba realized there was a treasure to be found nearby. Now her girls were a little older, she could take on academic and mentoring responsibilities in the burgeoning area of providing advice to post-secondary young men and women with the same ambition to help address the myriad problems that faced individuals as they tried to cope with the vast spectrum of crises facing them. There were needs for contact with a mature field worker, one who could visit students working in local settings where the presence of an experienced social worker was essential as a part of their vocational preparation. Zelda became that person.

It was a perfect match. Zelda was a splendid choice for a young university seeking to develop a capacity in a comparably new discipline, in a community rife with the challenges of a diverse population. In Winnipeg there was also the rising conflict between aboriginal people and newly arrived immigrants, and increasing numbers of individuals suffering the trauma of abused treatment on another continent and searching for happiness in a new land — a veritable mélange of needs that cried out for attention and understanding. Zelda had excelled in Toronto amidst the shambles of human survival and the accompanying trauma left by the Holocaust. Now she was drawn to the service of young people preparing themselves to enter a very different kind of fray and she found particular satisfaction assisting such undergraduates who would be facing the conflict and confrontation inevitable in a frontier-like municipality, one with a violent past but now on its way to becoming a modern late-twentieth-century metropolis.

As well, this "field worker" assignment suited her schedule because her employment time could be flexibly moulded to meet the needs of her family. Indeed, the family took on a new style. When not rehearsing, Victor worked at home and often fed the children breakfast or lunch when Zelda rushed off to her assignment of the day. Zelda was home for dinner before Victor took off for another rehearsal or they both went off to a concert.

By the 1950s, both Victor and Zelda had accepted the fact that being a conductor in a country of few, but widely distributed symphony orchestras, and as well maintaining a career that must include performance opportunities overseas, meant there would be times each year when Zelda would have to take over complete responsibility for the home. She accepted that and it was a likely circumstance that she could handle with grace and effectiveness. The Feldbrill's became a closely knit family unit that Victor and Zelda cherished as the prime source of their daily delight. Their daughter Aviva remembers her own experience after she herself, through marriage, came to be a part of an arts-oriented family. She puts it simply: "Unlike most comparable people engaged in show business, we were a real family."[4]

Even before leaving Toronto, Victor had come to realize there was one piece of furniture that a new artistic director of a major orchestra in a significant city needed — a grand piano. It was more than just an instrument that might grace an elegant living-room or be valuable as a motivating factor for two children interested in a keyboard performing experience rather than that of a stringed instrument. Victor, with his virtuosity on violin or viola still very much intact and never having to rely on a keyboard to reveal the secrets of a new score, had never become a slave to the pianoforte. However, he was now a commanding community figure in the musical life of a significant Canadian centre and there would be gatherings in his home at which a great concert pianist might well be the central attraction as a guest performer with his WSO. Victor needed a grand piano.

A CBC piano tuner indicated the availability of such an instrument. A lady whose husband had died was in the process of offering for sale one that she cherished but for which she now had no use. It had been well cared for and well used in the past. Victor's friend and colleague, Glenn Gould, proclaimed it a fine example of the kind of musical asset that Victor was seeking. There was only one problem. The value of the instrument and the price, the five thousand dollars being demanded, was far beyond the Feldbrill budget. Victor was not about to put his well-being at financial risk for what seemed an unaffordable icon related not to his family's needs but to the position of musical leadership that he had assumed.

An extraordinary example of kindness and generosity ensued. The owner discovered who the potential buyer was and the straightened circumstances in which he found himself. She virtually gave the piano away knowing it would have a good home and a caring owner. Victor and Zelda expressed their eternal appreciation, enjoyed the moment of ownership ecstasy, and the grand piano was soon on a van making its way across northern Ontario to the Canadian West.

~~~

The late 1950s and early 1960s were happy years for the Feldbrill clan. Both Zelda and Victor were enjoying all the unfamiliar sights and sounds of a new home city. They soon had a close circle of friends who saw them not as professional associates, but as intimate companions. And family life thrived. Indeed, Saturday became "family day" and it was normal for the Feldbrills to arrive together at a downtown restaurant for a weekly celebratory luncheon. There was also time on that day for excursions to local galleries and museums or a trip to nearby parks and recreation areas for picnics. It was a time that Victor guarded jealously. He had always been close to his first child, Debbi, but now he developed a special relationship with Aviva in the knowledge that his absences in the early days of her childhood had created a chasm he wished to bridge. These experiences enabled the family to withstand the negative features of Victor's tenure as conductor of the WSO in the mid to late 1960s, when circumstances intervened to erode the initial delight of his welcome to Manitoba's capital city.

Indeed, these years seemed filled with one success after another. It was not just the concerts that were receiving warm reception. It was the fact that Victor's plans for expansion and performance improvement were coming into being. However, there were clouds appearing in the bright skies of western Canada. It was true that even though outstanding musical evenings took place in the smaller concert hall of the Civic Auditorium whenever the professional nucleus of the WSO performed, there were times when the audience was too small to make it financially viable. Too soon that program had to be cancelled. That was tragic because the intimate surroundings were so much more conducive for the smaller chamber orchestra and for the groupings of duos, trios, and quartets that could be formed to create varied and exciting programs.

As well, the limitations of the concert hall were such that Victor realized that adventurous repertoire for the larger orchestra could not be played. Nor would the acoustics allow smaller works from the modern era a fair hearing. Often modest contributions of Canadian composers, as well as those with international reputations in Europe and Asia, simply could not be performed. This pushed Victor to become even more determined to achieve an acoustically friendly venue to replace the hopelessly inadequate Civic Auditorium. It made more apparent Victor's argument for the building of a completely dedicated orchestral venue devoted to the playing of great symphonic music.

Indeed, at one of the special concerts in the smaller venue associated with the Civic Auditorium, the *Free Press* critic Kenneth Winters could scarcely contain himself within his normal journalistic reserve over "the stunning performance of the Handel Viola Concerto," and emphasized the importance of the combination of "excellent acoustics, solid gold program and the generally efficient playing under Victor Feldbrill." On that same night, listening to the sound of reduced orchestral forces playing the Beethoven Symphony no. 7, he reported he had been "moved by a performance that was almost consistently first-rate." The venue and the virtuosity of his professional nucleus had allowed Victor to take the last movement at such a clip that he literally "stole the show" as "the music came flying off the page. It was a real performance"[5]

In another such special concert, critic S. Roy Maley was ecstatic, making use of such terms as "superlative," and Winters again effused about "the solid, careful work" and "the buoyant, rhythmically exciting playing of a program well-planned in its moods and textural contrasts." These concerts in the smaller auditorium served the purpose of revealing what sound and quality of playing would be possible if the WSO was fully contracted and performing in an appropriate concert hall. The Winnipeg critics became Victor's allies in this sector of the battle to improve the listening experience of Winnipeg citizens.

With all these disadvantages, in the midst of his first season Victor could revel in the fact that the first eight concerts for Winnipeg students had already drawn some six thousand young people and could take some pride that the orchestra had received "a tremendous reception from these students many of whom were having their first listening experience with a symphonic ensemble." One of those listeners was Bill Richardson, eventually to become the host of *Saturday Afternoon at the Opera* on CBC Radio 2, who was present at one concert at which he felt Victor had skillfully aroused the audience interest by short, pointed, and informed comments about each of the selections on the program. Richardson was also present for a disaster beyond Victor's control. At one performance there was a ballet segment that included dancers who aroused wild levity among students who had not been prepared by their teachers to realize that the human body could be trained to express in movement the thoughts, interactions, and emotions to be found in the "Music of the Dance" symphonic program. Richardson remembers the hysterical laughter that had greeted this segment of the program because of teachers' inadequacy.[6]

By April 1959, there was unanimous confidence that the WSO had completed an outstanding season. At the final concert of the subscription series, an evening that included the Sibelius Symphony no. 2, *Tribune* critic S. Roy Maley described the work as the climax of the evening. The concert "had ended with a triumphant ovation for its musical director, Victor Feldbrill.... The musicians joined with the audience paying Mr. Feldbrill a tribute he richly deserved."[7] In typical self-effacing fashion, Victor passed on these accolades by congratulating the astuteness of his audiences and the "hard work and devotion of the excellent instrumentalists who make up the WSO." Even the vision of the board of directors was acclaimed and shared in that moment of triumph. More than mere nostalgic wisdom led critic Kenneth Winters to observe to the author that Victor had been "exactly the right person at exactly the right time" in the WSO's checkered history.[8]

Looking back over the initial season, Victor could expound at length on the success of his formative plans for the WSO. It had included, in his own words, "a liberal spicing of the unknown." He had doubled the number of concerts for children and by the end of the first full season some nineteen thousand had heard their city's symphony orchestra. He had initiated concerts for the most difficult age group ... the teenager. He had developed concerts with a repertoire that could excite entire families who might come together to enjoy music, at what became a family pops series of concerts. He had just begun the process of serving people in the province of Manitoba beyond the capital — both Lynn Lake and Brandon had been visited by the WSO. Such special concerts had also been artistically success-ful. Most heartening of all, though, was that the increase in the number of subscriptions for the coming season was the greatest in the WSO's history.

Now able to think about the patterns of activity for the coming season, Victor could once again promise that children's concerts would increase, the number of youth concerts would be maintained, special concerts of the WSO professional nucleus would continue, and the commitments to Canadian composers, the playing of some five compositions as a part of the regular series, would be enhanced by the commissioning of a Winnipeg-born composer, Barbara Pentland, to write a symphony. Most dramatic of all would be the increase in touring, both in the province — to Brandon, Verdun, Dauphin, and Flin Flon — and outside — to the Lakehead and Kenora in northern Ontario. (In the case of Brandon and Dauphin, the WSO visit became an annual event.)

There were always difficulties that had to be expected. At Kenora there was only half an audience but Pat Bourgeault, in the April 11 edition of the *Kenora Daily*, made the point that in a bingo and hockey town the WSO had played a "thrilling concert with an excellent choice of program." She could not restrain her admiration for the conductor "with a wonderful personality who introduced each selection." At the next visit, she predicted, there would be a full house.

Yet the signs of trouble ahead continued to gather. Victor's expres-sion of discontent over the Civic Auditorium was palpable and became a kind of mantra as he discussed the orchestra's future. Many looked for-ward to a resolution of that problem but others resented the expense the building of a new hall would incur even if the federal and provincial contributions, encouraged by the eventual Centennial celebrations, bore the major fraction of the cost. Of course, controversy soon began over the location of the Civic Auditorium's replacement and merchants who benefited from the auditorium's present location were loath to see the orchestra's performing venue move. As well, the need for a larger orchestra, one that could play the symphonies of Sibelius, Mahler, Bruckner, to say nothing of the orchestral operatic music of Richard Wagner, was apparent. The need for additional players to be fully under contract to the point that the term "nucleus" would no longer apply to any minority or majority of WSO musicians was becoming a constant theme, particularly as the size of the orchestra's budget rose yet the WSO continued to receive considerably less financial support from the Canada Council than the TSO, or the Montreal and Vancouver Symphonies. Victor made the case that the WSO, with as active a program but fewer sources of corporate donation, could never raise the sums of private money that the other "big three" could amass. Yet the WSO was expected to achieve the same level of excellence. Equal support to major orchestras from the Canada Council became his solution but one that had no hope of achieving in the political context of arts funding in the country.

Most controversial of all was Victor's intransigence regarding the WSO's constant performance of contemporary music, particularly the compositions of his Canadian "friends." This element of his plan had political and ideological overtones. His position was that if the music itself had integrity and was skillfully written, it must be played.

His opponents saw a conspiracy that smacked of revolutionary societal change. Alas, this debate eventually took place but the effect was a rejection of all change on the part of some later additions to the WSO Board and even a few early supporters of Victor's plans could be seen to be less attracted to his repertoire.

The immediate challenge in the summer of 1959 was the occasion of a royal visit. Queen Elizabeth and Prince Philip were to hear Victor's work with both the WSO and the TSO — an extraordinary feat for the busy conductor who had already agreed to teach at the University of Manitoba's summer schools and bring his WSO strings for concert appearances as an element of his participation in the program. Victor's agenda was to ensure that the Queen and her entourage heard some compositions by Canadian composers.

His Toronto appearance with the Bach Society during the royal tour was of special interest. The *Toronto Telegram*'s George Kidd commented that "the entire program conducted by Victor Feldbrill was generally a rewarding one" and that he had assured that soprano Lois Marshall received an excellent accompaniment "by giving 'special' attention to orchestral detail and ensuring that shading had exceptional care." The *Globe and Mail's* John Kraglund was even more flattering, expressing the opinion that the fact "the evening sounded like Bach can be attributed to the concise, self-effacing direction of Mr. Feldbrill. He drew from his players one of the best balanced and most stylishly paced performances of the season." William Krehm, writing for the *Toronto Daily Star*, observed:

> He gave us a measure of his growing stature as a conductor in the Bach cantata, *Sleeper's Wake*. Always an excellent hand for keeping an orchestra coherent and articulate, Mr. Feldbrill has moved on to the more elusive phase of a conductor's art — the molding of a phrase and the imparting of a mood!

As the Queen moved across the country she inevitably made her way to Winnipeg. There, once again, was Victor Feldbrill, leading another symphony orchestra, this time his WSO. Actually, he was present yet again in that city, though this time invisibly. The music for the Royal Winnipeg Ballet, also in performance before royalty, was conducted in person by Victor's old *Navy Show* colleague Eric Wild. However, in his absence the rehearsal of the accompanying ensemble had to be carried out by no other than Victor Feldbrill.

The WSO command performance that Victor presented included what S. Roy Maley called an "inspired offering" of Tchaikovsky's *Romeo and Juliet Overture*, which was "thrilling and vivid." The responses of the Queen and her consort to all of these performances were as one would expect — regally enthusiastic. On that note ended the long and dramatic first Feldbrill season in Winnipeg.

However, it is often the second season that predicts the success of a conductor's tenure on the podium before an orchestra (not unlike the experience of a rookie hockey or football player). The exuberance of the initial year can be attributed to the euphoria of a new beginning, but a blasé comfort level quickly blunts the excitement of that opening season and the slow erosion of expectations and accomplishment ensues. Victor, who from the outset had indicated that building a major symphony orchestra was a long-term goal demanding years of time-consuming hard work, was determined this would not happen.

At the opening concert of his second season he programmed a favourite composition of both his audience and himself — the Dvorak *Carnival Overture*. With its glorious melodies, its lush orchestration, and its composer's association with the North American context, he could not go wrong with Dvorak. A Feldbrill coup was the presentation of Glenn Gould's debut performance of Brahms's Concerto for Piano and Orchestra no. 1, a stunning experience for both orchestra and audience.

S. Roy Maley needed no prodding to witness the impact of Victor's selection of the Mozart *Jupiter Symphony* as the conclusion of the concert:

> I was constantly struck by the high level of proficiency and musicality to which Conductor Victor Feldbrill has brought our Civic Orchestra ... he so effectively captured the spirit of the work, made each point with such purposefulness and sensitivity and brought out its drama ... he stressed the lyric elements without any way neglecting the strength of the score and achieved a thrilling climax in the vigorous and vibrant final movement.[9]

However, it was at the next concert that Victor had programmed the Bartok Concerto for Orchestra, a composition he knew well from his broadcasting experience. Not only was it a work that could arouse an audience, with thematic material that engages any attentive listener, but it gave every instrumental section in the orchestra an opportunity to shine forth with its most thrilling virtuosity and its most enthralling sound. Victor believed that the WSO was "up to it." Subscribers would be reminded yet again how far the orchestra had come in its pursuit of performance excellence. Jeffrey Anderson, replacing the *Free Press* regular critic, Kenneth Winters, could bring himself to comment that the "looked for quality of the playing has already made itself abundantly evident."[10]

Although S. Roy Maley found the performance "surprisingly brilliant ... intense and dynamic throughout," he picked up on a Winters theme — the Bartok had proven the orchestra needed about twenty more players to successfully climb the heights of the late nineteenth and early twentieth century romantic repertoire that provided such powerful and climactic moments.[11]

Victor was forcibly reminded of this WSO size limitation frequently through these years as every few months he was invited back to conduct the TSO for one or another event. In that city, the entire orchestra was under contract, and the orchestra was considerably larger than that of Victor's WSO. In early 1960 it was "good old reliable Victor" who was called upon to conduct what was certainly a creditable outreach concert but one that generated considerable debate about the matter of artistic integrity. The concert was sponsored by the Metropolitan Police Association and was presented in Maple Leaf Gardens — a hockey rink of mammoth proportions, scarcely an appropriate venue for the playing of symphonic music. Yet there was a community support aspect to this invitation that could not be ignored. For years it was to be an annual event in Toronto and in criticizing this venture's unseemly venue one had to remember that for most of a decade the Metropolitan Opera was to pay its annual tour visit to that same hockey palace on its way through the city to other centres in northern New York State and beyond.

It was John Kraglund, a severe critic in past reviews of Victor's conducting capacity, who bathed Victor in deserved but rather surprising accolades, noting that he had drawn from his players "sparkling interpretations." Udo Kasemets, a prominent Canadian composer as well as a critic, provided the reason for the successful presentation: "Between the TSO and Victor Feldbrill there is always a feeling of affection. They make music with mutual understanding." It was clear on these occasions that Victor was keeping his options open regarding his relationship with this orchestra with which he had established such a long and productive history.

Back in Winnipeg, Victor was continuing his mission to play the works of Canadian composers and maintaining the momentum of his first season. His reputation was rising exponentially. It was composer John Beckwith who first made the calculations that Victor and his WSO were playing more Canadian music than all the other major orchestras in the country combined. For the 1959–60 season, Victor had determined that, in spite of opposition, he would feature the works of Harry Somers, and the subscription series began with his *Passacaglia and Fugue* along with a playing a few weeks later of John Weinzweig's Divertimento no. 1 for Flute and Strings by members of the WSO's contracted core. These were both works Victor was to take on tour in Europe and Asia.

But problems arose with the Barbara Pentland commission for a symphony. The new *Free Press* critic, Jeffrey Anderson, proclaimed it "tedious and confusing" with a particularly venomous description of the third movement as "vulgar." When, a few days later, Anderson described a Clermont Pépin offering by the WSO as "derivative, pretentious, a piece of modern academic patchwork," the debate was finally on about contemporary Canadian music. Victor took on Anderson over the "derivative" slight, pointing out that every piece of creative work builds on the work of previous artists, but from this point it was about whether Victor could hold out against a gathering storm of resentment over the performance of Canadian music — and at what cost.

Victor was constantly disappointed by the reaction of critics to the Canadian works he programmed. There seemed to be a constant undercurrent of resentment over his efforts to bring the creative efforts of Canadian composers to his audience. There was also a strong difference of opinion over the critic's proper function that Victor courageously addressed publicly — a foolish course some would say in the light of the capacity of a regular critic to demean every future concert effort of a permanent conductor week after week. Victor argued with Kenneth Winters that a critic had the responsibility to have studied the score, even listened to the orchestra in rehearsal, before dismissing the efforts of a conductor and his orchestra to interpret a new work intelligently. Winters, well prepared musically, responded that a critique of a concert should be nothing more than one person's reaction to the listening experience shared by every other audience member. Victor disagreed and expressed the view that a series of critical reviews of concerts that failed to recognize the challenges of acoustics, the rehearsal limitations, and the orchestral losses of key players, were unhelpful. These problems, he felt, should be acknowledged and recognized in any intelligent review. Victor was convinced that people depended on the comment of knowledgeable critics to understand the complete role of an

orchestra in any community. Indeed, Victor proposed the ultimate threat
— he offered to write a column titled "The Artist Answers the Critic" in
response to newspaper reviews, whether adulatory or savage, in succeeding
editions of the *Tribune* or *Free Press*. It was not an offer that was received
with any serious enthusiasm.

The CBC entered the fray of assessing Victor's early success in the
spring of 1960 with an article in the *CBC Times*, headed, "It Couldn't
Be Done (But He Did It)" — an account of Victor's programming of
Canadian musical works, pointing out that if he remained ten years he
would have introduced some fifty or sixty Canadian compositions and an
equal number of contemporary works from around the world. Victor had
an opportunity to commend his Winnipeg audience, who had "gone wild"
in support of a particular selection of contemporary music that a Toronto
audience had rejected by walking out during its initial hearing. Feldbrill
made another point — that audiences should have the opportunity to judge
Canadian music after "repeated hearings" and concluded with a statement
some Winnipeg listeners did not want to hear: "I feel a great responsibility
to the Canadian composer of symphonic music."

The summer of 1960 was the most important for the future of Canadian
composers. Louis Applebaum was a Canadian composer noted mostly for
his background music in film, radio, and live theatre — in particular the
Stratford Shakespeare Festival in Stratford, Ontario. He was determined as
music director of that festival to bring together contemporary composers
from around the world for a special gathering of creative music-makers. He
tried and failed to produce Shostakovich as his drawing card but a number of prominent composers from foreign countries came nevertheless. The
conference was a great success. In fact, many years later, in listing his lifetime accomplishments, Louis identified his part in making this happen as
the one action he felt most proud to have taken. The Canadian composer,
for the first time, came to realize that he or she was just as able to create
good music as those from other countries. This event changed the entire
environment of music composition in Canada forever.

Victor would play a major part in the presentations of new Canadian
music at Stratford. He was called upon to conduct virtually every orchestral
concert. As well, with his new reputation as a champion of contemporary

music, he was placed on a panel discussing the problems of contemporary composers. He took the opportunity to advise composers in a practical fashion about how they could best assure themselves of having their compositions played. First, "make sure the manuscript score is legible ... make sure that all the corrections are made before rehearsal — that time is too valuable to spend on simple clerical errors," and he pleaded with the gathered composers to "take orchestral performers into their confidence, rather than conductors, for many have never been instrumentalists and therefore are ignorant of the possibilities and difficulties involved in playing the various instruments." It was good advice from a knowledgeable source.

Feldbrill was one of the few who saw the significance of the Stratford Composer's Conference. He met, while there, Alfred Frankenstein, the music critic of the *San Francisco Herald*, who approached him after a performance with the question, "Where did you get these players? I've rarely heard such enthusiastic playing." He predicted, as one who had heard previously only the name of Healy Willan as a Canadian composer, that the conference would exponentially increase awareness of Canadian music-making.

Victor was quietly ecstatic. He felt that no one had come with an axe to grind ... the atmosphere among the composers had been "wonderful" and it had been inclusive of all innovators — accepting even those for whom electronic music was the future. He had found the whole Stratford conference "refreshing and stimulating."

The debate around the playing of Canadian music would end in Winnipeg only when Victor Feldbrill left that city some years later. Ironically, although Victor lost the battle to secure a firm commitment, he won the war. Eventually, Winnipeg became known across Canada for its nurturing of Canadian composers and their work. By the 1990s, another distinguished conductor, Bramwell Tovey, with the help of composer Glenn Buhr, was able to establish a WSO "New Music Festival" that has become a fixture in the life of the Winnipeg musical scene, one that was to provide a continuing pressure on every orchestra in the country to feature the work of Canadian contemporary composers. Without the determination to face all opposition for a full ten years in the late 1950s and throughout the 1960s, the foundation would not have been laid upon which such a festival could be built. It just took time, along with a slow realization that there were compositions that deserved attention from Canadians interested in understanding, through contemporary music, themselves and the wonders of their own country, as well as the diversity and difficulties of the world they lived in.

There were memorable moments in the early 1960s — an exciting time in Canada, when the entire nation began preparing for the Centennial. Victor was at the centre — admonishing any artist planning to go to the United States to remain in Canada to take advantage of whatever opportunity that could be garnered from the event. Like his colleagues who did remain, Victor believed Valhalla was imminent. It turned out to be an "impossible dream," but in the efforts to make the dream reality the centennial celebrations did more to advance Canadian confidence in itself than could have been imagined. As author Paul Schafer was to comment years later to the author, "Would any of this have happened if it had not been for the pioneering work of people like Victor Feldbrill?"

By the 1960s there emerged extraordinary musical presentations that thrilled audiences and raised the bar for anything the WSO was to attempt in the future. An early concert in the 1960–61 season included the Vaughan-Williams *London Symphony*. Beneath an appropriate headline, "London' Surges to Life Under Feldbrill's Baton," S. Roy Maley declared this offering the "most brilliant and polished of the evening," and added that Victor's "interpretation left little to be desired." It was his opinion that Feldbrill "has never given greater evidence of the 'musicianly' control of his forces … the music of this finely wrought work leaped to life in a stirring vital performance."

In a later concert that year, Maley commented upon Feldbrill's leading of the orchestra in Berlioz's *Symphonie Fantastique*, suggesting that "he also disclosed more temperament and imagination than observed previously during his Winnipeg regime." In the concert that began 1961, the *Tribune* critic also found a lesser-known work to have achieved monumental proportions. Performing Bloch's *Schelomo Rhapsody* with Leonard Rose as solo cellist, "Victor Feldbrill and the orchestra provided an opulent tonal background, projecting with superb skill all the barbaric splendour of the great modern orchestrations."

That year saw major guest conducting opportunities come Victor's way and remain throughout the decade. Toronto invitations had come every year, at least one but more often three or four. In December of 1961, the TSO asked him to conduct a Sunday pops concert with a substantial repertoire that included Tchaikovsky's *Marche Slav*, Beethoven's *Fidelio Overture*, Kodaly's *Dances from Galanta,* and Wagner's *Prelude to Act III of Lohengrin.* Mary Simmons, a soprano of some reputation, was the soloist, whom John Kraglund felt had been provided "a balanced, thoughtful support" by conductor Feldbrill. Once again, conscious of Victor's presence from afar, Kraglund wrote that, "He has become an efficient, workmanlike conductor," and that his reading of the Kodaly was "outstanding for its clarity, rhythmic precision and subtle shading." These appearances on the distant podium like that of the TSO led Victor to realize that being a freelance conductor was a real option for his future.

A second significant guest appearance took place in association with the Quebec Symphony Orchestra late that year. There was to be a performance in Trois Rivières and one in Quebec City. With the knowledge that the eminent Alexander Brailowsky was solo pianist and with Weinzweig's score *Edge of the World* in his briefcase Victor had every reason to feel confident. The review in Trois Rivières contained the accolade *"Victor Feldbrill possède les qualités d'un grand chef d'orchestre."* Quebec City's *L'Évenement-Journal* simply translated the Trois Rivières assessment as the headline to its review, but went much farther.

> The subscribers of the Quebec Symphony had occasion to become acquainted with the young Toronto-born orchestral conductor Victor Feldbrill. Pupil of Pierre Monteux, Mr. Feldbrill has all the qualities of a great orchestral conductor, a sure technique, dynamism and a remarkable musical sense. Under his baton the musicians brought forth all the characteristics and grandeur of the works on the program.[12]

By 1962, Victor was receiving recognition from conducting ventures both at home and abroad that reflected well on the WSO. The CBC had been central in achieving Victor's appointment in 1958. Now there was an opportunity to take advantage of his presence in Winnipeg by including him in a program, the "most ambitious of its type ever produced in North American television." Featuring the symphony orchestras of Toronto, Montreal, Vancouver, and Winnipeg, the series would amount to forty-six hours of symphonic programs and would be introduced by the CBC in a documentary, *The Portrait of an Orchestra.* Victor had no hesitations in placing his WSO in that company and, once again, his program performance compared most favourably with the best of Canada's symphonic orchestral producers.

That same year saw the continuation of a close relationship with the outstanding international "star" solo pianist, Byron Janis. Victor had by now established his reputation as a model conductor of an orchestra accompanying a soloist, whether vocal or instrumental. Many conductors have little interest in this necessary function; indeed, in some cases, they prefer to hand off the role to the orchestra's assistant conductor. By their attitude in rehearsal, conductors can convey disinterest and thereby ensure a second-rate concert performance of concertos that may be in some cases the major work on the program.

Victor, from the outset, had a belief that the concerto repertoire was just as deserving of first-class presentation as any other genre program selection. Janis, after a concert that had included an outstanding rendition of the Schumann Piano Concerto, had declared his enthusiasm for Victor's talent: "the inspiring feature is that you have a splendid young conductor in Winnipeg. Mr. Feldbrill and the enthusiasm and high spirits of his players is so evident that the soloist performance is affected." This liaison of soloist and conductor resulted in an extraordinary return engagement at which Janis played three very difficult and demanding third concertos, by Beethoven, Prokofiev, and Bartok, making up an entire concert program. The audience reaction was staggering ... ovation after ovation — a new level of excitement in a city in need of such inspiration.

It had been significant in 1959 when Glenn Gould wished to launch his first performance of Brahms' magnificent Concerto no. 1 that he had chosen to do so with Victor Feldbrill and the WSO. By the 1960s, Victor's commitment to concerto musical literature became broadly recognized. It meant that his audiences experienced the guest appearances of the finest solo performers in the world throughout the 1960s.

It was in the spring of 1963, just five years into Victor's decade-long stretch as conductor of the WSO that the orchestra became involved in a research project of the major periodical serving the North American symphony orchestra community — *Musical America*. The purpose was simple. A better understanding of the role of the symphony orchestra in the life of the host community was essential. Everett Helms, editor-in-chief of the periodical and a recognized American composer and music critic, proposed to examine not only the paragons of the North American orchestral performance scene, like the New York Philharmonic, but as well smaller, perhaps more challenged ensembles struggling in a modest municipality. These orchestras were particularly vulnerable in seeking to survive the assault of lowering budgets and doing so at a time when new technologies were crowding out the more traditional forms of performance or in some cases providing savage competition from the broadcasting initiatives of the major orchestras. Were these lesser orchestras going to survive when the Cleveland or Philadelphia orchestras could be heard and eventually seen in the living-rooms of subscribers to local orchestras across the entire continent?

As a strategy to assess the health of "off the main stream" symphonic music, Helms chose to examine the WSO as one of five centres in North America in a review process sponsored by the American Symphony Orchestra League. Winnipeg would be the only Canadian city so treated. As an appropriate beginning he chose to attend the final concert in the 1962–63 subscription series on April 11. It was a good choice, featuring the highly acclaimed Philippe Entremont as piano soloist playing the Prokofiev Concerto no. 3 and concluding with the Tchaikovsky crowd-pleaser, the Symphony no. 5.

Helms was delighted with the performance of the concerto. In an article appearing in the *Musical America* publication he observed that "Feldbrill maintained an excellent balance between orchestra and piano and produced a very well integrated dialogue between these two elements."[13]

However, it was in the Tchaikovsky that Helms could judge the quality of the WSO most accurately: "The performance made me forget that one has heard it 4,872 times [Perhaps something of an exaggeration]. It was a natural performance with plenty of tension, but no 'hamming,' plenty of expression, but no emoting."[14]

Helms found the entire listening experience "fresh, healthy, virile and satisfying." He concluded his assessment with words that expressed enormous confidence in the orchestra:

> To sum up, Victor Feldbrill is unquestionably a very talented conductor who knows what he wants and how to get it. He conducts for the music and for the orchestra, not for his audience. Yet his stage personality is not by any means academic. The results are natural and highly musical.... Winnipeg is to be congratulated on having him.[15]

It was no accident that Victor had included in that program a short composition, *Overture for an Unwritten Comedy*, written by the most well-known Canadian composer of the time, Healy Willan. It was the Feldbrill touch — that Canadian composers should be included in as many concerts as possible. Little wonder that Helms could bring himself to comment, "If we don't hear a good deal of Victor Feldbrill as a symphony conductor on the international scene, I'll eat my hat."

One might have expected that such a public evaluation from such a source would have given the board of the WSO an enormous infusion of confidence. Within two years, and with the next contractual arrangement with the conductor looming, the board, much to Victor's horror, was writing letters to musical luminaries in Canada and the United Kingdom, requesting an assessment of Victor's role in the symphonic world. The results were predictable. All responded with comments indicating high respect for Victor's ability and performance. Conceding that "most of the players in any orchestra have ambitions to wave the baton," Sir Ernest MacMillan wrote:

> From the first time I saw Victor I was convinced that he, more than any of our players, had the natural ability necessary for this office and his subsequent career has convinced me that I was right. He has the musical knowledge, the discernment and the diplomacy that orchestra conducting demands ... since his appointment in Winnipeg he had vastly improved the playing quality of the orchestra.[16]

Sir Ernest went on to express "regret he [Victor] has lost a number of his best musicians," but reported that he had heard "nothing but favourable reports of his work." He was admired particularly in regard to "the inclusion of the works of our own composers." He went on to indicate his distress "to hear that Victor had been under fire from critics, both professional and lay ... and that it would be most unfortunate for the Orchestra were you to lose him."

A similar request for assurance to Hugh Davidson, music program organizer for the CBC International Service, elicited a similar response. He replied, drawing into his circle Canadian composers (for example, Barbara Pentland and Murray Adaskin) who had worked with Victor: "They were overjoyed with the musicianship, discipline and enthusiasm, both of the group and the efficient and musical way in which Mr. Feldbrill rehearsed and conducted them ... as a musician I find Victor Feldbrill, sensitive, hardworking and courageous."17

Letters to individuals associated with his conducting for the BBC brought forth similar responses. The letters gave no basis on which the board could not extend Victor's contract. However, there were clues even in the most positively supporting missives that told some of the tale. One comment that Victor was "perhaps less glamorous than some of the brilliant visitors inflicted on the Montreal Symphony," and the constant references to his "courage" were indicative to board members who indeed wanted "glamour" and were not interested in "courage," at least not as it might relate to the programming of modern works. The whole process revealed the extent of the deterioration in confidence on both sides after the first five years.

One thing was certain. It was apparent the halcyon years were over. The final years at the WSO would be a burden to both the board and the conductor. Victor, however, was determined that all that had been achieved would not be lost and that there would be no damage to the high quality of the playing the orchestra that had been achieved. Orchestral music in one of Canada's major cities would never be the same as before Victor's arrival. As well, he had set a new standard to which Canadian contemporary composers could point in their efforts to defy recalcitrant boards, managements, and unwilling players in order to secure the performance of Canadian works.

Nearly four decades later, in March of 2004, the WSO invited Victor back to its podium as a part of his eightieth birthday celebrations. It was a gala event and one highlight of the occasion was an interview on the local CBC station conducted by James Manishen, now a senior artistic adviser to the WSO and a long-time colleague of Feldbrill.

Indeed, as an aspiring teenage clarinet player Manishen had first performed for Victor in a Winnipeg Symphony Youth Orchestra. His defining moment had come when, as a totally untried musician who, upon the resignation of the incumbent clarinet player in the WSO, had been selected by Victor as a replacement in spite of his youth and inexperience. Manishen had never forgotten Victor's act of faith in his possibility as an instrumentalist who displayed intelligence, skill, and commitment.

Manishen was confident in his introduction to the CBC interview in stating that in 1958 Victor had ushered in a new era in the WSO's short history. Specifically, Victor had "taken a fledgling WSO from a mere collection of musicians to being a truly professional ensemble."[18] He stressed two major contributions — the extraordinary improvement in the playing of the orchestra and the enormous task of successfully securing a concert hall for the city of Winnipeg. It was an interview that recounted the tributes penned by Manishen's own review in the *Winnipeg Free Press* of that evening's performance, and was titled "Conductor Soars above Nostalgia Concert Far Beyond Feldbrill's Homecoming":

> One of the great and rare pleasures at concerts is bring in the presence a veteran musician whose notable skills remain undiminished by time. As conductor Victor Feldbrill embarks upon the final week before his 80th birthday, his guest appearance showed him as vital as ever.... It was a concert as rich and rewarding as could be. Feldbrill is permanently bonded to the WSO ... its music director during the years 1958 to 1968 pivotal ones that ... saw the orchestra grow artistically as never before. He opened the Centennial Concert Hall. His career in prolific service of Canadian music can only be described as incomparable.... It was an afternoon of first-class music-making by an eminent Canadian who hasn't lost a step and an orchestra who knew it.[19]

On the CBC program *Metronome* of Saturday April 27, 1968, Neil Harris put the case directly:

> It is rather a cruel blow that after having struggled for ten years to make music in the wrestling arena they call the Winnipeg auditorium, he now relinquishes his orchestra just when they have a proper environment. To all those who say that the Orchestra has never sounded better, Mr. Feldbrill is saying this is the way it has sounded all along. You've just never heard it before.
>
> It is impossible to exaggerate the contributions Mr. Feldbrill has made to Winnipeg music. When he arrived here, our Symphony was a semi-professional organization struggling to provide Winnipeg with one of the symbols of a civilized city. Through his amiable dedication, he has placed the Orchestra on a professional basis, he has wrangled grants from the Canada Council, he has built a new audience through school concerts and free Sunday afternoon "pops" concerts, he has programmed more new Canadian music than any other conductor in the country, and he has instilled a new attitude about music in Winnipeg.

But even all that, in Mr. Harris's view, was not his greatest achievement:

> Mr. Feldbrill's major contribution has been, in my opinion, his insistence on professionalism. He has demanded that musicians be paid-professionals so that they can devote the time necessary to give professional performances. In demanding this kind of professionalism from his orchestra, he has paid us the highest compliment by assuming that we deserve the best.

Nothing that transpired after his 1968 resignation could take away the enormous triumph of the Feldbrill first half-decade that had transformed the musical life of a prairie city.

CHAPTER 12

"I Should Have Left!"

In a new millennium, looking back over several decades of extraordinary music-making, Victor Feldbrill could place his unique experience as artistic director and conductor of the WSO in some context. In his first few years, expansion of his vision, warmth, and appreciation had characterized his relationship with his orchestra and its board. He was in no doubt that he had achieved an extraordinary improvement in the work of the WSO and had introduced an enormous breadth of new repertoire that contained the music of twentieth-century composers from around the world, but particularly those who were Canadians.

He had made a remarkable intervention in reaching out to previously untouched adult audiences and had, in particular, initiated an amazing number of Winnipeg children and youth to the joys of symphonic musical expression. Victor could take credit for touring the orchestra outside the city to rural communities, where for many, attending a symphony concert had been a previously unattainable dream. Victor could also feel that he had reached a summit of success and that only a diminishing of his satisfaction could be expected. Yet the supreme moments of musical euphoria went on and on with concerts that surprised and delighted his listeners.

It is the fate of artists in any discipline to find themselves uncomfortably confronted by the walls of comfort and satisfaction that appear to damage virtually every human enterprise. Artists are automatically their own worst enemies — any achievement will signal the need for further creative change and challenging development. However, it soon means that old allies become new enemies as every step forward, no matter how seemingly logical and necessary, will arouse the opposition of those disciples who have become familiar and pleased with the heights already scaled. Every artistic victory over that complacency comes to have a cost. Forward movement invariably comes to mean the loss of support. There is an inevitable erosion of that warm confirmation that initially comes from a phalanx of welcoming allies. Inevitably, artists are lured into a context of believing that they can overcome those weaknesses of the human spirit they have encountered in others, and that, with a little patience, a unique paradise can be created. It was this remembrance of such discontinuity that Victor saw coming to a head by the mid-1960s. There remains no bitterness, but with calm statement of reality he sincerely believes that he "should have left after five years in Winnipeg. But the family was so happy, the girls doing so well in school and Zelda was coming into her own as a social work mentor and adviser. I had to stay!"[1]

Winnipeg was no easy place to become "the conductor." It was not a large, prosperous city with an army of well-to-do music enthusiasts ready to donate liberally and enthusiastically encourage others to provide the largesse upon which a symphony orchestra depends. By Victor's arrival in 1958, the WSO had certainly been given an adequate start on the road to orchestral competence and was aspiring to become a central agent in the cultural life of the community. But it had but a decade of performance under its belt! Two major arts organizations were already in place in the city

— the Manitoba Theatre Centre and, surprisingly, in what was so close to being a frontier community, the Royal Winnipeg Ballet. One might have expected a symphony orchestra to have had decades of presence before an internationally recognized ballet company would emerge, but it had not happened that way. In 1958, the question was whether there was room in the performing arts spectrum for a symphony orchestra at all.

Even in the latter years of the twentieth century, Winnipeg was still the wonder of the North American artistic world. Cities of that size might possibly have one performing arts organization at the international level of excellence, but not three such institutions. Using the presence of prestigious arts institutions as the criterion and taking size of population into the equation, Winnipeg is still Canada's foremost arts centre with outstanding opportunities in the visual arts as well as excellence in theatre, dance, and musical performance readily available.

There are those who believe that it is the circumstance of Winnipeg's isolation that demands such a response — that Winnipeggers had learned many years before that "doing it yourself" was the only course either in the arts or athletics. Yet in the case of orchestral music that isolation was a major factor in making it difficult for WSO conductors to replace instrumentalists, absent temporarily as a result of ill health or on a more permanent basis in the case of those players who had decided to move to a more mainstream urban centre. In spite of these limitations, it seems that Winnipeg has a special motivation in the fact of its isolation to create and develop the institutions that are essential to the expression of a rich cultural life.

At the time of his arrival Victor was faced with a motley collection of fine musicians. To create a worthy orchestra would demand a continuing commitment on their part — and resources to make it happen. For that reason, the placing of well over half of its players on a twenty-six-week contract (like the entire complement of the TSO and Montreal Symphony Orchestra) was a most important first step.

Expanding the performing activity was the only way to increase revenues to cover the costs in the short and long run, even if in the short run it would put even greater pressure on the budget. As well, governments at all levels had to be brought onboard to make an appropriate contribution. Victor's timing was perfect. By the end of the 1950s, a Canada Council for the Arts had been formed to provide support from Ottawa, and soon after that the Manitoba Arts Council, one of the first such bodies at the provincial level in Canada, came into being. By the 1960s, even municipalities were participating in providing arts funding. Even so, it was a constant struggle for Canadian arts organizations in communities faced with the disadvantages of access only to sparse populations and with enormous geographical spaces to cover in so doing.

There were difficult decisions that had to be made in the early '60s and later in the 1970s, when restraint replaced the period of growth and expansion. Performance excellence meant more and better instrumentalists and these could best be found in orchestras serving larger cities. Yet compared to New York, Philadelphia, or even Toronto or Montreal, Winnipeg was massively undeveloped in terms of the presence of large and prosperous corporations and foundations. But those very orchestras sometimes toured through Winnipeg, and the classical music enthusiasts wondered why these orchestras from such cities sounded so much richer than their WSO. Victor, while improving the existing WSO sound, would soon tell them why.

There was another aspect of arts administration in a smaller city — there was no possibility of solving internal confrontational issues quietly and privately. The inevitable conflicts within institutions soon prominently appeared in the pages of Winnipeg's two major dailies, the *Tribune* or the *Free Press*. That could be counted on!

In Winnipeg there was a long tradition of "in your face" politics. A mid-nineteenth-century rebellion in a Red River settlement had eventually allowed Winnipeg to take its place as the capital of a new province in a new national union. Decades later, a general strike in the midst of the triumph of Bolshevism in Russia after the First World War had occurred, not in Toronto, Hamilton, Montreal, or Halifax, but in Winnipeg. Trade union solidarity was seen as a reason for confidence in fighting any perceived injustice in any situation that invited a confrontational response. Indeed, the very centre of the radical left in Canada was North Winnipeg. The nation's most distinguished social democrat before the emergence of the incomparable Tommy Douglas had been J.S. Wordsworth and Winnipeg was his political base.

The city was proud of its unique politically activist tradition that included the work of Stanley Knowles, another paragon of left-wing politics who certainly had propelled Canada toward more progressive, socially responsibly policies — but had proudly participated in a style of direct political action that had an impact on the nature of any process of resolving Winnipeg controversies in the arts as well as virtually every other societal sector.

Music, like virtually every human form of expression has always been created and performed in a political context. "Serious" music had gone through an unparalleled political phase throughout the early and middle years of the twentieth century. Hitler's love for Wagner's compositions was but the edge of the realization that musical preference had political overtones. The banning of music written by Jewish composers in the Third Reich (that had included the works of Mahler and Mendelssohn) had not resulted in a reciprocation on the part of the Allies with the banning of Bach, Mozart, and Beethoven, but there were doubts throughout all the conquering Allied countries about the roles that composers like Richard Strauss and a host of performers, such as the renowned Elisabeth Schwarzkopf, had played amidst the horrors the short-lived Third Reich had inflicted upon Europe in the 1930s and '40s. An aspect of the "de-nazifying" of Germany in the second half of the 1940s had been a major intervention in the musical life of Germany, both the East and West sectors, particularly by American occupying forces. Victor had witnessed this phenomenon both in Germany and through his presence at the famous Concertgebouw performance in the Netherlands after the conclusion of the war.

Stalin's intervention in the Soviet Union's music-making of Prokofiev and Shostakovich proved it was not only right-wing politicos who had measured the impact of music on the political scene. The twentieth century initiated a debate about whether the nature of music composition in every jurisdiction had a political extension about which music lovers, whether creators, performers, or listeners, needed to be aware. With no evidence, there were those who believed that the apparent conflict that seemed a characteristic of music in the mid-twentieth century was an attack on the civilization they knew that emphasized melody and orderly rhythm. Others saw in the seeming formlessness and apparent dissonance of twelve-tone or serial writing of musical composition simply an appropriate response to the perceived limitations of traditional classical music in dealing with a frenetic and violent modern world.

Victor, with his years in the United Kingdom and Europe during the war, was familiar with all this baggage that music and other art forms had gathered, but he believed in the ultimate triumph of great music, whether it be the works of old masters or contemporary composers, over the perversities and irrationalities of violent and destructive human behaviour. He was determined that he would not be restrained by past events or present tensions. All good music deserved to be played and he was drawn particularly to Canadian creative spirits who were, after 1945, emulating the style and substance of music their colleagues were producing in foreign lands.

Even in North America, Aaron Copland, certainly the dean of American composers in the middle years of the twentieth century and a great supporter of Franklin D. Roosevelt's intervention on the side of the arts in his fight against the injustices and stupidities of the Great Depression, had his troubles with the House of Representatives Un-American Activities Committee in Washington, D.C.

In the politically charged atmosphere of Winnipeg, even the selection of repertoire was an intensive extension of ideological meaning that was not as obvious in other Canadian communities. Though he never commented on this aspect of possible contention, the confrontation over "too much Canadian contemporary music" had this underbelly of suspicion around Victor's perceived alliance with radical views. Victor, with his European experience, recognized this danger, but could only ignore these charges if the full musical listening needs of Winnipeggers were to be served.

There was no doubt that Victor was ploughing new ground in Winnipeg — particularly in the matter of supporting his belief that fair wages for honest work, even in the arts, was simple justice. And his choice of repertoire, so different from his predecessor's concentration on the mainstream Teutonic tradition, had to do with a belief that all music, like all rational opinions, had a right to a hearing. Indeed, he was determined to expand the listening tastes of every Winnipegger who would attend his concerts.

Yet Victor was drawn to the repertoire that included the less aggressive and more intricate selections of French composers as well as the climactic and melodic Russian composers. He believed that justice demanded that Canadian orchestras give a voice to Canadian composers. "Who else would do so?" was his constant query. It was not just the unfamiliar sounds, the less melodic styles and the more complex instrumentation that brought about the tension of Victor's latter years in Winnipeg. It was the largely unexpressed sense that he was interrupting the flow of comfortable, traditional, easily listenable repertoire and replacing even the familiar sounds of Elgar and Vaughan Williams with compositions that, for example, spoke to the erosion of empire rather than its celebration. In short, Victor's repertoire choices were seen to be fuelled by a vision of a world of greater equality and a more compassionate social environment. He was supporting that mission through the playing of these more complex Canadian works. Though it was much more than simply "left-right politics." It was no mystery that John Weinzweig was of a radical and intellectually questioning bent of mind. Though Victor's enemies might express these predilections more as a personal preference for the unfamiliar and challenging, it was not entirely inconsequential that Victor Feldbrill wanted to play the music of these musical social activists.

Predictably, in light of his sense of mission, Victor came into conflict even with other musical activities that were both prestigious and well-established in the city, in particular the Manitoba Music Festival, an event that traditionally dominated Winnipeg's musical life for several weeks each year. During those weeks, virtually nothing else musical could transpire. As well, Victor had a problem with the whole connection of music and competition. He had witnessed the worst aspects, the "turn-off" of young people to serious music as a whole when confronted with endless rehearsals of a single selection for performance before a panel of often faceless judges. He had suffered with the losers, some of them in tears, after a particularly cruel assessment, too often by an "expert" flown in from the United Kingdom. Such events had brought not the joy of music performance, but rather had surfaced music performance's capacity to bring pain and humiliation.

Through a casual conversation in a Winnipeg friend's home, Victor discovered his host's son's open hatred of serious music. A simple question revealed the reason. Were you in a music festival performance and had a teacher tell you not to sing? The lad was thunderstruck. That indeed was the cause of his anger. Before he left Winnipeg, Victor watched the young boy create one of the finest collections of classical music recordings to be found in the province while becoming an enthusiastic supporter of music performance of all kinds in the city.

Yet as a critic of the festival tradition, Victor conceded that he had seen success in competition result in a "take-off" of a young musician's career after a brilliant presentation and a rave review. He remained convinced that this identification of talent and intelligence could be achieved in a less competitive context that celebrated the accomplishment of making music rather than the sorting out of winners and losers.

Victor was also concerned about the way music was "used" in such competitions. He had initiated a tradition of featuring acceptable winners of a certain category at student concerts — but often he was confronted by a winner who could play only a single movement of a concerto. Victor, who loved that repertoire, found himself conducting a performance that had lost its wholeness and thus its intelligibility, in the name of promoting a virtuoso pianist or string player who had been a music festival winner. In the intimate setting of Winnipeg, his concern was soon broadcast abroad and represented yet another strike against his unquestionably splendid record as a conductor and artistic director.

This issue was hurtful for Victor, as no WSO conductor could have given more attention to the importance of having guest soloists from the Winnipeg community, including musicians who were regularly part of his orchestra often occupying first chairs in the various instrumental sections. As well, he regularly played the works of fine local composers. One of the most prominent was Madame S.C. Eckhardt-Gramatté, the creative spouse of the Winnipeg Art Gallery's director, Dr. Ferdinand Eckhardt, and Victor gave the first WSO performance of her Concerto for Trumpet, Clarinet, Bassoon and Orchestra and the world premiere of her Concerto for Orchestra.

There were, of course, the music critics, particularly those associated with the *Tribune* and the *Free Press*, S. Roy Maley and Kenneth Winters (who was in Winnipeg for most of Victor's tenure). Both were highly respected and had a loyal following. Conductors and performers rarely engage in public confrontation with journalists in their role as music critics. The reality is that the critic not only has the last word, but likely the word engraved in print, and any conflict between performer and critic, especially in the case of a resentful regular reviewer, can result in a spate of negative reviews that can damage the artistic reputation of even the most talented performer. Victor was a rarity in his willingness to "take on" the critics for any lapses in judgment he felt to be unfair or unwarranted. It was also Victor's view that music critics were typically much too preoccupied with the literary opportunities that the newspaper column offered and were too often attempting to follow in the footsteps of George Bernard Shaw, whose music reviews were masterpieces of a quality that would have assured him eternal prominence even without his prolific theatrical offerings. Victor was sure that the truth was often sacrificed to the question of "how the review is going to read," and the "invention of new turns of phrase" inevitably became paramount to the disadvantage of securing a clear, positive observation of what the concert was seeking to achieve. As well, he expressed some dissatisfaction about the fact that visiting ensembles were treated much more gently by critics, who placed much higher expectations on the WSO than could be met given the limitations posed by the inadequate budget of the local ensemble.

At times, the confrontation reached unparalleled levels of vituperation. In his review of a concert in January 1965, Kenneth Winters referred directly to the controversy in his *Free Press* review, indicating that there was "a feeling abroad these days that Conductor Feldbrill and the Orchestra should be getting more encouragement in the press ... I share the feeling ... when are they going to start deserving it?" He went on to claim that the WSO had become "stodgier than for several seasons" and while conceding the financial constraints, concluded that "a standstill has been reached. How does one encourage a standstill?"[2]

Sometimes, Victor's allies came to his side, writing letters that referred to Winters quite unfairly as a "so-called music critic, the worst of its kind in North America," but such confrontation only raised the stakes of the battle and these struggles did not endear Victor to those who represented his best chance of reaching the Winnipeg public. There is a cost to such engagement in public controversy and Victor paid the price for expressing his views so bluntly and so dramatically, or indeed, for having over-zealous supporters ready to raise the temperature of every dispute over music performance.

Victor, on arrival, had moved quickly in sorting out the organizational direction that made possible his hopes for orchestral quality. But even that most necessary step had within it the seeds of tension. There were still some thirty or more players who would not be a part of the professional nucleus, that is, not under any contract. Victor saw the "nucleus" as a beginning and eventually hoped to see the entire orchestra under contract — but financial pressures held him back. The "non-professionals" had to play the same music as the "nucleus" performers in the program for full orchestra. But these non-contract players had to work every day to make a living outside the WSO. Thus, their time for personal rehearsal was limited and the conductor was asking them to play very complex contemporary music, which some believed made unreasonable demands on their capacity to perform at the highest level. As well, rehearsals had to take into account the work schedules that placed these individuals at some disadvantage in relation to their orchestral "nucleus" colleagues. Victor bridged the gap with his considerable experience in dealing with musicians and their representatives, but the opportunity for those outside the "nucleus" feeling diminished on occasion, was certainly present and became an unfortunate aspect of the political dynamic of the orchestra.

There were individual cases of confrontation that were unavoidable. The leadership of the incumbent concertmaster is an essential element in the musical governance and inspirational source within any symphony orchestra. Victor found at the first rehearsal, to his horror, that the WSO concertmaster was, first, a very prominent political and social figure in a city in which his position and status were widely known and rightly honoured, but had a vibrato in his violin performance that damaged the tonal quality of the entire first violin section of the orchestra. It was an intolerable situation that had to be resolved as quickly as possible.

Thus, on his arrival, Victor was faced with having to replace the most prominent member of the orchestra, one whose wide recognition for civic political involvement was respected and appreciated. (At one point, he had been elected to the provincial legislature.) Victor was successful in removing the flawed incumbent after three seasons and recruited a splendid violinist from the Vancouver Symphony — Lea Foli.[3] But it was not without consequences among those who felt that the sound of the orchestra should be sacrificed in the cause of the proud reputation of this public figure prominently displayed in its membership ranks.

The boards of arts organizations are necessary but troubling entities in every jurisdiction. They are essential as keepers of the public purse when major donations from government represent a good portion of the operating budgets of theatre and dance companies or symphony orchestras. As well, private donors and foundations need to have a window on the decision-making process of such agencies. The membership of these boards is a problem. They must include membership on the part of the donors but also must include in their numbers people who care deeply about the artistic mandate and its expression. Maintaining the balance was and is today not an easy task.

The WSO Board that had invited Victor to take over by a unanimous vote was a splendid combination of local businessmen, CBC production personnel, and community music enthusiasts who understood how orchestras functioned, along with a number of individuals who were simply loyal volunteers.

But the turnover of board membership is inevitable and in most cases much to be desired. However, new people have different commitments and expectations. Invariably, different values and priorities emerge and the conductor may be faced with a revolt in the ranks of the very people to whom he must look for support and to whom he is legally responsible. In a large metropolis, the various confrontations and accommodations that must be reached never become public. In Winnipeg, even if conflicts did not always play out on the front page of the *Free Press* or *Tribune*, these differences too often were the subject of widespread public knowledge, often through rousing Letters to the Editor or articles in major community publications that took one side or the other.

Equally damaging can be the conflict of artistic leadership and the managerial and administrative focus of arts organizations. Victor, for a host of reasons, came to believe that the incumbent WSO manager was undermining his position. Even the laudatory comment from touring successes failed to be conveyed either to board members or the local press. Offhand deprecatory remarks from management figures were given credence by repetition throughout the community. This type of standoff could not go on indefinitely but the resolution of the conflict came only in Victor's last year, when Leonard David Stone was hired and his presence augured for peace and deeper understanding in place of tension and confrontation in the musical scene that faced Victor's successors.

Eventually Victor found himself engaged in debates in board meetings around such issues as the playing of encores at the end of performances. There were some board members who saw the promotional value of a regular encore at the conclusion of every concert. Victor was adamant that after a major symphonic work there should be no trivialization of the total listening experience by the playing of a "lollipop" (as Beecham identified the short, melodic offerings he sometimes used to end his concert programs). Victor, who had carefully and thoughtfully programmed every concert program to achieve the most effective climax, one that would most dramatically impact itself upon the audience, was outraged by this defilement of his purpose and refused to compromise. He even embarrassed one recalcitrant board member who was describing his trip to the British National Theatre to watch Lawrence Olivier's performance as the title character in *The Merchant of Venice* by asking him whether this popular thespian, at the conclusion of the play, had quoted a jolly limerick or two before the audience finally allowed him to leave the stage. The point was driven home but at a price.

Even more disquieting was the furor over the regular playing of "God Save the Queen" at the opening of every concert. By the 1960s, it was very much out of fashion, particularly in Britain, where Victor was quite familiar with orchestral practices. When he decided that this abeyance to a nationalistic symbol should cease in Winnipeg as it had in other concert halls around the Commonwealth, the uproar was considerable. The issue and its resolution aroused all the powerful but normally latent feeling about the Empire and encouraged confrontations between those audience members with old traditional expectations and the recently relieved new-comers for whom this practice was quite irritating. The differing views raised all the shibboleths of left-wing leanings that could be directed at those not wishing to wear their patriotism on their sleeves by those for whom these symbols were their only protection against the complete triumph of "radical" predilections that had infected the community of Winnipeg. It became a *cause célèbre*, a controversy that neither Victor nor the WSO Board needed in the context of gathering support, especially financial donations, from every corner of Winnipeg society. It was simply a soul-destroying "lose–lose" battle, with no winners in sight. In the end, Victor got his way — the British national anthem was played only at the first concert of the season — but again victory came at a price.

Throughout the final years of his contract, these and other issues around repertoire and concert style and practice surfaced month after month, much to Victor's frustration. These normally latent divisions within the Winnipeg community could significantly undermine even the making of good music.

Victor knew that the Ukrainian community had a reputation for nurturing great choral music. This sizeable Winnipeg minority had a famous choir that Victor wanted to use in a work that featured a demanding bass line perfect for the men who were part of the Ukrainian Male Chorus. But there was in place a commendable Philharmonic Choir and among its members were those who resented any seeming displacement by another collection of voices, even though Victor wished only to add to the quality of a single dynamic presentation and certainly not compromise in any way the splendid sound he was seeking to achieve at the regular performances of the Philharmonic Choir. Yet, innocently, he was intervening in the latent competitiveness of choirs that should have no place in the making of great music, but, alas, does! Victor won his battle — the Ukrainian men sang with the WSO, producing a glorious sound, but the struggle against inclusion of "outside" choristers eroded the positive nature of the entire enterprise. This issue came up again with Victor's presentation of the Beethoven *Choral Symphony*. Additional singers produced a memorable performance. Yet once again there was a loss of support that threatened all that he had achieved.

It is paramount that the artistic director has complete responsibility for the individual concert programs. By the latter years of Victor's time in that post, even this principle was in danger of being breached. Victor had been successful in securing for a concert appearance the Amadeus String Quartet, one of the finest chamber ensembles on the international touring circuit. These musicians came because they wanted to reunite with Victor who had joined them in Vienna on one of his European visits in the 1950s. It was a courageous choice. There are orchestral enthusiasts who cannot abide the "preciousness" of the string quartet. However, although it would indeed play as an ensemble in one the great Schubert classics, Victor wanted to engage the first violin and violist in a performance of one of the treasures of the orchestral repertoire, Mozart's glorious Concertante in E-flat Major for Violin, Viola and Orchestra, another first performance for the WSO. The presentation was a triumph. Kenneth Winters wrote ecstatically of the orchestra's "sensitivity and dignity, skill and warmth," and concluded that the orchestra "gave as delightful an account of Mozart as I can remember."[4]

However, as Victor conducted he was aware of the unpleasantness that the announcement of his coup in seducing the Amadeus Quartet to travel to Winnipeg had caused at the board meeting. He had been grilled and questioned, the most discouraging of the latter process being the query, "Who are the Amadeus Quartet?" The assumption emerged that if the questioner had not heard of the ensemble it could not be very good. But behind this farcical interchange was the realization that the distance between certain members of the board and the conductor was widening.

Yet throughout all these tensions and confrontations, the WSO and its conductor continued to provide outstanding concerts. One reason shines forth — Victor's reputation as a conductor of outstanding accompaniments to outstanding international instrumental and vocal soloists. John Fraser, a Toronto critic, had referred to Victor as a soloist's "dream conductor." An Isaac Stern or a Byron Janis and their agents knew that in Winnipeg there would be a splendid, sensitive, balanced performance that would satisfy, indeed inspire, both audiences and musicians. That became known as a given and was an enormous advantage as many performers were not anxious to take the extra time to visit an isolated city in the Canadian West and face incompetent accompaniment in the bargain. And in spite of all the controversy over a host of issues, the great music continued. The list of outstanding concerts performed by world recognized musical figures could not be denied. In every way, the orchestra was reaching out to ensure that the great symphonic repertoire of the ages was played by the greatest internationally recognized interpreters.

Nevertheless, by 1965, with all this tension, it was time for a showdown. Victor expressed his anger and frustration in what was most certainly the most direct and focused commentary on the behaviour of a board of an arts organization that could be imagined. He termed it a "Report to the Board of Directors from the Music Director," dated November 1965. In light of the fact that few on the board had been in place in 1958, when Victor had agreed to come to Winnipeg, some historical background was necessary. At that time the orchestra had normally played only ten subscription concerts and perhaps three student presentations annually. Within a year, he had raised the number to sixty such presentations and the years of expansion and significant improvement had begun. He pointed out that "then came the frugal years," reminding his board of a motion that had been passed "that the size of the orchestra be decreased, that salaries of the players be decreased." Though there had been no follow-through "the whole idea of expansion came to a standstill." In spite of his personal outrage, he told them, "I have made every attempt possible not to let this 'image' [of the presence of a fine orchestra] down in the public eye, as many of you are aware." However, he added, "in this respect some of you have indeed let your organization down."

Victor conceded that no conductor is acceptable to everybody but in his view it was the "responsibility of Board Management to present a united positive front to the public regardless of what is going on behind the scenes." He made a serious charge that "a subtle but deliberate attempt to undermine the 'image' of the conductor has taken place." He placed specific evidence before his board colleagues. News of his triumphant European engagements the previous summer were not included in the WSO concert programs and Columbia Artists Agency, a prestigious organization presenting artists across the continent, had been informed that Victor "would not be around" to participate in future decisions about musical development in Winnipeg.

The criticism of orchestral quality he felt to be particularly unfair. Major orchestras still played in Winnipeg on tour across the continent. Board members continued to question why the WSO could not sound like these visiting American ensembles. Victor could only respond that there were "30 reasons, nearly all in the string section" — a reference to the constant loss of fine violinists, "plus salaries in other orchestras two or three times higher than what we pay" — a reality that affected every section of the orchestra. He reminded his board members that he had "voluntarily postponed a raise in his own salary so that an extra dollar or so a week could be added to some of our musicians' salaries." He recounted his efforts to find sources of fine instrumentalists, for example, "at the New England Conservatory in Boston," but had to concede that though there had been a noticeable improvement in the brass and woodwinds, he had been unable to solve "the viola and harp problems." However, with low salaries, there could be no major developments, and Victor told the board, "'[it's] your decision' ... my initials are V.F not J.C. I cannot create miracles."[5]

It would be wrong to conclude that the WSO Board of Directors was unanimous in its determination to change Victor's course on these various matters. Leonard Isaacs, board member and director of the University of Manitoba's School of Music, by the end of 1965, had had enough. In a letter to the board chairman, R.W. Richards, he took on the critical voices of the community as well as his colleagues on the board, making the point that "no doctor or lawyer would tolerate the destructive criticism from non-professional sources." He found no evidence to support any of the criticism Victor was facing. In fact, he stated, "I can only regard expressions of non-confidence as being without professional foundation." He then proceeded to provide a review of a recent performance which he described as "unified and stylish, out of which the soloist's parts sang and soared like angelic voices."[6] There was certainly no universality in the board opposition to Victor's efforts, and there was even less indication that represented the orchestra members or audience, but there was reason to consider moving on.

By 1965 Victor had decided he would not seek any further extension to his contract, but would complete his tenure in 1968 and from that point would turn to other interests that would bring artistic delights without the pressure of satisfying a board that not only expressed impossible expectations but undermined the capacity of the conductor to make the improvements they desired. He looked forward to embracing the role of a free agent, indeed a free spirit, able to establish himself as an available guest conductor and accept short-term contracts with various orchestras, and, as well, to set a course toward becoming an educator.

During his time in Winnipeg, Victor had been presented with a Concert Artists Guild of the U.S.A Award in recognition for his work done on behalf of young people, "to assist them to reach their potential as artists." He was the only Canadian who had ever been honoured in this way and it led him to include as a priority in his future the education of children and young adults. His love of children and respect for their needs had been described by virtually every observer as one of his strongest attributes. Victor took every opportunity to reach out to them — it was always a central focus of his work. However, teaching in a university while still conducting was an enticing possibility.

For Victor, having turned forty, decades of career options loomed ahead. He was determined to make the best of this spectrum of exciting experiences that he hoped would stretch out before him. He did so without fully realizing the dangers that were contained in resigning from a position of considerable prestige when, in Canada, there were so few opportunities for a comparable position or level of remuneration. It led to a difficult period of doubt, disappointment, and dismay that affected Victor's entire family. These reactions were abundant even while all the accolades were descending upon him.

Nevertheless, the intense commitment to the performance of Canadian music never wavered even as his days in Winnipeg came to an end. In this regard he became a national hero. Indeed, many of Victor's absences from his podium and his city were the result of invitations to perform the repertoire of Canadian composers across the country. For example, in February 1963, Victor was invited by the Canadian League of Composers to conduct the Montreal Symphony in an all-Canadian program that included the music of Alexander Brott, Morel, Pepin, Somers, and Schafer. The *Montreal Star*'s reviewer, Eric McLean, recognized the singularity and importance of this event in the musical life of the nation and what it said about the pathetic state of regular Canadian orchestral music performance: "There ought to be a law against the kind of concert that was given last night at Plateau Hall [a complete program of nothing but unfamiliar Canadian music]. The law should rule against the circumstances which make such a concert necessary."[7]

Two years later, in October 1965, the CBC hired Victor to conduct a program of entirely Canadian works. Freedman's *Images*, Adaskins's *Saskatchewan Legend*, Archer's Divertimento, and Pepin's *Guernica* were the offerings for a national broadcast. Once again it was Victor who was perceived, particularly in Winnipeg but also across the country, as part of a conspiracy devoted to the cause of securing the performance of music by Canadians no matter the cost in terms of audience desires and predilections.

There was another irony in the mix. As a result of this obsession, Victor had been successful in securing a special contribution to the WSO from CAPAC, one of the major bodies responsible for securing compensation for artists, in this case, Canadian composers, whenever their work was performed. It gave a thousand-dollar grant to Victor's WSO for their willingness to program a selection of Canadian music (and bear the overtime costs of rehearsal). Even though his enthusiasm for performing Canadian music brought modest financial gain to the orchestra, Victor received few plaudits for so doing.

It was in 1967 that Canada's composers came to his side. Perhaps the award that Victor most came to value was that of the Canadian Music Citation from the Canadian League of Composers. He was the first recipient and only orchestral conductor who ever received this award. It was presented to him on the stage of Toronto's largest and most prestigious performance venue, the O'Keefe Centre. Srul Irving Glick, a splendid composer, read the citation. The award had been established to honour "a musician who has shown dedication and outstanding achievement in performing Canadian music ... who has consistently programmed Canadian music ... and has presented it with dedication and enthusiasm to the public ... and has interpreted it with conscientious fidelity." It described Victor perfectly.

The League gave this award to only three Canadians — one was Robert Aitken, a fine instrumentalist who has given his life to the encouragement of the performances of Canadian composition, and Mary Morrison, a splendid soprano who sang and encouraged the singing of Canadian vocal music and then went on to become an instructor to dozens of Canadian professional singers at the Faculty of Music, University of Toronto, who in turn were to sing Canadian works on the world's stages. The selection of Victor as the initial recipient had been a political action. It was a statement that here was an orchestral music director who had made a commitment to the creative spirit of Canadians and was a symbol of what the country could be if a similar commitment was forthcoming in every centre where an orchestra, a choir, or an opera company was to be found. It was Victor's finest hour as his time in Winnipeg drew to an end. The award came to be a reminder of the singular recognition of his composer colleagues as well as a symbol of Victor's ongoing struggle to perform Canadian music from podiums across the country. Unfortunately, it must be said that it did little to inspire other conductors to emulate his determination to perform the works of Canadian composers.

There was splendid irony in the timing of the Artistic Director's Report in 1965. A particularly extensive two-week tour had been planned for the spring of the WSO's 1964–65 season. The orchestra would visit twelve cities in the northwestern United States, just the second of such tours for a Canadian orchestra. (The TSO had made one such foray some years before.)

The WSO tour was a brilliant success. At the University of South Dakota at Vermillion, there was an audience of nearly three thousand people. As one observer pointed out, the WSO "gave its most stirring performance of the tour." It was here that the WSO was asked if it would consider being the resident orchestra for the local university. A WSO supporter reported that "our conductor was especially applauded for his vigorous conducting and commentary prior to each selection ... introducing each number as if presenting a gift to an audience anxious to receive it."[8]

In Minnesota, Victor was described as making "succinct and appropriate" comments on the composition or the composer listed in the program: "The audience approved of this practice ... it helped provide a better rapport between them and the music." It was not a normal procedure for Victor, but he realized he was performing before audiences whose experience of the classics was meagre indeed. A local critic observed that "Victor Feldbrill is a top-ranking conductor. He knows the limits of his orchestra as well as the strengths that he has exploited to the limit."

Critics in these communities "gave praise to Winnipeg for having such an orchestra." The difficulties were not inconsequential. In Worthington, Minnesota, the concert was one hour late in starting as the tour bus had engine trouble. In South Dakota, a twenty-two-inch-deep snowfall in the Black Hills delayed the orchestra's arrival, but the two concerts went on and were wildly cheered.

As the WSO press release reported, "Reviewers used such phraseology as 'musical brilliance and artistic joy,' 'brilliant performance,' 'wonderful, intense, exciting and varied program, well-balanced orchestra,' and a 'rare treat.'" The *Austin Daily* was quoted as stating that "the important point was that the Winnipeggers made a genuine hit. They have stature and vigour and a fine Conductor and repertoire."[9]

The orchestra members were enthusiastic ambassadors distributing to audience members Centennial pins (inviting potential tourists to historic celebrations of Winnipeg's beginnings) and information about the city's hosting of the upcoming Pan American Games. It was estimated that thirteen thousand people had heard the orchestra in twelve concerts in communities that were anywhere from a mere four inhabitants to communities of fifty thousand people. As well, Victor had ensured that the inhabitants of these states had heard one piece of Canadian music — John Weinzweig's *Edge of the World*, which one reviewer described as a "hit" that "made use of the wide range of tone colour in the melodic line as it passed from one instrument to another."

There was irony in the fact that this triumph had come from serving audiences in the United States. Victor's relationship with the United States was highly ambiguous. He most certainly appreciated the recognition that the American Symphony League had bestowed upon his orchestra and had no reluctance in developing most ambitious tours of the northern American states. He recognized the affinity in challenges faced by these Americans who shared the topography of the central region of the continent with his own audiences in Manitoba and other western provinces. They, too, lived in a cultural desert, a state that had once been the common experience for all Canadians across that 49th parallel.

While artistic director in Winnipeg, Victor had accepted membership on the executive of the American Symphony Orchestra League, the only Canadian conductor invited to serve on this body to that point in time. He developed warm friendships with conductors of American symphony ensembles and learned much about the American musical scene. He expanded his enthusiasm for the music of Aaron Copland, whom he had met at Tanglewood many years before.

But he knew other composers, like Leonard Bernstein and Alan Hovhaness, whose music he had played and whose patriotism had been questioned by the Senator McCarthy assault on free expression, musical as well as literary. These investigations had undermined the American culture of tolerance and openness during the post–Second World War years. The mindless fear of a communist threat of world domination had made the United States an unpleasant destination for seemingly radical composers and performers of their music. He certainly celebrated the comparative Canadian tolerance that allowed for such breadth of thought and expression. One night in the late 1960s, he received a telephone call at his Winnipeg home from a significant American symphony orchestra. He was asked if he would be open to an invitation to become that ensemble's conductor. It was minus thirty-five degrees Fahrenheit in Winnipeg in the midst of a normal frigid Manitoba winter. As well, it was becoming cooler in the Winnipeg musical environment. The caller presented a seductive invitation from an orchestra with a more generous budget, playing in the much warmer climate of the southern United States. As well, he was aware that such an appointment would ensure a host of guest appearances with prestigious orchestras across the United States.

Victor was flattered. There had been an effort by Sir Adrian Boult and Herbert Howells to keep him in Britain. Canadian colleague Robert Farnon had remained in Britain and done well. But Victor, like many creative and talented Canadians who remained to create the cultural explosion in post-war Canada, was determined to stay in his native land. With little hesitation he turned down the invitation. "I did not want my children to grow up and remain in the United States." That statement revealed a swath of justifications. Certainly Zelda, within her family's commitment to socially aware politics, would not have been comfortable. And there was Victor himself. He had become an outspoken, articulate leader in his country, prepared to confront governments for their parsimonious treatment of the arts and performing arts institutions. He saw problems in the American setting he would not want to tackle. It was not only his preoccupation with contemporary repertoire, but, by this time, his enthusiasm about his trips to the Soviet Union. Though critical of the repressive political system he found there, Victor had commented generously on the artistic strengths he had experienced. He would have been a target in the United States for the radical right and he had no interest in playing that role. He stayed in Canada and it was his base of operation for the rest of his career. He was simply unwilling to consider the offer even from an American orchestra that promised more remuneration, wider career choices, and a warmer climate.

A perusal of the WSO programs indicates the extraordinary breadth of repertoire that Victor had brought to his Winnipeg audiences. The central German repertoire had been played liberally under his predecessor, but there was little of the music of French composers who had come to the fore in the nineteenth and early twentieth century. Victor had programmed these composers and insisted upon rehearsing his players relentlessly to achieve the appropriate sound he wanted. For a January 1963 presentation of Ravel's *Daphne and Chloe Suite No. 2*, the result was evident. S. Roy Maley commented:

> Under Victor Feldbrill, the performance had the high
> crest of sonority, the sensuous languor and the authority

of distinguished performance ... as well as the truly allur-
ing and ear-filling sonorities of the orchestration with its
gurgling woodwinds, sighing strings and ecstatic harp ...
one of the best performances ever given by the WSO.[10]

And the Russian repertoire was extended significantly. The year 1963
saw a stellar performance of the Shostakovich Symphony no. 5, one that
indicated "how far the WSO has advanced in technical and musical skills
since the performance given in 1957...."

By the end of that year, Victor had had mounted a performance of Ralph
Vaughan Williams's Symphony no. 4, a presentation that Kenneth Winters
regarded as a "turning point," where "the orchestra had reached its stride"
since the beginning of the concert season. The following January, Victor provided memorable performances of three major symphonic works from three
different musical cultures and had distinguished his orchestra in so doing.

While Victor was becoming the national figure devoted to the perfor-
mance of Canadian works, most often for the first time, this attention was
also being directed at works by well-known composers of other nations.
Bartok was given a considerable number of initial WSO performances
(Concerto for Orchestra, *Dance Suite*, Divertimento for Strings, Rhapsody
no.1 for Violin and Orchestra) and attention was directed toward Benjamin
Britten (*Sea Interludes from Peter Grimes*, Serenade for Tenor, Horn and
Strings, *Variations on a Theme of Frank Bridge* and *The Young Person's Guide
to the Orchestra*.) Even Brahms's Double Concerto for Violin, Cello and
Orchestra, his *Tragic Overture*, and Symphonies no. 2 and 3 had never been
played in Winnipeg before. Perhaps even more surprising for an orchestra
in a Commonwealth country was the previous absence of Edward Elgar's
Cockaigne Overture, his *Enigma Variations* and his Concerto for Violin and
Orchestra. Victor had been relentless in filling in the gaps of nineteenth-
century composers who had received little attention from the WSO. For
example, even Rimsky-Korsakov's *Scheherazade* had never been played
before by the WSO and Victor rectified the absence of that popular work.

An indication of the broad reach of Victor's programming is the fact
that he also introduced twenty-one works by Mozart (including eight symphonies) that had never been heard in Winnipeg. The Haydn Symphonies

no. 15, 88, 93, 96, and 103 were all also performed there for the first time during his tenure. Most dramatic in his contributions of little-known compositions were the works of Ravel, almost ignored before Victor's arrival. He added to his audience's experience the composer's *Daphnis and Chloe Suite no. 2*, the Introduction and Allegro for Harp and Orchestra, the Piano Concerto in G Major, and his *Rhapsodie Espagnol*.

Popular composers like Schumann had nine works never performed by the WSO and there were five works by Prokofiev similarly treated. Indeed, as one would expect from a conductor intrigued by modern works, Richard Strauss had his Concerto no. 1 for Horn and Orchestra, *Don Juan*, *Four Last Songs*, and *Til Eulenspiegel*, chosen to be performed by Victor along with Stravinsky's *Circus Polka*, Concerto in D for Strings, Concerto for Piano and Winds, *Petrouchka Suite*, *Firebird*, and *Symphony in Three Movements*.

There were represented a host of composers whose works had never appeared on WSO programs. For example, Aaron Copland, the most popular of American classical composers, was introduced by the playing of his *Appalachian Spring*, the *Suite from Rodeo*, and his *Fanfare for the Common Man*.

What this array of "new music" meant for both orchestral members who had to learn all this repertoire and for subscription audiences who were invited to expand their understanding and appreciation of these unfamiliar compositions was an individual matter, but it followed the path that Victor wished to take — the expansion of the conscious performance and listening experience of everyone involved, both performers and members of the audience.

Many of these first performances received enthusiastic response from curious subscribers and even critics. Berlioz's *Symphonie Fantastique* was given a "superlative" performance to conclude the season (1964–65) with "high distinction." S. Roy Maley went on to say,

> Feldbrill's reading was remarkable for its delicacy and suggestion in passages of a more subtle nature. He eschewed the usual highly coloured, slashingly painted, mural-like concept of the *Fantastique* and instead created a series of all-together engrossing chiaroscuro studies.[11]

Victor, while recognizing the pressure to scale the mountains of great new works and the extra attention it demanded of each audience member, was convinced that artists needed this variety of musical experience to grow, and listeners' musical lives would be gloriously enhanced. They would inspire each other with their willingness to seek out change and accept positive development, something that might not be achieved by the playing of the Beethoven Symphony no. 5 for the hundredth time.

In 1968, there was the inevitable farewell concert in Winnipeg. It was, of course, in the new concert hall that Feldbrill had fought to have built against considerable odds. At one point in the half-decade campaign, it had mysteriously slipped off the list of priority items the municipality was struggling to place before the province and the national government. Only a gathering in Victor's living room and a full press on the agendas of every level of government brought the mission to a successful conclusion. Victor and Winnipeg and all its citizens received the fine, single-function, acoustically thrilling Centennial Concert Hall. And it was here that Victor's long-term contribution to Winnipeg's culture could be properly recognized decades after his departure.[12]

The program that Victor conducted was warmly received. All the political figures of the municipality of Winnipeg were present, as well as a splendid array from the provincial government of Manitoba. There were the speeches of appreciation from an array of distinguished Manitobans extolling all that Victor had done, and the response of the members of the orchestra was particularly animated. All in all, it was a farewell concert to remember — in the new Centennial Hall, with acoustics that could enhance rather than diminish the sound of a good orchestra.

The most dramatic intervention came to the audience, who opened the evening's program to find a list of all that had transpired in the ten years of Victor's presence in the city of Winnipeg.[13] It was a staggering record of accomplishments that illustrated what one human being with passion and ability could do, even when faced with enormous odds that too often frustrated his efforts. More than any sound that instruments or the human voice could have expressed, it was a catalogue of what Winnipeg would be losing when Victor and the Feldbrill family returned to Toronto.

CHAPTER 13

Louis Riel and the World of Opera

Before Victor departed Winnipeg, he was confronted with an opportunity to participate in one of the most exciting moments in the musical life of Canada — the mounting of a major production of a new Canadian opera by the nation's foremost ensemble — the Canadian Opera Company (COC), based in Toronto. It was to be part of the COC's major contribution to the country's 1967 centennial celebrations and it was assumed that after a run in Toronto's O'Keefe Centre it would be toured at least to Montreal's Expo but possibly to the United States and abroad.

The work was to be written on commission by one of Canada's most prestigious composers and a good friend of Victor's, Harry Somers. The composer had made one point very clear: even though Victor would be based in Winnipeg throughout the planning and rehearsal stages and for a year after the Centennial presentation, Harry wanted him to conduct the production of his opera. He knew he could trust the one conductor who had made the playing of Canadian music his central cause and calling, and there was to be no substitution of his involvement in the launching of this his major work.

There was a warm response from Victor. By the mid-1960s, with all the tensions around the relationships with the WSO Board, a major project beyond Manitoba was a perfect distraction. As well, Victor needed to know what direction he should be planning to take when his time in Winnipeg concluded in 1968. He was determined to make his gifts count in the years that lay ahead.

A newly composed Canadian opera represented an option, indeed was a symbol of a new path — a concentration on musical theatre, one he needed to consider, one of several that came to mind in the years before ending his tenure in Winnipeg. By 1966, sorting out his future was the central focus of an apparent mid-life crisis that contained a realization that after 1968 there was a terrifying prospect of unemployment facing him, but as well a positive, exciting opportunity to make a major shift in his life work.

Any effort to analyze the quality of a career in mid-stream must be shaped by an appreciation of the values and expectations of the individual being considered. Upon reviewing Victor's life, one might, for example, be led to believe that the height of Victor's career was that of being the artistic director and conductor of the symphony orchestra of a major city in the very centre of Canada. A misleading conclusion might be reached that, at the age of only thirty-four, Victor had reached the "mountain-top" of his career, and that now, at forty-four, his subsequent vocation had gone into a decline. Nothing could be farther from the truth.

The more accurate assessment, based on Victor's philosophy and behaviour, leads to a different conclusion. If the metaphor of scaling mountains must be maintained, Victor's tenure in Winnipeg can be viewed much more accurately as a plateau of achievement from which a series of further triumphs could be launched. The future might have much more to do with performance of the great music of his country and a forging of an influence on the quality of its musical presentation through the teaching of the young and less to do with administrative trivia in one community. Through the process of presenting music in the decades that remained, he could play a part in developing the culture of his entire native land. This path represented his basic values, which had less to do with status and power and much more to do with fashioning the cultural landscape of Canada.

Indeed, Winnipeg, surrounded by vast stretches of water and flat lands, visually modelled his situation, allowing him to see intellectually what might be accomplished in the world of musical composition and performance even beyond the borders of his own country. For example, that city had been paramount in centring his attention on the ways in which young people could be drawn into a delight in musical performance that would change their entire future. In reaching out to these young people and children and recognizing the context in which they were developing their interests, he had come to understand how concerts that brought families together to listen were at the pinnacle of the strategy for reaching new audiences upon which every orchestra must depend. As well, in Winnipeg, his encouragement of the performance of contemporary and especially Canadian music had come to be seen as essential if music was to become part of the lives of both music-makers and their audiences.

Unexpectedly, Winnipeg had become a launching pad for a series of projects that gave greater significance to the use of his time and talent than he assumed any specific leadership role as a conductor and/or an artistic director for a single music organization could.

The remaining decades of Victor's long and active career were not filled simply by building a musical empire of one sort or other, nor were they restrained to that of devoted tenure upon any one podium or another in any particular city, region, or country. Rather, Victor focused on the essentials necessary to maintain the cultural contribution of ensemble performance that would also display the outstanding instrumental virtuosity in dozens of symphony orchestras across the country. He put his attention to the strategies for developing new audiences in a variety of venues, focusing especially upon the young. He promoted Canadian musical expression which was accessible but also directed toward the creation of a planet that emphasized peace, justice, and goodwill. These were the years where he did so in the context of his own personal lifestyle, which included a commitment to the strength and unity of his own family, one that could be an inspiration to other colleagues and audience members facing the challenges of surviving in a fast-paced, technologically obsessed environment, one that was dramatically overtaking the arts community and the society of which he was a part.

⋙

There were continuing basic preparations that Victor needed to address before he could make any decision about his future after the WSO. It could be said that Victor had more professional experience in musical theatre than in any form of musical expression. The years in the pit for *Meet the Navy* had taught him a great deal about this genre of music-making, even if that particular production was closer to musical comedy or, more accurately, vaudeville.

However, his experience in this field went much farther back. Indeed, his first conducting experience had taken place when he found himself in front of the Harbord Collegiate student orchestra playing in Gilbert and Sullivan operettas presented nearly each year of his high-school career. The product of these two extraordinary British figures was not truly operatic, yet surprisingly many of the skills and attitudes that surface in *Tosca* and *Rigoletto* and even *Die Walküre,* can be found within the musical expression and the theatrical movement to be found in the *Pirates of Penzance* or *H.M.S. Pinafore.*

Perhaps the most obvious contrasting element in these theatrically staged forms of expression to that of orchestral performance is the collaborative nature of such presentations. A dominant over-arching ego of either soloist or conductor cannot survive the test of the collaborative approach demanded by theatrical forms of musical expression. Victor, from the outset, had forsaken the recognition of his considerable talent as a solo violinist, and had found his way into the orchestral environment or, failing that, into the precious world of chamber music ensembles — duets, trios, quartets, and quintets. Victor revelled in the give and take of debate and discussion and the collective experimentation that resulted in a more co-operative synergetic interpretation of a musical work. This kind of democratic procedure could not work in the large orchestra any more than pure Greek democracy of the city-state forum could be introduced into the workings of a massively populated industrial nation. He knew that opera, though, demanded the presence of a creative team with many talents that had to be included in the vision of any successful production. For good reason Victor was drawn inexorably to the orchestra pit of the operatic instrumental ensemble.

After he had returned from the war to the facilities of the University of Toronto's Music Faculty and the Toronto Conservatory, it was to Nicholas Goldschmidt, the conductor of the Opera School, he was assigned by an overly pressed Ettore Mazzoleni for instruction in the techniques of conducting. Though, in Victor's view, that linkage had produced little, he did remain the concertmaster for the Opera School Orchestra, observed the Goldschmidt performance, and, on occasion, replaced him on the podium. There were satisfying moments on the university campus, in Hart House, and downtown Toronto theatres. Indeed, one of Victor's earliest public conducting experiences had been a Hart House concert performance of *La Bohême*, excerpts involving students from the Opera School.

Victor soon realized that there seemed little future for any Canadian conductor who wanted to put grand opera as a high priority in his working life. In Ontario, before the 1950s, opera had been confined to a small group made up in part by fairly recent immigrants, who, thankfully, had decided to move the CBC toward radio performances of opera and in some cases into the hallowed halls of academe on the university campus.

Thus it could be said that even by 1951 there was little live opera on public stages even in major Canadian cities and there was little opportunity for any young conductor to find an opening and begin to gain experience in what was most certainly a complex process of preparing oneself for the special challenges of that genre of music-making. In practical terms it was apparent that at the University of Toronto Goldschmidt could handle all the conducting chores, and he remained in place until just before Victor moved to Winnipeg in 1958.

It was in 1956 when Victor returned to Europe for further study and another opportunity to measure his skills with those graduating from the universities and conservatories on that continent that a series of circumstances associated with admission complications resulted in his landing in Salzburg and the classes of Meinhard von Zallinger, the music director of the Munich Opera. The work being addressed as the test piece was

Mozart's *The Magic Flute* and within a few days Victor had so impressed von Zallinger with his progress that he received an invitation to conduct a segment of the final gala concert. There was disappointment on both sides when Victor had to decline the invitation in order to return to Canada and an engagement he had contracted on home territory. The session with von Zallinger ensured that Victor's interest in opera never diminished throughout the rest of the '50s and '60s.

Even while in Winnipeg there had been two occasions when Victor was contracted to provide the accompaniment for Canadian Opera Company touring productions. In the early years, as Canada's national opera company, there was pressure on the COC to bring opera to those in more remote areas of the country ... a role that was eagerly accepted. Where there had been no opera presence, busloads of singers now arrived with minimal sets and costumes, but no orchestra. The presentation was reduced to a piano accompaniment or a local ensemble like the WSO if there was a Victor Feldbrill able to gather and conduct the local musicians. In October 1963 it was Mozart's *Cosi fan tutti* in Winnipeg's Playhouse Theatre, and the COC director, Herman Geiger Torel, was delighted with Victor's performance with his WSO players and became Victor's advocate as an opera conductor. The audience response was electric. Critic Kenneth Winters recorded in the *Free Press* that "the opera was extremely well accompanied by local players under Victor Feldbrill," and that his conducting had been "crisp and delicate ... there was no gainsaying that he swept the whole opera along in a warm and lively fashion."[1] Not only was the evening a delight, but the WSO Endowment Fund was advantaged by the addition of a few thousand dollars.

More and more, opera excerpts appeared on WSO regular concerts, often with local singers as well as international operatic "stars." Even overtures and segments from Wagnerian operas demanding large orchestral forces were played at subscription concerts. For example, the *Overture to Rienzi*, one of Wagner's most often played selections, opened a November concert to which Victor had attracted an associate, cellist Leonard Rose, to return to Winnipeg to play the Brahms Double Concerto for Cello and Violin with concertmaster Lea Foli.

At this time, Victor began to establish a national reputation as having a special strength in accompanying opera soloists. John Fraser, a Toronto critic, had already proclaimed him Canada's "dream conductor" in this role: "He permits the orchestra to express the subjective as well as the objective values of the music to be fulfilled ... frees his orchestra of any extraneous brilliance or volume that would detract from the performance."[2]

When, two years later, Victor made similar arrangements to bring the COC touring ensemble to Winnipeg to produce *Die Fledermaus*, it was well attended and enthusiastically received. Kenneth Winters did not appreciate the selection, which he described as "really just an operetta," but indicated that its success on the Winnipeg stage was the result of the "crisp support and guidance provided by the orchestra and Mr. Feldbrill.... Indeed, these were what carried the day."

Though this opera did not meet the Winters standard for this genre of music-making, it proved so popular that a decade later the Manitoba Opera Association (MOA) decided to mount it once again for three performances. The MOA management, remembering Victor's previous leadership of the COC production, called upon him (by now a faculty member of the University of Toronto as well as a part-time conductor with the TSO) to return to Winnipeg as the opera's conductor. It was a fine production that much benefited by Victor's presence on the podium. It occasioned a very warm review by Chester Duncan on CBC's *Arts National*, broadcast coast to coast. He began by commenting on how much he hated opera as a genre but continued to give a heartfelt accolade to Victor's performance.

> My last word on this production is personal. I am proud to regard Victor Feldbrill as my friend, but when I heard this transparent score approached with such bite, crispness and charm I feel that merely to say I admired it is not enough. Victor Feldbrill's work in *Die Fledermaus* was undoubtedly the most musical and intelligent thing in the whole show.[3]

Victor's decades-long contact with the COC, along with that company's confidence in his capacity, was of paramount importance in the most prestigious operatic event of his life — the creation and performance of *Louis Riel* as the COC's major contribution to Canada's centennial celebrations in

1967. There were good reasons for composer Harry Somers's confidence in Victor's ability to bring dynamic leadership to the enterprise. Their friendship went all the way back to the early 1940s when they were both in secondary school. Just as Victor had represented Harbord on the TSO's Student Concert Committee in the 1940s, Harry had represented East Toronto's Malvern Collegiate. They had met once again in the late 1940s at the Conservatory. Harry's decision to be a serious music composer had left him in somewhat poverty-stricken circumstances that made him dependent on work outside the world of music. In fact, Harry Somers was identified in the media as both a talented Canadian composer and a highly competent taxicab driver.

Victor had, by the 1960s, been promoting Harry's music for some years. He had played some part in convincing the COC that commissioning an opera would be an appropriate response to the nation's anniversary and that Harry would be the perfect composer of such a work. Actually, the COC decided to commission two operas. Raymond Pannell, an active composer, was asked to provide a second opera based on a play called *The Luck of Ginger Coffee*. It turned out to be a poor choice. As Morey and Schabas relate in their volume on the COC,

> *Ginger Coffee*, which opened the Centennial season at O'Keefe, was disappointing, being in great part a rather ineffective play with music that owes much to Menotti, Weill and Bernstein.... Its interest depends on words sung, but many of these were lost in the vast O'Keefe Centre. The work also lacked operatic drive, for want of a better word....[4]

This disaster left the landscape clear for what Schabas and Morey, in their description of *Louis Riel*, refer to as an "all out success ... one of the COC's finest achievements." After only twelve hours of rehearsal, it was plain that the work would be the pre-eminent COC production, one that not only would be the feature presentation in the Toronto COC season but would be the city's main presence in Montreal's Expo musical events, where an array of six of the finest opera companies in the world were putting their best feet forward on the occasion of Canada's hundredth birthday.

It was ironic that the selection began with a profound questioning of the appropriateness of Louis Riel being the subject matter of a celebratory production. (He was, in truth, finally hanged as a traitor and his conviction and execution had been the theme of almost a century-long confrontation between English- and French-speaking Canadians from coast to coast.) It was suggested that only over-serious Canadians would present such an opera at such a time of celebration!

Yet the work portrayed all the conflicts that have been at the country's very centre from its beginnings and Mavor Moore, with Jacques Languirand's assistance, provided a libretto that captured the tension. Somers's score was brilliant, one for which "Feldbrill skillfully worked out the many diverse elements."[5] Director Leon Major, designers Murray Laufer and Marie Day, and conductor Victor Feldbrill made a splendid team. They were all committed to a collaborative approach from the beginning and shared a single view of what the opera was designed to achieve. Rather than producing an historical account of French-English differences, the opera engaged the tragedy of a troubled man's efforts to bring democratic ideals to an empty land. That land was eventually to become central to the union of British colonies that eventually formed the Dominion of Canada. The libretto was clear and Somers was prepared to allow Feldbrill the freedom to adjust the orchestration when it seemed too strong to allow the full understanding of the text. Thus, Victor truly became a member of a creative staff that produced a sensation!

It came about with great difficulty. With two new productions, as well as an array of more popular operatic works in the COC's season, there was not sufficient time for rehearsal. As well, Victor was still ensconced in Winnipeg, responsible for what was happening in the city's Civic Auditorium, organizing the WSO's response to the Centennial and overseeing the transition to a new orchestral venue that he had successfully steered into being. However, with the commitment of both performers and technical staff, the rehearsals went magnificently.

Trish Baldwin is the highly respected managing director of the world-renowned Toronto-based Tafelmusik Baroque Orchestra. However, as a clarinetist on the University of Toronto campus in the 1970s, she played in Victor's TSYO as well as the UTSO. But her memory goes back even farther to the time when, as an eight-year-old child, she was taken to *Louis Riel* rehearsals by her mother, an active COC volunteer assisting with comforts for orchestra and singers during scheduled breaks. Trish was allowed to sit in the auditorium out of the way of everyone. She was transfixed. She was moved mightily by Victor's "passion for the music" and impressed with his sensitive handling of the orchestra players: "He was so patient working the players through all this unfamiliar music."[5] As a member of his youth orchestras in later years, she realized that she wanted to make music or work to have it made for the rest of her life. She eventually abandoned wind instrument performance and now lovingly manages the baroque orchestra Tafelmusik — a national cultural treasure based in Toronto but touring the world and playing in the finest venues.

Harry Somers was ecstatic that he had brought Victor onboard. In an interview on CBC Television, Harry made the point that he already knew Victor well. Somers appreciated the fact that Victor encouraged composers to attend rehearsals of their work — unlike colleagues who often barred them from any presence. But more important for Somers, "he knows every single nuance of what I am seeking to achieve."

Louis Riel received more attention than perhaps any other opera presented in Toronto. It was revived the following year (1968) as part of the regular COC subscription series and again in 1975 when it could be offered to the Kennedy Center as a gift to celebrate an American national anniversary.

The re-mounted *Louis Riel* exuded all the values of a repeat production. On that occasion, in the February *High Fidelity* magazine, critic Harold Schomberg proclaimed that "in addition to stage direction more adept that I have seen on the operatic stage in years, Conductor V. Feldbrill seemed in total control of the rocky rhythms of the complex score." In that same year, Riel returned to the O'Keefe Centre and Victor found himself conducting the TSO, at that point in time the COC's "pit" orchestra. It was said that he led "with even greater authority," and John Kraglund of the *Globe and Mail* commented on the "precise and enthusiastic fashion" of Victor's conducting.[6] William Littler, referring to *Riel* as "music drama" rather than opera and under the headline "Craftsmanship in Louis Riel Stands out in Polished Review," made the point that "Victor Feldbrill was leading the Toronto Symphony with even greater authority."[7] One American critic suggested that he would be ecstatic if an opera of this quality could be composed for the anniversary celebrations of America's beginnings.

Even more surprising, in 1969 *Louis Riel* was telecast on CBC to the entire nation. Finally, on the hundredth anniversary of Riel's death, the Canadian Music Centre released a recording of a CBC pickup from the Kennedy Center stage production on October 23, 1975. Nearly four decades later, it could be said that Harry Somers's *Louis Riel* is still the high point in the commissioning and performing of Canadian opera. Not until 1994 and the production of Randolph Peters's *The Golden Ass*, with the story and the libretto provided by Robertson Davies, was there a comparable homegrown success.

The first years of the twenty-first century have seen a stream of Canadian operas arrive on the nation's stages. Along with the staggering flow of Canadian opera singers, they signal the possibility that opera, like choral music, may be a genre of music-making appropriate to the strengths that Canadian composers and performers possess. Unfortunately, the circumstances producing such an opera thrust came too late for Victor. The triumph of *Louis Riel* could not be sustained until more wealthy opera companies arrived on the scene who could take chances with fragile box-office receipts. For decades after this success, it was still a time to feature the Verdi and Puccini operas whose well-worn and familiar tunes ensure a full house.

Victor's interest in conducting opera was certainly whetted by the success of *Louis Riel*. Even before he left Winnipeg he had another project on his plate. An English composer, Humphrey Searle, had composed *Hamlet*, a work with an English libretto that as of the late 1960s had not been accepted by any opera company in the United States, Britain, or in continental Europe (though a version in German had been presented in Hamburg). It was based, as one would expect, on the magnificent Shakespearian play that confronts nearly all English-speaking students at some point in their learning lives. However, as much as composers had admired this great work, putting it to music had been an elusive prospect. The Opera School on the University of Toronto campus, after Arnold Walter and Ezra Schabas had met with Searle, decided that it wished to give this monumental work its first hearing. Needless to say, it was a daunting task, but the expected arrival of Victor Feldbrill on campus in 1968 would provide a respected conductor who would no doubt give the performance all the excitement that *Louis Riel* had provided.

As it turned out, the production was not a success, but Victor earned the admiration of the composer, who felt that the Toronto presentation, as a result of Victor's efforts, had been more successful than a subsequent London Covent Garden effort. The unfortunate fact was that the text had overwhelmed the music. The libretto was caught up in the play's poetry, following too closely the words of the bard. The music could not elevate the experience, the unforgettable lines suffered unforgivable diminishing and the expectations of a dramatic and theatrical triumph were unfulfilled. Victor was deeply disappointed.

Victor's return to Europe in 1968 and 1969 with the support of the Senior Artist Award from the Canada Council was also to some extent a diversion from the negative aspects of seeking to give too active leadership to the WSO. Though there had been generous recognition of his work, there was still the residue of bitterness associated with the coming break. It was difficult to forget the hurt and humiliation of all the conflicts and, though public celebration of his achievements took place, the disappointment remained even to the point of damaging the warmth of the Feldbrill household. To some extent, going to Europe as an element of his departing year in Winnipeg was a defence against permanent damage to his psyche.

Things were not made easier by the fact that Victor's future was still quite uncertain. He was approached by Winnipeg music lovers even in European cities who expressed their disappointment at his leaving. These encounters brought back sad memories on every such occasion. It was not clear, for example, just what his role would turn out to be in Toronto, the only community that he had considered an appropriate future home for his family. Yet all the conducting positions of interest to him in that city were occupied. Though Niki Goldschmidt had left, there was no indication that the Opera School was deprived of the conducting skills of numerous replacements. Ettore Mazzoleni remained in place on the Toronto campus. It was in this state of mind that, while driving to Toronto with his car filled with paintings and other valuables, he learned of the tragic loss of "Mazz," his mentor and friend, under the wheels of a car. Now Victor would be returning home to Toronto devoid of the presence of both Mazzoleni and MacMillan.

The loss of these two giants was easier to bear once the family had arrived back after school ended and Victor's sister Eileen had found her brother and Zelda a lovely home at 170 Hillhurst Boulevard in North Toronto. After a single year in high school, Debbi could go off to university, but Victor had to fight the Forest Hill Secondary School administration to secure an appropriate grade entrance in a junior high for Aviva. Ontario, being the only province with a Grade 13, had disconnected its system from that of every other province in the country, making transfer from other provinces to Ontario and vice-versa more complicated than it needed to be.

The award from the Canada Council made it easier for Victor to share his hesitations about his gradual transition while in London, England — his "favourite city by far" — and among old colleagues of some two decades at the BBC, especially after a particularly warm welcome transpired in the city's orchestral establishments he knew so well. One of his first stops was the Festival Hall where his closest colleague Sir Adrian Boult was conducting. Victor said it was like going "home." At the BBC he encountered CBC producer Jeff Anderson who introduced him to his broadcasting colleagues as "the finest conductor Canada possesses." But his ultimate destination was to be Sadleir's Wells and Covent Garden and the study of opera being produced at its highest level. There was another agenda in Victor's mind. If things did not work out in Toronto, he wanted to examine whether there might now be a future for him conducting in Great Britain and Europe. Obviously he needed an effective agent who would look after his affairs across the ocean.

There was yet another purpose to be served by his trip to Europe. *Louis Riel* had been such a success at home that it might become a sensation in Europe if only he could find a number of opera houses courageous enough to experiment with a touring production from Canada.

He had complete confidence in both the quality of the work and his Canadian colleagues' capacity to produce world-class performances. In his travels during these weeks, he approached the management of Covent Garden as well as those of opera houses in Brussels, Amsterdam, Geneva, and Lyon, all to no avail. The name Louis Riel meant nothing to Europeans who had never heard of this obscure character or his pathetic little rebellions in the remote parts of North America. In fact, Victor was very persuasive about the quality and relevance of *Louis Riel* and was very close to winning the day but lost the support of Canadian External Affairs officials who decided to assist the sending of a French-speaking cultural entity, *Les*

Grandes Ballets Canadiens. Politics in bilingual Canada had trumped the opportunity to present a great work in Europe and Britain.

There was obviously too much to do in one trip, so the Canada Council Senior Artists Award became a support system for a few weeks across the ocean both in the fall of 1968 and, as it turned out, the spring of 1969. At Covent Garden, it seemed fortuitous that the first production whose dress rehearsal he should view was his old favourite, *The Magic Flute.* While he was there he met contemporary composer Humphrey Searle whose score of the opera *Hamlet* he was studying. He was able to point out a number of mistakes and Searle was "grateful and amazed" by Victor's command of the work. As for the Mozart opera in rehearsal, now being readied for opening night, he informed Zelda that he found the tempo "overly pushed ... with speed taken for brilliance." [8]

However, Victor's attention had now to be directed toward the fundamental flaws that infected opera productions in virtually every country he visited. For example, he found the sightlines of the staging failed to provide a clear view of the conductor for either the soloists or choristers. Acoustical problems affected the balance of sound. This was happening in established opera houses, a structure that did not yet exist in Canada, where the genre was forced to endure traditional theatre stages, if lucky; if not, school gymnasiums. Yet that same stage at Covent Garden was the setting for a "magnificent performance of Aida," with "a Triumphant March that looked believable ... not something out of Disneyland." [9]

From London it was off to Hamburg, where from his hotel Victor viewed a full-scale protest of terrifying dimensions involving "hundreds of police," on behalf of what cause he never discovered. The city's opera house was new — the historic opera venue having been destroyed by British bombs in the 1940s. However, the post-war structure was wonderful, with "rich wood and continental seating." It was a great place to start, to be followed by opera houses in Brussels, Amsterdam, Düsseldorf, Munich, Geneva, Zurich, and Vienna. Scandinavian and Italian opera venues would have to wait until April 1969.

In Europe, Victor found what could only be called an opera industry. Virtually every urban centre of any size was expected to have an opera company operating nearly year-long. There were permanent conductors in some cases, but as well a coterie of travelling conductors, directors, designers, and singers who moved from one location to another, few of whom had any real involvement in the community served by any one of these operations. He found the quality of the work of these smaller opera companies was very uneven, moving from the magnificent to the abysmal.

Too often operas were mounted with little rehearsal and it showed up in choruses that were "ragged," orchestral ensembles that were "indifferent," and soloists whose voices were not matched by any theatrical skills and seemed strangely uninvolved in the drama at hand. With all the effort that Victor had expended on *Louis Riel* in the months before the centennial year, he had felt himself at the centre of a splendid production and was quite confident in the assessments he was making of other operatic efforts. Even though most of his time was spent in major prestigious opera houses in Europe, overall he found himself profoundly disappointed.

Of special interest though, he found in Europe there was a commitment to new twentieth-century opera and that there were generous subsidies that could allow productions that drew small audiences and few box-office receipts. Unfortunately, he also found massive self-indulgence that did the genre of opera no great favour. It became his view that, large or small, opera companies were putting on too many productions that were minimally rehearsed. In some cases the community's symphony orchestra was in the pit, but beyond that role they might play only a dozen regular orchestral concerts in a season — much to the disillusionment of many musicians who were committed to the symphonic repertoire. Their frustration affected their performance of the operas. In other houses he saw singers whose presence onstage could only be explained as misplaced loyalty for fine performances in past seasons. Even the opera house in Hamburg presented a soloist playing the role of a Tristan who was "gross, uninvolved and sang out of tune."[10]

Victor was particularly appalled by the results of inadequate directions from conductors. On another occasion it was plain that the chorus in *Madama Butterfly* was "sloppy" because sightlines made it "damned difficult to see the tempo," and "the soloists with excellent voices were frustrated because conductors never gave the singers a chance to make a musical phrase."[11]

He found conducting colleagues who were solidly prepared and others in the pit learning the score as they turned the pages. The frantic schedules of those companies playing an eleven-month season ensured there were disasters galore. Yet it was apparent to Victor that in Canada lengthening the "on-stage" time for individual opera companies was essential if real progress was to be made.

He met Canadians performing on European stages wherever he travelled, reminding him of home and increasing his desire to be with Zelda and his girls. It also convinced him that in Canada there were in place misplaced granting council policies, both federal and provincial, giving generous support to Canadian singers to train abroad but providing minimal commitment to support opera companies at home in Canada. It meant that all the investment in talent and musical intelligence was benefiting opera houses across Europe. Victor even threatened to confront the secretary of state, Gerard Pelletier, with this reality when he returned to Canada.

On occasion there were moments of hell on the rehearsal stage that completely infuriated him:

> The Italian conductor Bruno Moderna was struggling his way in the pit to such a point that the orchestra and chorus lost all discipline — the orchestra played anything it wished (sounded like a bad high-school orchestra). The people onstage kept talking and joking and generally not giving a damn.... Not once were the singers and the orchestra together and aware of what horrible sounds were coming from the stage and the pit![12]

In the three hours that Victor remained on site there had not been fifteen minutes of operatic music. He attended the performance and concluded that the production was beyond redemption. Yet in that same opera house a performance of *Salome* was "truly great."

In Munich, Victor was warmly welcomed at Salzburg by his teacher from some twelve years earlier, Meinhard von Zallinger. His opening comment, "You were one of my most talented people," gave Victor a positive jolt at a time when his confidence was on the wane. In this case, Victor was confronted with a conductor who knew exactly what his role should be. As he wrote to Zelda, "He balanced the volume for each singer — it was fascinating to hear." [13]

Incidents from these travels enabled Victor to realize his own impact on those he had worked with and helped to shape his decision about his future. In Munich, it turned out that the timpanist had played under his baton through the original presentation of *Louis Riel*. He was ecstatic about the quality of that Canadian experience and informed his colleagues of Victor's "greatness." At the same time, Victor felt he impressed other local luminaries with whom he was conversing with his uncompromising analysis of the state of European opera. One director, Alfred Knopf, also in Munich, wrote to him after such a discussion: "If there are people of your calibre in Toronto, I would not mind going there to work in the opera department — there is rarely such honesty and perception here." [14]

Victor came to the conclusion that in Canada "we could do opera properly because we are not tied to any dead tradition." In Europe he had seen opera at its best and worst. There were moments of elation that had lifted his spirits and moments of despair where the "rot" had taken over.

While still in Munich, Victor had developed a strategy in his observation routine. With confidence in the artists who were in the trenches with whom he conversed, he was learning about European opera "from the bottom up."

"I am absorbing a great deal of the 'routine' of the pit through osmosis," he told Zelda. Even in Munich he had been disappointed in the "lack of involvement and absence of projection" in some of the productions. Conductors seemed untouched by the needs of soloists. In the *Marriage of Figaro*, Victor felt the tempo was so fast that the arias became "unsingable."

Victor chose to visit Augsburg, near Munich, where he met Peter Ebert who had taught at the Opera School in Toronto and had expressed the hope that he would like to return to that institution. For good reason, "Your conducting of *Louis Riel* was incredible" was his welcome comment and he hoped that this event presaged real progress in the making of music in Toronto.

All the positive things were not just happening to Victor. It was in Augsburg that Victor received the note from Zelda describing a moving moment in her professional life. At a school where she had been working, a child she had spent many hours mentoring saw her enter, ran and threw his arms around her, and told her just how much he loved her. She was overwhelmed and deeply appreciative of this gesture. This was also an indication of what she was doing back home and a reminder to Victor that he had a spouse back in Canada making a monumental contribution to other peoples' lives. Perhaps there was a lesson for him in his search for meaning in a future in music.

Finally, he reached Vienna and its Opera House. But even at this paragon of opera offerings he watched a *Don Giovanni* that was "amateur" and "unbelievably stupid" and a production of Verdi's *Falstaff* that completely missed the "hilarity" it should express. In short, the initial contact had left him "cold ... there were no fires being lit."

Yet things could change within a single night. "There was a production of *Rosenkavalier* that sent me into a veritable orbit ... it was visually breathtaking ... with an orchestra of eager players," all members of the Vienna Philharmonic. This sound could indeed be replicated in Canada. His assessment of the production was that "it was the orchestra that was the star." [15] Ironically, many years later that was where Toronto's COC would find itself when it turned out that Richard Bradshaw's development of the orchestra into a splendid-sounding virtuoso ensemble was indeed the place to begin.

Victor would return home via Amsterdam, a city that for him contained not great opera as much as his close wartime friends, the Boosts, with whom he wanted to keep in touch. They found him tired and somewhat depressed — his state of mind was affecting even his physical appearance.

In the spring of 1969 he returned for another visit but found no earthshattering resolution to the universal problem of presenting a complex genre that, without almost limitless funding and profound commitment, was beyond solution. However, what stuck Victor dramatically was the dead weight of the past and how it bore down upon singers, instrumentalists, directors, conductors, and designers alike. The European response was to do more — an eleven- or twelve-month performing season, along with an annual schedule of twenty to thirty operas being mounted, often with disappointing results (if not complete chaos) onstage. That strategy must be avoided in Canada.

In the spring of 1969, it had been back to Europe and its opera houses, but not without feelings of remorse that on occasion threatened to overwhelm him. His first letter to Zelda spoke of his two lives — the one *with* his family and the other one that was preoccupied with only writing to his family.

Then it was back to London's Covent Garden, where he came upon rehearsals for the opera *Hamlet*, the very work he had premiered (in English) in Toronto. There Victor met total disbelief that he could have miraculously "pulled off" the opera in six weeks of rehearsal with the UTSO and singers from the Opera School. He had audio tapes that revealed the quality of the performance: "It was the talk of the town among the opera sophisticates." He had also met the conductor, Edward Downes, and watched him conduct a rehearsal, discovering that "he had fallen into the built-in trap of settling into a monitory tempo. There seemed to be no contact of podium and stage with the singers still relying on the prompter's box for cues."[16]

It did not bode well for Searles's opera. It was mounted but failed to find any place in the opera repertoire at Covent Garden or elsewhere. Victor had acted as an adviser in the latter stages of rehearsal and he became known as the result of Searles's introductions as "the Canadian, the conductor who did such a brilliant job on my *Hamlet* in Toronto."

It was a vote of confidence in the mind of a man whose expectations of himself had been damaged and whose complete recovery was yet to come. He found the opera community of Covent Garden most appreciative of his efforts. To Zelda he could observe that these were the signs of "the respect of creative people who make all the struggle worthwhile."[17]

Then it was once again back to Munich and von Zallinger. His disappointment with European singers elicited a surprising comment that Feldbrill found quite fascinating: "No opera schools in Europe are preparing students as thoroughly as North American schools." It was a comment that Victor recalled when the graduates of the University of Toronto Opera School began to dominate European, and indeed American, opera stages in the late twentieth and early twenty-first century.[18]

Victor then went off to Rome, Milan and La Scala, and eventually Geneva, Switzerland. By this time he believed that the opera picture was becoming quite clear in his mind. "I think I should have an interesting report to make," was his conclusion.

Victor came to believe that Canadians could produce opera at the pinnacle of international standards. He had just come from an experience with the COC and had worked with brilliant people who cared deeply — from technicians and orchestral musicians to the artistic director. In retrospect, there had been freshness and a spirit of delight in the work, particularly the experimentation he had witnessed and been a part of. With adequate resources he believed Canadian creativity would shine through. Victor was sharing a new confidence that was spreading from all the success of the centennial events of 1967. Perhaps this optimism was premature, but Victor had a vision of a country devoted to the presentation of its culture. His experience in Europe had convinced him it could be so. In 1969, however, and in spite of the triumphs of 1967, there was little interest in this vision. Indeed, these were years of reduced funding for the arts in the wake of the centennial expenditures for celebration that could not be maintained. The solution was that arts institutions, and especially opera companies, must become more entrepreneurial and the private sector must pick up more of the costs. That did happen in the later decades of the century, but it was not fast enough to make best use of the contribution that Victor had prepared himself to make.

There were opportunities once he was in Toronto and easily available to the Canadian Opera Company. A year after his return, he conducted the National Arts Centre Orchestra as the pit band for a COC production of Mozart's *Don Giovanni*. William Littler appreciated the "light, lively texture" of the "fine, swift and neatly woven" orchestra, claiming it to be "the real hero" of the evening, under Victor Feldbrill's baton.[19]

It was followed a year later by Feldbrill's podium leadership for a COC Toronto mounting of Lehar's *Merry Widow* (once again, like *Riel*, directed by Leon Major) and later in Ottawa with the NACO in the orchestra pit. Tuneful and gorgeously presented, critic Lorna Bettes could nonetheless see the role that Victor was playing: "Feldbrill allowed time for the music to expand often to the point of achieving a sumptuousness, yet conjured up rhythmic sparkle that constantly delighted."[20]

In 1973, Victor had taken the challenge of conducting another COC production of a Canadian opera, *Héloise and Abelard*, with the score composed by Charles Wilson and the text created by Eugene Benson, a writer of some stature in the Guelph community. It was not a great success; indeed, John Kraglund commented that the opera had been held together by Victor's "way with a contemporary score." The most positive review came surprisingly from critic Harold Schomberg, writing for the *New York Times* of October 19, 1973, who commented, "Victor Feldbrill conducted with superb efficiency…." Perhaps that was his way of commenting on the limited quality of the score.

In the fall of 1974, Victor continued to indulge his interest in opera by conducting that most popular of all operas — Bizet's *Carmen*. It was not a memorable event in the COC's history, though John Kraglund did comment that Victor had been successful in "getting crisp, well-balanced playing from the TSO" in the orchestra pit.

It was clear that Victor had learned a great deal about opera from his European travels and this showed in his opera conducting of the early 1970s. The expected "output" in Victor's mind of his subsidized tours of the opera houses of Britain and Europe was a report to the Canada Council that would transform the opera scene in his native land. In fact, all that was really required by the council was an account of his use of the funds that had been provided. As it turned out, his observations and recommendations were of little interest to the Canada Council. The time of progress and expansion was over now that the centennial year celebrations had passed by. Opera, the most expensive of all the forms of performing arts genres, was not a popular place for investment in the 1970s.

It turned out that *Louis Riel* was Victor's crowning achievement, one in which he distinguished himself as a conductor of opera. Leon Major, the director, credits Victor for much of its success: "Victor had the ability to breathe with the singer. Being a violinist, rather than a keyboard artist, he fully understood the importance of the legato line. He also was sensitive to the needs of individual singers while recognizing his responsibility to keep it all together."[21]

Even though his observations were enormously valuable to those to whom he communicated verbally, the timing of his report to the Canada Council had come at the wrong time. Canadian opera companies, including the COC, were not far enough along in their development, and the granting agencies were not yet capable of providing sufficient funds.

As well, there were no champions of the kind he was seeking "on the ground." He wanted to encourage the creation of great opera performance, but from composition to production. He wanted Canadian opera to be in the hands of Canadians. At the COC in Toronto, the 1970s brought a new artistic director, Lotfi Mansouri, who convinced himself and many Canadians that there were no Canadian designers or directors and few singers who could reach his standards of excellence and thereby fill the unresponsive space of Toronto's O'Keefe Centre with great sound. Many of those Canadians prepared by Herman Geiger-Torel for a career in opera simply disappeared and were replaced by citizens of other lands.

There was, however, a "swan song" for Victor, in collaboration with Harry Somers, of *Louis Riel* fame. It was in the 1980s, when Lawrence Cherney and his Soundstreams entrepreneurial operation, as a part of the Sharon Temple initiative just north of Toronto, brought librettist James Reaney and Somers together to create an opera. It was called *Serinette*, a small but beautifully presented depiction of the life and times of the Children of Peace, who had created an extraordinary structure that had become a venue for glorious music. It was carefully prepared with a two-week workshop in 1989 and given nine performances in July 1990 at the Sharon Temple, with Victor Feldbrill on the podium. It was also recorded for broadcast on the CBC and released as a two-CD set, the first opera to be given such wide attention. Indeed, in the new millennium, a concert version of the piece was presented in Toronto's St. James Cathedral to the delight of a large and appreciative audience.[22]

However, it was a very special story, tied to a very particular venue, and without the full commitment of an opera company it had a limited life on stage. It was the final operatic moment for Victor, but one he treasured in company with Somers, Reaney, Cherney, and a small cast and orchestra that had produced a veritable "gem" and a recorded version that showed that this genre could become a source of pride for Canadians in both the east and west.

By the end of the century, a new vision and new people like Richard Bradshaw would bring into question the attitudes that were holding back the enormous possibility that Victor and his analysis of the world of opera, along with the experience of *Louis Riel*, would hold for the future of opera in Canada.

CHAPTER 14

Inspiring the Young

As Victor prepared to leave Winnipeg, there was unanimity on one aspect of his contribution to the musical life of that city that was celebrated with not a single dissenting voice — his extraordinary outreach to children and youth. It was plain that in Victor's view, the minds and spirits of the young could be reached — but only with the finest works of both historic and contemporary composers, and with the best performances that he could coach from his instrumentalists in the WSO. This was no small task, as "kids" music was considered by some musicians as "throw-away" time, a time when players could relax and enjoy the luxury of less demanding standards of performance.

This demeaning attitude toward the young is not a disease that afflicts only music practitioners. Throughout the arts, there has been a tendency, now thankfully in decline and close to extinction, to regard the serving of the young mind as most certainly a trivial enterprise compared to that of reaching out and inspiring the mature, who hold power and influence in our ship of state with its emphasis on economic prowess and political astuteness. At the lowest level of justification, it is these people who command the capacity to reward, both individually and corporately, those who give their lives to the art of making music. Understandably they must be rewarded!

A most unfair picture, but when one compares the public or private support (if any at all) that has been directed to children's literature, children's theatre, and children's musical performance in mid-twentieth-century Canada, it was invariably minimal in most jurisdictions. The finest performance and display of children's creative talent received little media attention, token grants, and insignificant corporate largesse. Nor did arts practitioners who gave attention to the artistic needs of young people expect rewards or attention commensurate with their commitment or creativity.

The last decades of the twentieth century saw the comparative obliteration of music in the schools when the competitive pressure of globalization and the technology that supported it captured the attention of most educational jurisdictions. There was little concern expressed about the impact on the learning lives of young people when the arts were de-emphasized and under-funded in our visual arts, music, or theatre classrooms from coast to coast.

There are two extremely close observers of Victor's career — his daughters, Debbi and Aviva, now having raised families of their own. His close relationship with them was rich in its quality and broadly contrasted in its nature. There is one matter upon which they are agreed — his work with children and youth was the most significant of all he did, more important than the awards he received for his efforts in the maze of activity which surrounds the world of orchestral performance, even more than his struggle on behalf of Canadian composers. Here his intervention was unique, deeply considered, and long-term in its reach. "He loves kids" was their chorus. Walter Homburger, the TSO's splendid administrative leader for so many years, can only explain it with a degree of disbelief: "At concerts he became one of them … he never lost his patience … he enjoyed their company both as individuals and as well their presence in his audience."

Victor made himself unpopular by constantly demanding adequate rehearsal for children's, youth, or family concert programs. As well, the repertoire for these presentations, he believed, must be appropriately accessible and not to be perceived as trivial or inconsequential. He was convinced that at an early age, these youngsters had sufficient musical intelligence to know when they were being patronized. In an early youth concert in his tenure in Winnipeg, the WSO played Smetana's *Overture to the Bartered Bride*, Mendelssohn's incidental music from *A Midsummer Night's Dream*, and Liszt's *Hungarian Fantasy*. Next came a favourite Feldbrill offering in such programs — the Tchaikovsky *Overture to Romeo and Juliet*. He knew the teenagers would know the story and might even have read excerpts from the play. To conclude the concert there was an unusual choice — a medley of songs from Lerner and Loewe's popular musical comedy *My Fair Lady*, but even that selection was given symphonic orchestral treatment by American composer Richard Rodney Bennett.

At the beginning of a series of concerts for young people, he often introduced all the instruments in the orchestra with a special attention to the groupings and the sounds they were capable of creating. Needless to say, Britten's *Young Person's Guide to the Orchestra* was often included in these programs and became the basis of this exploration. Often concerts emphasized themes around melody, rhythm, or harmony — the very makings of musical presentation.

Very soon after his arrival in Winnipeg he had been invited to speak to the I.L. Peretz Folk School parents and he chose to base his remarks on the topic "Music and Arts in Your Child's Development." These parents were knowledgeable but Victor had thought through very carefully the message he wanted to leave with them: music and the visual arts were central to the acquisition of a mind that would gather wisdom and compassion from every minute of time singing and playing. To deprive children of that opportunity was, in his mind, criminal in the broadest sense of the term. They were being robbed of what through the ages has been the road to intelligent thought and understanding. We now realize that Victor was prescient in his recognition of the importance of the early years in the learning life of every child, when windows of the mind are open, never to happen again in the same manner and to the same extent. It was then that music should be introduced to every child. He made it plain that this would be a commitment in the years he would devote to making music in Winnipeg.

The ideas that by the 1990s had become the stock in trade of progressive educators on every continent were being presented not by a career educator but by the conductor of the local orchestra. Victor had raised the flag and this speech gave integrity to everything he did with young people for the entirety of his time in Winnipeg. It was little wonder that the TSO realized during his time away from Toronto that his absence both from programming and performing for young people could not be sustained, and they invited him to return and conduct frequently those programs directed at families, children, and youth. Little wonder that once his tenure with the WSO had ended, it was youth programming at the TSO that would entice Victor to resume his career in Toronto.

During Victor's early years in Winnipeg, the WSO presented a series called Music for Youth, which featured programs such as Mendelssohn's *Italian Symphony* (complete) or the first movement of a Mozart violin concerto played by a local young artist who had reached observable heights of virtuosity and deserved a chance to perform — a common occurrence at such concerts even though Victor preferred to play every composition in its entirety. Young people, Victor believed, could be trained to expect the performance of a full symphony rather than just popular movements if assisted in their journey with a few well-chosen words.

Victor believed that it was most important that he prepare the listening audience with a spoken narrative that gave them clues about what they were to listen for. In the same program there were short but pungent commentaries about composers and their times that aroused the receptivity and curiosity of those sitting before him. His favourite strategy for the young listener was to compare the symphonic offering with a drama, beginning with the introduction, then the plot development, and eventually the appropriate climax to the story expressed in musical terms rather than verbally as they would expect in a play on stage or television. Children, and often accompanying adults, were engrossed, focused, and often entranced by these interventions.

Just as with radio, step by step, as the concert series progressed he moved toward programs that were more challenging to his youthful audiences. He had earned his spurs in the frantic radio broadcasting studio when in the mid-1950s the over-committed Geoffrey Waddington had often handed over a single concert or a series of CBC Ontario school broadcasts to Victor. Waddington knew the production schedule was brutal but had enormous confidence in his young protégé. There were inevitable moments of chaos. On one occasion, the orchestra was gathered in a makeshift studio over the University of Toronto Banting Institute's collection of cages containing birds and animals for medical research. The rehearsal began at 7:30 a.m. and the broadcast went live at 9:30 that same morning. It was an opportunity for a live cock to make an inappropriate intervention in the orchestra's rendition of *Morning,* a segment from the Greig *Peer Gynt Suite,* much to the amusement of the players and the despair of the technical staff.

Influenced by the CBC National School Broadcasts, and broadcaster Rex Lambert in particular, Victor was impressed by what could be achieved through the quality of the spoken word, often issuing from the lips of a famous radio actor such as John Drainie in programs skillfully produced by talented storytellers like Len Petersen, both of whom were already legends of "on air" presentation. For Victor, each program was part of a pattern of understanding. For example, the orchestra might play a single but successive movement over four programs, but then, on the fifth occasion, provide the entire Haydn or Mozart symphony along with reminders of the times of the composers' lives and the audiences they would be serving in their own day. He would often trace the history of music virtually back to prehistoric performances in cave dwellings to the delight of youngsters for whom early human beginnings held endless fascination.

Victor came to realize that he had an endemic problem on his hands within the schooling system. In his efforts to promote series of concerts for children, youth, and families, he became aware of the wall that existed between the music practitioners in the school classrooms and rehearsal halls and the performance spaces into which he was attempting to draw them. It was clear that the teaching of music was too often in the hands of disappointed aspirants to a professional performing career. Victor was prepared throughout his career to visit schools when he sensed that students were being deprived of a musical experience based on such reasoning; as one teacher expressed it, "These kids do not need to attend concerts. They have all the music they need or want right here in the school."

Fortunately, Victor had his own rich experience upon which to draw. He had manufactured his own musical life around the performances to be found in Toronto park bandshells, in the cheaper seats of Massey Hall, and at Varsity Stadium. His first opportunity to conduct beyond the Harbord auditorium had been at a TSO young peoples' concert at age eighteen. He never lost his appreciation of the elements in music that had fascinated him from the outset — the contrasts of sound, of rhythm, the thematic repetitions and key changes that transformed what he was hearing and how he felt about it. He knew this was the "stuff" of a child's interest that could be moulded into a presentation that created an excitement both over radio and on concert stage.

Victor believed that direct contact with professional music-making could raise students' attitudes toward musical study and presentation wherever they were involved. When he discovered in the late 1960s that his return to the University of Toronto's Faculty of Music might include a role that would enable him to influence the thinking of prospective school instructors intent upon achieving a teaching certificate, he was drawn even more enthusiastically to a return to his home base of Toronto. He took on that task for almost a decade and a half, with astonishing results.

Perhaps his greatest asset was, in fact, his willingness to spend time with teachers in the field and listen to their tales of woe. They were, of course, overwhelmed by the numbers of students, each one with differing learning needs, with little time for preparation and personal renewal. In many cases, they were faced with inadequate resources, either in terms of space or in terms of adequately repaired instruments. His interaction with hundreds of teachers made him aware of the roadblocks to creativity they encountered day after day and made his teaching intensely relevant.

As well, he realized that his students were trapped by a system of post-secondary preparation that was obsessed with survival techniques. It focused on transmitting a basic understanding of the workings of the spectrum of instruments that would be encountered in any school program that offered orchestra or band performance. Victor tried desperately to shift attention to the meaning of musical sound, to the interpretation of the musical score, but it was made extremely difficult by the ultimate reality that the educating of the young was a process that was provided with only minimal investment. The rhetoric of those who knew how important this experience of music could be in the support of a civilized society failed to make a difference. It was Victor's continuing mission to remove that dissonance that remained between words and deeds in matters that affected the learning experience of children.

Teaching within any university's faculty of music was itself a challenge. The post-secondary academic focus on the written and spoken word and on the intensive research process led logically to a hierarchy of discipline prestige that emphasized and rewarded the purveyors of traditional studies in the liberal arts and sciences. Inevitably, instrumental or choral performance in music was found at the bottom of the pyramid of priorities that received recognition in terms of space, time, and resources in every university. Even within the music faculties themselves, those staff associated with aspects of musical study that mirrored the academic emphasis assumed control. The course and programs in history, theory, and harmony were more at home in the university than those who "merely" taught students how to perform in the concert and recital hall. Victor resolved that inevitable conflict in his own mind by ensuring that his efforts were directed to the rehearsal process and the performance on the concert hall stage at an intellectual level that neutralized the inevitable criticism of academics.

Even more surprising, Victor discovered that in the administrative offices of both the WSO and later the TSO he was often confronted with considerable disinterest in the role of providing active leadership in programming for young people and encouraging their attendance at concerts. Orchestral members and management had their priorities, and the major focus of a world-class orchestra was that of confronting the greatest music written before audiences of peers and accompanying the pre-eminent soloists on the concert circuit, whether in Winnipeg or Toronto. Victor was determined to see that his students shared that excitement.

Fortunately, having arrived back in Toronto, Victor found that he had allies already awaiting his return. At the TSO, there was a coterie of young women who cared deeply about the musical lives of their own children and those of other music enthusiasts. They acted as the engine of commitment within the ranks of the TSO volunteers who were determined that the orchestra would reach out to children and youth in a more focused way. For them, Victor's appointment as director of youth programming was a godsend. They soon invited him to meetings of like-minded young women and soon he was attending regularly. Victor knew they were his strongest supporters and through them he could eventually mount an impressive array of interactions with young people both in the concert hall and with smaller groupings of TSO instrumentalists, in gymnasiums, cafeterias, and classrooms within the schools of the city.

A leading figure in the assault on the traditional mindset of orchestras was Andrea Alexander, who later became a member of the Honorary Governors' Circle of the TSO and a major contributor to the cultural life of the city. For example, she worked tirelessly with Niki Goldschmidt in his passion to make Toronto the scene of choral festivals that drew ensembles from around the world. Her colleague and as determined an enthusiast was Marion Langford (another future Honorary Governors' Circle member), who found that she had children of her own with obvious musical intelligence and enthusiasm and was determined that they were going to be served by the TSO to which she had already given so much of her time, energy, and financial support. With allies like these, Victor could not fail, and the children's and youth programming took on new emphasis until the TSO became a leader in this aspect of orchestral outreach across the continent.

At the same time, Victor realized that there was a price to pay for his preoccupation with the music listening life of the young. The accolades of the music critics, the attention of journalists, the images on the television sets, were directed to those who were part of a phenomenon he had come to detest — the unrelenting pursuit of international fame and fortune by conductor colleagues touring around the world from one orchestra to another. The ease of transoceanic flight had turned them into "names" for whom spending their lives on airplanes and in airports became the measure of their success. The conductors prepared to concentrate their talents on the development of a particular orchestra, on the education of its audience over a long term, and on an active commitment to the young, were forced to compete with those engaged in the highly "hyped" continuous perambulation from orchestra to orchestra and concert hall to concert hall around the planet. This contrast of attention by public media that profusely celebrated this mainstream presentation and ignored the more developmental elements of music performance also demeaned those concentrating on the enrichment of the lives of young listeners.

These were the considerations that influenced the quality of Victor's planning of his future in music. He believed there could be a legitimate process that focused on the development of audience understanding and appreciation of musical expression. The programs in a series of concerts were not just about performing an array of orchestral gems from the enormous repertoire of the ages. There must be an evening of thoughtful presentation of music that brought every individual audience member to an aesthetic climax and into the street appropriately inspired to lead a more productive and more caring life. But it must also be part of a long-term strategy that included the encouragement of contemporary composers who were using the language of music to express certain truths that needed stating. As much as the perfection of all this was beyond all practical possibility within the importance of recognizing the realities of the box office, the predilections of famous soloists, Victor was not prepared to forsake that ideal. For Victor it was the focus that gave his life as a conductor an integrity that went beyond the ovations and the occasional but appreciated recognition of his talents. It meant that he would be consigned by his own values to the responsibility of reaching out to children and youth with a passion. Indeed, Victor became the conductor for whom the outreach of great music to young people became a "magnificent obsession."

The rewards were evident. It was to become a normal occurrence for him to be approached on the street, in the subway car, even on his occasional airplane trips, by people who simply had to tell him how their lives had been changed by a concert they had attended as a teenager some twenty, thirty, or forty years before. He became not only the "reliable" Victor, the conductor who could be called upon to replace any other conductor who was indisposed and invariably knew the scores of the musical selections that had been programmed (in some cases already rehearsed), but as well the conductor who was comfortable occupying a podium for concerts devoted to the development of children and young people. The WSO artistic leadership convinced Victor that he had ambitions that went beyond position and title; although he was to be eventually appointed as the resident conductor of the TSO and, on a short term, was to take over the leadership of both Orchestra London (Ontario) and the Hamilton Philharmonic Orchestra, he left no doubt that these commitments were not his major focus. He wanted to be perceived as the conductor who cared about orchestral music and its composers and the audiences that they attracted both present and future. After Winnipeg, he made it clear he had no ambitions to be the artistic director of any orchestra in any formal sense of that terminology.

Most important of all, Victor realized that the most effective way of attracting young people to symphonic music was by encouraging their participation in the performing of great music. As a result he conducted youth orchestras and occasionally even high-school ensembles, culminating, in terms of prestige, in his being by far the most called-upon Canadian conductor of the National Youth Orchestra in its initial stages of development.

Victor discovered that the most effective path to the love of music was to be found in the process of actively making it. His arrival in Winnipeg had been heralded by an invitation to an international music camp in North Dakota. His reputation had arrived before him. He had earned it from his work with the UTSO as a recently graduated high-school student and before his war service. Victor had returned to Toronto and as a guest was soon conducting the Opera School and the Conservatory orchestras, all filled with young people searching for the meaning of the enthusiasm they felt while performing great music. He had even been invited to schools that wanted to demonstrate the prowess of their own orchestra before parents, trustees, and friends. He was aware that with the paucity of orchestras and audiences, some of these musicians would not be able to find employment as instrumentalists ... but they would be magnificent audience members and would encourage others to join them.

He saw another use for the amateur youth orchestra — it could be used to train future conductors. That had been his route to that role. The rehearsing of professional orchestras was extremely costly and Victor's immediate contribution to the North Dakota camp had been an insistence that a handful of young, aspiring conductors be invited to participate in its activities. "Where else could these young prospective conductors learn their craft?" was Victor's question to those in charge of the event. It was an unpopular question for boards and management figures of orchestras across not just Canada but North America. Even at this stage in the national pride of place in the post–Second World War world, the podiums of major orchestras in the United States were filled not by Americans but by Europeans. Canada, too, was bent on following this tradition. As a start toward building a coterie of Canadian conductors to whom orchestras could look for leadership, who could be a better subject of attention than a man or woman who had spent years playing in a youth orchestra as well as occasionally standing on a podium before it?

It was in 1960 that Walter Susskind, recently appointed as conductor of the TSO and already a figure of some consequence, having played a major role in the creation of a national youth orchestra seeking to entice gifted young instrumentalists in Britain, witnessed the enormous possibility of such a training opportunity in a country with a plethora of such young performers. He had come to realize that it could mean an even more dramatic intervention in a country that had not yet produced sufficient numbers of fine musicians to fill the ranks of its few symphonic ensembles. Indeed, in the major English-speaking city, Toronto, the few reliably gifted were rushing from one ensemble to another, from rehearsal hall to the CBC broadcasting studio, with little time to think carefully about the making of music and ensuring there was time for individual rehearsal.

The pressure in the 1960s was relentless and with a burgeoning postwar Canadian Opera Company along with a newly established National Ballet Company, both in need of fine accompanying orchestral support, the situation was desperate. When his friend Lou Applebaum was asked to investigate the problem and produce a report, he recommended the establishment of a second symphony orchestra in Toronto. Victor not only supported the idea, but was prepared to be its conductor once his Winnipeg responsibilities came to an end. Unfortunately, the recommendation of the Applebaum study went nowhere. There were scarcely resources to support the single symphony orchestra in the region.

There was another reason to believe that the development of more young instrumentalists was necessary. In the early 1960s, changes in the school system related to the enhancement of vocational education with its promise of employment opportunities had miraculously released from the federal government enormous sums of money both for appropriate capital construction (machine shops and typing rooms) and for needed equipment for instruction. Although the manufacturing of consumer goods was in the minds of the initiators of the federal Vocational Training Act of 1961, music rooms filled with strings, brass, woodwinds, and percussion instruments appeared on sites of the nation's secondary schools. It became evident that a major thrust in the preparation of orchestral instrumentalists in Canada was essential and the creation of a national youth orchestra could be a part of solving the major problem. Thus, after an initial effort was made at the Stratford Festival to make all this happen and when the second session was to be mounted at Christmas 1960, it seemed logical to invite Victor Feldbrill, along with a French-speaking colleague of considerable reputation, Wilfred Pelletier, to join him in the familiar facilities of the Royal Conservatory of Music in Toronto.

Following the example of Britain, the emphasis would be upon rehearsing these brilliant young musicians, carefully selected from across the nation, until, after a few days of intensive work, a program of great music could be presented to an audience not only of friends and relatives, but one including a curious general public, as well. Even music critics were invited to the concluding gala event and they enthusiastically accepted.

Feldbrill and Pelletier chose the repertoire very carefully. That first public exposure before parents and friends, along with invited music critics, would virtually decide the future of the entire enterprise. Victor and his colleague would share conducting duties but the quality of the music had to be beyond reproach and must serve the instructional needs of the participant. Feldbrill and Pelletier chose Mozart's *Overture to the Magic Flute*, with its glorious melodic lines and seemingly simple but transparent harmonies. It was a wonderful but unforgiving opening for any concert. A major feature must, however, be the performance of an extended work, one quite beyond the ambitions of any high-school orchestra. The choice was that of Beethoven's Symphony no. 5, demanding all the musical intelligence these young musicians could muster, and, as well, Tchaikovsky's *Overture to Romeo and Juliet*, with its lush dynamics and glorious climaxes. It would stretch these young people beyond the repertoire of any orchestras in which they had played, and would challenge their prowess as potential professional symphony orchestra players. The hope was that they would strengthen the ranks of the burgeoning numbers of ensembles being developed across the nation. Victor's record of involvement on six occasions as one of the conductors of the National Youth Orchestra in its first decade of existence was an indication of his commitment to its success and a record of participation that would stand for many years.

At this first real opportunity for the orchestra to be appreciated, there would be three performances in three days in Toronto, Montreal, and Ottawa. The initial concert would take place in Massey Hall. It was attended by composer John Beckwith who was obviously impressed with Victor's involvement. Under the headline "It Was a Concert of Splendour and Determination," Beckwith wrote:

> Victor Feldbrill had obviously aimed for a performance that would respect the composer's wishes as to tempo. He reasoned correctly, I think, that if some of the advanced string players were not able to keep up, their impressions as performers of this important work [a Beethoven symphony] would from the first be a stylistically accurate one.[1]

In the early days of 1962, Feldbrill and Pelletier were conducting an ensemble now more assured by the success of their first concert experience to Montreal. With the same program as the orchestra had played in Toronto, there was once again a standing ovation and, as noted by Walter Christopherson in Montreal's *Gazette*, there were significant moments during the post-performance applause when the players refused to accept the audience response, indicating their wish only to "applaud and cheer" their two conductors.

Eric McLean, the *Montreal Star* critic, was singularly moved to write, "under Victor Feldbrill and Wilfred Pelletier, they prepared a performance which without any concession to their amateur status or lack of experience might be compared with the best orchestra concerts this country has to offer."[2]

In Ottawa, at the Capital Theatre, G. Gordon Lennox, the *Ottawa Journal*'s music critic, effused, "It's just a miracle what has happened this week." He went on to point out that, "A good deal of Canada's musical future is right here today…. The results are proof of the quality and number of young musicians in Canada — and we haven't even scratched the surface yet … maybe this will awaken the country for the need for more financial backing."[3]

It would take more than a national youth orchestra revelation to move the political system, but during the 1960s the prospect and reality of centennial celebrations did actually release funds both from federal and provincial levels. Little went to the National Youth Orchestra (NYO) even though it was apparent that with more time for rehearsal even greater heights of performance excellence could be made possible.

The first session with the NYO had set the pattern and it was now established. At Easter, most of the young people would be brought back together at the University of Montreal for a comparable experience.

Victor, more than any other Canadian conductor, saw in this experiment not just a measure of the excellence of young people that could be emulated in dozens of communities across the country, but as well a means of providing a Canadian presence in the nation's symphony orchestras. Eventually the NYO became the most utilized source of fine instrumentalists to be hired by Canadian orchestras. But Victor never allowed these considerations to divert the purpose of the NYO — that of serving the young musicians in the present in the knowledge that as human beings and productive citizens their futures would be deeply influenced.

By August 1962, the NYO was once again gathered in Toronto for a week of intensive rehearsal. Although the ensemble had only two years of operation, there were already graduates providing recruits for Canada's orchestras and raising the level of performance in a few of the civic orchestras just beginning in a number of smaller communities. On this tour, the NYO would visit the city of Buffalo, New York, just across the border near Niagara Falls, and would also play a concert in nearby St. Catharines, Ontario, and then in Stratford. The repertoire was even more ambitious. Victor had inserted a Canadian work — *Saskatchewan Legend* — by West-Coast composer Murray Adaskin, along with Handel's *Suite: The Faithful Shepherd.* The climax of the program was a favourite Feldbrill offering, Tchaikovsky's Symphony no. 5, a work that normally occasioned a standing ovation but required enormous attention to orchestral dynamics. The *Toronto Telegram* critic, George Kidd, appeared in Buffalo and submitted a review that pleased every player, but particularly conductor Victor Feldbrill, who Kidd recounted had given "through his players, an overall reading that contained authority, drama, and emotion. It was the type of ensemble playing that could bring tears to the eyes of the listener." [4]

The Toronto *Globe and Mail* had sent John Kraglund to cover these NYO concerts. He had observed the opening rehearsal some days earlier and at the Buffalo concert had viewed the results. He wrote that Victor Feldbrill had moulded these young people into an "amazingly uniform orchestra." When the NYO played back in Stratford, he proclaimed their concert "the outstanding performance of the season," and recognized Victor's role: "Through his work [with] the orchestra, he had proved himself a conductor to compare with the best Canada has to offer." [5]

However, it was Z.H. Lampert in the *St. Catharines Standard* who unleashed the most unrestrained accolade. Of the Tchaikovsky item on the program, he wrote, "It worked up to a tremendous climax that for sheer, thrilling beauty, will be hard to ever surpass ... with flowing, happy music pouring forth from the very souls of these young people, it was a brilliant occasion." [6]

Certainly these experiences enhanced Victor's sense of well-being at a time when his work with the WSO was going well, but these opportunities to lead the NYO later in the 1960s also provided solace when times darkened in Winnipeg. It expanded his reputation as the nation's pre-eminent conductor of youth orchestras.

On the NYO podium he had the exhilarating feeling of making a contribution not only to the musical careers of these young instrumentalists but also to the improved sound of orchestras across the country. For the remaining decades of his career, at every guest appearance on Canadian orchestra podiums Victor was invariably greeted by old NYO alumnae from across the country. These occasions became warm reunions graced with joyous reminiscences that reminded Victor that he had indeed changed the lives of many young people and simultaneously improved the quality of symphony orchestras in every part of Canada.

Victor's crowning experience with the NYO came in 1965 when an extended tour of performances culminated with a visit to several Maritime communities. On that occasion, Zelda, Debbi, and Aviva accompanied Victor on the bus from place to place. Their interaction with the young players from every corner of the land was cherished in the warm memories of the entire Feldbrill family. It was a moment of revelation for Debbi and Aviva to see the respect and adulation their father inspired in these teenagers, an age not normally given to an easy response to adult advice and direction. Little wonder that his daughters came to believe that working with young people was truly the culmination of Victor's conducting career.

Other examples of this penchant for youthful musical performance abound. Even after his close relationship with the NYO receded, he never passed up a chance to be at the Banff Centre, where there was a particular interest in youth. For example, in 1983, when the Calgary Philharmonic Orchestra, in conjunction with the Banff Centre, created an orchestral program for that years' Festival of the Arts, Victor was back on the podium.

These sessions with the NYO were enriched by Victor's past commitments, but in the 1960s they also had an enormous impact on his vision of his own future after his WSO experience was completed. In the depressing last years of that decade, when it was not at all clear where Victor's career was going and when the WSO Board appeared to have lost interest in his genius (the search for a new conductor having taken over as their primary priority), working with young people took on an aura of professional salvation. Although he responded to media questions about his future with the answer that freelance conducting would be his main commitment, it was also clear that his life must be filled with aspiring young people pursuing their career choices in the presence of his mentoring.

Suddenly, returning to Toronto offered that opportunity. The TSO reminded itself that it needed someone of Victor's calibre on a more continuing basis to attract youth to its concerts. Almost simultaneously, the Faculty of Music at the University of Toronto, filled with Victor's former colleagues, saw an opportunity to bring Victor onboard. They not only wished to utilize his flood of experience before orchestras in Canada and his knowledge about the challenges of artistically directing a major ensemble, but, as well, his awareness of the realities of opera performance, learned both from his European studies and his experience with *Louis Riel.*

Thus in 1968–69, when offered both a role as special adviser of youth programming with the TSO as well as roles through the Music Faculty as conductor of the UTSO and a position teaching in the "Mus. Bac" Program (a program designed for students planning a career as a music teacher), Victor did not hesitate. It was a collection of activities that would engage his time for fourteen years, until the late 1970s; this time also saw him take on an expanded role with the TSO that ultimately took him to the position of resident conductor.

Yet leaving Winnipeg was a sad time for the Feldbrill family. There were so many friends, so many memories of wonderful musical experiences. The Feldbrills had become a close family, with Zelda delighting in her work with Manitoba University's Department of Social Work and the girls, now old enough to enjoy concerts to the fullest, joining their mother in the audience at the Civic Auditorium.

That last year, with Victor absent so much in Europe, seemed to presage another phase when the family would be fragmented. The prospect of freelancing across Canada and the United States along with his annual commitment to the BBC possibly expanded to include all of Europe, Victor's longer absences seemed to be an assured element in the family's future. Before the Toronto situation resolved, Victor poured out his feelings of depression borne of his uncertainty about his future to Zelda, who responded with consistent love and support for whatever might come, but also with a plea that Victor decide on what he really wanted to do and be.

It was a terrible time for Debbi and Aviva, now angry teens about to lose their friends, their school, and their familiar home in the pleasant neighbourhood they had come to know in Winnipeg. Victor realized that the pursuit of his "cause" was damaging the sense of well-being of those he loved most. It came to a climax while the moving vans were loading the furniture and his girls were surrounded in the back garden by their friends. Victor was devastated by the disappointment and despair his girls revealed in that dramatic moment. "It was the only time I ever saw my father cry," was Debbi's memory of the occasion.

For Victor, the rebuilding of his family became his first priority, outranking even the assumption of his new career in Toronto, a career that would last more than a decade — with the exception of occasional absences of a few months, he remained in that city until he was in his eighties.

CHAPTER 15

Toronto — A Return

Victor was returning to a very different Toronto than he had left in 1958. By the late 1960s his "home town" had seen an amazing expansion of artistic expression. There were more art galleries, more musical groups (both choral and instrumental), and many small non-profit theatre companies operating in abandoned warehouses and factories. These new cultural expressions were being funded, if sufficiently qualitative, by an arts councils and/or a cultural ministry at both the federal and provincial levels, thus giving some hope and expectation that there would be long-term development. Even individual artists with strong creative capacities were being identified and assisted. As well, inspired by government support, the

Canadian private sector had begun to emulate the funding generosity to artistic initiatives that could be expected from American corporations in communities south of the border.

Also, as Canada's major industrial, commercial, and financial centre, Toronto was becoming the preferred destination of the many people coming to Canada from around the world, many attracted by the burgeoning artistic scene. While in Winnipeg, Victor had continued to lead a small number of TSO concerts each year, returning to his family with tales of massive and exciting changes that he had witnessed in Toronto during each visit.

The 1960s began with an expansion to the educational system that reflected the demands of a more learning-based economic scene around the world. The problem of finding employment, especially for native Canadians, was becoming a national preoccupation, one that created a need for more adequate job training for countless new industrial enterprises, most centred in Ontario. Shocking as it seemed, it was plain that young immigrants coming from European countries were better prepared for work in industry and commerce than native-born and educated Canadians. The federal government's Technical and Vocational Training Assistance Act of 1961 released federal money into the provincial schooling systems, which unexpectedly spilled over and created a surge in instrumental music opportunities for secondary-school students whose interest in making music had replaced their enthusiasm for more recognizable preparation for jobs in the manufacturing and resource-development sectors. Ultimately, this new interest and the need for prepared arts teachers produced an academic position in the University of Toronto's Faculty of Music, one that was perfect for Victor, one that would make use of both his talents and his experience.

He was not about to abandon his central commitment to orchestral conducting, however. In Winnipeg, he had justified his decision to leave by proclaiming his determination to pursue a career of guest conducting that would take him across Canada and beyond. The opportunities and necessary remuneration for a Canadian so disposed was patently insufficient. It was a stretch as yet to find enough Canadian orchestras on the lookout for a conductor for single concerts and as yet little chance of finding American orchestras seeking such assistance.

Victor, in his forays to Britain and Europe in 1968 and 1969, had sought to engage an agent who might represent his interests on that continent, but with little success, even though he had by this point linked with a concert agency, Ingpen & Williams, an entrepreneur arts operation that would manage his interests at least in England. However, European conductors were present in sufficient numbers that the prospect of paying the transportation costs of transatlantic flights from Toronto for guest conductors was manifestly unlikely. Victor was unable to find an equivalent figure to Ingpen & Williams on the European continent. Except for his annual gig with BBC orchestras in the United Kingdom, an extremely important aspect of his career across the Atlantic, there was no regular and continuing employment to be found across the English Channel.

During the 1960s and '70s Victor had continued to appear before various Canadian orchestras on a fairly regular basis. Indeed, he found himself being approached to sit on juries for orchestras like the Victoria, Saskatoon, and Regina symphony orchestras, who were seeking new leadership or wanted his expertise as a consultant on any number of matters. It was clear that he needed a base of operations in Canada that only Toronto could provide. He had become famous for his willingness to respond to the frantic telephone calls from orchestral managers in need of a replacement for an ailing conductor or to fill a date that was now open as a result of the regular artistic director's desire to be elsewhere. Now he wanted to make guest conducting a larger part of his career.

In the light of these considerations Victor was pleased to accept an invitation to return to the University of Toronto campus that he himself had attended some two decades before. He had been back for only two years, when music critic William Littler wrote an extensive article about Victor in the *Toronto Star* under a headline that proclaimed, "He's a Conductor Without an Orchestra, But Still Victor Feldbrill Is a Happy Man." Littler recounted that in the final stages of Victor's departure from Winnipeg there had been considerable surprise in Canada at his leaving. His affinity with the WSO had become as recognized in Canadian music circles as the connection of Arthur Fiedler with the Boston Pops or Leonard Bernstein with the New York Philharmonic was to serious symphony orchestra devotees in the United States.

Victor had justified his departure by claiming that "he wanted to do more" but the WSO's budget had proved incapable of further expansion. As well, it was clear, as Victor put it, "I needed a break from the constant pressure of being an artistic director." The Canada Council Senior Arts Award had allowed him to spend time in Europe visiting opera houses, but on a longer-term basis he realized that he needed "the stimulation of a Toronto." His reasoning exposed the glory and the frustration of creativity. It was best celebrated in a context that allowed continuous interaction with other creators and too often these people were gathered in large cities — in mid-twentieth-century Canada this meant Toronto.[1]

Littler's extended article went on to describe Victor's role at the University of Toronto's Faculty of Music as that of teaching conducting to a new wave of young people, enriched, it appeared, by his own reputation and continued participation as an occasional guest conductor with the TSO. As well, Victor's experience at Tanglewood, Hilversum, Maine, and Salzburg had given him insight to what could be achieved in a classroom setting that included actual involvement in the practice of music-making. Now he was asked to provide a similar experience over a full academic year. Instead of a handful of students, he would now be faced with groups of thirty or more, all clamouring for his individual attention. He was coping with the underside of universal education, which was establishing its presence even in the University of Toronto's Faculty of Music.

Victor saw that there was a particular need to assist individuals who were already or were about to become choral conductors either in schools or in the community. There was the reality that many of these conductors would be simultaneously leading both an orchestra and a choir, particularly if they ventured into the literature of the oratorio, such as *Messiah* or *Elijah* as the culmination of a season's musical expression. It was a special interest of Victor's and made his work particularly relevant to many teachers, especially to those who would be in smaller schools in the province, where only one music teacher would be available to conduct both the high school's choir and its orchestra.

Lee Willingham, now providing leadership in music and teacher preparation at Sir Wilfrid Laurier University in Waterloo, Ontario, was one of Victor's graduates. He became a music coordinator in the Toronto area

Victor Feldbrill with colleague, British conductor Sir Thomas Beecham, 1957.

Victor Feldbrill receiving a pie in the face from Toronto Symphony Orchestra flutist Nora Shulman at the Christmas Box Concert, 1976.

Victor Feldbrill with Diane Krall and Robert Farnon at the latter's eightieth birthday at the National Arts Centre Orchestra Concert, 1997.

Victor Feldbrill conducting the University of Toronto Symphony Orchestra, 1943.

Victor Feldbrill conducting at the Canadian National Exhibition bandshell, 1963.

NATIONAL YOUTH ORCHESTRA OF CANADA
EDWARD JOHNSON BLDG. — TORONTO, 1962

Victor Feldbrill with members of the National Youth Orchestra, 1962.

Victor Feldbrill, with singer and comedienne Anna Russell during rehearsal for a television show with the Toronto Symphony Orchestra in the 1970s.

Victor Feldbrill conducting the National Youth Orchestra, 1964.

Victor Feldbrill with comedian and violinist Jack Benny after the Toronto Symphony Orchestra's Pension Fund Concert, *circa* 1971.

Victor Feldbrill assisting guest artist Anne Murray button her sleeve at a TSO Pension Fund Concert, May 3, 1974.

Victor Feldbrill with Ella Fitzgerald after a Toronto Symphony Orchestra Pension Fund Concert, May 23, 1975.

Victor Feldbrill with Canadian contralto Maureen Forrester after concert with the Winnipeg Symphony Orchestra, 1967.

Victor Feldbrill in rehearsal with Luciano Pavarotti for a Toronto Symphony Orchestra Pension Fund Concert, April 11, 1976.

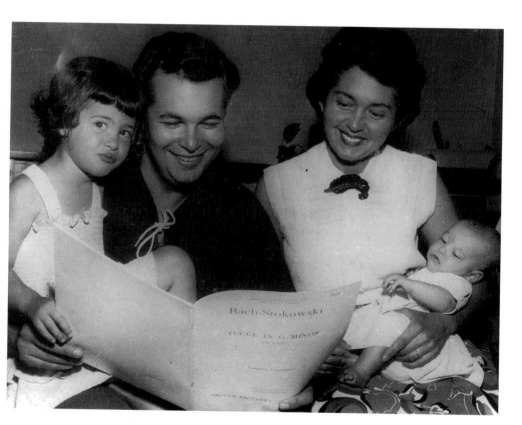

Victor and Zelda with Debbi and Aviva, 1954.

Feldbrill and student Kayushi Ono in May 1980. Ono would go on to become one of Europe's most important opera and symphony conductors.

Zelda Feldbrill with Japanese child proposed for adoption.

Victor Feldbrill conducting the Geidai Philharmonia, Tokyo, 1985.

Victor with his beloved Zelda, 1990.

Victor with companion and inspiration, Mae Bernstein, 2005.

Debbi's family. Front row (left to right) Erin Goodman with son Bradley on her lap, Dr. Ted and Debbi, Danny Goodman with Zachary on his lap. Back row (left to right) Naomi Orzech (holding Dylan) and Dr. Neil Orzech (holding Abbey).

Aviva's family. Front row (left to right) Stacey (Joshua's wife) holding Joseph, and Aviva. Back row (left to right) Jake, Herbie, Benjamin, and Joshua.

and while there established an outstanding choir, the Belle'Arte Singers, an ensemble made up largely of teaching colleagues, which toured and recorded extensively and effectively. Willingham's memory of his classes with Victor is indeed vivid. "He gave us the tools," is his considered judgment. "He could really teach us how to conduct. Even today I still use his cueing techniques when teaching my own students." These comments illustrate the long-term impact of Victor's work of a decade and a half at the University of Toronto.[2]

William Littler's assessment of Victor's predicament of being a conductor without an orchestra was slightly misleading. In fact, along with his academic appointment he had come to the University of Toronto as its first "conductor in residence" with the particular responsibility of giving leadership to the UTSO. No longer a student-run operation, the orchestra had been taken over by the Faculty of Music and was now ready to play a more active role in the musical life of the city. With an infusion of instrumentalists now engaged in preparing themselves for a career in the orchestral field of music presentation, the orchestra was dedicated to higher standards of virtuosity and the performance of a more demanding and qualitative repertoire.

It would have been more accurate for Littler to have written that Victor had no established professional orchestra completely under his direction, though he had never been very far from the podium of his beloved TSO even throughout his Winnipeg years. In 1970, the year of the Littler article, Victor was to conduct the TSO six times, in three student concerts and three children's concerts at Massey Hall, to say nothing of informal groupings of TSO players on various school premises. The following year, as his programming for youth expanded, he would conduct fourteen concerts at Massey Hall — seven student concerts and seven children's concerts — in addition to six concerts at Ontario Place, Toronto's newly constructed summer recreational man-made island on the waterfront.

Obviously, the TSO was making considerable use of his services as a guest conductor, while his main titular role was now that of director of youth programming — a role that also encouraged him to commission new works for children's programs. Another of his responsibilities in that position was having to deal with all the accolades and the complaints of those who were dissatisfied with his choice of repertoire, his selection of solo artists, and his handling of sometimes recalcitrant audience members.

An example of a highly supportive letter came from a Mrs. Alex Mills of Don Mills, a suburb within the city of Toronto:

Dear Mr. Feldbrill,

This has the distinction of being my first "fan" letter. We were so impressed by yesterday's Young People's Concert that I felt I must write to convey my appreciation to you and the Symphony. I was a Charter Subscriber to this series so have attended almost every one of the concerts over the years with all of our six children. We have enjoyed them and are tremendously grateful for the introduction the concerts gave the children to good music. All of them now play instruments and the older teenagers play in several bands and orchestras and are TSO Subscribers.

But to get back to the performance yesterday. It seemed to me (and our eight year old) to be the best yet! The format and music chosen appealed to everyone in the audience and even captured the unusually somewhat noisy neighbours. We were both sorry when the concert drew to a close.

Much to our delight I found our Katie humming "The Stars and Stripes Forever" all the way home in the car. And as soon as we reached the house everyone had to hear Katie's account of Tom Kneebone and "The Sorcerer's Apprentice."

If we are in any way a representative sample of your audience — our enjoyment must have been shared by everyone there. I think you've found a good formula. Keep up the good work.

Yours very truly,
Jane Mills

Needless to say, all the missives from listeners were not as positive as the letter from Mrs. Mills, but rarely did a disapproving response arrive to dampen Victor's enthusiasm for his role as director of youth programming.

Indeed, negative comments tended to come not from patrons but from music critics. Of one of Victor's young peoples' concerts, the comments of *Globe and Mail* music critic John Kraglund raised a considerable uproar. The headline over the review, "Music Animals: Kiddie Turkeys," was particularly resented. An elementary teacher, Mrs. Judy Anderson, wrote to Victor on behalf of four of her students who had been angered by the Kraglund article, which had in its text a somewhat deprecating opinion both of Victor's introductory comments and his music-making. Mrs. Anderson went on to express her views that Kraglund's negative description of Victor's short speeches about each musical selection were inaccurate and the reviewer's comments "were not only unfair but untrue." She wrote a letter to Kraglund himself indicating that she rarely agreed with his critiques but in this case "took exception to both your point of view and your conclusions." She found the headline implied "an insult to the children" and proceeded to analyze Kraglund's opinions about the appropriateness of Victor's repertoire in the light of her own research into the views of the children she taught. It was a devastating commentary. As a teacher who had arranged for eighteen students from her Grade 4 class to attend the entire series of concerts, she was capable of a well-considered intervention that deserved to be heeded.

Mrs. Anderson took the trouble of having the letters her students had written copied and mailed to Mr. Kraglund for his edification, along with a most impressive researching of the responses of her students to each selection on the program, noting that his perceptions of the popularity and appropriateness of various elements of the program were simply wrong and in conflict with all her research of her students' opinions.

Victor was naturally delighted with this show of support and ensured that the entertainment editor of the *Globe and Mail* received a copy of all this material. Needless to say, it was not an action which enhanced his popularity with one Toronto music critic, whose capacity to degrade his public performances for years to come was apparent. Those years included a large number of TSO appearances, but also concerts of the UTSO, the ensemble that Littler had failed to mention in his article, thereby seemingly dismissing in his definition of a symphony orchestra the very orchestra that Victor had accepted as his major responsibility upon his arrival at the university in 1968.

The repertoire was now very much based on educational rather than recreational principles. Victor was determined to transport his students down through the centuries and across a broad spectrum of orchestral programming choices. In a single program in his early years he scheduled Stravinsky's *Greeting Prelude*, Tchaikovsky's *Roccoco Variations*, with Jean Howarth on cello, Ravel's *Daphne and Chloe Suite No. 2*, and concluded with Brahms's Symphony no. 4. This was a program that would challenge any professional orchestra, but whose presence had seemingly been discounted by the music critic of Toronto's largest newspaper. On that same evening Victor had, predictably, included a Weinzweig selection, *Dummiyah*, to ensure that his student musicians were aware of his support of Canadian music, an extension of expectation that very few of his colleagues on podiums of professional or partly professional orchestras felt was necessary to complete any concert program. Indeed, Victor even commissioned special music for TSO programs during these years, including Harry Freedman's *March* and John Beckwith's *All the Keys and All the Bees*. Both were warmly received by appreciative audiences.

In his review of the above concert, though, William Littler was right about the proper basis of any assessment of the concert program's value:

> The point of student concerts, however, is to challenge players and this Feldbrill certainly did. For them to respond so well to the voluptuous sweep of Ravel's *Daphne and Chloe Suite No. 2* was remarkable to behold. And for them to make such an intelligent job at the tone clusters, microtones and waves of vibrati embedded in John Weinzweig's *Dummiyah* was a tribute to Feldbrill's tutelage.[3]

At a concert in the fall of 1974, critic Ron Hambleton was particularly taken with the UTSO's performance, which included Howard Cable's *Newfoundland Sketches* and the Khachaturian Concerto for Violin and Orchestra and concluded with the Sibelius Symphony no. 1. His review's conclusion was adulatory but perceptive: "But beyond all that is the fact that in Victor Feldbrill we have a musician around whom the music that Young Canada want to make, can crystallize."[4]

The UTSO concerts became significant campus events, with increasing interest on the part of university students seeking an evening of pleasure. The campus newspaper, *The Varsity*, on October 31, 1975, carried a review that reflected this renewed involvement. It began by commenting on the "enthusiasm" and the "sense of excitement generated by conductor and players," resulting in the orchestra's successful performance that took in the "sweep and broad outlines" of the Ravel *La Valse.* By 1976, Victor was challenging the UTSO to perform works of considerable virtuosity, such as the Bartok Concerto for Orchestra, Stravinsky's *Rite of Spring*, and the Beethoven's Symphony no. 9 (Choral). Indeed, his reputation for bringing along young musicians through demanding repertoire reached the British Isles and he was engaged in these years to conduct a series of concerts presented by the Academy Orchestra of the BBC, really an orchestral training ensemble created to supply able musicians to the various orchestras whose concerts Britain's national broadcaster made available on air throughout the year.

By January 1974, Victor had made another step forward as the TSO's missionary in the field of youth outreach. He had approached Walter Homburger who agreed that a youth orchestra could be formed that would bring together the best secondary-school students and recent graduates as an ensemble that would advantage young people who, in school orchestras, had been and were being held back by less gifted instrumentalists. The headline in Toronto's *Globe and Mail* simply announced that "TS Plans Formation of a Youth Orchestra," and the article revealed that Victor would be the orchestra's conductor. Soon the initiative was to be welcomed on all sides. James Westaway, TSO Board Chair, explained the rationale: "Young instrumentalists would be exposed to both the teaching and practical expertise that Victor Feldbrill and his faculty (drawn from the TSO orchestra) possess." In doing so, Westaway proposed that "the TSO would be building on Feldbrill's unique rapport with our community's young people." He was sure that Victor's presence would "undoubtedly add immensely to this new undertaking."

The first season of operation for the Toronto Symphony Youth Orchestra (TSYO) would be in the 1974–75 orchestral season, and the new ensemble of players in their late teens and early twenties would perform a series of three concerts each year, one of which would be in association with the regular members of the TSO. Walter Homburger, who had supported the idea from the outset, commented that it would give the young musicians what membership in the National Youth Orchestra could not — "full year round training." Regular weekly rehearsals would take place from September to May, supplemented by weekly sectional rehearsals. It would be a demanding schedule that would test every member's commitment.

The creation of a youth orchestra would, in fact, place a major time demand on the shoulders of its conductor at a time when his commitment to the work of the TSO had increased exponentially. However, Victor was ready to make that effort in the light of all the benefits that the presence of such an ensemble could bring. Not only would young prospective orchestral musicians develop more quickly and hopefully find their way into the TSO, but young solo instrumentalists and vocalists, particularly those in Toronto, could find another platform to express their talents and prepare for a solo career. Victor was already making use of children's and youth concerts to present young Canadians planning to pursue a solo career, thus providing them with an opportunity to face an audience in less forbidding circumstances than in a regular concert in a subscription series directed at mature, but perhaps less forgiving listeners.

Victor saw yet another advantage. There were young, aspiring composers who could benefit mightily from hearing their own music played. Victor believed deeply in the need of both mature as well as burgeoning composers to experience the sound of their music. Until then, the notes on a page had insufficient meaning and often students of composition who knew all the rules could produce a score that was either unplayable by instrumentalists or unconvincing to its listeners! Victor's work with established composers like John Weinzweig and Harry Somers had proven that there were often adjustments to the scores of new compositions that could be made on the rehearsal stage, with the composer present and invited to comment on what he or she was hearing.

In 1975, as evidence of his continuing commitment to young composers, and despite the fact that the youth orchestra was being created at that point, Victor convinced the TSO that they should be prepared to play a newly created student composition at a regular concert. Victor had set up a jury made up of Harry Freedman, John Beckwith, and John Weinzweig to select the composition for performance. It all came about but was too much of a risk for it to be a regular occurrence at an existing series of subscription concerts. However, a well-rehearsed youth orchestra could play that role more often and at considerably less expense.

As well, having a youth orchestra was politically astute. The TSO, along with the Montreal Symphony, were the leading and dominant orchestral ensembles in the nation. This step put the TSO into a leadership role in developing young Canadian musicians. Other orchestras would certainly benefit, particularly those newly established and able to pay only minimal salaries to some and none at all to others. For Victor, it meant that not only would his TSYO be seen as a leader in the particular field of youth instrumental and orchestral development, but he would be able to continue to indulge his interest in the development of such organizations long after his days of employment with the TSO had ended. Indeed, his reputation in this field of endeavour became as singular as his role as Canada's pre-eminent conductor of Canadian contemporary repertoire. Within a couple of years Victor was being invited to conduct at the Quebec Festival of Youth Orchestras as a result of his position as the founder and leader of the TSYO. Even before that, he had been invited as a "world status conductor" to perform with gathered youth orchestras at a festival mounted in co-operation with the Banff Centre for the Arts.

Victor was now launched on another definable cause — that of interacting with young people in order to improve the standard of Canadian orchestral players and in so doing enhance the quality of performance of the nation's orchestras from coast to coast.

It would not be easy to launch such an ensemble. The inaugural concert of the TSYO in early February 1975 was somewhat of a disappointment. Headlines in both major Toronto newspapers — "Youth Orchestra Too Much Too Soon" and "Youth Orchestra Really Wasn't Ready" — exposed a common theme of discontent. Certainly, Victor had placed enormous expectations on the shoulders of these young people. Their first program included Shostakovich's *Festive Overture*, the Bach *Passacaglia and Fugue* arranged for orchestra by Leopold Stokowski, and the Dvorak Symphony no. 6. Also included, of course, was an obligatory Canadian work, Morel's *Antiphonie*. It was quite an expectation for a group of young instrumentalists who had only just met a few months before and whose only experience had been that of playing each week in a school auditorium.

However, by April of 1975, the orchestra had come a long way and such selections as Ralph Vaughn Williams's Symphony no. 2 (*London*) could be given a strong performance. As usual, a Canadian work was given a place on the spring program and Harry Freedman's *Tangents* was well played. By March of the following year, the orchestra could play for a single evening in the TSO Student Concert Series. At another concert, accompanied by TSO regular members, the TSYO played Rimsky-Korsakov's *Russian Easter Overture* and Tchaikovsky's suite of ballet music from *Swan Lake*. The concert concluded with Beethoven's Symphony no. 5, in which the audience was confronted with two full orchestras producing a dynamic volume of sound in Massey Hall that had rarely been heard before.

Trish Baldwin, the young child entranced by Victor's performance as the conductor of the COC opera *Louis Riel*, was now playing clarinet in this orchestra as well as the UTSO. She was once again ecstatic about her conductor's insistence on excellence and his gentle, thoughtful, sensitive interactions bar by bar through the difficult passages on every page of the score. Eventually, the embarrassing interludes when individual instrumentalists failed to come through — missing an entry, obviously losing their place in the score, or failing to watch for a particular cue — disappeared. She observed as the increasing loyalty and respect for Victor's leadership engaged every player. These elements of civilized music-making, as well the expectations of excellence and commitment, were her legacy from these Feldbrill orchestras and they positively affected her ensuing career as an orchestral manager of Canada's pre-eminent baroque orchestra, Jeanne Lamon's Tafelmusik.[5]

This enthusiasm for young people and the music they played continued in the heart of a man who had conducted that age group for several decades, well beyond any thought of retirement. Since shortly after Zelda's death in the mid-1990s, he has shared his life with an extraordinary woman, Mae Bernstein, who, early in the summer of 1996, accompanied him to a one-week music festival at Camp Manitouwabing, near Parry Sound, Ontario, where Victor was asked to rehearse an ensemble of young people and conduct a concert for parents and friends on the last day of the camp's session. She watched day after day, overwhelmed by the commitment these young people had to the music they were playing. Mae, a fine amateur violinist herself who had played in orchestras of modest accomplishment, knew how much angst was being expended on this process she was witnessing.

At the beginning the sounds coming from the instruments of these young people had been truly awful, but Victor never relented … nor did he become angry. Slowly but surely he overcame. They learned to listen as well as play. They learned to follow the precise movements of his baton. From a rabble of gifted but collectively incompetent band of instrumentalists, they became an ensemble. She was witnessing the Feldbrill touch that cared for little else at that moment but the music and those who were making it. He showed no concern for his reputation as a conductor or his own image as a performer and what people might think of this terrible noise emanating from the rehearsal hall. He aspired to give these young people the experience of achieving the very best in their capacity as individual players but more important as members of an orchestra. With a few hours of preparation, at the end of the week they would be expected to reach professional standards and provide splendid renditions of Godfrey Ridout's *Fall Fair*, Schubert's *Unfinished Symphony*, and Bizet's *Carmen Suite*.

More important, they would then go back to their schools across Ontario as ambassadors of a splendid classical music sound and instrumental expression and provide an example of that devotion to hundreds of other young people. They might never play in such an ensemble again — or, in a new century they might go on to become members of that spectrum of orchestras now to be found playing in every sizeable municipality in the country. All of them had the potential of becoming more knowledgeable members of audiences who not only would enrich their own lives, but enhance those of others around them. He was involved in making a difference in the quality of life of nearly one hundred young people and he knew it.

Mae Bernstein was in shock at the end of the concert that concluded their week together with the young people making up this curious, momentary makeshift symphony orchestra. For doting parents, the performance was a sensation. The audience was ecstatic, but Mae was appalled that no one had thought to record the entire afternoon. Someone should have kept this experience of glorious music for posterity. More important, it would have been possible to send a copy of the disc to every member of the orchestra for them to take back to parents or close friends who missed the performance, to their schools, or to individual music teachers. In her view, these discs would be cherished as treasures for the rest of their lives — a record of excellence, of sensitivity, of collective caring about the great examples of human creativity on their music stands. Mae was right but, alas, neither the financial resources of the sponsoring organization nor the general understanding of those responsible had led to the production of a record that would have been a testament to what a group of talented young people could accomplish under inspired leadership.

During those years, the TSYO continued to improve. Of great importance were the weekly sectional rehearsals. Victor had drawn the finest musicians from the TSO ranks to work with individuals and small groups. The names of Pratz, Lipchak, Kernerman, Monahan, Weait, and Rittich were already legend in the process of building a fine senior orchestra, and, more important, had demonstrated a love of teaching the young. When the two orchestras, the TSO and the TSYO, came together for a concert it became an event in the Toronto musical calendar that was not to be missed.

Though Victor gave up his responsibilities at the TSO in 1977, it was not until 1978 that he relinquished his relationship to the TSYO, and only when he could not be sure of his regular presence in Toronto. He felt he could give up his administrative duties with the TSO because he had by then put the programming for children and youth on a steady path that others could follow. But he was reluctant to lose those magic moments with the TSYO members as they struggled to become competent and committed members of a symphony orchestra.

Perhaps most surprising of all was the fact that during the years in the mid-1970s when he was developing his TSYO, Victor's role had expanded most dramatically. What in 1968 had begun as a part-time role as director of youth programming alongside his considerable, but not overwhelming, duties as a guest conductor, became more than full-time work. Along with his work at the university and COC guest appearances, the workload became impossible to accommodate. It was William Littler, considering the totality of Victor's responsibilities, who commented that if he had not been in place in the Toronto of the mid-1970s, he "would have to have been invented."

A perfect example of his influence can be found in his proposal to Walter Homburg that the TSO establish a "Light Classics series on Saturday nights."

Victor was increasingly conscious of the fragile nature of TSO audiences. Their members tended to be older and had been brought along through children's and young peoples' concerts in the past. He knew that there must be no addition to the deficit — the series had to be reasonable in its cost to the audience member and thus must be sold out. There could be no expensive "name" guest artists but there must be a solid repertoire of selections with tune, rhythm, and varied instrumental colour that would attract ears that had possibly never heard a symphony orchestra before. It was also an opportunity to display Canadian performers and music by Canadian composers. Most important, this audience must not be played down to! Walter Homburger agreed ... and the series sold out. "Light Classics" concerts still grace the TSO offerings each year and continue to attract young audiences, well into the twenty-first century.

However, in the mid-1970s, a threat to the TSO's well-being came to a head and tragedy overtook the orchestra.

Karel Ancerl had been attracted to succeed Seiji Ozawa as conductor when the latter left to take over the San Francisco Orchestra at the end of the 1968–69 season. It had been a fortunate choice. After the somewhat inexperienced but exciting young Ozawa, it was felt that the TSO needed the solid, mature leadership of a conductor who could bring to the orchestra the knowledge and experience of a distinguished career in Europe. Under his tutelage, the orchestra could develop even further in the direction of performance excellence. And indeed the orchestra did excel in those years ... both under Ancerl's and on many occasions Feldbrill's batons.

However, Ancerl's health was considerably compromised and in 1973 he was hospitalized in Toronto in considerable discomfort. It was known by this time that the TSO would be touring Europe in the fall and it was hoped that recovery of its conductor would be the result of his hospitalization. In the light of Ancerl's obvious ill-health and the realization that access to Victor's conducting skills might be even more crucial, the board had appointed him associate conductor in the spring of 1973. It was accomplished in the shadow of a provision that his appointment to this position would not indicate any expectation of succession to the conductorship either upon Ancerl's retirement or his withdrawal as a result of ill-health. Indeed, Ancerl indicated that he would not seek a further contract beyond the 1974–75 concert season. The issue of replacement became significant when on July 3, 1973, Karel Ancerl passed away in a Toronto hospital. Fortunately, the TSO had Victor in place and under contract. Indeed, on the day after the maestro's passing, Victor was named resident conductor.

There were those who failed to understand the reluctance of the TSO to allow Victor any expectation of assuming the conductor's role and the assumption of musical direction of an orchestra which by the 1970s he had served in one way or another for some three decades. There were many factors. They included the presence of the colonial mind that in North America believed such a prestigious position as the conductor of the TSO belonged to a figure who had excelled in the home of Western classical music, such as western Europe or at least the United Kingdom. Victor was a local boy — born, bred, and educated in downtown Toronto. There was an expectation in symphonic circles of the need for a maestro whose wisdom, charisma, and experience could be sold to an audience and the orchestra's financial contributors. A Canadian could not even be considered.

The TSO was taking the traditional position of virtually every Canadian symphony orchestra in its selection of an artistic director and conductor. In those years, the National Arts Centre Orchestra in the nation's capital also found itself looking for a new conductor, and as author Sarah Jennings points out in her book *Art and Politics*, "a solid European-trained leader steeped in the romantic repertoire" was sought. The centre had the same expectations in the 1990s when another search was being carried on.

Victor will not articulate any recognition that anti-Semitism has ever been a problem in his career, but others are not so sure. As a sector, arts organizations were normally the least affected by such prejudices, yet even in the last years of the twentieth century prestigious American-Jewish conductors had been known to change their names and composers had been known to convert to Protestantism. Women certainly felt the impact of gender prejudice as it affected leadership positions in arts organizations.[6] It has been the pride of the twenty-first century that dancer Karen Kain is the artistic director of the National Ballet of Canada and Jackie Maxwell has reached that same pinnacle at the Shaw Festival in Niagara-on-the-Lake. However, being Canadian was a sufficient disability, and other such forms of perceived inappropriateness were unnecessary to assure his being overlooked for the TSO's artistic leadership in 1973.

The personal popularity of the only successor to Ancerl "on the scene" was quite beyond question. An appeal to his willingness to save the orchestra replaced the provision of any hope his own presumed ambitions might be rewarded by the TSO. Probably a more aggressive personality would have taken advantage of the predicament of the TSO, but Victor was not of that ilk.

There were other reasons, perhaps more than enough to justify the cooling of any ambition that Victor might have had to take on such a responsibility. He had been outspoken on issues that bothered the managements of orchestras by the 1970s. He had openly criticized the minimal salaries and restrained length of the concert season — both devoted to limiting the impact of salaries on the orchestra's budget and keeping its musicians in poverty. It was generally assumed that conductors were part of management and it was their responsibility to keep the orchestra budget under strict control rather than worrying about the economic well-being of the players. But Victor could never lose the influence of his roots — that of playing in the string section of the TSO and other ensembles in his early years and sharing the poverty of the orchestral musician even in times of general economic growth and national prosperity. Again and again, whether in Winnipeg, London (Ontario), Ottawa, or Hamilton, he was to side with the players in their disputes with orchestral management on the matter of just remuneration.

Also, he had this obsession about the importance of including the works of Canadian composers in his programs. He was openly critical of Canadian orchestras' resistance to carrying out what he believed to be an appropriate commitment to the performance of Canadian works. It was not a popular position among orchestra board members, untutored and frankly nervous about "new" music of any kind, and sure that empty seats and lower box-office receipts would ensue from any appearance of an expansion of commitment to the works of Canadian composers. (On these matters, it must be said, he was taking positions that were unpopular with some orchestral musicians, as well.) It was a stand that ultimately came to be seen as undermining any enthusiasm for the steady, reliable quality of work, with the more popular concert series drawing new audiences, especially among the young. Ironically, the disinterest in contemporary music and the continuing reliance on the "old" but popular classics both in concerts and recordings may have had much to do with the decline of support for symphonic music as the twentieth century ended.

There was also no doubt that Victor was not the most popular figure on the podium in the eyes of Toronto critics. The development of his career had worked against him in that he had attained an image of enthusiasm for a particular role — as the conductor of pops, youth, and children's programs. Today, some thirty years from the events of the early 1970s, the mention of Victor's name arouses the memories of that role. Val Saunders, a valuable associate of Ezra Schabas when he was principal of the Conservatory, immediately seized on the words *nurturing* and *caring* when the Feldbrill name emerged in a casual conversation about his relationships with young listeners and players. During a flight to Florida, when recognized by an attendant, Victor was summoned to the cockpit by a pilot who regaled him enthusiastically with stories of his love for classical music which had resulted from his attending student concerts in Massey Hall. Such moments became regular occurrences in Victor's life. But the effect of this iconic recognition led to a tendency to trivialize his talents as an interpreter of major symphonic works that were the fare of the major subscription concert series — a process that did not take place when he was conducting major symphonic works in the British Isles, Europe, and later Asia. There the reviews of his work were not composed in the context of a reputation for enhancing the listening life of the young and possibly their accompanying parents, but on the same basis as other outstanding guest conductors from around the world.

Of course, it did not help that Victor had a reputation for "taking on" the music critics, both in Winnipeg and Toronto. Critics, by definition, feel themselves badly used, unappreciated in their roles of providing continuing evaluation, but in so doing engage in unpleasant criticism of popular entertainment figures. Victor, unlike most artists, was quite open in his occasional lack of respect for their efforts and, on occasion, their integrity.

Victor's persistent advocacy of more generous support for the arts from Canadian governments and their agencies did not help his cause. He had made it plain that the power of the major institutions gave them an advantage in seeking funds. He had supported the underdog, the smaller and less powerful WSO, against the comparatively well-situated Montreal

Symphony and TSO. Once again, it was a public position that diminished his likelihood of ever gaining support for an exalted occupation of a major conductor's post in Canada's most prestigious orchestra.

Even in the equality-driven, pro-democratic, anti-social-class atmosphere of the post–Second World War period, it was a fact that Victor was a Toronto boy from a poor family whose musical beginnings were to be found in the violin section of the TSO. In a former British colony that had retained a non-hereditary class system, it placed him at an enormous disadvantage in securing such a post. It takes no acceptance of Marxist rhetoric to realize that Victor, even if he had fought relentlessly for the position of conductor, could not have "made it."

To be fair, Victor himself suffered from the same illusion — that someone else with international credentials was necessary — and accepted the position of resident conductor without protest. The TSO, in his words "needed a world-class conductor," and he felt that, even with all his experience in Winnipeg and in European circles, and the flattering opinions of distinguished colleagues abroad, he did not qualify for that designation in the competition for the position of regular conductor of the TSO.

Before the TSO could seek out its next conductor and artistic director, there was the need to establish some feeling of confidence in the immediate leadership of the orchestra. Fortunately, the orchestra was not in financial crisis and indeed had registered a surplus during the last year of Ancerl's tenure. A host of guest conductors- — in reality, a phalanx of hopeful applicants for the job — was arranged through the expertise of the inimitable Walter Homburger. As part of the strategy for establishing continuity and calm, once again Victor was there to save the day, with no expectations of tomorrow.

The first crisis to be faced in the summer and fall of 1973 was the fact that in just a few months time a tour of the major centres of Europe was to take place. It had, of course, been arranged with the expectation that Karel Ancerl would be leading the orchestra. Walter Homburger was able to secure the services of Kazimierz Kord, a European conductor of some distinction, but there were those both in the orchestra and among its friends who questioned this decision and openly wondered if it would not be more appropriate to have both a Canadian conductor and one well known by the TSO to take over the tour. To that question, Victor generously placed the blame on the European entrepreneurs who had arranged the tour, indicating his understanding that he had no public reputation to market in Europe and the tour's success depended on full concert halls for a Canadian orchestra that had not yet established a reputation across the Atlantic.

Victor accompanied the orchestra, but played no role, not conducting a single performance, not even in a lesser venue on the continent. It was not a role he appreciated, being the non-conducting resident conductor, but he occupied his position and was there if Kord had been indisposed in any way. The tour was a resounding success, with standing ovations in nearly every centre visited. However, in private correspondence with Zelda, Victor could comment on the playing of a Berlioz *Roman Carnival Overture* that was "so slow it nearly fell apart," of the wrong entry by a first desk player in Godfrey Ridout's *String Études*, of a Schumann piano concerto that was "not together," and a Shostakovich symphony in which the tempo "was all over the place." To be sure, in the process of making these observations Victor may have been visibly disturbed, but he was most certainly publicly silent.

When the time came and Andrew Davis was securely in place as the TSO's conductor, with no expectation of reward, Victor tendered his resignation as resident conductor. He made the point that the newly appointed conductor was now himself "resident." His letter of resignation was received with some relief by a board that appreciated the extent of his contribution and had thought there might be an expectation of some considerable recompense for his successful occupation of a position that Victor himself had described as a "difficult and at times a thankless job." He had been forced to encourage certain retirements and although he was enormously successful in attracting outstanding replacements, like cellist Daniel Domb, trombonist Gordon Sweeney, and especially flutist Nora Shulman, there was always cause for complaint for one reason or another. To handle all this in the context of an artistic leadership that was obviously short-term and minimally honoured by its own designation (the term "resident" had its own definition problems) was an extraordinary achievement. Certainly one man recognized that fact. James Westaway, the board chair, in a letter of appreciation, congratulated Victor on everything he had done over nearly half a decade to bring the TSO through its time of troubles. He was not alone in recognizing the extraordinary contribution that Victor had made.

～～

For Zelda, the 1970s were also years of outstanding professional accomplishment. She had left Toronto for Winnipeg as a mother of two young daughters. She had been convinced that with an active and often absent husband, she must give her full attention to Debbi and Aviva and had taken leave of her professional duties in the early 1950s. It was even more important that their need for her attention be accommodated in a new city so far away from home. However, she had every intention of resuming her social work career when the opportunity arose. And so she did, at first in Winnipeg, on a part-time basis, where combining social work with the mentoring of future professionals earning their first degrees provided particular satisfaction.

Even with all her family and professional duties, Zelda was able to provide enormous support to Victor during the difficult times in the latter years as the WSO's artistic director, and she had every reason to believe that being back in Toronto would help to quell any feelings that he had failed in Winnipeg.

However, after the family returned to Toronto, Zelda realized that she had two mature daughters — one soon to enter university and a second coping with secondary school. She could now return to her mission as a social worker on a full-time basis. Happily, she found a role that exceeded expectations.

The Toronto Board of Education, like many other such boards in larger jurisdictions, was reaching out for more effective ways of reaching students disconnected from the positive impact of the school as their place of learning. Greater understanding of the learning process was bringing to the surface the fact that realities outside the school environment — in the home or neighbourhood, for example — had an impact on how effectively children and youth learned. Lack of motivation rather than the lack of intelligence was seen as having much to do with the fact that so many dropped out of school as soon as it was legally possible. Yet, it was clear that the school did not have either the understanding or the resources to address this broad range of needs that students expressed, often through negative behaviour and intentional absences from class. Teachers had neither the training, nor in many cases the interest, to become involved in the well-being of a students' family life — many were hungry and not appropriately clothed.

Teachers had a responsibility to cover the curriculum, judge the performance of students, and keep order, surely a sufficient demand upon their energy and intelligence day after day.

School attendance was the only legal pressure that could be exerted to a certain age, and as the economy became more diverse and demanded more professional training and more classroom time, keeping kids in school became a national priority. Suddenly the involvement of other professionals became imperative. Psychologists and social workers were seen as partners in developing a support team and parents were seen as members of a supportive enterprise geared to retain young people in school for as long as they could benefit both intellectually and socially.

Zelda saw in this shifting of school priorities and practices an opportunity to make use of her training and experience in a way that would benefit the life chances of those she had always cared about — children from lower income and broken families already handicapped by an environment that provided no inspiration to attend school or learn while there. Attendance departments and mental health units were combined to establish new student service operations and in some problem schools filled largely with children from low-income and single-parent families, the needs were massive. These schools, then referred to as "project schools," and later renamed "inner-city schools," were provided the extra funds for supporting the presence of psychologist-social worker teams. Here was a situation that Zelda saw as an opportunity to make use of her special experience, preparation, and deep caring. Giving children and young people a second chance through interventions that involved parents, teachers, and educational administrators might advantage these young people. It was a role in which Zelda would come to thrive, and she seized the opportunity with an exhilaration and tenacity that was electric.

She took her place at the Park Street Public School, which served children from the Regent Park complex — a large concentration of low-cost housing that had been built after the Second World War. In that position she found that she interacted not only with parents and teachers but served as a mentor to countless numbers of social-work students from the University of Toronto, there to "learn the ropes" of coping with the new expectations of those who had chosen this vocation.

It was a challenging role. She had to convince teachers and principals that this special program would not undermine the school's disciplinary regimen, or hold inappropriate young people in the school settings both to their own disadvantage and in some cases leading to the disruption of the learning of other students.

As well, Zelda was faced with the fears of teachers and administrators who thought that inviting parents into the school decision-making process was an affront to their positions as professionals. Very soon, a wise and diplomatic Zelda developed a reputation for confronting uncooperative school staff members and winning them over.[6]

When Rosemary Hazelton, an experienced professional social worker who had graduated from a BSW program in Edmonton and worked in Saskatoon before coming east, met Zelda in the early 1970s she soon became a friend and colleague: "Zelda was my model."[7]

Perhaps more than anything else it was the energy and commitment of "a dynamo" that she brought to the job which impressed her colleagues. That and the sense of social justice she brought to every task: she was not just a facilitator … she was an advocate. These children were victims of a social system that ensured inadequate learning — poor health, poor housing, and especially in winter, inappropriate clothing. Zelda was there for them when they were faced with unfeeling teachers and administrators. She had all the right words and attitudes, she was aware of all the networks — how to bring the right people together who could support individual students.

It was ten years later that Dr. Esther Cole, a psychologist, encountered Zelda in the Regent Park school community. She was still there in that same school. Others had come and gone — many choosing to move to more socially acceptable neighbourhoods with a less troubling clientele. But Zelda stayed year after year.[8]

Esther Cole was particularly taken with Zelda's relationship with the school parents. To them she was not "Mrs. Feldbrill," but simply Zelda. She even "dressed down" to ensure that they felt comfortable in her presence. Her noon-hour fare at "brown bag" multi-disciplinary committee luncheon meetings with parents was always one boiled egg and a modest sandwich. When conversation became hot and heavy she could demonstrate to parents how to achieve their goals without confrontation. To clarify an issue on the agenda being addressed in expert jargon, she would, with an injection of "what you mean is," admonish the professional who was engaging in diminishing the concerns of mere parents. Eventually there were mothers who became so obviously adept and effective that they were offered employment as assistant teachers in school classrooms. Invariably they were enormously helpful as classroom bridges across the chasms that existed between parents, teachers, and professional social workers.[9]

Esther Cole was amazed at the degree to which Zelda could separate her work among the disadvantaged and her role as the wife of the now illustrious Victor Feldbrill. She never referred to that aspect of her life as a way of levering her desires into influence, no matter how honourable the expected result. Her role as head of the family was never shrugged off lightly — she was proud of her daughters, and her husband's determination to become Canada's foremost conductor was an ambition she fully shared. Yet her role as a caring professional was the power that guided everything she accomplished beyond her home.

The return to Toronto had been a wise decision for Victor. Not only did it bring the satisfaction of mounting podiums before enthusiastic young players but as well the opportunity to be a guest conductor of the finest orchestras in Canada. Almost a decade and a half of teaching students who were determined on a career that would include the conducting of orchestras and choirs and who would, in turn, influence the lives of thousands of other young people, was a special role he enjoyed enormously.

For Zelda, it was a time of extraordinary professional satisfaction, bringing understanding and comfort to both underprivileged young people and their parents, thereby lessening the impact of the injustices of an often cruel society.

Although they never saw themselves as a "team," their combined contribution to the life of Toronto and beyond, was great.

CHAPTER 16

Have Baton, Will Travel

Victor was clear on one point: to be recognized as a symphony orchestra conductor required considerable travel. It is true that there were examples of conductors of orchestras, often in smaller municipalities, who had withdrawn from touring and remained on one or two podiums over an entire career. The reason behind such behaviour might be an extraordinary commitment to a particular collection of musicians or to a particularly beloved community. It might have much or little to do with the excellence of the conductor's skills.

On the other hand there were orchestral conductors who never took on responsibility for the well-being of any single orchestra but remained available to a number of orchestras. This is particularly true in the world of European opera or orchestral performance and Victor saw the advantages and disadvantages of that process during his tour of European opera houses in 1968 and 1969. That strategy was more possible on that continent, where distances between music centres were less challenging, making it possible for agents to organize tours for conductors that could involve several orchestras and opera houses. For a North American, particularly a Canadian, conductor the distances between orchestral concert halls were almost always immense. To the disadvantage of Canadian conductors, it was often simpler for orchestral and opera house managers in this country to adopt a north–south approach to finding guest conductors by reaching over the Canadian-American border where nearby performance venues might reveal a conductor whose travel costs would be more reasonable.

With the latest twentieth- and twenty-first-century communication and travel technology, distances have vanished as factors in determining the availability and ensuring the presence of guest conductors. Until his arrival in Winnipeg, Victor's prowess as a conductor was known essentially across Canada and internationally through his CBC radio and television work, to be more specific, his frequent appearance as conductor on various CBC Radio educational programs, particularly school broadcasts. In the evenings he could be found conducting the orchestra on one or another of the outstanding adult programs for which the CBC had become famous internationally (for example, *CBC Wednesday Night* and *CBC Sunday Night*), and the concerts were often interspersed with discussion or theatre presentations. To be added to that kind of work was, after 1957, the annual trip to Britain and the BBC network programs.

Victor's appointment in Winnipeg had ended his working career as an orchestral player. Now he had become the conductor and the music director of a major ensemble in a substantial Canadian city, indeed, a provincial capital. It was a prestigious appointment that had succeeded in attracting the interest and subsequent invitations to guest conduct from orchestras across the nation. Indeed, the number of requests grew exponentially to the point that Victor had to adjust his response to this sudden shift of attention. His central philosophy of what the core of being a conductor and artistic director should be — that of developing an orchestra's search for excellence in performance over a substantial period of time — could be jeopardized by frequent trips to orchestras across Canada and over the border to the United States. The exposure of conducting in different regions of the country was often not sufficient justification for all the time and energy that transcontinental travel entailed and the absences from the WSO such effort demanded.

However, there were other considerations. On occasion it was an appeal from a Canadian composer who wanted to have Victor conduct his or her work. Even more often it was a frantic call from an orchestra's general manager who could not mount a scheduled concert within the crisis of a sick or otherwise unavailable regular conductor. On such an occasion, managers realized that the availability of a replacement in Canada with a broad knowledge of frequently played scores and proven competence on the podium was a rare phenomenon, and immediately raised Victor's name. Sometimes it was the need to have a conductor who had a reputation for presenting concerts that reached out to audiences unfamiliar with symphonic repertoire. At other times young people were the potential listeners and Victor's expertise on the podium was essential to bring off a successful program.

For Victor, throughout the 1960s, there were regular guest appearances in Toronto with his TSO. It could be two, three, four, or more concerts each year, in this case motivated quite openly by Victor's appeal to younger and obviously "new" audiences. These gigs were important to Victor, who, though he had a renewable contract in Winnipeg, had to be aware of the long road extending into the future once the second five-year stint as conductor had concluded. The possibility represented by the musical life of Toronto was most certainly an attraction. As well, Victor was determined to keep in contact with a city that contained both his and Zelda's family and a host of friends they had made in the immediate post–Second World War period.

A welcome guest appearance for Victor was that of leading one or another BBC orchestra in Britain. His friendship with Sir Adrian Boult had led to introductions to the musical leadership of a broadcasting network on which the CBC was based, one that had orchestras playing "on air" concerts from London, Manchester, Bristol, Glasgow, and other British centres. Victor became a valued member of the guest conductor contingent on which the BBC relied. His reputation for repertoire expertise was expanded and his capacity to secure competence and even excellence with minimum rehearsal time became legendary.

Victor's attitude to guest conducting abroad was also made manifestly dichotomous by the fact that it meant inevitable absence from Zelda and the girls. During the passionate, nearly daily correspondence measured in war years while Victor was ensconced in *The Navy Show*, Zelda and Victor had promised each other that they would spend the rest of their lives in physical and spiritual intimacy only possible through a mutual commitment to be in each other's presence. In the post-war years Victor had reluctantly but necessarily spent months away preparing to be a conductor by engaging in one or another learning experience in Europe or the United States. Now they were facing the reality that his being a symphonic conductor at the level that Victor demanded of himself meant that he would be away more often than he wanted to be. Extended periods of several weeks a year were resented but recognized as unavoidable. Fortunately, for Zelda, the presence of the girls and then the extended family she cherished made it more tolerable. As well, her commitment to her own career eventually connected these absences to her being present in Toronto. It made those trips they eventually shared, to Europe, to Japan, and to other venues they could both enjoy, even more treasured and pleasurable.

More profound than his personal distaste for placing distance between his family and himself was the conflict that guest conducting created between his own philosophy of the conductor's role and that popularized by the media. He sincerely believed throughout his life that an artistic director/conductor's main role was not that of providing a unique physical demonstration of dominance from a podium. Rather, it was about creating a context which would attract the demonstrated creativity of the orchestral collective and make a statement to the community about the great music being played month after month, season after season. It was this kind of commitment that could change the lives of both musicians and listeners.

Essentially it was about ensuring that the focus was on the music and the musicians. Only they could produce the sound that could give life to a composer's understanding of the very nature of being. The conductor/artistic director role was that of developing, week by week, month by month, and year by year, the quality of sound and the intensity of interpretation that would allow this to happen. To be successful, a conductor with that philosophy had to be present, but not at every rehearsal and performance, as creativity can be a momentary as well as a continuing phenomenon, and the presence of a great guest conductor can energize an orchestra. Victor had brought Monteux and Barbirolli to Winnipeg to do just that! However, the permanent conductor/artistic director must be there on the podium to work with purpose and focus, not just with the entire orchestra but occasionally with every section of instrumentalists and with individual players, until the ensemble reaches its height of possibility. Victor resented conductors who took on two or three orchestras at the same time and flitted back and forth by plane, never establishing a presence with any one orchestra that was sufficiently long and intense to exude any caring about its development of excellence.

As well, Victor believed that every orchestra should have a unique and recognizable sound, the result of that continuing collaboration of conductor and instrumentalist he appreciated so profoundly as an orchestral player himself. The practice of sharing a conductor's energy and creativity among a spectrum of orchestras invariably ensured that there was a loss in distinctiveness that could only emerge from an intimacy and shared pride of performance whenever the particular orchestra played. When he lost confidence in his capacity to maintain a positive board-conductor relationship as an outcome of his work, he turned rather to a style of guest conducting that he made legitimate by another definition — that of a guest on the podium. With skill, experience, preparation, and determination he found that he could reach an orchestra very quickly, establish his expectations with few words and minimal physical gyration, and thereby secure a quality of performance that often brought unfamiliar audiences to their feet.

The irony of Victor's career was the bizarre reality that the adulatory reviews he received in Britain, Belgium, and then in the Soviet Union, and that he would receive years later in Japan, were bestowed to a much lesser degree upon him in Toronto, the city where he chose to base his career for the majority of his life. He came back from most of his concerts in foreign lands energized and enthusiastic about his chosen career, ready to face the less enthusiastic local reviewers of his TSO ministrations.

This in itself encouraged him to believe he had much to give that form of orchestral leadership. He knew he had spent much time conquering the complexity of a vast spectrum of musical scores and he had proved that he had an unusually steep learning curve in addressing new works. As well, the intensity of his commitment to Canadian compositions gave him a special role to play as he moved across the country. Eventually, he developed a repertoire of Canadian music that simply "travelled well." Harry Freedman's *Images*, John Weinzweig's Divertimento no. 1 for Flute and String Orchestra and his Symphonic Ode, Howard Cable's *Newfoundland Sketches*, Harry Somers's *Lyric* and *Passacaglia and Fugue*, Godfrey Ridout's *Fall Fair*, and Pierre Mercure's *Kaleidoscope* were examples of music from Canadian composers that could be learned within a short rehearsal period and were accessible to unfamiliar audiences. Often when he followed his normal style and included a Canadian piece amidst other recognized masterpieces, surprisingly, the applause of the audience was more intense for the unknown Canadian fare than for the traditional offerings.

For the first couple of years in Winnipeg, Victor had understandably stayed close to home, conducting virtually every concert in the multiple series he had planned on his arrival. Except for concerts back in Toronto with the TSO and in youth orchestra festivals both far and near, he largely remained on his familiar Winnipeg podium.

In March of 1960, however, he was contacted by the Edmonton Symphony to conduct a concert. There he was close to home, which made the decision to accommodate this date much easier. In that case it was a matter of replacing a guest conductor, the distinguished international figure, Sir Bernard Heinze, who had fallen ill. The climax of the evening's concert was the Tchaikovsky Symphony no. 5 — always a crowd pleaser. Victor had been offered the opportunity of changing the program but declined with the comment, "Let's not rock the boat," indicating that he would prefer to leave the program intact and have the orchestra work on that already arranged repertoire more intensely in the limited time he had with them rather than begin rehearsing new compositions at the last minute.

The concert was an outstanding success. Victor was called back on stage four times throughout a standing ovation. He was particularly moved to discover that orchestra players were joining in with the applause and loud bravos. With all his determination to remain with his Winnipeg orchestra, he began to see the advantage of occasional absences, especially if he could find adequate replacements. As well, he had become aware of the fact that there was a long period from April until September when the WSO was virtually silent and his presence was not so essential.

In the summer of 1960 he was back in Britain with an invitation to conduct the Manchester BBC Orchestra, a fine ensemble prepared to compete with any on the British Isles. It was on this occasion that he was able to bring Zelda and extend the visit to include Amsterdam and a host of other European cities.

He returned to Ontario in August of 1960 with his family in order to conduct many of the concerts associated with the International Conference of Composers organized in Stratford by his friend Lou Applebaum. A pattern developed for future summers that allowed him to visit both the Vancouver Music Festival and the Canadian National Exhibition in Toronto, invitations that tended to come annually in the early years of that decade.

By the summer of 1961 Victor had also invited to conduct the Quebec Symphony Orchestra. It was the first of a series of appearances in "*la belle provence*," where he found the audiences most responsive. Indeed, he was proclaimed to "have all the qualities of a great conductor" by the *L'Événement-Journal/Le Soleil*.[1] This event was the first of a number of opportunities through which Victor became well-recognized as a conductor of choice for such celebrations held during the summer months.

On a 1962 trip that included a period with the National Youth Orchestra, Victor accepted an invitation to conduct the Montreal Symphony Orchestra in a concert on Mount Royal. The concert featured Louis Quilico, a Canadian baritone developing a growing international reputation as an artist in a number of opera centres, and the selections Victor chose for the concert were well-received. Here again, the critics and the players were enthusiastic about this young, little-known Canadian conductor who was so proficient and appealing.

Near the end of that summer, Victor was back at the Canadian National Exhibition Bandshell, where "the orchestra responded to Mr. Feldbrill's carefully modeled interpretation, suavely directed with playing of matching, clarity, grace and vigour."

It was a substantial program, one that Victor tended to bring to informal holiday concerts. Brahms's *Academic Festival Overture*, George Gershwin's *Rhapsody in Blue*, and Mendelssohn's *Scottish Symphony* were all included in the program. The trip allowed yet another family reunion with friends and family in Toronto and reminded his colleagues in the eastern Canadian musical community that he might be available in the future. Significantly, he found he invariably received more attention in his identification as the permanent conductor of the WSO than he could have expected as an occasional TSO guest conductor.

As the decade progressed, the concerts at which he appeared as guest conductor became increasingly prestigious. In 1963 it was the Canadian League of Composers who brought him to Montreal to play programs of Canadian music. He had become its champion and this event was central to the development of a consciousness about the presence and strength of the country's creativity in producing fine orchestral music. In a few weeks, he returned yet again to the C.N.E. Bandshell in Toronto, this time for a concert sponsored by the Musicians' Union. A further concert in Montreal was reviewed by Frances Goltman, who effused, "We have never heard a better summer or winter concert or such a receptive audience." [2]

His increasing tour schedule of the entire WSO in the 1960s had the effect of placing attention on Victor as a possible guest conductor with a variety of orchestras. In 1966, a few months after a WSO visit to Saskatoon, the city's symphony orchestra attracted Victor's presence as a guest on its podium. Indeed, he became a kind of resident adviser to western provincial symphony orchestras in handling a number of issues, particularly helping them in their search for a regular conductor or new orchestra members. He generously passed on contacts with musicians he had encountered and whose musicality he had come to respect even though he could not himself offer them a position. Indeed, his interest in being close to prairie orchestras continued even after he had moved back to Toronto.

In April 1975, the manager of the Regina Symphony called him. They were in some trouble. Their conductor had left suddenly in the summer of 1974. The programs had been set for the coming season and conductors had been found for all but the final event. It was to be the climax of the 1974–75 subscription series, and a performance of the Beethoven's

Symphony no. 9 (Choral) had been scheduled. The Regina Symphony Chorus was insufficiently rehearsed and thus totally unprepared to take on that challenge. As well, the orchestra did not have the instrumental forces to give the solid sound demanded by the work. Victor dealt with the crisis with an immediate decision that in this case only a change of repertoire could answer the problems presented by the monumental expectations that had been aroused. Mendelssohn's *Elijah* was substituted and the concert closed out the season with a sense of accomplishment.

Even into the 1990s, Victor was asked to replace an ailing conductor in Ottawa. (He had already conducted the National Arts Centre Orchestra in a special anniversary concert during a management-performer dispute in 1989.) It was a special Open House occasion. The review of the concert by Joseph Siskind appeared in the *Ottawa Citizen*:

> Feldbrill and the members of the orchestra responded to the soloist's [Jeffrey Kahane] contribution [Mozart's Concerto no. 25] with delight and the entire performance was an unalloyed pleasure.... The sound of the Schumann was rich, filled with warmth that would have been inappropriate earlier.[3]

This willingness and growing enthusiasm for conducting as a guest had important ramifications. It was a time when cultural interchange seemed a useful strategy in replacing the Cold War with a society more attuned to peace and universal brotherhood. It was a cause that had Victor's complete support.

With what came to be known as the Cuban Missile Crisis erupting shortly after Victor's arrival in Winnipeg in the late 1950s, it was a time of wide recognition of the fragile nature of human existence on the planet. The atomic blasts that had levelled portions of Hiroshima and Nagasaki in 1945 had revealed the extent of devastation and loss of life that humankind had discovered but even these events were insignificant compared to the nuclear weaponry that had since been developed. Not even the separation by oceans gave any hope of avoiding the ultimate fate of deadly rocket attack. During those days of the Cuban Crisis, millions of people in every corner of the planet looked beseechingly to the skies and wondered whether this was their last look at the glory of the universe revealed in the panoply of stars and planets. For Canadians it was a revelation to discover that these thoughts were focused on the dangers of attack just a few miles from the shores of the North American continent. Indeed, there was now nowhere to hide!

The alternative stance of mutual fear of retaliation did not, by itself, assure total avoidance. The search for common ground and a basis for trust had to accompany terror as a strategy to avoid the ultimate confrontation that threatened the survival of the species. There had been cultural exchanges in the days before 1960 but the Cuban Crisis had certainly aroused a greater interest in this form of raising understanding and mutual respect.

Thus it was in 1962 that Victor received a letter from Canada's External Affairs Ministry inviting him to consider an invitation to be a guest conductor in the Soviet Union to balance a visit that a Soviet orchestral conductor was making to Canada's West hosted by the Calgary Symphony Orchestra. Victor was certainly the most experienced and significant figure in the region, with a reputation for both the successful touring of his orchestra and guest appearances. As well, he was acquiring the experience of conducting abroad in an unfamiliar culture and a reputation for civilized behaviour in difficult circumstances that might arise on such occasions.

Most exchanges between East and West had been individual artists, like Glenn Gould, who had established an enviable reputation as a performer. Music was itself an international language and had none of the limitations of interpretation that touring theatre engendered. However, there was some question about sending conductors who would face large numbers of instrumentalists with no capacity for discourse through a shared language on which to base interchange and understanding. But, as Victor insisted, the shared musical score was itself an international language that revealed not only the sounds but the universally recognized symbols that indicated the composer's wishes to performers in any country or region about the dynamics or the rhythm that was to be expected. The fact that conductors spoke through visual expression rather than words made such an exchange potentially effective. Far more important would be the communication skills that revealed attitudes to orchestral musicians that exposed the visiting conductor's respect and appreciation and Victor had developed the body language to express his commitments to music and its makers in every imaginable setting.

As well, Victor knew the repertoires that Canadian composers had by this time created and had achieved a fine reputation for performing these works. It was an opportunity for guest conducting that had enormous extra potential. It would expose the fact that Canada had a cultural reality unlike the appearance of a single virtuoso solo instrumentalist or vocalist and would influence the thinking of Soviet Union orchestral composers and musicians as well as audience members about the nature of this northern landscape across the Arctic Circle. Thus, even by the 1960s, Victor had joined a number of artists in developing a pattern of touring abroad that eventually became a major element of their lives and careers.

He was placed in the hands of Canadian Embassy cultural attachés who, once the issues of financial responsibility were settled, looked after every detail of his foreign visit, ensuring that his needs were accommodated by similar officials in the host country. The first visit in 1963 would be to conduct the orchestras in four centres in the region of the Soviet Union known as Ukraine — Lvov, Kiev, Zaporizhzhya, and Odessa having the ensembles that were available.

Canadian Embassy officials came to realize that, in Victor, an artistic treasure existed beyond their expectations. He was the foremost exponent of Canadian contemporary orchestral music. In a country that had produced Shostakovich, Prokofiev, and Khachaturian, along with a considerable spectrum of lesser but recognizable composers, Russia, along with Britain, had assumed international leadership in producing a great twentieth-century repertoire during both the pre–Second World War period and the years after. Russians would be impressed by the knowledge that Canadians were also in the mainstream of musical composition. The 1960 international gathering in Stratford had proven the existence of a cadre of competent Canadian composers and Victor was also articulate and appealing as a speaker and could remind them of that fact simply by programming selections of these composers. The initial tour was a resounding success.

There was, however, a darker side to all this manifestation of cordiality and goodwill. Victor was now in the hands of bureaucrats in a country with a record of hostility toward the West and its values and behaviours. There existed a distrust that could include visiting artists, even those from Canada, who represented a capitalist rapproach to economic realities that included the making of music. They must be watched carefully. Victor was subject to continuous formal and informal monitoring of his every movement. As well, there were restrictions of those movements. Often there were sudden changes in his travel arrangements that embarrassed even the interpreter who accompanied him throughout his visit.

Only the inevitable incompetence of national systems of surveillance made it possible for him to behave with normal casualness. On one occasion, the control of his movement was obviously designed to prevent his observation of Soviet defence installations, but the intelligence system broke down completely. On May Day, 1963, in Odessa, a city with important harbour facilities that he was intended to avoid, Victor was placed in a hotel room that overlooked the entire waterfront area. He was even allowed to walk freely around the streets of the city with a camera hanging about his neck.[4]

It was fortunate that in Odessa he encountered the celebrated Russian violinist Igor Oistrakh. He, as well as visiting with family, was playing a recital, one that as it turned out had given him little satisfaction. As he put it, "Only in the trivialities did the audience come to life." He was unable to attend either of the Feldbrill concerts but was quite aware of the impact that it had on the morale of the orchestral musicians whom he knew well. As he said, "It was one of the greatest successes heard locally in many years."

The second Odessa program included the Mozart *Prague Symphony* along with Mercure's *Kaleidoscope*, a composition that once again was popular with both the audience and the orchestra members.[6] The program concluded with Berlioz's *Symphonie Fantastique*, a favourite of Victor's, given new exuberance by an orchestra that had played little of the French repertoire over the years since the Communist Revolution. The orchestra demonstrated a lack of rhythmic discipline but Victor recalls that "many of the players had thronged to tell him [the manager] that they had really enjoyed playing with me." The manager had even dropped by the hotel to tell him how much the orchestra "respected me not only as a musician but as a human being." Little wonder that the experience led Victor to express to Zelda his intense sorrow that she could not be there with him.[7]

Victor's observations of the musical life of the Soviet Union were pungent and informative. He was fascinated with the city of Odessa itself, its architecture, and its pride in its past. Unfortunately, it did not have one of the best orchestras he was to find in that part of the Soviet Union and he soon discovered why that was the case. The region apparently produced fiddlers for string sections of orchestras like some American communities develop baseball players and some northern Canadian towns contribute hockey players to their country's sporting culture. It ensured a flood of excellent violinists to the region's symphony orchestra string sections but left weaknesses in other sections, meaning that the Odessa Symphony was not as balanced and exciting as, for example, the Kiev Symphony Orchestra.

Overall, Victor found that even in a country with an unparalleled musical heritage, there could be terrible orchestras — largely, as one would expect, in smaller communities. Indeed, in the hinterland these lesser ensembles seemed uniformly pathetic. Yet, he found that usually the string sections tended to be very strong, with less virtuosity to be expected in the woodwind and brass members of the orchestra.

No matter what the quality of the orchestra, Victor realized his mission was that of endearing himself in such a way that even without any Russian language skills, good musical performance could emerge. His informal style based on an intimate understanding of the internal dynamics of an orchestra, along with a friendly demeanor would attract the best response and the finest sound. Again, even in the city of Odessa, after several days of rehearsal, the performance was warmly received by an audience that filled the hall. As a gift, Victor presented a copy of a signed photograph to the leading members of the ensemble and in so doing revealed an aspect of Soviet anti-Semitism that he had not expected to find. On the copy to the Jewish concertmaster Skazunetsky, he penned a few words in Yiddish. The recipient was visibly moved and showed it to every other orchestra member of Jewish background. They were emotionally moved to see their if not illicit certainly diminished language written on a document in their own corner of the Soviet Union.[5]

Victor had been fortunate that the first stop on the tour, Lvov, was a beautiful city, once called "a miniature Paris." Unfortunately, its glamour had been allowed to disintegrate during and after the Second World

War. Even its musical heritage, one which included evidence that Mozart's son had once taught music in that city, was in a sad state. There was little pride left in the members of the city's symphony orchestra. The players were unhappy and surreptitiously approached Victor for advice on how they might move on to a better musical life. They were curious about working conditions for orchestral players in Canada, particularly the nature of their remuneration. Their enthusiasm for moving to Canada cooled somewhat on discovering that Canadian musicians were often on a six-month contract that forced them to find other jobs between April and October. They were shocked to discover that Canadians did not listen to music twelve months of the year as they did in Russia. It was clear that the Lvov players were treated like civil servants on a regular yearly salary and worked every day, rehearsing every morning and afternoon five days a week. Their questioning had revealed reasons both to leave the U.S.S.R. and also to remain there.

Victor's two concerts in Lvov were characterized by overflow audiences. He had fashioned a repertoire that spread itself across a collection of favourite selections — a rousing beginning with Beethoven's *Egmont Overture*, followed by Tchaikovsky's *Romeo and Juliet Overture*, a Chopin piano concerto, and again Canadian composer Pierre Mercure's *Kaleidoscope*, the latter with some embarrassment on Victor's part when he discovered that U.S.S.R. performances provided no royalties to the composer. The concerts had concluded with César Franck's Symphony, and the standing ovation that the performance elicited became an enduring reaction wherever he conducted in Ukraine.

Kiev was to be the pinnacle of his tour, described by Victor as another "magnificent city," where he was again to conduct two concerts. He was impressed by the quality of the orchestra. Indeed, he expressed the view that it "puts every orchestra in Canada, except the Toronto CBC Orchestra, to shame." Once again, he was taken with the sound and responsiveness of the strings. At the first rehearsal, after the initial read-through, the musicians gave him an ovation. Through an interpreter, they assured him that "though they had played the Berlioz 'Fantastique' under many conductors, Victor had put new life into it." The Kiev concerts were a "fantastic success." The audience kept breaking into rhythmic clapping and shouting after every number.[8]

Victor was including Canadian contemporary compositions in each of his programs and it was noticed by the local composers' association. It was in Kiev that he was invited to dine with local members and engage in a discussion of modern classical music. The opinion seemed unanimous — that such music, "twelve-tone," as it was identified by the Soviet contingent, was decadent as well as unattractive and inaccessible by the common people. Victor was aware, of course, that the Stalinist regime had moved against the two most prestigious Russian composers, Shostakovich and Prokofiev. As major purveyors of musical talent, they were expected to produce music of the people, thereby eschewing the compositional techniques of the capitalist West. Throughout the discussion, Victor kept his composure through the rants of Soviet composer after composer. He began his contribution with a simple question: "How did you like the Weinzweig?" (The Kiev concert had included the Weinzweig Symphonic Ode.) The gathered composers expressed their positive reaction to the work, to which Victor replied, "Well, that is twelve-tone"![9]

Once again, once all the public activity concluded, loneliness and the need to share overcame Victor: "Once the children are grown up, you will go everywhere," had been his promise to a Zelda back home in Canada.[10] That statement had to be amended to "when you are retired" after Zelda resumed her social work career in Toronto.

By early May, Victor was in Zaporizhzhya, an industrial city, the last stop on his tour. Here he found an orchestra almost beyond redemption. The only positive sign was that he had almost limitless time for rehearsal. The orchestra needed every second. It was completely undisciplined. After an hour of rehearsal, the player's representative announced a "break" of ten minutes that stretched to twenty before the players found their way back to their music desks. Victor's impatience was palpable and he announced through his interpreter that he could not conduct the orchestra under these conditions. Referring to the strong factory presence in the city, he exclaimed, "You cannot bring the style of the assembly line into the concert hall." There was stunned silence. Then one player began to clap. He was joined by a second and a third. Eventually, the entire orchestra was applauding and Victor was overcome by their support. From that moment there was no further interference in his rehearsal schedule and he had the orchestra firmly under his control, ready to accept his leadership. The concert was as enthusiastically received as in the previous cities, but Victor recorded his private disappointment. It was "far from a standard I would call good," was his assessment in a letter to Zelda.[11]

This first tour in 1963 had been such a success that, as the situation in Winnipeg soured in the mid-1960s, Victor began to think of the possibility of expanding his commitment to an international guest conductor role in the future. Now he had contacts and invitations to return to the Soviet Union. The main problem would be his distaste for any more absence from Zelda and his family.

However, both the Canadian and Soviet embassies were determined to have him back to the Soviet Union and began the process of planning his return, this time to cities in the Georgian region. Rather than a spring tour, the event would take place between mid-December and early January of 1967.

Victor did not find it as satisfying as the first tour. He arrived in Moscow in the midst of a major two-day snowstorm. Then it was off to Baku, where he was faced with an orchestra that was reluctant to follow his baton. He had to push hard to get the musicians' attention. Yet, at the end of the rehearsal, instead of a dispirited exit of players, "they applauded loud and long … and I was pleasantly surprised." However, it was not before he had challenged the entire structure of the orchestra. He observed the main problem to be totally inept leadership. His strategy was that of changing the seating arrangements on the spot, and instantly demoting the concertmaster who Victor perceived to be totally ineffectual. (Victor was later to discover that his position of leadership had more to do with his political affiliation than his artistry.)

The Baku concert concentrated on Beethoven — his Concerto no. 3 for Piano and Orchestra and his Symphony no. 1. From the point of view of the audience reaction it was a "huge success," but he wrote to Zelda, "I'm not happy about it. I hope the other orchestras are better."[12]

In Tbilisi, he was determined to challenge the orchestra by programming the Bartok Concerto for Orchestra, even though the published version of the work had not yet reached the Soviet Union or the orchestra's library. Thus, the performance had to be based on a manuscript copy that was illegally copied, much to Victor's distress. During performance, there was a minor disaster when the bassoon player responsible for a fugal phrase had to be kicked awake by his own colleague in order to make his contribution. However, in a second concert in Tbilisi, he found the Sibelius Symphony no. 2 "brought the house down."[13]

On Christmas Day in 1966, Victor, disconsolate and lonely, wrote to Zelda complaining how strange and inappropriate it was for him to be away in the midst of the paramount Canadian holiday season. It was an absence he obviously deeply resented and was determined should not be repeated.

The Tbilisi orchestra was "not so good" but Victor was particularly outraged by the casual attitude to the question of copyright that was also revealed by the illegal copying of Pierre Mercure's *Kaleidoscope* before rehearsal could begin, avoiding the normal distribution of appropriate purchased copies from a Canadian publisher. As well, he had a pianist performing the Brahms Concerto no. 2 who insisted on playing every movement "presto" until Victor was forced to show him the specific tempo marking of the composer. Even with extensive rehearsal he found that to his horror, in performance "the orchestra did some stupid things."

The last stop on the tour was Minsk, where Victor did find a better orchestra. At all times, reaching the orchestra without a command of its language did create problems. He had programmed a Brahms symphony and was seeking to secure the full, warm, sensuous sound from the violins and cellos. He received the reaction he desired by repeating "Tutti, Like Oistrahk" and "Tutti, Like Rostropovich." The string sections got the message and the reaction to the Brahms score that Feldbrill had wanted was achieved by concert time.

In short, from this tour, Victor became aware of the pitfalls, particularly when he was visiting a different culture graced by an unfamiliar language that placed him at the mercy of interpreters who had but minimal experience with music and its making. He also came away from the Soviet tours with an awareness of how difficult it was to perform in a state with a dissimilar perception of the meaning of democracy and the impact it could have on the lives of musicians and composers. Yet he also discovered the extent to which a shared love of music enriched and liberated musicians who, in spite of the pressure of ideology and militaristic rhetoric, became his friends and colleagues.

The Soviet Union tours were to profoundly affect Victor's future. He had experienced a sense of mission in a world seemingly inching toward violence and nuclear annihilation. In the 1960s these exchanges of artists were the hopeful light on a very black horizon. He had seen the impact of war on the lives of innocent people, largely women and children, and that had influenced his decision to visit the Soviet Union. It is impossible to weigh the role that artists played during these decades we call the Cold War in creating a shared base of respect for human life and civilized behaviour. The rhetoric of violence, the actions of the CIA and the Pentagon, and the horrors imposed by Stalin and his successors, all promised a terrible future that in some small part was avoided by the many interactions of artists and creators during that almost half-century of tension.

As for Victor, the last years in Winnipeg were too busy to encourage any further effort to extend his international conducting presence beyond his annual trip to the BBC. However, the memory of much that transpired in the Soviet Union remained sweet and appealing, and he was determined that at some point he would expand his life mission to include major interventions in the field of guest conducting and eventually teaching abroad, in countries where he could experience a culture different from his own.

CHAPTER 17

An Invitation to Japan

As the years of the twentieth century's seventh decade sped by, Victor could point with pride to the hundreds of young people who had left his youth ensembles to take their place in the growing number of vastly improved professional orchestras both in Canada and abroad, or to those instructing and leading secondary-school and community orchestras across the land. As well, these were instrumentalists engaged in music education who were joining a growing number of colleagues in Canadian orchestras who cheered the appearance of a Canadian contemporary composition on their music stands rather than just mildly approving or demonstrating outright hostility of previous decades. In this way he had permanently changed the landscape of music in his native land.

When this work was expanded by his intense commitment to the National Youth Orchestra and the number of graduates emerging from the NYO, the TSYO, and the UTSO to join Canadian symphony orchestras from the West Coast to the Maritimes became extraordinarily prolific, he had every reason to feel pride in the role he had played. Every Feldbrill guest appearance across the country became a reunion with the many graduates from his university classes, and from the TSYO, UTSO, and NYO rehearsals and performances. These occasions led him to realize that he was at the centre of progressive and positive improvements in orchestral performance in Canada. For Victor, the question arose whether he could have a similar impact on another country and its culture.

Along with these encounters with the greater excellence in the symphonies he was involved with came a sense that he was improving the quality of orchestral conductors at all levels. His University of Toronto classes were fountains of inspiration where the basic techniques of the baton were being slowly passed on to new generations.

The 1970s provided another plateau in Victor's career with the assumption of the role of resident conductor of the TSO from 1974 to 1978. He had rescued the TSO from what could have been a major setback when Maestro Karel Ancerl died suddenly in the summer of 1973. There was no other person in the wings with Victor's understanding of the internal conflicts and drama, and he knew how to prevent situations that could negatively affect morale and ultimately the performance of the entire ensemble. It was no surprise then that Walter Homburger turned up at Victor's home on the morning after Ancerl's passing and appealed to all the love and loyalty Victor felt toward an ensemble that he had either played in or led over a quarter of a century.

Victor's contribution in the role of resident conductor was unique. He had the intimacy and self-assurance to carry out this most difficult position — that of giving leadership to the orchestra without having the authority that a regular, full-time conductor could have provided. After four years of stellar service he was able to step down with grace and elegance. So, with as little drama as possible, Victor calmly resigned his position once it was obvious that Andrew Davis was in place and could perform all the functions of conductor and artistic director. He left an orchestra that Davis (today, Sir Andrew) could lead with distinction and effectiveness for nearly a decade and a half. Yet Victor did remain part of the team as far as outreach was concerned and, at least for a short time, as the conductor of the TSYO.

≈≈≈

The 1970s were good years for the Feldbrill family. Zelda was playing a respected role in the schools of Toronto and was also providing leadership year after year to students of the Faculty of Social Work at the University of Toronto as a mentor and adviser. It was a time when the value of the graduates from this once-questioned form of preparation became established and the importance of the presence of professional social workers was increasingly being recognized. Her colleagues found that her previous work with Holocaust survivors in post-war Toronto, her special contributions in Winnipeg, and her enormously effective role with at-risk students in Toronto schools had been extraordinarily valuable and she was recognized even beyond her academic community as a cool, thoughtful, sensitive, and enormously effective practitioner-educator.

These were also the years in which the two Feldbrill daughters completed their formal educations, got married, and established families. Victor and Zelda were incredibly proud of their girls. They became grandparents and the new additions to the family brought special moments of delight into their lives.

However, as the decade came to an end, Victor faced a challenge that compared to any he had previously encountered. It came at the right time, and revealed an entirely new direction he might take on the international stage.

In 1978, Victor accompanied the TSO as a member of their leadership team (but without any conducting duties) on a tour of the Far East that included Japan. Unbeknown to him, conversations took place that would involve him and present an opportunity he could not reject, one that would dominate the 1980s as his most demanding commitment.

A year before, two Japanese students who had arrived at the University of Toronto's Faculty of Music in order to study violin and to play in the

UTSO contacted their past instructors back at home. They recounted their good fortune in Canada where they had been privileged to have before them a conductor who seemed to know all there was to know about playing in the string section of a symphony orchestra. They had become enormously impressed with Victor's leadership and the efforts he had made to reach them and overcome their limited capacity to speak the English language.

These students were close to their former professors at the Tokyo National University of Fine Arts and Music and had maintained a regular correspondence with professors Iwasaki and Fukui. In one of their letters they spoke highly of this popular conductor/professor at the University of Toronto, a Victor Feldbrill, who was in their opinion a quite proficient faculty member as well as an outstanding conductor. It was one of those coincidences that changes lives.

At that moment, Professor Fukui, an international figure of some consequence who was familiar with the music scene in North America, was some eighty years of age but fluent in English. He was relied upon by the cultural attachés at the Canadian Embassy in Japan for advice on ways in which arts events might strengthen the relationship between Japan and Canada. It was a fortunate moment in time as there was a priority in the Canadian Ministry of External Affairs that Professor Fukui came to believe might be exploited. The year 1979 was the fiftieth anniversary of the establishment of formal relations between Japan and Canada. Here was an opportunity to arrange an exchange of artists that might be the beginning of an effective form of celebration.

When Victor appeared with his TSO colleagues in 1978, he was propositioned by these Japanese professors to return to Japan the following year to engage in more than a mere short-term visit. He was asked to be involved in a full-term guest professorship that might lead to an even longer and more profound commitment. If the idea was to build a bridge of musical understanding, then several years of presence would be required, and it appeared that Victor had been singled out as the perfect informal ambassador by the prestigious Tokyo National University of Fine Arts and Music (now the Tokyo University of the Arts).

Fortunately, at the Canadian Embassy, Second Secretary of Cultural Affairs Alan Jones was prepared to go through all the intricacies of diplomatic interaction to make such an event happen. Even more surprising was Jones's willingness to be Victor's ally in advancing the knowledge of Canadian music in Japan. He was to assist Victor in bringing his close composer friend Harry Somers to Japan to support his strategy to play his composition, *Lyric*, with the university's Geidai Philharmonic Orchestra. He also wished to have Harry's violin sonata played where local composers could hear and appreciate his work. Victor, with his many contacts with Radio Canada was able to bring recordings of Harry's works to Japanese shores. Somers could thus become a beacon to the greater appreciation of Canadian music and could thereby represent his composer colleagues as an admirable example of Canadian musical creativity.

In 1979, when he returned to Japan, Victor was able to arrange for a presentation at the Nippon Press Club and invited members of the Japanese League of Modern Composers and the Japan Society for Music Education as well as composition students at Tokyo University to attend. The lecture was a sensation and both Victor and Harry Somers were introduced to Japanese composers and composition faculty, including Professor Fukui, who had been in negotiation about the possible invitation of a Canadian guest conductor as a guest professor at the Tokyo university for some time. Fukui, confident from his contacts with former students in Canada, informed the Embassy that he knew the person the university wanted as their guest conductor in the years ahead — Maestro Victor Feldbrill in Toronto. With his knowledge of Canadian music and his interest in contemporary composition, Victor was the perfect choice.

Alan Jones was followed at the Embassy by yet another figure, a cultural attaché, John Sloan, a man of extraordinary dedication. He joined this stream of officials who, over the years, would encourage and assist Victor in his efforts to bring great music and a unique quality of learning to Tokyo University and its faculty and students, and, as well, to advance the knowledge of Canadian music through his position as guest conductor before a host of audiences of orchestras he would come to conduct in Tokyo and across the nation.

To provide immediate evidence of their respect for all Victor had accomplished, shortly after the lecture it was arranged that he be transported to the Tokyo City Hall and there be presented with a City of Tokyo

Medal with a citation that recognized all his many years of work with young people. There could not have been a more appropriate honour at this time in his career.

Victor would return in the spring of the following year for a number of weeks before the formal contract for his service could actually be put in place. When all the arrangements were completed, Victor would take on a role he came to cherish — that of a conductor/professor. In the interim he wanted to assure his Japanese hosts that his enthusiasm was in no way waning as the long process of formal negotiation went on and his presence even for a few weeks was a definite asset in bringing the university–government discussions to a successful conclusion.

It could be said that Victor's 1979 visit was a dress rehearsal for the prospective years in the 1980s that were described as his "cultural re-birth" by Canadian colleagues. Though his Japanese hosts were sure they had the right man, they were taking no chances. The initial position at Tokyo University was termed a "visiting professorship," in which he would assume responsibility for conducting the university's professional symphony orchestra, the Geidai Philharmonia, as well as three orchestras of student instrumentalists. In addition, he would provide seminars for those students intent upon acquiring conducting skills in an advanced class in orchestral leadership.

Victor had not realized what a wealth of professional symphony ensembles were based in the nation's capital. There were some ten in number, including the Tokyo Metropolitan Orchestra, the Tokyo Symphony Orchestra, the Tokyo Philharmonic, the Japan Philharmonic, and the New Japan Philharmonic. As well, in the university there were outstanding choral forces capable of performing the Bach B Minor Mass or the Verdi Requiem with the Geidai Philharmonia. Each of the Tokyo orchestras had an audience that filled the hall for their concerts. As well, the major internationally recognized orchestras — the Boston Symphony, Vienna Philharmonic, and Philadelphia Orchestra — included Tokyo on their itinerary for any tours of the Far East. Victor was astonished at the amount of orchestral performance he found in Tokyo: "The excitement never seems to diminish." He also realized that the success of his Tokyo experience would be judged by his work with the array of Japanese orchestras in that city and others beyond the capital that made up the Japanese orchestral musical world.

Victor returned alone on April 18, 1979, though he had been determined to bring Zelda. However, she could not free herself until later in the spring. He was welcomed at the Tokyo airport by Canadian Embassy and university officials (including not only the head of the conducting department but the concertmaster of the Geidai Orchestra, as well). Within a couple of days, he was welcomed by the president of the university, whose office was, in Victor's words to Zelda, "the size of our house." Then it was off to a drop-in visit with the third-year student orchestra and, by the end of the first week, to a concert by the NHK Symphony Orchestra — a superb broadcasting ensemble, beside which Victor had to admit the TSO would be considered a good "provincial" orchestra. On the podium on that occasion was conductor/composer Krzysztof Penderecki, leading the orchestra in a program of his own music "with impeccable precision."

Victor began his work with the third-year student orchestra and at the first encounter found the musicians "very formal." He chose an initial challenge that would convince them he was serious — the Beethoven Symphony no. 3 (*Eroica*). Before a note was played, Victor explained the meaning of *forte* in a Beethoven composition and the contrast in sound to that same indication of volume and articulation in a Mozart or Schubert score. He then emphasized the importance of the achievement of balance between sections and "soon they were mesmerized by the sound they were making." Tokyo University's Professor Endo, the head of the conducting department, was ecstatic. Rarely had he seen his students at a rehearsal so animated and enthusiastic. Even the visiting German professors, who had arrived to watch the Canadian conductor who might become their colleague, were impressed.

One element of the Japanese style that Victor found difficult to change was the predominance of the brass sections, seated as they were on raised pedestals and seemingly unconscious of their capacity to overwhelm the strings and woodwinds. He wanted more restraint from that section and in order to make a statement, he had their elevation removed (as he did with the percussion section) and placed them in such a way that they were encouraged to listen and blend with the other sections. The physical rearrangement worked. (Years later, Victor was to discover that other Tokyo ensembles had removed the raised platform on which brass players had been traditionally placed and had achieved the similar orchestral balance.)

By the second month Victor was also working with the second-year orchestra and, though they had already rehearsed the Schubert *Unfinished Symphony*, "he could not believe how badly they played the opening." His solution was simple — he literally took the orchestra apart and worked on each section separately, but insisted on the other sections carefully listening as he took each through the opening bars and ultimately achieved the tone and flexibility he desired. Soon individual sections of the other student symphony orchestras were requesting separate rehearsals.

With all the years of conducting young people in Canada and, on occasion, in the United States and Britain, Victor had never encountered such eager response. At the end of rehearsals, entire orchestras "burst into applause and foot stamping." To Zelda he wrote, "they respond so well and so readily that it is a joy."[1] Often, Victor would look around at rehearsal and find the hall half filled with students from other years and other music classes. On one occasion he took the third-year orchestra through a reading of the Brahms's Symphony no. 1 and the students sitting in the hall rose as one to give a standing ovation.[2]

Again, the response was unanimously animated. The concertmaster of one orchestra commented that the ensemble had learned more in six rehearsals with Victor than they had over the previous two years. Even the orchestra's librarian joined in: "They are willing to play their hearts out for you." Very soon there was a response that drifted across the entire campus. "They 'ruv' you" was Professor Endo's interpretation of these events, but the Canadian Embassy official who had played a major role was more lucid: "Vic, I don't know what you are doing but the word is out that a real firebrand has hit the Tokyo University of the Arts."[3] It was clear that Embassy officials and Tokyo University students and faculty all wanted him back.

It would be 1982 before all the formalities could be observed and a formal professorship could be arranged. In the intervening years, Victor remained in close contact with his hosts. It was partly a matter of clearing Victor's schedule as well as concluding the endless negotiations within the university to find an appropriate place for all of Victor's talents. Meanwhile, as he introduced new repertoire to orchestras before his appointment, he ensured that Canadian composers were receiving attention. In one letter to Zelda, he asked her to phone Harry Somers to tell him "that the Geidai Philharmonia had applauded his piece *Lyric* after we played it today."[4]

Victor was also giving seminars to students who had hopes of becoming conductors. It was not baton technique that was missing. Rather it was essential that he push them in the direction of searching out authentic individual interpretations of the works of Western masters — a direction that was not comfortable in the context of a society emphasizing collectivity and personal modesty rather than individual achievement.

To increase his familiarity with the Tokyo musical culture, Victor often appeared as a listener at every concert he could find being performed across the city. On one occasion, he found a well-known British conductor leading the NHK Symphony in a performance that he could only describe as "awful." The orchestra was "ragged and rough in everything they played." It was a popular program — the Beethoven Symphony no. 8 was the centerpiece, with British favourites from the pens of Vaughan Williams, Elgar, and Britten making up the rest of the program. "I got better sound out of the third-year student orchestra," was Victor's assessment of the concert.[5]

It was not only the student response that was paramount in determining the future of Victor Feldbrill at Tokyo University. The assessment of the members of the Geidai professional orchestra was central to the decision that might lead to an appointment at the professorial rank. The rehearsals had gone well but the concert performance would be the real test.

Victor's immediate response to the first 1979 concert was positive. There was a full house — even more patrons than had come to hear Penderecki and the NHK Symphony a few nights before were in their seats. As well, the orchestra had come through: "The orchestra played beyond what happened at rehearsals and retained almost all I had been striving for, i.e., style, blend and precision." At the end of the concert, "the audience went wild and would not stop clapping." Victor's encore was the moving and melodic Samuel Barber *Adagio* and "it brought the house down." Throughout the thunderous applause, in deference to the man who they felt had achieved the miracle, the orchestra members refused to stand to accept the accolades. The only way Victor could end the evening was to take the concertmaster by the hand and physically lead him to the stage wing. It was the last step in the process of deciding Victor's future role in Tokyo. It had been a triumph.[6]

A Canadian Embassy official, John Sloan, heard from the university president that "the Geidai Orchestra has never sounded as well under any conductor in all its years of existence." However, it was the good opinions of the orchestra members that Victor most treasured. The first clarinetist put it best: "Mr. Feldbrill, I have to speak for all of us, especially the woodwinds when I tell you that you are the first conductor who has made us sound like a real instrument and for that I thank from the bottom of my heart."[7]

From this point there was little doubt that much of Victor's time in the 1980s would be taken up by his responsibilities at Tokyo University. The Canadian Embassy felt they had pulled off a "coup" — a Canadian had been found who could not only bring excitement to the musical life of Japan but one who could introduce that nation to the works of Canadian composers.

Victor had realized that it was essential that he return to Japan year after year until the appointment was actually in place. That would reveal his enthusiasm and assure the Japanese he was still anxious to come. Thus, in May of 1980 he was back in Tokyo for a short visit, to maintain his contact with the university and to lecture and meet with students and faculty.

At the top of the list of engagements in 1981 was the Tokyo Metropolitan Orchestra and yet another ensemble in Sapporo. Again, these events went well. The collective assessment of the musicians was that he was "an excellent conductor, a superb musician and a real gentleman."[8]

Although Zelda had been able to join Victor for the last month of his 1979 visit, the remaining months of absence from Toronto in the years 1979 to 1981 had been deeply disturbing for Victor. More than ever he missed Zelda whenever her own professional duties kept her in Toronto rather than allowing her to be with him in Tokyo. The separation from his children, their spouses, and the growing number of grandchildren made his loneliness even more intense. Their expectation was that she would be retiring from her work and would be accompanying him to Japan, but things were more complicated than expected. She had to get herself extricated from her academic and mentoring responsibilities. And for Zelda, separation from the rest of the family was a problem. Aviva, especially during the time when she was pregnant and shortly after, seemed to need her mother's presence, and Zelda treasured this new intimacy with her daughter.

As well, she knew that she could not spend her time in Japan with no role to play but that of being Victor's wife. Indeed, people at both the university and the Canadian Embassy, as well as new friends in Japan, made it clear she would be welcomed as an instructor in English conversation by a host of individuals associated both with the university and the Embassy. There emerged a campaign to attract her enthusiasm. Victor was determined to find a role that would satisfy her determination to be useful and make a contribution. Reading the local English-language newspaper, he found an advertisement expressing the need for English-speaking social workers. When she arrived, Zelda followed up by telephoning the employment agency and was hired on the spot. She would be working with social workers engaged in the placing of children for whom adoption was desired. In some cases she was working with Embassy staff people seeking to return home with a Japanese child. She spent three days a week carrying out what she found to be a most satisfying job.

Victor was elated. Her work was an important element in Victor's strategy to shift his direction toward the pursuit of an international career. He had discovered in 1979 that without her his loneliness was "the worst I have experienced" and the presence of Zelda was essential to his desire to seek new horizons. However, besides the issue of presence and intimacy, there were also economic considerations that had to be faced. Victor realized he must find activities that would add to his income. He could not consider returning to the University of Toronto. As well, as he put it succinctly to Zelda, "the CBC has all but folded for any conductor and guest appearances are almost non-existent." He had decided that after decades his radio and television broadcasting opportunities were diminishing. Thus, his work in the media as well as his academic life was coming to an end. In straight economic terms he could only advise Zelda, "The Japanese thing cannot go on forever — let's make the best of it while it lasts."

However, for Zelda it was a time of retirement and also one of re-evaluation. During these years she wrote with some passion as Victor proceeded to move in the direction of the appointment in Japan. The reality that this would lead to increased and lengthy absences from home could not be softened for her this time. She realized that in spite of the joy she felt being with Victor, the Japanese position also represented separation from the rest of the family and their familiar community. In terms of his thought of pursuing an international conducting career, "Is this what you want?" was her constant question.

For Victor this query challenged his own sense of mission as well as the love he had for his family. Victor's eventual reply revealed his distaste for what seemed his only alternative to his Japanese commitment — "being the old reliable at the Toronto Symphony." His situation in Japan stood in considerable contrast. "Here they can't wait to work for me." Victor went on:

> And darling, I've been knocking myself out for years for this kind of respect and recognition. No, it does not compensate for my family, but once you are with me, a lot of that will be overcome. Does that make sense? Please tell me what you feel about this. I can hardly wait for your letter so we can carry on some sort of dialogue.[9]

In that same letter, Victor could take some relief in the fact that through all this discussion, their affection for each other had miraculously survived: "I'm happy to know that we mean so much to each other…. I love you more than words can say."

However, the interchange about the future continued. Victor worried constantly: "At home, I would be sitting around waiting for the rare CBC bone to be thrown my way. The TSO remains constant so far but no one can predict how long that could go on. This [his work in Tokyo] could be an exciting way for a few years."[10]

Once again, his letter could conclude with the statement that after nearly fifty years of commitment, "we have each other and nothing is worth more than that."

In 1982 he could sense that a new opportunity to conduct extensively across the entire country of Japan was emerging. As well, he was becoming more deeply involved in the affairs of the Tokyo University orchestras; indeed, he was conspiring to give the Geidai Philharmonia its own reality, by changing its image to that of an orchestra in its own right, not just a university add-on ensemble that was easily confused with student orchestras. He also shifted the emphasis on academic-year-based student ensembles by reducing their number from three to two and insisted on a process that focused on the effective preparation of students and connecting them to the world of symphonic music "out there" rather than that of everyone "moving together," lock-step, through the university orchestral performing experience. It solved the problem of there not being enough talented students in particular sections of the orchestras to make up three ensembles. Victor expected a revolt from his colleagues but was pleased to find that they agreed completely with his proposals.

Yet with all these triumphs he could not lose the sense that he should be at home in Canada with his family, devoting his time to the culture to which he had already made such a contribution. On March 28, 1985, he would write to Zelda, "It's time to come home for good." Just three weeks before, realizing how orchestras must plan their seasons ahead, he had written to Walter Homburger to inform him of his decision in the hope that there might be a place for him in the TSO's future plans. He was far from being finished with Japan or the Far East, but he now knew where his greatest satisfaction would be found — in his country, in his province and its capital city, and most of all, in the midst of his family.

CHAPTER 18

The Far East

It was not until the fall of 1981 that the *Globe and Mail* informed the Canadian public of Victor's Tokyo University appointment and quoted him on his enthusiastic perception of the nature of his role. In the article, he emphasized one particular aspect that had attracted him. In contrast to the atmosphere of confrontation often found in North America between conductor and orchestra members, he stated that "musicians tend to regard conductors as teachers over there. The conductor is not the natural enemy of the orchestra in Japan." It was a tradition that Victor wanted to test.[1]

In the article, Victor made it very clear that he was weaving himself a lifestyle that still included Toronto, where his daughters and their spouses along with his grandchildren lived. It would still be his home and his artistic base even though more than six months of his year would be spent in Japan. However, it was quite clear that for the next few years he would give special attention to the cause of enhancing the role of symphonic music in the land that he and Zelda had now come to love.

It was made obvious that the role that the Tokyo University of Fine Arts and Music envisioned for Victor had two major elements. The university considered itself the most prestigious source of training in the musical arts in the country, with a mandate to enhance the knowledge and technique of the graduates in presenting Western music as an element in Japan's broad and comprehensive culture. With meticulous care, a process had been constructed by the university that brought able instructors from abroad who would bring their expertise in European music performance to Japan. To that point, the invitees had largely been brought on the assumption that the most prolific and recognized composers and the most famous performing artists had come from western Europe. For the first time, the university had looked east to North America, and the first Canadian to hold such an appointment in the conducting department of the music faculty was Victor Feldbrill.

For Victor, there was an opportunity to participate in the education of both instrumentalists and audiences over an extended period, along with an active interchange with the community of Japanese composers.

Certainly a most attractive aspect of the appointment was the expectation that Victor would be conducting student orchestras as well as the Geidai Philharmonia, the university's professional orchestra, in its annual series of concerts. He had no intention of withdrawing from occupying the podiums of the professional symphony orchestra at a time when he was at the height of his conducting career. As well, he would be conducting not one student orchestra, as he had at the University of Toronto, but as many as three student orchestras — one from each academic year in the program. Later, on Victor's advice, this number was reduced to two such ensembles, each with its own rehearsal and performance schedule. It was as though this appointment had been created for him. It combined his desire to be an active conductor of major orchestras as well as his delight in working with young people.

His accommodation in Japan was completely looked after. He, and when possible, Zelda, were living in an apartment owned by the university, in a "House for Foreign Professors." In an effort to keep Victor and Zelda comfortable, a member of the faculty had visited them in their home in Toronto and had photographed every room. When Victor and Zelda reached their abode at the university, their familiar electrical appliances had been replicated for their convenience in their new Tokyo apartment.

Not only were all the amenities provided but trips to the important historic sites in Japan were arranged upon request. The Feldbrills would play the unfamiliar role of being tourists as well as employed visitors. Inevitably there were occasional bureaucratic interferences, but on the whole the Japanese obsession with avoiding conflict and confrontation worked well for Victor and Zelda. When together they were in a veritable heaven on earth, but still had those months each year back in Toronto where they could enjoy the company of their growing family. They had no hesitation in playing the role of doting grandparents; indeed, they did so with evident satisfaction and delight.

Zelda was thrilled with the opportunity to visit Japan and to be present over an extended period. As Victor remembered, "She loved it there ... the civility ... the respect for personal space ... the warmth of the people." It was not long before she found her own niche — in the world of social work she so loved: "It was her way of being useful and engaged, especially when I was conducting orchestras in other cities." [2]

The visit in 1979 had been a dress rehearsal for all that was to occur in the 1980s. The Japanese appointment became the dominant challenge in Victor's life. He was expected to lecture students on occasion in Canadian music and its composers, doing so with a broad stroke, making reference to the vast nature of Canadian contemporary music writing. He contrasted the contained island context of Japanese composition with the Canadian composer's passion for openness and dramatic effect — the result of the influence of living in a huge country of magnificent beauty with a splendid contrast of climate and geography. He used the compositions of Somers, Archer, Pentland, Freedman, Weinzweig, Cable, Beckwith, Applebaum, and Schafer to illustrate his point. He made it clear there was no "Canadian school" of composition but that there were common elements that surfaced in the work of these and others, but with significant differences as well. It was indeed a series of lessons on the patterns of creative music-making that had given dynamic inspiration to the building of his Canadian repertoire.

However, it was the conducting that particularly excited Victor. As well as the three (later two) student orchestras and the professional orchestra, there was also the opportunity to conduct several ensembles which graced the capital city of Tokyo and other cities of any size in the country. The orchestras associated with the university, even the Geidai Philharmonia, were, to Victor's delight, available for the performing of student compositions. As well, the orchestra was devoted to the training of student conductors, a role that Victor had also taken on as part of his academic duties. He was engaged in their preparation and it was deemed essential that they spend some time on the podium, coaxing sound and movement from their fellow student instrumentalists and even from the faculty colleagues in the Geidai Philharmonia (a role no professional orchestra in Canada in Victor's experience had ever agreed to assume on a regular basis). This was made possible by the fact that some members of that Geidai Philharmonia were also on the faculty roster of Tokyo University and performing student compositions was considered a part of their academic responsibilities.

This experience would be no holiday from the frantic pace of musical life in Toronto. It was a demanding academic experience he had agreed to be a part of, yet one that satisfied the main objectives of his life in music performance. Of course, one of the major challenges would be that of communicating, both as a lecturer and conductor, when he had no facility in the Japanese language. There were those in his conducting classes and orchestral ensembles who did, in fact, speak English. Though their traditional Japanese humility forbade them to seek distinction apart from their colleagues by indicating any superiority in the speaking of the English language, they could be enormously helpful in passing on the more demanding expectations of their animated Canadian conductor who was limited to articulating his thoughts through his baton alone.

Many visitors to Japan resent the imposing formality which characterizes relationships in that country but Victor handled these elements of cultural style quite well. He did not emulate the brashness of the stereotypical North American; indeed, his own reserved nature was one of his endearing qualities on the Tokyo campus and beyond. Nor did Zelda in any way have any aggressive attributes that could offend Japanese sensibilities. They were the perfect couple for the role they were playing as ambassadors of Canadian goodwill, a point the Embassy officials appreciated immeasurably.

A memo from External Affairs, dated June 19, 1979, had succinctly described Victor's early days at Tokyo University in the most generous terms, stressing his success with the Geidai Philharmonia. After comments extolling Victor's knowledge and enthusiasm came a glowing assessment: "Orchestra members were quite open in their admiration of his musical ability and as the end of his stay approached it became obvious he would be asked back again at the Tokyo University of the Arts. It was agreed that the orchestra had played the best they had for some time under Feldbrill."[3]

* * *

Upon his return to Canada in 1979, Victor had taken the initial step in preparation to free himself to accept a position in Tokyo — he sent his resignation to the dean at the University of Toronto's Faculty of Music, Gus Ciamaga. He could state without hesitation that he had found "his time at the university enjoyable and rewarding." He could also take some pride in the fact that during what would eventually be fourteen years of service he had trained some 480 orchestral students and could report that he could now find University of Toronto graduates of his classes "in nearly every orchestra across Canada." It was a statistic he could regard with signal pride — one that decades later represents a magnificent contribution to the musical life of the country. He concluded by informing Dean Ciamaga that the 1981–82 academic session would end his work at the University of Toronto.

On the evening of April 4, 1982, in the MacMillan Theatre on the University of Toronto campus, a special concert took place. Music critic Ron Hambleton described it as "a grand farewell Victor gave Toronto." It was also Victor's last concert as conductor of the UTSO, and with the playing of the massive Mahler Symphony no. 2 (*The Resurrection Symphony*) it was an event to be remembered, one that included not only his orchestra but the University Singers, the University of Toronto's primary choral ensemble, as well. Hambleton went on to inform his readers that over the years Victor had taken this orchestra through some seventy-four major orchestral works: "It was impressive to see him surrounded by this battery of young musicians, even more impressive to hear the work come to life under his baton. The choral work was outstanding and the ensemble rose to the challenges presented by the resonant score."[4]

Not to be outdone on this festive occasion, Arthur Kapitanis of the *Globe and Mail* proffered his own set of statistics that of the hundreds of student conductors in Victor's music education classes, there were many now leading secondary-school orchestras across Canada. Even in the shadow of all this achievement, Kapitanis had wondered whether on this occasion the student ensemble could possibly address this monumental work: "Would they bring *The Resurrection* to life? As it happened, they played and sang as well as Feldbrill could have dreamed ... the strings had bite and body, and the collected winds detonated some of Mahler's grandest climaxes with hair-raising energy."[5]

It was only a few days later that Victor was back in Japan, enjoying a reunion with Tokyo University's professional orchestra, the Geidai Philharmonia. There was a concert coming up and he had scheduled Mussorgsky's *Pictures at an Exhibition*. He wanted to shift the orchestra's preoccupation with the German repertoire and introduce them to the descriptive emphasis of this work from a major Russian composer. It suited his purpose perfectly. It was not without a little "quiet tirade." Victor remembered that the Russians had been the enemy of Japan, especially since the beginning of the twentieth century. However, one of the delights of working with this "in-house" ensemble was "his wonderful feeling to be able to work with this professional orchestra in an atmosphere of limitless rehearsal time." He was determined to achieve perfect intonation and a "sustained orchestral sound that sings" and it would take that extra rehearsal effort to make every player aware of the sound Victor was seeking. Eventually, after the performance, later in May, he could say that the strings "glowed with warmth" and that indeed "you could see the Gates of Kiev." The players were ecstatic over the quality of their performance.[6]

At the next Geidai Philharmonia concert, Victor programmed the Mozart Concertante for Winds and Orchestra (using principals of the Geidai orchestra). The impact was obvious. The quality performance not only raised the self-confidence of the orchestral players but elevated their morale as well. The attitude of the orchestra toward his conducting continued to please Victor: "They want criticism — what a contrast to the atmosphere at home." He had found he could be away from the orchestra for months and return to carry on as if he had never left.[7]

Victor found that he had a major challenge with the students intending to become conductors. Their instruction had led them to concentrate on arm and hand movement with little attention to music interpretation. He was determined on his return to change that preoccupation and he spent many hours concentrating on the individual reaction to musical text — an emphasis that Japanese musicians with their tendency to elevate modesty and restraint, found difficult.

There was another area that needed Victor's attention. His students had little experience with collective orchestral sight-reading. It was not the custom for conductors to take orchestras through an uninterrupted initial run-through of a composition without previous preparation. He stressed the advantage of this technique of introducing players to the challenge of addressing unfamiliar music.[8]

While in Japan, Victor never missed a chance to hear visiting orchestras under the batons of distinguished conductors as part of his role as an educator seeking to instruct other conductors. Often the concerts were "a complete bore," but a visit by the Bamberger Symphony Orchestra convinced him that an international presence could be a satisfying role. The orchestra "played magnificently" under Eugen Joachim, now eighty years of age, a man whom Victor called "the last of a breed of excellent conductors from Germany," and he waxed enthusiastically about his "incredible shading of the colours of the music and the real control of the climaxes."[9] Victor never lost his capacity to revel in the wonder of a true genius and he transmitted his excitement to his students.

He passed on to the Kajimoto Agency, which was handling his external conducting, that he could take limited time from his academic duties to carry out conducting invitations in other Japanese cities. He made it clear that when there were clashes, his academic duties took precedence. Yet, as early as 1982, he could proudly inform Zelda, "I've got as many guest spots as I've had in three years in Canada [excluding TSO gigs]."[10]

In 1983 Victor was invited to conduct Beethoven's Symphony no. 9 (Choral) on eight occasions by different Japanese orchestras over a period of some six weeks (from November to January). This massive composition was played obsessively by Japanese orchestras, sometimes as many as fifteen times in each performing season, which ran from November to January to sold-out audiences. There is nothing to compare with this preoccupation with a particular composition on this scale in any other jurisdiction in the world. (Perhaps the closest approximation might be the inevitable multiple choral performances of Handel's *Messiah* that choirs in the English-speaking world perform every Christmas season.) A.D. Gibson, in an article in the *Asaki Evening News*, questioned Victor regarding the ability of each orchestra to be "up" for every performance of the work. Victor reply was very straightforward: "This symphony fills the halls ... but more important, the music that is produced is as fresh and vibrant as any works played throughout the year." Could it be that the text of the final movement emphasizing the brotherhood of humankind had special relevance to the people of a country that has the distinction of containing the only victims of atomic bomb attacks and thereby a notion of what a future nuclear war would be like?

Victor found that although the members of the orchestras he rehearsed had virtually memorized every note of the Beethoven composition, they insisted upon playing every bar in every rehearsal nonetheless. "They approach each performance as a new experience," was his conclusion.[11]

⚊⚊

By 1984, Victor was expanding his horizons in Asia by accepting a conducting opportunity in the Philippines arranged by Canada's Ministry of External Affairs. It was not an invitation he relished. He was aware of the negative world view of the Marcos régime and wanted no part of any performance that would seem to give support to the corruption and political oppression that was so much a part of that country's troubles. The Canadian Embassy assured him that there would be no possibility that the ruling family would be present. Indeed, the invitation was centred on his ability to transfer his musical talent and experience to an inexperienced orchestra. He was to work with the Philippine ensemble for some ten days, extend the ensemble's repertoire, provide an opportunity for the orchestra to sample examples of Canadian creativity, then conduct a concert that provided evidence of his success. On that basis, Victor accepted.

He placed before the orchestra a demanding task — to conquer Richard Strauss's *Death and Transfiguration* along with Canadian Pierre Mercure's *Kaleidoscope* and to end the evening performance with the Brahms Symphony no. 2. The *Manila Daily Express* covered the concert, and its reviewer, Rosalindah Orossa, wrote of the Strauss: "With little physical movement, Feldbrill set a clear, precise, steady beat and extracted robust sounds — massive, solid and cohesive from the players." Of the Mercure composition she said little, except to indicate her pleasure that "what Feldbrill admirably succeeded in doing was to galvanize the ensemble into a tightly knit and clear articulation." Brahms received even shorter shrift: "The baton wielder miraculously delineated each melodic line or curve for audience discernment." One could not escape the conclusion that in spite of the conductor's dislike of the Philippines political situation, the orchestra had learned its lessons well.[12]

By March of 1984, Victor was coming to the conclusion that he was losing interest in international guest conducting unless he was in front of a first-rate orchestra. The pressure and frustration of coping with second-rate ensembles when there were language blockages as well, were simply no longer attractive enough to compensate for the exhausting travel and continued absence from Zelda and his family.

His decision in this regard was strengthened after 1987. His work in Japan went so well that the Canadian Embassy, hand in hand with the Chinese government, contacted Victor, offering him a series of concerts over a three-week period in China, initially to be one in Beijing and one in Tianjin. Not only was he hesitant about the quality of the Chinese orchestras, he had decided he wanted to make a commitment that went beyond a handful of concerts to one that included the influencing of the quality of conducting and performing in the communities he was visiting. As much as he insisted, the provision of seminars for conducting students who might be interested and willing to benefit from his experience did not come off. With the co-operation of the Canadian Embassy and the Chinese Broadcasting Symphony Orchestra, he had high hopes that the first concert, now to be in Tianjin (and to be televised), might provide such an opportunity. It was not to be. There were no potential conductors on site. As well, the orchestra turned out to be very poor and Victor found he was "back to basics" if anything of musical quality was to be transmitted.

The Tianjin concert was well received but was far from Victor's standards of performance expectation. It was now on to Beijing where he had scheduled the Mozart Symphony no. 35 and as his Canadian composition, John Weinzweig's *Symphonic Ode*, the latter no doubt perceived as "capitalist music" yet ironically written by one of Canada's most respected left-wing radical artists. As the concluding selection he had chosen the Sibelius Symphony no. 2 and as an encore he had prepared an orchestral version of a Chinese folk song arranged by a local composer. The Chinese Broadcasting Orchestra was one of China's finest. The reaction of the audience was jubilantly positive.

However, Victor was once again disappointed in the quality of the total experience. He was treated royally and the orchestra was most enthusiastic. But the musicians, though willing, had been rendered incompetent by the country's history. The Cultural Revolution had savaged the orchestra's capacity to play Western music. Ideology had triumphed but competent musical expression had been effectively undermined. Active musicians had been declared enemies of the people and had been sent into the country to work in the fields. By definition, members of orchestras playing Western music were seen as disloyal. As with university academic disciplines in the 1980s, music performance of Western composition in China was in tatters. As Victor reported, the Chinese orchestra lacked basic tuning procedures and failed to observe simple time values. Sadly, the impact on the quality of the composition being played was negative. Members of sections had no idea which section had the theme of the piece being played. Victor was confronted with total chaos.

Needless to say, the tour was, in Victor's eyes, a trying time. There was not enough opportunity to shape these ensembles into effective musical instruments. Though his concerts were greeted with considerable audience and orchestral enthusiasm, he felt that his standards had not been reached.

Victor's Canadian colleagues had become aware that he was seemingly invisible in Canada for several months each year. In an article in the March 1984 periodical *The Canadian Composer*, music reviewer Arthur Kapitanis repeated the view that Victor was easily Canadian music's "most dedicated podium spokesman." He then outlined Feldbrill's success in playing Canadian music outside Canada with a list of the well-travelled compositions by Somers, Weinzweig, Freedman, and their colleagues that Victor had featured and focused on in the Japanese music scene. In particular, Kapitanis quoted Victor's description of the encouragement given by the Japanese music faculties to write for the symphony orchestra — in contrast to the Canadian scene where he felt that the composition of music for full symphonic orchestra was being de-emphasized. Composition departments in North America were advising students to concentrate their attention on chamber music for solo instruments or for duos, trios, quartets, and quintets, where the likelihood of the composition being played before an audience was significantly greater.

Kapitanis described the process by which a panel of faculty from the music department would select the compositions of two students whose compositions would, in a single morning, be played by the Geidai Philharmonia in an auditorium filled with fellow students and faculty members. The process would have included a meeting with Victor and the student composers several times before they appeared with their compositions. On completion of each composition's performance by the Geidai Philharmonic, audience members and orchestral players were invited to critique the selection. It was a methodology that Victor thought deserved replication in Canada with perhaps the cost of orchestral members being supported by special grants from provincial arts councils and the Canada Council for the Arts. The Kapitanis reaction to this determination to encourage creativity was, "Little wonder that Tokyo attracts the best outside talent from all over the world. And the best just happens to include Victor Feldbrill."[13]

Two years later, Rick Kardonne, writing in *Lifestyle* magazine (Spring Issue, National Edition), also set the record straight with an adulatory article that began with the question: "Who is the most honored and sought after symphonic conductor in Japan? The answer: Toronto's own Victor Feldbrill." The author pointed out that Tokyo outstripped New York in both area and population, but unexpectedly also in its passion for symphonic music. Kardonne outlined the outstanding success Victor was having in what he perceived to be a conductor's paradise, a contrast from the

North American context of competition and an individualistic artistic life that seemed dominant. He quoted Victor's description: "The complete dedication of all the musicians in the orchestra to work to regard each other as colleagues is a way of life. The atmosphere at the rehearsals is one of constant learning. It's very refreshing to have this 100 percent attention. Yet the atmosphere is more relaxed with them than expected."[14]

It was Kardonne's assessment that it was in this less aggressive and less confrontational atmosphere that the Feldbrill philosophy and style could thrive.

While Victor was focusing his attention on the musical life of Japan and receiving the accolades from that country's music lovers that he received the highest civilian honour his own nation could bestow — an appointment as a Fellow of the Order of Canada. It was the ultimate irony that with all the work he had accomplished to enhance the role of the Canadian artist and the improvement of the quality of presentation of Canadian orchestras, this citation emphasized his work in another country. It stated:

> Victor Feldbrill teaches at the prestigious Japanese University ... conducts the best Japanese orchestras ... uses his very influential position to assist Canadian artists in performing in this part of the world and thereby introducing Canadian contemporary music to audiences and in so doing supports the Canadian Embassy's cultural activities.[15]

It was an occasion at which a number of eminent Canadians were so honoured. William Davis, a most distinguished premier of the province of Ontario, whose contribution to the cultural and educational life of the country in the 1960s and '70s was being appropriately recognized. As well, June Callwood, a social activist whose work on behalf of the marginal and the forgotten, such as battered women and victims of HIV-AIDS, was another recipient. Betty Oliphant, whose contribution to the founding of the internationally recognized National Ballet School could scarcely be measured, was present as an Order recipient, along with author

Timothy Findley, a giant literary figure of the age. Both represented the best of Canada's cultural community. Victor would certainly have known another recipient, Mary Jolliffe, from his Stratford days. Her passion for the promotion of theatre and its management had successfully launched the festival. Most appropriate of all was the presence of another appointee, the composer André Prévost, whose music Victor had conducted. Victor was in good company indeed.

Just a year later he became the first recipient of the Roy Thomson Hall Award. Nancy Westaway and her colleagues had established this prize to recognize musical figures who were perceived to have enhanced the musical life of Toronto. As a distinguished volunteer leader, she had remembered the 1970s and the enormous efforts that Victor had put behind reaching new audiences and as well recalled the role Victor had played in holding things together at the TSO when Karel Ancerl had suddenly died. Her citation remarked on the fact that Victor, in order to accomplish such feats, "must be a psychologist as well as a communicator, to shape the orchestra for excellent performance, to teach, to reactivate, inspire, and to do so with a joy and love of music." As well, she recounted, he had revealed "the courage to play new music, to do so with a twinkle in his eye." She, too, emphasized his international role: "His approachable personality, his infinite patience and his outstanding technical abilities have taken him away from our Music Faculty at the University of Toronto, to Japan where he motivates young conductors."[16] The *Toronto Star* headline on the front page of the February 18 edition announced the presentation of the award and put it simply that Victor had been honoured for his "outstanding contribution to the city's musical life."

It was appropriate that on an occasion in which he was in Toronto receiving honours rather than in Tokyo, he conducted the TSO and received a splendid review from Arthur Kapitanis. The program included a performance of Mussorgsky's *Pictures at an Exhibition* that Kapitanis described as "a corker." He continued, "Seldom has the TSO responded as energetically to Feldbrill's demands and seldom has Feldbrill's interpretation held itself together with such a convincing sense of grandeur."[17]

Victor's contract with Tokyo University was renewed for 1985, '86, and '87. However, he had decided that Canada would be his home and his place of operation beyond that year. His Japanese colleagues were disappointed. Giving him their highest accolade through the reaction of Professor Endo, they expressed the view, "We want you to die here." However, Victor was adamant. From that point he would accept guest conducting appearances on a short-term basis only. As one would expect, these opportunities came as the 1980s wound down and the '90s emerged.

Though his academic role would disappear, the greatest advantage for Victor would be that he could continue to conduct the fine orchestras that Japan offered. As the 1980s rolled on, Victor had become increasingly familiar with the enthusiasms of Japanese orchestras and audiences and the means by which he could extend his repertoire choices to bring both enjoyment and inspiration. As well, his attention could continue to be focused on one of the main reasons for his presence since the 1970s — the improvement of the various ensembles with which he was connected, particularly the Geidai Philharmonia and Tokyo University student orchestras. As early as 1982, that latter element of his presence was being recognized. The reviewer for the *Japan Times* commented in some appreciation for his efforts after a student orchestral concert:

> The Canadian conductor's forthright interpretations were executed with vigor and considerable aplomb by his instrumentalists and graduate students.... Feldbrill showed taste and a fine sense of balance and the orchestra played cleanly for him.[18]

Indeed, a respected music reviewer in Japan, Marcel Grilli, was driven to a comparison that did not endear him to the many other orchestras in Tokyo. Feldbrill's third-year student orchestral ensemble performance had "sounded as good as some of the professional orchestras in this metropolis," and concluded that "both conductor and players are to be warmly praised for the generally high standards their work reflected."[19]

A few years later, Grilli reviewed Victor's performance of the magnificent Shostakovich Symphony no. 5 with the Tokyo City Philharmonic Orchestra. He remembered that he had heard this piece played by the New York Philharmonic some years earlier and had been deeply moved by the work. He found, however, that in Victor's presentation "there were many moments when I felt as affected as on the first occasion." He went on to state:

> Professor Feldbrill's fine control of rhythm secured some splendid climaxes, as well as contrasts of texture and dynamic. He also succeeded in securing admirable response from his players. Having heard a previous performance by the Tokyo City Philharmonic (under another conductor), I must confess I approached this concert with some misgiving. I was greatly rewarded.[20]

Victor programmed a great deal of Brahms in his Tokyo concerts. As the decade ended, he was invited to conduct the 330th subscription concert of the Tokyo Symphony Orchestra. Both the Brahms third symphony and his first piano concerto were scheduled and the reviewer praised Victor's interpretation as "quite agreeable and pleasing recognizing that Brahms's deep and dignified tone was so well presented through his obvious understanding of the uniqueness in the sound of Brahms's music."[21]

One of the last concerts that Victor gave during his tenure at Tokyo University was in September 1986. M. Uno, the critic for the most impressive of Japan's musical periodicals, covered this concert of the Tokyo Philharmonic Orchestra in the city's Festival Hall. He termed it "a superb concert" and supported his opinion in most laudatory language: "The purity of sound and the tight ensemble playing was in sharp contrast to the usual standard of this orchestra. The dramatic change was entirely due to its excellent guest conductor Victor Feldbrill."[22]

His enthusiasm for the repertoire was evident. The performance of Debussy's *Afternoon of a Faun* occasioned the comment from Uno that "rarely have I heard this piece so well performed in Japan."

Victor was to return year after year to conduct single concerts in Japan. But the time for long absences from home and family had ended. He would now be back in Toronto, with no specific appointment at hand. However, his focus had changed yet again. He would find that his talents were to be engaged in continuing to enhance the well-being of Canadian orchestras that needed the kind of leadership for which he was now famous.

CHAPTER 19

Assisting Canadian Orchestras

During the late 1980s, Victor celebrated his sixtieth birthday. He had by this time developed an enviable reputation both abroad and at home. He had completed several years of acclaimed leadership in Japan and experienced forays into the Philippines and China. He was never to completely abandon that part of the world even though from that point Toronto was to be his home and his base of operations both in a personal and professional sense. Throughout his years abroad he had maintained his connection with the past and the TSO. He regularly conducted concerts, particularly those whose programs seemed to be unusual, or ones being performed in somewhat exotic venues that had to be flexibly accommodated — for example, an Ontario Place outdoor presentation area with a revolving stage and the making of music amidst the presence of noisy sporting events only a few hundred yards distant.

Sometimes his life between Tokyo sessions seemed particularly frantic, especially when they were accompanied by annual concerts with the BBC that were in competition for his time with commitments in Canada. For example, in 1980, not only was he conducting a Manchester BBC Orchestra on radio but the nearby Northern College of Music engaged him to conduct a demanding program that included the Brahms Concerto no. 2 for Piano and Orchestra (with Stephen Hough as soloist) and the Beethoven *Egmont Overture.* In addition, appreciating Victor's commitment to contemporary composition, Northern College added the Tippett Symphony no. 4 — not an easily conquered work for young musicians not yet fully launched on a career in a professional orchestra. Yet Victor took on the latter work with considerable delight.

Back in the late 1970s, Victor had found Orchestra London (Ontario) was searching for a new conductor and going through the normal hesitations that orchestras experience when seeking new leadership. Help was needed but Victor made it clear that he was not interested in accepting a position of artistic directorship with any ensemble. Equally typical of his mindset, however, he was willing to help the orchestra find its way to a new level of performance in its leaderless interim. In 1979 he had realized that although there was universal enthusiasm to arrange his presence as both an academic and a conductor at the Tokyo University of Fine Arts and Music, it would be two or three years before all the niceties of such an appointment could be resolved. In the meantime he could assist Canada's Orchestra London. With this very narrow window of opportunity he accepted the role of acting music director of that ensemble with responsibilities to provide conducting services (which meant he would be on the podium or others who he had contracted would be) for all of fifty concerts and accompanying rehearsals. He would assume responsibility to audition and employ musicians and to plan the season's array of programs, ensuring that they would be attractive and enticing. This he did while simultaneously withdrawing from his University of Toronto duties, restraining his services to the TSO, and directing his thoughts and energies more particularly to the work he was anxious to accomplish in Japan.

Once it was plain to orchestra managements in the 1980s that he was available for several months in Canada each year, there were calls on his wealth of conducting experience and reputation for quality performance; as well, he became a source of consultation and a purveyor of valuable advice. It was a role that Victor performed with enthusiasm and dedication. If there was a crisis, even a specific concert that posed a problem, Victor was there to fill in and overcome all kinds of obstacles. For example, even before his formal Tokyo appointment, the Niagara Symphony had scheduled, as a climax to its 1979–80 season, a performance of the Brahms *Alto Rhapsody* and the composer's *German Requiem*. The venue was Brock University in St. Catharines, where there was unfortunately only a hopelessly inadequate gymnasium available for orchestral performances. With only ten days' notice, Victor achieved what was described by reviewer Lorraine LePage as "a remarkable balance between the choral and orchestral presentations." Of the requiem, she could report, "The Brahms selection survived the condition of the hall extraordinarily well which can only be attributed to the skill of Victor Feldbrill."[1]

That same spring he was still conducting Orchestra London and on the April 23 and 24 concerts, reviewer Richard Newman commented on his response to possible disaster most enthusiastically. Victor had been confronted with a disappointment when "star" cellist Leonard Rose had to be replaced at the last minute with a much less prestigious soloist. In one reviewer's opinion, "It was one of the best concerts of the year — and one of the most thoroughly musical ... indeed, the Bloch *Scheloma, Rhapsodie Hebraique for Cello and Orchestra* produced one of the finest performances of the season."[2]

It was not just great performances that Victor was providing in London, but a new sense of direction that was influencing the morale of the orchestra and its supporters. On his arrival he had publicly announced that if the community did not financially support the orchestra, then it deserved to lose it. He made Londoners aware of the fact that though he had conducted many fine ensembles, London's symphony orchestra was one of the most proficient he had experienced.

His message to board members was direct and unsolicited — and to some unwelcome. In his view the contract players who made up the

London Sinfonia and formed the professional core of the symphony "were seriously underpaid," a condition that could also have been described as "below the poverty line." In the battle to save the orchestra now going on, Victor had proclaimed as the heroes of the struggle those players who had stayed on in spite of the sacrifice it represented, in order that the orchestra might survive.[3]

His ministrations came to involve not only the Niagara Symphony and Orchestra London, but the ensembles that served Hamilton and Ottawa, as well. In each case, his efforts were directed toward the continued cultural health of the city as host of an orchestra that was central to its musical well-being. He had by this time conducted virtually every orchestra in Canada and was totally aware of the many factors which could result in the demise of even the most able and seemingly indestructible institution. Most important of all, he himself had come from the ranks of the orchestra and understood the veritable seething morass of personalities as well as the professional agendas present in the minds of its players. These challenges must be confronted if a great ensemble was to be created and maintained anywhere on the planet.

In short, there could be no institutional manifestation so complex, varied, and potentially volatile as a symphony orchestra made up of as many as a hundred highly trained musicians, ambitious for the most idealistic reasons, rightfully proud of their competence, yet at the same time expected to remain humbly subservient to the collective cause of creating great music. On top of all that, at that time they were invariably less well remunerated than any other such collection of comparable professionals.

Victor realized from personal experience that many of those musicians had to carry the lifetime baggage of having aspired to, but having failed to achieve a career as a solo instrumental performer. Thus, a part of the dynamic of every orchestra was the fact that many of the members could see their presence in an orchestra the result of both perceived and real failure. Indeed, even at the best of times, the presence at concerts of a Yo-Yo Ma, a Midori, or a James Galway was a reminder to many orchestra members of some of those career disappointments.

Victor truly believed that the role of orchestra player could not be celebrated if it was seen as a diminished place in music performance and

therefore merely the outcome of the blasted expectations of solo prominence. Being part of a fine ensemble had to be recognized as an opportunity
of building a valuable and proud career devoted to the performance of the
greatest music ever composed. But when the existence of that very ensemble was added to the general despair, and a reduction of minimal remuneration was considered as a legitimate strategy for financial survival by board
members and local newspaper editors, the morale of orchestra members
was at even greater threat. In the circumstances of orchestral disruption,
Victor's concept of the role of a conductor was to quell the internal politics
of disappointed and disillusioned individual orchestral members and provide the challenge of achieving excellence as a common enterprise, thereby
ensuring that the making of glorious sound was not forgotten. Only in that
context could individual or ensemble healing be initiated and have some
measure of success.

Unfortunately, Victor knew that too often in these circumstances of
crisis the conductor became the lightning rod when such a cauldron of
dissatisfaction and disillusionment set off explosions that made continued
performance quality questionable at best, patently uninspiring and deadly
at worst. If the orchestra in trauma could bring itself to play at its highest capacity, both audiences and players could survive the disruption of
a labour relations breakdown. The conductor who has the respect of the
musicians could alone bring a solution to the dilemma of broken dreams
and lost opportunities and thereby set the orchestra on the course of creating the excitement of making music that expresses the truths about human
existence that are beyond mere words. The composer's genius must become
the common ground upon which the synergy of orchestral performance
takes on its own energy and dynamic and strangely becomes the foundation
of the mutual respect and common accord upon which the future of the
enterprise can be built. It was Victor's unique combination of understanding of orchestral integrity, caring, and dynamic drawn from his experience
in the ranks that would allow him to perform this unique role.[4]

Victor realized that such dalliance in the murky waters of collegiality
carried great risks. Top-down dictatorship may not produce the most efficient outcomes but it produces the most predictable results on a short-term
basis. Democratic and collegial procedures are messy and time-consuming,

indeed can lead to disorder and anarchy. But Victor found that he could discover through inviting written missives what the performance enthusiasms of his players might be. He tried to comply with their wishes.

The miracle of great music performance transpires when the virtuosity and genius of each individual orchestra member conspires to create moments of true inspirational music-making. In the midst of the despair of a dysfunctional relationship that results in the silencing of an ensemble, the conductor comes to accept the ultimate responsibility for the failure to ignite the minds and spirits of the contending parties. These were the challenges that Victor faced on each occasion he ventured into the uninviting but necessary process of trying to help an orchestra.

Victor, by the 1980s, had developed a sense that he could play a positive role as consultant and adviser that included raising the level of music-making of disturbed and troubled ensembles. Thus, he allowed the continued presence of such an orchestra in the community to become a matter of concern to aware citizens, creating a context in which anything but the continued performance of a fine orchestra in a particular community would be impossible to conceive.

In the fall of 1988, Victor was intervening in the affairs of a West Coast orchestra that needed some attention — the Victoria Symphony Orchestra. Victor had been commissioned to perform with yet another ensemble in a leaderless state searching for a conductor. His first concert appearance was a success, with reviewer Adrian Chamberlain terming his rendition of the Mozart *Jupiter Symphony* a "barnstormer," the result of "his concise conducting ensuring that musical nuances are brought out and acquire a life of their own."[5]

When Victor was approached for an interview by Chamberlain, he presented her with a list of changes he would introduce if he were to be ensconced as the orchestra's artistic director. First, there would be no weeding-out process. He expressed his surprise at the fine quality of the musicians. The orchestra was made up of "really dedicated players ... indeed, they are wonderful," was his assessment. Typically, his first priority would be to give the musicians a raise in pay (core professionals in Victoria were at a poverty line level of twelve thousand dollars for a thirty-two-week season).

His second step would be to enlarge that core of professionals. He had scheduled the Schumann Symphony no. 2, and insisted upon achieving a "full, unforced sound," the result being that there was the impression that two extra players had been added to each string section. "The extras were absent — the sound was there," was Chamberlain's comment. But Victor had illustrated the importance of a richer sound if performance of a full repertoire was to be achieved.

Third, he would make the orchestra then serving the British Columbia capital the province's symphony orchestra by introducing extensive touring. His proposition was that every centre in the province should be visited by the Victoria Symphony each year.

Finally, the building of a fine concert hall in downtown Victoria was a necessity. Victor was extrapolating from his Winnipeg success in dealing with the problems of a Victoria Symphony he now had found capable of making great strides, but labouring in an inadequate venue. However, even in the terrible acoustics of the present hall, Chamberlain was impressed with the performance, and commented, "Toronto's Victor Feldbrill is a terrific conductor who knows what he is doing and the results of the concert showed it."[6] The performance and the Chamberlain consultation represented a significant intervention in the affairs of an orchestra in need of guidance and although the advice might not be completely accepted, Victor was creating a positive environment in which debate, disagreement, and reconciliation were more possible.

⁂

The National Arts Centre in Ottawa is a unique structure in the cultural life of Canada. Staggering as it may seem today, before the Centennial Year there had been no appropriate venue for the performance of quality music and theatre in the nation's capital. A group of Ottawa women decided to change that disgraceful situation and, commandeering a prestigious figure, Hamilton Southam, and a highly respected prime minister, Lester B. Pearson, both blessed with cultural awareness, they set about creating a splendid venue to serve both theatre and music (and dance, as well) just a stone's throw away from Parliament Hill. They hoped that the preparations for the Centennial Year would thus create a cultural atmosphere that could serve the citizens of Ottawa in both official languages equally well.

The National Arts Centre that eventually came to be built — admittedly two years after the Centennial Year — was the result of outstanding Ottawa women who expressed appropriate outrage that a middle power on the international stage like Canada had a capital city that was pathetically served by the arts. It was plain that there should certainly be a place where the finest expressions of Canadian cultural achievement could be showcased not only to Canadians, whether civil service or parliamentarians, but as well to the representatives of foreign countries in the embassies based in Ottawa, to say nothing of the string of visiting dignitaries who had some degree of presence in any national capital.

Realizing that a resident orchestra in such a music venue would be a necessity, Southam engaged Lou Applebaum, composer and arts administrator *par excellence*, to act as an adviser in matters associated with music presentation at the planned National Arts Centre. It was Applebaum's view that the provision of an orchestra was essential, but in order not to arouse the opposition of forces behind the TSO and Montreal Symphony Orchestra, who would resent yet another full symphony orchestra with whom they would have to share minimal federal resources for costs of operation as well as limited commissions for programming from the CBC, the National Arts Centre's orchestra should be a very different entity seeking distinction of a different kind on the world stage. It would be an enlarged chamber orchestra, often referred to as a Beethoven-sized ensemble, putting its attention to the baroque repertoire but with the capacity to expand its membership when great compositions from later centuries were to be performed. Most important of all was the challenge of assembling a splendid coterie of fine musicians. Mario Bernardi, a Canadian with a splendid reputation as an orchestral conductor in the United Kingdom, was given the task of auditioning the prospective players and thus creating this fine ensemble.

As well, it was in Applebaum's mind that this national expression of quality musical performance could be toured at minimal cost, compared to that of taking a full-sized symphony orchestra. If the orchestra could actually appear in municipalities across Canada, it could be truly "national" in its impact. It was all very logical but did not take into account the reduced support for the arts which characterized the 1970s and '80s. These changed circumstances allowed the deterioration of the hopes and aspirations of both Applebaum and Southam as well as their immediate successors who would be responsible for the National Arts Centre enterprise.

Victor had been invited to conduct the National Arts Centre Orchestra (NACO) on several occasions and had developed a warm relationship with many of the players whose loyalty had been tested all too often in the decades that followed the establishment and the first halcyon years of the new ensemble. Ken Murphy was the first manager of the NACO and in those first glorious years called on Victor often to take his place on the podium. In his mind, the reason was obvious — he was "very good" in terms of technique, he knew the repertoire, and the players "liked him very much."

By the mid-1980s, confrontation over inadequate recompense was the order of the day, with an intractable administration that was the bane of those who saw a positive future for the NACO. It was into this later period of uproar that Victor found himself drawn.

In the fall of 1989, the orchestra had decided that withdrawal of service was the only solution to the dispute around both recompense and a host of other irritations. The members of the orchestra, realizing that subscription holders would be deprived of the concerts they had purchased, proposed to play these concerts at a local high school. However, there was no similar generous response from management. Instead there was intransigence. The result was anger from patrons and the general public, including even Hamilton Southam, now long absent from NACO leadership but who felt it necessary to express his horror at the behaviour of the management of the day. He strongly supported the orchestra members' determination that the dispute would not sever the outpouring of Ottawa citizens' generosity of spirit toward the orchestra and its outstanding quality.

The main question became that of unearthing a conductor for the performances which were being planned. It was the view of the National Arts Centre administration that conductors were part of management and any and all conductors engaged for succeeding seasons were by definition part of that management team. It all came to a head when orchestra members asked Victor to conduct the first of such "outlaw" concerts. (Unfortunately, under the circumstances, this was an historic twentieth-anniversary concert with the identical repertoire of the orchestra's first performance.)

There was every reason for the players to make Victor their choice as conductor. Not only was his leadership a guarantee of artistic merit but Victor's often expressed attitude toward the well-being of orchestral players was well-known from coast to coast. He was the orchestral members' ideal advocate for a living wage as no other major figure in Canada's music world could claim. However, it would be an involvement that some orchestral board members and managements would resent deeply — for surely the conductor's appropriate stance should be that of restraining the financial expectations of musicians/employees, not encouraging their desire for ever more remuneration.

In this case, Victor was in a complicated position. If he accepted the invitation to conduct the NACO members' concert he would be following his conscience and his belief that orchestral musicians deserved adequate compensation for their efforts, their long period of preparation, and their experience. Yet, having agreed to conduct a concert in the next year's regular NACO schedule, he was seen as part of the management's future artistic thrust. The National Arts Centre managerial leadership, in the context of normal negotiations, had a point. As part of the campaign to defeat the orchestra members, the board threatened Victor with negative consequences if he conducted, using a normal clause in his contract that deprived him of the right to lead any local competing ensemble. In this case, the competition was being provided by NACO players acting on their own behalf rather than as employees of the National Arts Centre. For Victor, this dispute had become an assault on his integrity as an individual but also a threat to his role of being a guest conductor with orchestras across the country. Victor did end up conducting the orchestral concert — in a nearby high-school auditorium — but fortunately the threat to his future relations with the orchestra did not materialize and he continued to conduct the NACO in succeeding years.

The issue was ultimately resolved and normal relations between National Arts Centre management and the NACO were re-established. The termination of the dispute actually heralded the most productive period of Victor's relationship with the NACO.

A few months later a special concert of Canadian music was mounted and held in the ballroom of the Château Laurier Hotel, just a short walk from the Parliament Buildings. The program was made up entirely of Canadian music and included Weinzweig's *Interlude in an Artist's Life*, Mathieu's *Les Preludes*, Lucas's *Macbeth Overture*, and Ridout's *Ballade*. The program was enthusiastically received and thereby revealed perfectly Victor's hopes that the NACO would take on the special responsibility of playing the music of Canadian composers with increased commitment and excitement.

Then, in 1992, Victor was contracted to conduct the NACO in what was a national tour. A project was needed that would restore the orchestra as a pre-eminent ensemble, devoted to the nation and not just the citizens of the country's capital city. What better way to demonstrate this role than to have the orchestra appear in cities across the land and play a repertoire that would reveal the splendid quality of this special ensemble? It would represent a reaffirmation of its original mandate as a national institution.

It was an exhausting experience but it did restore and enhance the reputation of the NACO. It could only be led by a conductor who had the respect and affection of the musicians (whose opinion of the management had recently been so badly eroded and had lost all credibility). Victor was determined that the NACO would live up to its earlier reputation as an international phenomenon devoted to orchestral excellence. There was even a raison d'être that was convincing — the celebration of the country's 125th anniversary.

The *Halifax Chronicle-Herald* announced that the NACO would perform in the Maritimes, and would include in its itinerary St. John's, Halifax, Sydney, Antigonish, and Charlottetown. Ultimately the NACO would conclude its tour in western Canada the following May. The tour would not include Toronto and Montreal, but smaller communities such as Baie Como, Chicoutimi, Rouyn, and Val d'Or in Quebec, Sault Ste. Marie in Ontario, Victoria and Prince George in British Columbia, and Saskatoon in Saskatchewan. By the tour's end, the NACO would have travelled twenty thousand kilometres.

However, it was not just the idea of a Canadian concert tour that drew the attention of NACO aficionados; it was Victor's determination to engage in an educational project in tandem with the concert performances.

Under the headline, "Conductor Feldbrill Shares Talent with Student," music reviewer Stephen Pedersen outlined Victor's master class schedule for potential conductors that would accompany the NACO performances. Victor was quoted as justifying this program as recognition that student conductors "never have had an easy time learning their craft and getting work in their own country." It was a reflection based on his own experience but it was accompanied by his dark observation that "things are worse now than when I started in the 1940s [almost a half century before]. The CBC was a wonderful outlet. Now it just picks up programs of already established orchestras and whereas it was once an institution that offered opportunities to hone ones' craft, all that is gone."[7]

When the NACO had performed in St. John's, giving what was described as a performance that "sparkled," the now famed Canadian pianist Louis Lortie was the soloist in the Mozart Concerto no. 24 in C Minor. Victor's masterly skill in accompaniment stood out: "The orchestra from Ottawa under the revealing direction of Victor Feldbrill was brilliant in support of Lortie being impressive in every movement, catching the various moods of the music in fine fashion."[8]

The reviewer, Welmer Biernaan, alluded to what was perceived an unusual programming choice in placing Mendelssohn's Symphony no. 1 as the climax of the evening. He conceded that it had worked well, but "would need to be given a reading of the kind offered last night by Feldbrill and the superior sound offered by the NACO." Accolades abounded. The *Charlottetown Guardian* commented on the orchestra's playing "with awesome virtuosity."

When the NACO played in Fredericton, it received a laudatory review under the headline "Orchestra Presents Magical Performance": "Maestro Feldbrill exacted a clean sound from the players, with careful attention to the dynamic contrasts and a blend which was perhaps the best I have heard from a symphony orchestra."[9]

There was comparable enthusiasm in the West in spite of difficulties that could not be avoided. Referring to the NACO as Canada's "Unity Orchestra," Victoria's reviewer Derek Barker had to concede that the city's Royal Theatre was only half full but that in spite of the disappointing audience numbers "it would be difficult to imagine a better, more convincing performance than that given of Mendelssohn's Symphony in C Minor."

In Saskatoon, a musical group performing in the basement of the auditorium forced Louis Lortie to interrupt his performance of a Mozart piano concerto. However, once the concert resumed, the orchestra was to play before a wildly appreciative audience.

It could be said that the NACO national tour was a triumphant procession, both in the east and west. It was a minor miracle that Victor could assist an orchestra to raise its reputation across an entire country, particularly in a decade when there was so much resentment against the federal government for failing to meet the expectations of virtually every region of Canada. Any Ottawa institution, even an orchestra, bore the impact of that discontent. However, in 1992, though there would be stormy days ahead, this effort to bring great music to cities across the land did raise the self-respect of the splendid ensemble that had been established as a delayed element of the 1967 celebrations. The NACO could be seen as a binding force in a country whose regions were desperately seeking reasons to stay together.

The tour intensified the affection that the NACO had developed for Victor's leadership. It was conveyed in an email from Evelyn Greenberg, a respected Ottawa musician and accompanist, who has remained closely associated with the ensemble since its earliest days. She refers to Victor as "one of Canada's most respected and passionate Canadian musicians." She states categorically that "there is no one who has worked with Victor that does not have positive things to say about him." He is simply "a good conductor."[10] In an interview, Greenberg remembered an occasion in the mid-1990s when the NACO had scheduled Trevor Pinnock to conduct an important concert with guest cellist Yo-Yo Ma. Pinnock was suffering from high blood pressure and a few hours before the concert was to commence, was advised by doctors that he must cancel his performance that evening. Victor was caught on the way out of his home and was flown to Ottawa. Yo-Yo Ma gave an informal recital until Feldbrill arrived at the National Arts Centre and, with no rehearsal, a splendid performance of Dvorak's Cello Concerto in B Minor was achieved. Even Yo-Yo Ma was impressed with the quality of the support he received from a breathless Victor Feldbrill.[11] The audience gave both Victor and Yo-Yo Ma a prolonged and well-deserved standing ovation.

Over the weeks of the 1992 national tour, Zelda had accompanied Victor and had become the orchestra's most popular bus trip companion and audience member. NAC musicians marvelled at the fact that she attended every single concert, encouraging Victor and the orchestra in every way. Though deeply moved, it was no surprise to Victor that the NACO opened its next concert season with a performance "in memory of Zelda Feldbrill," after her death in 1995. It was the only way the NACO could express its respect, yea, more, its love for Victor and his beloved spouse.

It was in 1989 that Victor was invited to take on a leadership role with the Hamilton Philharmonic (HPO). He was asked to become interim music adviser, then music director, with the responsibility to achieve a smooth transition from the Boris Brott years to those that were to follow under a new conductor. Hugh Fraser, a dominant figure in the cultural life of Hamilton and a music and theatre reviewer and commentator, wrote perceptibly that the HPO was "looking for its future."

The orchestra and the city had achieved the impossible in the previous decade — a fine symphony orchestra in a splendid Hamilton Place devoted to the task of enhancing its sound. The city of Hamilton was known as a "hard-hat" town of monumental dimensions industrially but with very little expectations of achievement as a performing arts centre. Not only was it assumed to be populated with people with few cultural interests but was too close to all the orchestral music, opera, ballet, and theatre that Toronto as a mega-centre could provide after a mere single hour's journey.

However, these were years when Hamilton had decided that as much as the opportunity for NHL hockey could be blocked by the presence of Toronto's Maple Leafs, choral and orchestral music could take place in the very centre of the city in a fine newly built concert hall to which the trade union movement, through its members, provided much of the capital.

The HPO had been through a period of enormous development to justify the erection of such a grand concert hall and to find an enthusiastic acceptance from the people of Hamilton. Certainly the new structure, which contained a most attractive art gallery, had been a major factor, along with a major redevelopment of the entire downtown, in creating a new image for this city at the western end of Lake Ontario. Boris Brott had all the entrepreneurial characteristics of one of the most musically animated families in Canada. He had placed the HPO at the very centre of the musical life of the city, taking the orchestra to industrial sites and commercial shopping malls to perform and through so doing, gained the attention and the respect of the entire community. Along with this came an expanded audience base and the financial resources to build a fine orchestra. After twenty-one years of service, Boris Brott and the HPO were synonymous with orchestral performance in the city of Hamilton.

However, after two decades, new faces of the board of directors with as yet unachieved agendas, a substantial deficit on the HPO books, and the presence of elements of discontent within the orchestra all came together to end a regime that had seemed to be endless in its expectations. A severance of relationships and a loss of communication had intervened to the extent that, with the resignation of Boris Brott, the future of the orchestra was very much in doubt. It was now leaderless and under the circumstances no sane person would have wanted to accept any invitation to provide that leadership.

Once again, Victor's strategy was that of securing the attention of the Hamilton public in general and the city's music lovers in particular. He lauded the HPO as a splendid instrument but made it clear that he had no magic wand. So, unless the Hamilton community wanted a symphony orchestra, it would simply die. He indicated that it would be a tragedy, as there was now in place a magnificent ensemble whose members were working day and night to save the orchestra in what he described as a "wonderful atmosphere of collegiality, cordiality and mutual respect." He made it clear that he was not interested in a permanent appointment as conductor himself, but was prepared to stay in Hamilton until the 1992 concert season ended to provide the stability in which new leadership could be found.

In the September 1990 edition of a local periodical, *Hamilton*, Victor was interviewed about his plans. His response was predictable. The Hamilton Philharmonic Orchestra was now in its third year without Boris Brott. In Victor's view the orchestra had become the "star" in the firmament and its continued presence could be attributed to the determination of its musicians to survive. Its members were phoning subscribers in order to secure their continued support. He saw his role as music director as one of building the image of that entire enterprise and his first step would be to increase the number of resident professional musicians, while keeping in place the existing core. This would stabilize the personnel complement for yet another year.

Victor set about establishing different series of concerts that would appeal to a wider range of audiences than a regular subscription collection of presentations might attract. The main series would offer six concerts at which there would be major works performed, including the musical presence of a Canadian contemporary composer at each one. Thus, Weinzweig, Somers, Ridout, and MacMillan would be given hallmark presentations by the HPO in his first season.

He also placed before the Hamilton community a series of special concerts, "Orchestral Favourites," of highly popular and accessible repertoire. For example, the evening devoted to *Down the Danube* was essentially an exploration of Johann Strauss waltzes and other popular fare emanating from that region of Europe. He conducted three Christmas presentation of Handel's *Messiah* with the established and respected and recently energized Bach-Elgar Choir, which included the highly acclaimed Richard Margison and Gary Relyea as soloists. Critics were exultant. One gave the presentation exhibiting "a miraculously supported line" a tribute rather than a critique. The music had been splendid!

> How come all the above? Because Victor Feldbrill was on the podium. with his finger on every pulse of the music. It's as simple as that. His tempos were ample and spacious, his conception coherent, he told the story magnificently. It was the finest *Messiah* I have ever heard.[12]

The *Hamilton Spectator*'s music critic, Hugh Fraser, described the Feldbrill-led HPO as exhibiting a sound that was "crisp and lively … more together and full of beans."

Fraser, while maintaining his distance as music critic, became a valuable supporter of Victor's management decision as well as defining his record of performance excellence. Although Victor was carrying the main load, the 1991–92 concert season included the involvement of five guest conductors that gave Hamilton audiences a broad range of qualities and weaknesses of conducting styles.

Though the Music Alive series of programs made up entirely of twentieth-century composers had to be given up, the Orchestra Favourites and children's Sundae Symphonies survived and prospered. Under the headline "Feldbrill Has the Orchestra Playing with Spirit and Joy," Fraser pointed out in his *Spectator* column that "a tremendous improvement in the string ensemble was apparent." As an example he referred to the playing of the Mozart *Haffner Symphony*, where he found "the taut, poised phrasing and fleet, elegant ensemble performance had marked a key fine reading" of the work.[13]

Victor encouraged the continuation of another Brott direction — that the HPO should play outside the city. Communities like Milton were encouraged to provide a venue and an audience and Oakville soon followed. Soon other nearby towns and cities were lining up for the following season.

In order to bring Hamilton back into the mainstream of orchestral presentation, Victor arranged to participate in an exchange of conductors with the Singapore Symphony Orchestra — an appearance in the Far East that went well by all reports but gave a new sense of international relevance to the health and well-being of the Hamilton Philharmonic.

By February 1991, Victor had informed the Ontario Federation of Symphony Orchestras that the HPO would host the annual Ontario Festival of Youth Orchestras. On that occasion he himself conducted the Hamilton Youth Orchestra in the Dvorak Symphony no. 8, as well as R. Murray Schafer's *Statement in Blue*. It was another strategy to place the HPO at the centre of a provincial orchestral initiative.

It surprised no one when just a few months into his 1990–91 contract, the board of the HPO announced that Victor's tenure as music director and principal conductor would be extended until 1993. As part of the announcement, Victor was quoted about his plans to feature outstanding Canadian soloists, including Joanne Kolomyjec, violinist Martin Beaver, and pianist Robert Silverman — every one also an international figure. Thus the Hamilton audience was guaranteed a consistent quality of solo performance at every regular concert. As well, Victor indicated that he would advise the board to include in its plans the hiring of a second conductor. It was an ingenious selection. He brought his old friend Howard

Cable, now a legend in his own time, on board to lead the orchestra in pop concerts with no fear of any loss of quality.[14]

An account of the concert Victor had scheduled at the Royal Botanical Gardens in Hamilton in May of 1991 occasioned Fraser's rumination about age and the making of music. There had been disparaging self-analysis by Victor about his approaching seventieth birthday and Fraser's response was direct and to the point: "He's one of the most taken for granted people in Canadian music. Always there, always excellent, but without a reputation for setting the world on fire ... Feldbrill can make this orchestra sound immaculate." Fraser had stumbled over the very point missed by many observers — the momentary "setting the world on fire" was replaced by a performance that had to do with the composer's genius and the sound of the orchestra.

The spring of 1991 was the right time to extend the reach of the HPO. The Royal Botanical Gardens had already been identified by Boris Brott as an appropriate venue, but Victor also exported a series of concerts featuring the music of Mozart to the citizens of Ancaster, Burlington, Stoney Creek, and to the Scottish Rite Cathedral in Oakville. Of the first concert, Fraser wrote, "Rarely has anything here sounded as precise, alive, committed and beautiful as the HPO last night."[15] Of a concert a week later in Oakville, Fraser described Feldbrill's rendition of the Symphony no. 34 as "absolutely thrilling in its energy, spirit and skill."[16]

It was not an accident that on June 7, 1991, Brock University in St. Catharines conferred a Doctor of Laws (*honoris causa*) on Victor Feldbrill. The university had developed its commendable criteria for this honour-ing of Canadian citizens not so much emphasized by other universities — the selection of people who had made a unique contribution to the region occupied by the university, in this case the Niagara Peninsula, which included areas that Victor and the HPO had served so well. In just a short time, he had enhanced the musical life of that region and was most cer-tainly an appropriate recipient.

By the fall of 1991, Victor's work was paying off. In the review of a concert which included, yet again, Applebaum's Concertante for Small Orchestra, and concluded with Beethoven's Symphony no. 4, Fraser could comment "what was thrilling was the logic, shape and excitement Feldbrill managed to draw from the orchestra … once more another absolutely first class concert." In seeking to understand the Feldbrill style, he sought the opinion of orchestra trombonist Mark Donatell, a respected musician who could be quite frank and open: "We know we are working with a leader who is very inspiring, very straight forward and a pleasure to work with." He then became even more specific: "When we go to work we're excited … he knows the music, he knows exactly how he wants it to sound … if he doesn't get it right away he works until he does and then says 'thank-you.' He is consistent and we know he respects us."

Oboe and English horn virtuoso Nancy Nelson had been a regular member of the Hamilton Philharmonic for some thirteen years before Feldbrill's arrival but it was his commitment to lead the HPO that decided her future with the orchestra. She had met him many years before in Winnipeg, had watched his career, and in spite of the "troubles" in Hamilton, decided she would remain in the HPO. Though years have gone by, she still thinks of him as a "fabulous" conductor as well as a "wonderful man." She feels she is not alone in this assessment: "He seemed to love as well as respect the people in the orchestra and was able to express that respect." In Nelson's case he had a work for English horn and orchestra commissioned for her — a divertimento by John Weinzweig. As well, there were performances she remembers with some emotion: "These were moments of musical ecstasy. For example, at the conclusion of a performance of *Messiah*, I found myself sobbing from the sheer impact of that magnificent music and the way we had played it!"[17]

Her sense was that Victor had developed a very special relationship with this troubled ensemble. There were obvious reasons. He was a temporary incumbent in the conductor's role and he was putting himself on the line for a few years in a situation that might not turn out well. The HPO was a smaller and more closely knit ensemble than, for example, the TSO. But most of all, there was a crisis that only the exemplary playing of great music together could solve. It created a bond that was unique and valued by all.

That same fall, while his attention was focused on the HPO, Victor was called upon by the Kitchener-Waterloo Symphony Orchestra to conduct a concert. In this case the orchestra was not in any state of crisis and Victor was able to concentrate on providing an outstanding program. He began the concert typically with a Canadian composer, Oscar Morawetz's *Overture to a Fairy Tale*, followed by a Mozart flute concerto and the Brahms *Variations on a Theme of Haydn*. He concluded with a Haydn symphony. A perceptive reviewer, Colleen Johnston from the *Kitchener-Waterloo Record*, recognizing that "what was impressive was the commitment Feldbrill got from the players," commented of the Brahms: "Feldbrill played on the contrasts of volume and timbre. He dwelled on them, he relished them and so did we. Feldbrill pulled energy and bite from the players."

Of the Haydn she had very determined views about its performance: "Feldbrill did something interesting and that was to read Haydn not as a bumpkin cousin of Mozart's but as though he were an uncle of Beethoven's. The playing with motives rather than melodies, the use of surprises — that and more was brought to our attention."[18]

The 1992–93 Hamilton Philharmonic concert season was to be Victor's last and he crowned it with the addition of three more concerts for Hamilton secondary schools and extending the HPO's commitment yet again to Oakville, Dundas, and even to the parking lot of Hamilton's Mohawk College. The board, as a gesture of appreciation for all he had done, appointed Victor as principal guest conductor for the 1993–94 season, even though by 1992 a permanent conductor had been selected. His presence, it was believed, would take the HPO through the next phase of its development.

Throughout these years the stream of Canadian music flowed unabated with Harry Somers's *North Country Suite*, Murray Adaskin's *Fanfare*, John Beckwith's *Round and Round*, Howard Cable's *Newfoundland Rhapsody*, and Harry Freedman's *Tableau* being featured along with selections from the composing energies of Ridout and Weinzweig.

It was in 1993 that Victor became aware of the fact that Lou Applebaum, a most popular composer and arts administrator, was dying of cancer. He was being kept alive by the excitement and purpose created by a commission that he and Mavor Moore had undertaken to mount a chamber opera based on the famous futurist fantasy *Erewhon*, to be given its debut performance in Victoria. Victor, who by this time was also conducting an ensemble of retired TSO string players, was able to commission a Concertante for Small Orchestra. It was based on themes from the opera and included a solo voice played by an English horn. Victor scheduled it again and again during Applebaum's last years — a tribute that only a composer could fully appreciate.

In the early spring of 1993, Victor faced a curious mixture of delight and sadness. He had brought an orchestra back to life and it was performing splendidly — on the other hand he was completing his contract, and conducting concerts as principal guest conductor would be his only role with the HPO from that point. As one would expect, the orchestra arranged a tribute to Victor at Hamilton Place. In May, the HPO mounted a concert that would illustrate the contribution that Victor had made. He would conduct a grand program which would open with the Beethoven Piano Concerto no. 4, a favourite offering that Victor sought to play whenever possible. The soloist would be Canadian pianist, Jane Coop, one of Victor's favourite performers. The climax of the evening would be the Beethoven Symphony no. 9 (Choral) with the Bach-Elgar as the chorus for the thundering final movement. The soloists were colleagues from Victor's past: Glyn Evans, Gary Relyea, Carol Ann Feldstein, and Rosemary Landry. It was a glorious occasion that marked the achievements of the past few years in Hamilton, but also signalled the quality that of a fine orchestra that would survive the difficult final decade of the twentieth century.

Hugh Fraser, the *Hamilton Spectator*'s music critic, in an end-of-year survey of great musical events in that city in the early 1990s, had identified Victor as Hamilton's Musician of the Year. His reasoning was perfectly expressed. He had taken the city's orchestra and performed with it splendidly at a difficult time, both financially and artistically, and done so in a period of slow economic growth that had affected the entire arts community nationally. His choice was universally accepted.

Appropriately, Fraser's nomination was based on musical achievement as well: "I haven't heard this orchestra ever play as well as this. In fact I haven't heard any orchestra play as well as this." In that retrospective commentary, tongue-in-cheek in the circumstances, he threw out impossible advice to a board in search of a permanent conductor: "If the committee searching for a new director quietly dissolves and we get to keep the treasure we have, I'll be quite happy...." That being impossible, the "lucky stiff [who is chosen conductor and artistic director] will get a really first class orchestra to conduct courtesy of Victor Feldbrill."[19]

Victor had accomplished these results without retreating from his most heartfelt principle — that musicians were being severely underpaid. Indeed, at one point in a HPO board meeting, one member had suggested as a strategy for dealing with a deficit the reduction of the payroll. Victor had been outraged and made it very clear that "if there is a penny taken from the paycheques of orchestral members, I am out of here, make no mistake."[20]

As his own farewell to Victor, Fraser wrote quite poignantly of his role. In his view, in the midst of a crisis that threatened the continuation of the institution, the HPO Board "had turned to the steadiest hand on a Canadian orchestral baton in the history of Canadian music." Playing with well-worn images, Fraser went on to say that Victor had been a "bridge over troubled waters," a "healer," and, "most of all an agent of excellence." He had guided the fine HPO musicians into an atmosphere based on "camaraderie all focused on the music." The orchestra had "become a team producing some of the finest music the orchestra had ever offered its public."

Fraser recounted the highlights — *Messiah* with the Bach-Elgar Choir, the Mozart Festival, "the three solid weeks of exposed music-making," and "the series concentrating on contemporary music that eventually had to be cancelled." Even the latter had been a triumph of sorts. The final peak was the successful conductor and composer's workshops that Victor had initiated with the HPO. Yet, above all, Victor had never faltered in his central personal commitment. Canadian contemporary music had continued to be part of all series he had initiated. As well, the orchestra had spread its influence to other communities achieving its stability in adversity and had never lost sight of its mandate.

His attention was not totally focused on bringing stability and direction to existing and troubled Canadian symphony orchestras. In 1993, Victor had become involved in the creation of another orchestra — the Toronto Senior Strings. The idea came from the mind of Ruth Budd, a renowned social activist who had spent decades in the bass section of the TSO and had reached retirement age as the 1990s began. A female bass player was an exotic specimen in a symphony orchestra, especially one who had a reputation for articulate and intelligent discourse in support of various liberal causes. When she indicated that a mandatory retirement age for instrumentalist members of a symphony orchestra was an enormous waste of human creativity and virtuosity, people listened. She founded a string orchestra and invited TSO colleagues who had been recently retired to join her. They would make music and show just what a contribution a group of mature musicians could make to the cultural life of her city. She needed a conductor and one who could command the respect of the fine players she had gathered. No other name was considered. Victor Feldbrill was her choice and that of her colleagues.

For a number of years there would be a series of afternoon concerts in St. Andrew's Presbyterian Church just across the street from Roy Thomson Hall. Although the concerts were available to the general public, the target audience was identified as senior citizens, particularly those for whom a short afternoon concert in an easily accessed venue would be particularly welcome. The tickets would be affordable so that no senior would be absent as a result of the cost of attending.

The response from retired string players was warm. Revered TSO retirees Stanley Solomon, Yascha Milkis, and Pearl Palmason and their colleagues were joined by fine additions from other professional orchestras in the Toronto region when necessary. The orchestra had a number of successful years. It was made possible because Ruth Budd herself looked after the details of administration and promotion. But it was the involvement of a prestigious conductor prepared to contribute time and energy without remuneration that made the project possible.

There was another agenda that Ruth Budd had in mind. She had always given her support to the TSO outreach programs that took musicians into the schools and into close and intimate connection with children. Ruth saw these Senior Strings concerts as an opportunity to present young virtuoso performers who needed both attention and the experience of playing with a fine orchestra led by a splendid conductor. As a unique form of outreach, elementary-school string students were invited to be part of the audience of every concert. Needless to point out, it was an initiative with which Victor Feldbrill was quite comfortable.

The first concert took place on November 11, 1993. There was a good crowd, the orchestra created a sound that had grace, sonority, and precision. It was a great beginning.

The second concert in June revealed that the orchestra with a mandate already declared to be that of providing exposure to Canadian composers, could indeed perform a Feldbrill program — in this case the Harry Somers *Little Suite on French Canadian Themes for String Orchestra* along with some Mozart and Holst's *St. Paul's Suite*. The soloist was a young graduate of the University of Toronto's Music Faculty's Performance Program, Darrell Steel, a fine bassoonist who played a lively Vivaldi concert. These young future soloists discovered what it was like to be accompanied by a first-rate ensemble led by an expert conductor.

After a number of years the orchestra became beyond the resources of its founders, but not before two fine CDs were produced and a grand finale was mounted. It was discovered that both Ruth Budd and Victor would reach their eightieth birthday in 2004. The final concert of the Senior Strings on May 2 of that year included the works of Purcell, Handel, Mozart, and Britten, along with a concerto that Kevin Budd, Ruth's son, played on the pan flute. It was the end of a decade of splendid performance by outstanding mature musicians and a cherished opportunity for many older music lovers who otherwise could not have attended such concerts in their latter years.

For Victor, it was an appropriate mission that he enjoyed enormously. He assumed correctly that his players were serious, indeed would give their very best in the context of all the wisdom and sensitivity of their professional performing careers. As well, he had no intention of addressing a repertoire that was overly familiar or lacking challenge. In March 1995 he presented them with a repertoire that was written entirely by twentieth-century composers, including Gustav Holst and Peter Warlock, along with Canadian composers Harry Somers, Godfrey Ridout, and Sir Ernest MacMillan. It showed the respect that Victor had for older colleagues with whom, in many cases, he had played many concerts. It also indicated that in the making of music, even age could not be used as an excuse for incompetence, lack of focus, or occasional disinterest.[21]

Ruth Budd's assessment of Victor's role with her Senior Strings was blunt. She had gathered the "stars" from the National Ballet, Canadian

Opera, and TSO, and with her advice they had chosen Victor. Her assessment: "they simply loved him."[22] He respected and honoured their years of contribution but then demanded excellence of performance of a significant repertoire as, in his mind, he would be conducting a gathering of professional instrumentalists. Once again, it was all about the music!

Even in comparative retirement in a new millennium, the state of symphonic music in Canada never left the Feldbrill agenda. Early in 2008, the CBC announced a new direction in its programming on CBC Radio 2, its classical music station. Existing live programming would be emphasized in the broadcast schedule instead of a concentration on the past. Daytime symphonic programming would be replaced with the inclusion of a broader, more varied, more multicultural repertoire. It was believed that more differentiated music would attract younger audiences and would replace the presumably deadening focus of the classics, both ancient and contemporary. For those whose quality of life depended on the assurance of fine classical music over the CBC network, it was an assault on their sense of well-being. To add to the sense of outrage felt by loyal listeners, the activities of the only remaining symphonic CBC orchestra still in place and still playing regularly in Vancouver would be discontinued in the fall of 2008, ending the corporation's final outpost for the commissioning and performance of Canadian works.

Though Toronto remains his home, Victor is not a full-time resident. Though often away in the spring, he and his companion Mae Bernstein returned to Canada and participated in a protest rally of music performers and avid listeners in a park beside the CBC building on Front Street on a May afternoon in 2008. Victor read a letter he had written to CBC management protesting what he proclaimed from his vantage point of some fifty years of broadcast conducting, what seemed the last retreat of the CBC from its mandate and its pride of past achievements. Not only was CBC Radio 2 to witness a radical reduction in classical music programming, but the last CBC orchestra in Vancouver was to be disbanded — the last example of a studio orchestra maintained by a broadcasting system on the entire continent.

It was a powerful Feldbrill statement ... but there was little hope that this orchestra, with its special role of playing Canadian contemporary music, would survive the latest assault, or that the broadcasting of great classical music would ever be seen as a high priority of a management focused as it was on commercial rather than public broadcasting values. Victor made his point clearly and cogently. Now reaching his mid-eighties, Victor had witnessed the glory days of the CBC and could only express his anger and disappointment at the cultural erosion these policies of a great Canadian institution represented. His presence at the protest rally was noted by the dozens of former students and orchestral players who greeted him with evident delight. It was a typical Feldbrill cause. Once again, it was the music that mattered!

CHAPTER 20

Celebration, Despair, and Retrospection

For Canada, the latter years of the twentieth century offered a swath of celebratory events for those engaged in the arts. The impact of the Second World War had initiated a number of institutional responses to artistic needs — both in terms of performing arts organizations created and concert venues built to house them. More important, an amazing number of the returning members of the Canadian Armed Forces had become the composers, performers, and arts administrators. These men and women made possible the explosion of cultural activity that characterized the Canada that entered the new millennium. Victor was one of those who had returned from the services prepared and determined to be a part of that development. It seemed that whenever there was a composer to be honoured, a performer's life to be celebrated, an institution or venue whose role was to be remembered, Victor was called upon to provide leadership. He had become such a recognized cultural figure, indeed such an icon, that it seemed manifestly appropriate that he be on the podium for any such event that was being staged.

There was so much to celebrate. Victor had been involved in those heady days at the University of Toronto and the Conservatory that followed the war and led up to and included the great national centennial celebration of 1967 and even the coming of the millennium, all encouraging recognition of the successful arts enterprises that now grace the lives of Canadians fortunate enough to have experienced them.

Victor's own career had been a manifestation of what these circumstances could encourage for a citizen committed to the use of his or her musical intelligence, creative urges, and productive talents. He had witnessed the contrast and participated in the activities that changed Canada from what many had perceived as a cultural desert in the early and mid-1900s to the rich and varied scene of the 1980s and 1990s. He became a major figure in the collective memory of those who had been a part of those developments that had changed Canada's culture beyond its citizens' imagination forever.

With all the challenges of varying political leadership and shifts in funding expectations, there were now more symphony orchestras and a transformation in the quality of their performance. There was little doubt that the repertoires of these ensembles had become more complex and sophisticated. Most important of all, Canadian works were being played, not in the number Victor would have wished, but at least more than in the decades before his emergence. Even his own career, the peaks were now more clearly recognized, such as the triumphs of his decade of devotion to the city of Winnipeg. His time as conductor was seen as the turning point in the WSO's institutional life.

In addition, his work teaching and conducting young people was felt across the land as more and more rose to prominence in orchestras from Newfoundland to British Columbia. Joan Watson, who has played principal horn in Canadian symphonies such as the Victoria, the Toronto, and today in the Canadian Opera Company Orchestra comments that in the 1980s and 1990s Canadian instrumentalists were winning even international auditions and taking their places in Canadian ensembles. Simultaneously, improved performances across the land were the order of the day. No wonder that in those years more knowledgeable and appreciative audiences and observers of the musical field were recognizing his influence on the richness of Canadian orchestral performance.

The appreciation of his contributions was, of course, a part of the growing realization that Canada was arriving on the international scene across the entire spectrum of cultural expression. The years following the Massey Commission and its recommendations for national investment in cultural activities had seen the massive expansion of creative forces in theatre and dance along with a staggering increase in the number and productive quality of literary figures; Margaret Laurence, Robertson Davies, Margaret Atwood, and a host of colleagues had joined the expanding army of authors now writing for English-speaking readers in lands beyond Canada. In the visual arts the Group of Seven and their successors had made a twentieth-century impact, and by the end of the century, music and dance had reached the stage of acknowledgement abroad.

The recognition of these efforts to increase and enhance the performance of contemporary classical music, to secure attention to the work of living Canadian composers, and to successfully encourage improved instrumental virtuosity invariably led to Toronto and to Victor Feldbrill. Thus, when celebration was timely, Victor always seemed to be there. Indeed, the event could be legitimized beyond any question by his presence and involvement. This pattern developed in the 1960s and continued into the new century.

By the 1970s, the first thrust of post-war graduates from the University of Toronto's Faculty of Music and the Royal Conservatory were now retiring or even expiring, along with, in some cases, the extraordinary figures who had provided them with inspiration. Indeed, on April 6, 1978, recognition of the retirement of faculty members Greta Kraus, Robert Rosevear, Pierre Souverain, and John Weinzweig was celebrated with a concert of the UTSO conducted by Victor Feldbrill. These faculty members had been called "salt of the earth," and their teaching in Toronto had established the standards of learning in method and technique that eventually had led to the city's recognition as a centre of North American music education leadership.

Of course, the grand old man of Canadian composition, Healey Willan, received special attention during these years. Willan had achieved worldwide recognition before the Second World War and even though his compositions were clearly focused on the liturgical needs of the Church of England, in the early 1980s the city of Toronto proclaimed an entire week to be named in his honour. Ensembles both choral and instrumental were requested to sing and play his music. Various choirs, orchestras, and chamber groups responded and, although most of Willan's output had been centred on the church choral community, Victor actively participated in the secular events that enveloped his city.

In that same decade, the Royal Conservatory celebrated its centenary with a concert display of many figures in Canada's performing musical life, including instrumentalists Arthur Ozolins, Robert Aitken, Zara Nelsova, Martin Beaver, and Steven Staryk, all of whom had been part of the RCM's illustrious past. Lois Marshall came out of retirement to sing a Schubert offering with the accompaniment offered by the renowned Greta Kraus. Canadian composition was appropriately included in the evening with a Freedman fanfare and a concluding commission, *Play On*, from Lou Applebaum that featured the acclaimed tenor voice of Jon Vickers. The performance brought the house down with its sly and clever references to the great tenor's leading operatic roles, including that of the leading figure in Benjamin Britten's *Peter Grimes*. Throughout the evening, it was Victor's role to conduct the orchestra whenever a segment of a concerto was chosen to illustrate the quality of a Royal Conservatory graduate soloist. Thus he shared the podium with Elmer Iseler, leading the Toronto Mendelssohn Choir, and with composer Lou Applebaum, conducting his own commission. The proceedings were saturated with the voices nurtured at the RCM — Glyn Evans, Janet Stubbs, Russell Braun, Catherine Robbin, Gary Relyea, Rosemary Landry, and other eminent soloists. It was a glorious occasion that honoured the enormous contribution of an institution with which Victor had been so closely associated.

A mere two months later, an event as never mounted before or since took place at Toronto's Roy Thomson Hall. The occasion was the retirement of Walter Homburger as the illustrious manager of the TSO. In reality it was a celebration of his extraordinary career as an arts entrepreneur whose presence had enhanced the careers of countless Canadian artists and had resulted in the development of the TSO as an internationally recognized ensemble. His success with the programming of the orchestra revolved around his amazing relationship with a host of great performing artists whose confidence in the TSO resulted in their frequent appearances in the orchestra's schedule year after year. A considerable number of these outstanding figures on the international stage were brought to Toronto for what was termed a "Great Gathering," a concert that featured the finest artists of the century together on a stage for a single evening devoted to Homburger's extraordinary contribution. On that single occasion, the Toronto audience was thrilled to hear Yo-Yo Ma, Zukerman, Perahia, Rostropovich, Rampal, Midori, Louis Lortie, and Maureen Forrester perform. Even though conductors Ozawa, Andrew Davis, and Elmer Iseler were there and participated, only Victor had been intimately involved with Walter Homburger throughout all four decades of his incumbency as the manager of the TSO. Walter and his wife, Emmy, recognized that special relationship. They wrote at the time:

> We are so glad you are able to take part in the March 9 [1987] celebration and value your great contribution over so many years.
>   Affection and love to Zelda and yourself,
>
> Walter and Emmy[1]

Victor, the ultimate orchestral accompanist, had a busy evening, and the Great Gathering was a glorious success. As music critic William Littler was to record, "there had been no event like it in living memory."

Those years in Canada's artistic life had seen the rise of philanthropists who came to match the generosity of governmental funding agencies and whose liberal monetary giving deserved to be recognized and celebrated.

On September 18, 1988, at the Bluma Appel Theatre on Front Street in Toronto, a tribute to Floyd and Jean Chalmers was presented. One of the significant "causes" that had attracted the resources of the Chalmers family had been the support of the COC production of Harry Somers's opera *Louis Riel*. Along with the original lead, Bernard Turgeon, the original conductor Victor Feldbrill had assembled a fine accompanying group of musicians to present *The Trial Scene*. It could not have been a more appropriate program, crowned as it was with a playing of Lou Applebaum's recently commissioned Concertante for Small Orchestra.

Of all Canada's finest arts administrators, Lou has been the closest adviser to the Chalmers family. It was evident that Canadians were not only becoming proficient in the presentation of great music but were also capable of celebrating those responsible for making it happen.

During the latter decades of the twentieth century and the opening years of the new millennium, even the most invisible figures in the creation of great music — the composers — were receiving some public recognition. John Weinzweig, the aging "dean of Canadian composers," had been linked to Victor since his days at Harbord Collegiate. The interim years had seen countless performances of Weinzweig's compositions with Victor on the podium, both in Canada and abroad. When the TSO decided to celebrate Victor's eightieth birthday in 2004, he realized that in that same year John Weinzweig would be reaching his ninetieth. Victor proposed that both birthdays that year be celebrated in a series of concerts that featured John's music. Thus came about the three TSO events that ensured the recognition of both Canada's most respected music creator and the man who had done more to see that it was played than any other conductor.

There were other celebrations of creativity in which Victor had some part to play. Just as with Lou Applebaum's pending demise some years later, Victor had become aware in the late 1970s that Godfrey Ridout, certainly one of Canada's most popular contemporary classical composers, was ill with cancer and unlikely to live much longer. Ridout's contribution to musical understanding had been prodigious over his many years as the TSO's program note presenter of the evening's musical fare in its concert program week after week. Victor reported Ridout's impending death to Walter Homburger and soon a TSO commission for a piece of music ensued in the context of a Toronto anniversary occasion, an orchestral piece that Ridout called *No Mean City.* Significantly, he dedicated it to Victor Feldbrill. For good reason! Victor, in spite of his willingness to perform the works of patently stylish modern composers, had never abandoned the works of a Godfrey Ridout who openly declared himself an anachronism, preferring to be a writer of compositions based on the patterns of the repertoires of previous centuries. His compositions were melodic and easily accessible and Victor played his works with obvious relish, *Fall Fair* being one of his favourites, particularly when on tour. The *No Mean City* commission gave purpose to Ridout's life and kept him going for several months. When his death finally came his family insisted that Victor conduct the recording of Ridout's works by the TSO soon after.

In the mid 1990s, there was yet another celebration of a Canadian composer — one with whom Victor had a unique connection. On the occasion of his seventieth birthday, at Victor's suggestion, the National Arts Centre Orchestra decided to present a complete program of Harry Somers's compositions, *The Spring of Somers.* With many years of close collaboration with the composer in mind, Victor was on hand to conduct the evening's proceedings. The concert not only recognized Somers's work, it revealed that a Canadian composer had produced a repertoire that could fill an entire evening's orchestral program and ultimately fill a CD, also entitled *The Spring of Somers.* Victor presented such proof by including his *North Country Suite*, Lyric for Orchestra, Suite for Harp and Chamber Orchestra, along with his Symphony no. 1. The Ottawa concert was a demonstration of how far Canadian composition had moved but one that has rarely been repeated by Canadian symphony orchestras in succeeding years. Nor have many CDs focused on the musical creations of a single Canadian composer been produced.

With all of Victor's attention to the city of Hamilton over the years, it was no surprise to discover that Victor was called upon when the city's most distinguished political figure, Lincoln Alexander, was celebrating his seventieth birthday that January (1992). How could a former lieutenant-governor of Ontario, a popularly elected Hamilton member of the Ontario Legislature, as well as the city's most popular citizen be adequately honoured? It was decided that he and his guests should be greeted by the Hamilton

Philharmonic Orchestra at a huge gala concert in Hamilton Place, a venue scarcely capable of containing the enormous army of Alexander's admirers.

Victor had been chairing a committee of the Toronto Women's Music Club that had been commissioned to select the winner of the first competition for string instrumentalists that had ever been conducted by that illustrious organization. Victor had heard the submission of a tape revealing a simply staggering performance by a competitor in the violin class and had made his decision. He determined that this individual should be his soloist at the Lincoln Alexander Gala Concert in Hamilton a few months later. Victor realized that performing with a full symphony orchestra at the Lincoln Alexander concert would launch the career of an unknown young instrumentalist more effectively than any other strategy that could be devised. The name of the sixteen-year-old in question was James Ehnes, a Canadian violinist of stunning proportions who has since become an internationally acclaimed soloist. That January, Ehnes played the Bruch Concerto no. 1 for Violin, and Victor was also able to sign him up for the first concert of the 1992–93 Hamilton Philharmonic season to play the Beethoven Concerto for Violin.

Most certainly, for Victor, one of the celebratory features in the latter years of a career in the arts largely devoted to the young is the knowledge that he has influenced the beginnings of a career developed by a talented and intelligent performer whose presence is being recognized both at home and abroad. Now, some two decades after Victor's introduction of Ehnes and the perceptive management of Walter Homburger, he is now a prime example of Canadian violin virtuoso performance excellence. He is quite open about the role that Victor played in his early years:

> I first met Victor I was in my mid-teens. Growing up in Brandon, Manitoba, I was surrounded by many fine musicians at the school of music at Brandon University. When Victor heard me, he decided to take an interest in my career. I had the great fortune of playing my first performances of several of the major violin concertos with Victor, first the Bruch, then the Brahms and the Beethoven. He also brought me as his soloist for my debut

with the TSO. Having someone like Victor supporting me created a great deal of interest with orchestras and promoters, and unquestionably advanced my career.... I learned so much working with Victor and gained a tremendous amount of confidence just from knowing that someone like him with his reputation believed in me as an artist.[2]

When it came to celebrating the fiftieth anniversary of Victor's own debut as a conductor of the TSO, the orchestra mounted three concerts that included in its program, along with the Sibelius Symphony no. 2, the magnificent lyrical and moving composition by Srul Irving Glick, *The Reawakening*. It was an inspiring piece devoted to the life of the spirit with all the commitment that Glick revealed through his works so tied as they were to the Jewish scriptures.

For two of the concerts Canadian cellist Ofra Harnoy played the Hadyn Concerto for Cello in C Major, and in the third concert Victor had to replace her with the young pianist Yuval Fichman playing a Mozart piano concerto. It was a special moment for Victor to be on the podium to receive the plaudits of his close TSO friends and colleagues and, as well, to be lauded by an audience who were aware of all he had contributed throughout the previous half-century.

By the 1990s, even arts venues were becoming historically celebrated, venues such as Massey Hall, located on Toronto's Shuter Street. The legendary concert hall opened in the last decade of the nineteenth century and had been the home of the TSO throughout most of its existence, as well being the Toronto Mendelssohn Choir's preferred venue. In 1994, though its role as the primary music performing space had been taken over by Roy Thomson Hall, it had not been torn down. With all its problems in terms of inadequate temperature control, lack of foyer space, uncompromising sightlines, and lack of parking, there were those who swore that the sound of the old hall was a treasure. This perception was strengthened when the "old lady of Shuter Street" was perceived to be more accommodating to the sounds of the orchestra than the new Roy Thomson Hall, whose acoustical difficulties were only solved by a successful renovation a couple of decades after its inauguration as Toronto's major orchestral performing space. During the succeeding years, Massey Hall has remained an ever-present venue, not only for a wide variety of popular music presentations but for political meetings and sporting events, as well.

When, in May 1994, a celebration was planned for the hundredth anniversary of this building's initial contribution to Toronto's musical culture, there was considerable enthusiasm. It was thought sufficiently important that Victor would conduct and demonstrate the remaining quality of this much-honoured structure as a concert hall. One of the more ironic twists was the program inclusion of John Weinzweig's ballet score, *Red Ear of Corn*, the very piece which had identified him as a dangerous revolutionary figure by American headhunters during the years of McCarthyism that followed the Second World War. No doubt the political rallies held within its wall by the Communist Party of Canada, as well as the Conservative, Liberal, and New Democratic parties, were being honoured by the presence of that now-familiar selection of Canadian repertoire. It was a celebration that conveyed many messages, all part of the story of a great building.

A mere year later, there was an anniversary concert for an orchestra Victor had founded and conducted in its early years — the TSYO. It had now been in operation for two decades (no doubt a surprise to those who first heard its feeble attempts in its first rehearsals). By the mid-1990s it had provided a glorious musical experience for hundreds of young musicians. Once again, it was Victor who was invited back as guest conductor to join with the incumbent TSYO conductor, David Zafer. The program opened with Sir Ernest MacMillan's *Two Sketches*, followed by the Sibelius *Finlandia* and *Karelia Suite*. The evening ended with the Shostakovich Symphony no. 5.

The celebration assisted in enhancing the realization that a significant investment had been made in young musicians and that this was the only path for maintaining interest in classical music, whose very continuance would become questionable in the century that was to follow.

As joyous as all these moments of celebrations were, the fact is that these years contained the overwhelming tragedy of Victor's life — the loss of Zelda in 1995. She was a vital, energetic seventy-year-old, retired from full-time employment, but just as entwined with her life "cause" — the support of people desperately seeking some meaning to their lives and hoping beyond hope that they might find someone who would help them understand and cope. She was still a missionary providing solace and an activist against those forces that drove people to despair and self-destructive behaviour. Her combination of academic thoughtfulness and practical hands-on assistance of people in the field, were perfection itself. With every client, she was always able to find her way to relevance and compassion, whether in Winnipeg, Toronto, or Tokyo. Her colleagues worshipped her and her students revered her presence, and yet there was a hard, tough centre of expectation of ultimate self-healing by the individual concerned that all of those who associated with her recognized and respected.

Miraculously, she accomplished her tasks within a context of a relationship that demanded she operate hand in hand with a public figure who was "on stage" whenever he walked outside his front door. However, she was a loyal supporter of her husband, despite the fact that he had chosen a profession that commanded not only his full commitment but demanded that much of his life be spent away from her, and often for extended periods.

But whenever Victor and Zelda appeared in public together, they were envied from all sides. Besides her willingness to be at Victor's side in a quiet and supportive manner, Zelda emanated a charm and an intelligence that captivated artists, musician colleagues, and audience members. In any gathering at which they might be separated, Victor's eyes constantly searched out her presence and their deep love for each other was patently obvious to every observer. In the 1990s they were interviewed for an article in *Fanfare* magazine. Their marriage had for decades been seen as a phenomenon — termed a "study in counter-point" by one author. At that time, they were actively engaged in renovating their home, not to accommodate their own needs, but to achieve more space for the increasing number of grandchildren, already some five in number. The children had become the central focus of both Victor and Zelda. This was particularly true for Zelda, who, when her daughters became mothers themselves, began to experience a new, closer bond with them. This awakened understandable disappointment in Victor on those occasions when their needs made it impossible for her to be in Japan with him.

Zelda and Victor were looking forward to celebrating the fiftieth wedding anniversary. Although they were married on December 30, 1945, they had decided to celebrate in the fall, instead — they tended to see their first meeting while at Harbord Collegiate as a part of a continuum that added years to their half-century of formal marriage. As the *Fanfare* article pointed out, "Their family is important to them," and they both made the point that they had "made career concessions in the past to accommodate family needs at the time."

They were quite open about the fact that there had been difficult moments. It had been "touch and go" in the early years. Indeed, Zelda admitted "that meant days when you had to walk another block to get cheaper vegetables at another store ... but we always managed." There had been monumental sacrifices, but it was clear that Zelda was proud of Victor's success. She was ready and willing to be quoted as believing, directly and simply, "I think he is terrific."

The author of the article sensed "a deep attachment these two had, built of shared years, both good and bad." There was so much they had in common — "a love of classical music, [and] a sense of responsibility to the community" being at the top of the list. But there were also day to day moments of happiness, the sharing of the pleasure of old movies and good books (the Marx brothers, Orson Welles, and *Citizen Kane* were mentioned). The writing of Margaret Atwood was also a common bond that provoked inevitable discussion. Finally, with Victor able to pick and choose his projects, to opt whether to remain in Toronto or spend a few days away, their opportunity to spend more time together could become a reality. The dream ended so rapidly.

Florida had become a destination of pleasure for the couple, and Victor had become wedded to time in the sun, particularly during the Christmas and Easter seasons. They craved the warmth that had departed the Canadian scene in the winter months and the delight of walking the beaches hand in hand. Back in the 1970s they had attempted to set up a holiday in the Bahamas with close friends and had found there was no accommodation in the Nassau community they had chosen. Along came a time-share arrangement in a Florida community and they invested little but enough to assume ownership, with the mortgage covered by the rental income. It meant that they had a place they could be sure of inhabiting for at least part of every year, even if it would be only a week or two at a time.

In February 1995, they had scheduled themselves to return home for a grandson's bar mitzvah. Only a week or so before, they had hiked together for three miles. But now Zelda was listless and easily tired. Days went by but nothing improved. Then she had several fainting spells. Victor got her on the plane in a wheelchair; she arrived home and was soon in a doctor's office. Lung cancer had taken over … in a woman who had never smoked. It was a slow but inexorable journey. Victor and their daughters were devastated. He made his home in her sick room.

On September 15, 1995, Zelda died, just three months before their anniversary. And so came to an end one of the most significant relationships to be found in the world of performing arts. Everyone around them would recall the total savagery of that broken intimacy and the impact it had on Victor, who was almost paralyzed with grief through the months that followed.

But Victor's life had to resume. His daughters, distraught by their own grief, helped their father through the next months. Eventually it came time to abandon the Florida residential retreat and remove the many possessions that were a constant reminder to Victor of Zelda's absence.

In one of a series of unexpected steps toward normalcy, Victor found companionship with a woman, Mae Bernstein, a widow who was mourning the loss of several close family members. It happened that she was a fine amateur violinist who had played in semi-amateur orchestras. Some six years after the initiation of her friendship with Victor, she received a letter from a friend in Florida, Ruth Stevens, opining the need of the local Lyric Chamber Orchestra for a real conductor. Victor read the letter and agreed to help out. It took only five minutes of the ensuing rehearsal together for the ensemble to realize it had found a leader beyond their highest hopes. The search was abandoned and Victor took over. He now had an orchestral conducting role that bridged his delight to be in the company of Mae and his appreciation of the warmth of the Florida climate.

A growing affection led to the uniting of two people whose sorrow for the past could be assuaged by each others' presence. A close partnership emerged that renewed the excitement of living for both. Mae describes herself as an impatient, feisty person whose likes and dislikes are easily exposed. Victor is the quieter and more composed of the pair, but the differences in their temperaments have become a basis for a new kind of love and respect that demanded no diminishing of the remembrance of past intimacies but provided a basis for a life together.

Victor currently has a condominium in Toronto. His two girls pointed out that it was manifestly unfair for Mae to be hosted in a home that had such intimate ambience with Zelda and Victor's past together. Selling the family residence and acquiring a convenient apartment was the solution. However, Victor and Mae spend some months each year in New York and the cold winters in Florida. But every important family affair or religious celebration brings Victor back to the family he adores and the community that has the greatest meaning for him.

Victor still conducts in Canada. Until very recently he led the Brantford Symphony — his friend of many years at the TSO, Nancy Westaway, ensured that her favourite conductor was on the podium before her community orchestra and Victor happily complied. Further, he still makes an annual trek to the Vancouver Academy of Music, where he is surrounded by admiring faculty and eager young instrumentalists determined to make their mark in the orchestral training program that Victor has led for decades. There are all kinds of conductors who would love to replace Victor — but none have greater respect for creative composers and the music they provide and no one cares more about the quality of its performance in Canada than does Victor. As director Jerold Gerbrecht points out, it is a rare one that has the decades of experience on stage that can be transferred to these future musicians to whom we will look for brilliance, excitement, and vision in the future. Gerbrecht speaks with awe at the continuing commitment that Victor makes to be in Vancouver each spring to guide the young instrumentalists in yet another leap forward in their desire to make orchestral music. Even well into the twenty-first century (April 2009) he carries out that commitment with the energy of a conductor half his age.

It was a member of the Hamilton Philharmonic, an orchestra that received loving care in the hands of Victor Feldbrill in times of despair and shared triumph in happier moments, who claimed that "he is the Isaac Stern of the Canadian music scene." This comparison surprised me.

Isaac Stern has long had the reputation of being a stellar violin virtuoso, also a veritable treasure in the chamber music performance community. But these distinctions are only a fraction of his impact on American music. He is known for his warmth and generosity toward young aspiring instrumentalists, his respect for contemporary composers, and his caring for all those involved in the world of American contemporary classical music. Ironically, today, there are those who would say that Stern's most notable achievement was that of saving Carnegie Hall, the most prestigious and historic performance venue in New York, from destruction (it was slated to be turned into a car park).

A second Stern comparison was even more convincing — their shared love of children. It was made by Ann Cooper Gay, a choral conductor who established a splendid reputation with several youth ensembles. Her analysis of her colleague was most significant. As a soprano soloist herself, she remembers warmly his "bringing together" all the forces that produced the *Riel* revival for American audiences in which she sang a major part. Stern, on an intermission feature for a television concert, stressed the point that his greatest moment in Carnegie Hall was when he experienced the hall filled with children singing their hearts out. Ann Cooper Gay also helps children find that magic of their own voices and as a former American citizen the name of Isaac Stern has monumental significance. Her description of Victor as a "fine human being who reaches out to choristers, indeed, hangs out with them waiting to go on stage," includes children, and has profound significance.[3]

Another voice, that of Janet Stubbs, an outstanding solo performer whose appearances with the Canadian Opera Company revealed that a Canadian soprano had the talent, the intelligence, and the presence to ensure a future in opera around the world, but who instead decided to make her contribution as a splendid arts administrator, mirrored Ann Cooper Gay in her assessment of Victor as a fine conductor of assembled voices.

Stubbs began her operatic career in the COC chorus in productions like *Heloise and Abelard*, *The Merry Widow*, and *Carmen*, and was stunned that "Victor actually knew my name. He treated singers with warmth — not always to be expected from orchestral people. He let you feel that you mattered." She went on to solo roles before her retirement from opera, when she took on the management of a foundation that supports the arts.

These perceptions of Victor seem to be universal and are recounted with pleasure particularly by those in the world of vocal solo music performance, many of whom had been embarrassingly buried by orchestras conducted by less sensitive occupants of the podium. As with Stern, the name Victor Feldbrill brings back memories of glorious afternoons and evenings with children and youths and sometimes parents, being enraptured by new sounds and the emotions they aroused. For these now mature concert attendees, Victor represents the open window on a lifetime of pleasure, a continuing experience of the magic of great music. For countless individuals it has added meaning to a life concentrated on those things that provide for the support of family and community. For others this contact with Victor is the basis of a relationship with potential loved ones that has brought delight and even intimacy.

For a sizeable number of musicians in Canada, Victor represents the initial experience of performing the music of the ages led by a baton in the hands of a professional conductor who really cared about the quality and meaning of what he was doing. Lawrence Cherney was an outstanding instrumentalist, but is recognized today more for his splendid leadership as the CEO of Soundstreams, a major arts entrepreneurial agency he founded to bring together musical groups, often vocal, from across Canada and the world to make music together at the highest level of accomplishment.

Lawrence met Victor when he was a teenager playing in the National Youth Orchestra. Victor was the featured conductor that year and Lawrence remembers the patience he was accorded as he sought to conquer a difficult solo, the English horn passage of the Berlioz *Symphonie Fantastique*. It was a defining moment. A negative experience might have closed off a career, both as an instrumentalist and an arts entrepreneur, and that would have left his country and his city the poorer. Yet there was with that infinite patience a toughness that insisted on a level of execution appropriate to a public performance, even when only the few days of rehearsal were available.[4]

More famously, the name Feldbrill is associated with the experience of hearing or playing an orchestral composition of a creative Canadian who was not only alive but lived in the same community as the listener or players. More than mere nostalgia is the continuing delight, as a member of an ensemble, the joy of discovering that there was in Canada a man who truly respected the orchestral performing arts and was prepared to fight for remuneration and conditions of work that made it possible. Victor may not have "saved" a Carnegie Hall (though without his determination, a Centennial Concert Hall would never have been built in Winnipeg) but his services to Canadian orchestras across the continent make the comparison nicely with Isaac Stern's role in the United States. Indeed Stern could be termed the American Victor Feldbrill.

However, there is so much more. Feldbrill had a vision that included the expectation of symphony orchestras in every region of Canada, employing splendid Canadian instrumentalists and including in its repertoire the works which expressed the culture of his native land. To do that he was prepared to defy symphony orchestra boards, endure absences from his family, accept the tiring necessity of travel and often uncomfortable accommodations.

Just how good a conductor was Victor? Accolades come from all directions. Every colleague mentions his steady beat, his knowledge of the score, his commitment to the intentions of the composers. Why then weren't orchestras from around the world clamouring for his services? First, he was a Canadian conductor, based in a country with virtually no recording industry that might have heralded his genius abroad. As well, as already mentioned, he had no stomach for the "hype" of modern marketing techniques or the excesses of theatrical interpretations, nor did he revel in the lifestyle of constant travel that would have brought him widespread attention abroad.

However, there is also another reality. A leading Canadian composer and musician, Victor Davies, identifies it making use of the term "mystery" as the key to the kind of conductor who receives attention in the Western world.[5] Just being "from abroad" was the first essential element in the sense of mystery, and Feldbrill failed to meet that criterion. As well, as Davies puts it, Victor did not encourage any "mystery" in his conducting style. He kept the score before him though his colleagues knew he was in command of every page. Even more significant was his distaste for all association with the commercialism that dominates the field of performance and is connected so often with the expectations of "pop culture," a style of thinking and performing that mirrors a world obsessed with raucous and arrogant behaviour and unjustifiable riches that counts for so much in a world that values those qualities in the arts as in every other aspect of life.

"Mystery" becomes part of the game of gaining attention in just that sort of world. It lies behind the comments from orchestral giants that he was altogether too "nice" on the podium. His alternative to that reputation could have been one for filling the souls of musicians with fear for their lives and careers. Instead it was for an especially kind and gentle treatment to nervous young soloists playing their first concerto with a conductor on a podium. One central performer and later executive with the WSO, James Manishen, called him "the finest accompanist I have ever encountered."[6] International vocal soloist Roxalana Roslak was chosen to sing in Somers's opera *Louis Riel*. It was her first experience as an opera singer and she was understandably terrified. In her own words she was "very young and vulnerable" and "no conductor could have been more supportive and helpful" than Victor Feldbrill, providing her with encouragement in what she was accomplishing every night of the production run.[7]

Indeed, there is a bevy of soloists, both vocal and instrumental, who join that chorus. In 1963, Gwen Thompson had won the Victor Feldbrill Cup in the violin class at the Winnipeg Kiwanis Festival. A solo appearance with the WSO was her reward and with Victor conducting she played the Lalo *Symphonie Espagnol* to great acclaim. She was to play in the National Youth Orchestra and other Canadian ensembles when Feldbrill was a guest conductor. Over many years she came to appreciate not just his role as an accompanist, but as a great musician "with an absolute love of music" that affected every performance. For her that was Victor's "charisma," a word she used quite consciously.[8]

TSO trumpet player and composer Johnny Cowell remembers Victor from his Second World War days with appreciation and warmth for the decency and respect for other colleagues that was so much a part of his public character. These were the attributes of a "reliable" figure who so often was the invisible treasure in the TSO team, one who had over those many decades played various roles, serving a host of needs that the orchestra came to realize needed his skill and attention.[9]

The word *reliable* becomes almost derogatory when seeking the commanding heights of those engaged in orchestral conducting. The relationship of player and conductor is filled with possible tension. Stanley Solomon was a valued member of the TSO for some forty-three years and principal violist for most of those years. He, too, refers to Victor's "reliability" (a term he uses as synonymous with "able to fill the seats"), while treasuring his half-century relationship as a chamber music associate and a member of an orchestra that played under his baton on countless occasions. In Solomon's words, he was a very popular incumbent on the orchestra's podium, even though popularity as a conductor can be perceived as "weak," "indecisive," and "uninteresting."

Solomon asserts that there is an ever-present tension between players and conductors created virtually by the definition of those roles. "Players blame conductors for their own shortcomings," was this veteran player's analysis. One could add that conductors, with responsibilities to address a broad repertoire, cannot follow the musical prejudices of nearly a hundred players and this may be a major problem for a Victor Feldbrill bent upon exposing audiences to contemporary composers — and Canadian ones at that![10] Popularity in the role is likely not "on" … but one soon recognizes that respect is more to be valued and the orchestras across Canada contain colleagues for whom "respect" and "Feldbrill" are interchangeable.

Certainly one of the attributes of a modern conductor is that of assisting in the raising of funds and attracting new audiences. John Lawson, a major figure in the musical life of Toronto as a Mendelssohn Choir singer and as a board member (and often chair and fundraiser for seemingly countless arts organizations and venues), recounts Victor's prowess in this unpopular task. At a concert of the UTSO there was a piano concerto played by a graduating student. The pianist was quite good — but the quality of the piano was appalling. After quieting down the applause at the end of the concert, Victor took the opportunity of addressing the audience about the pathetic instrument that the Music Faculty of the University of Toronto was obliged to use and appealed for financial help to buy a proper Steinway. Sitting next to John Lawson was a music lover who was so moved by Victor's appeal that he donated the entire cost of a splendid instrument. Few conductors would have taken on that responsibility — even fewer would have been successful.

Victor had accepted a Roy Thomson Hall Award for his enormous contribution to music but, uncharacteristically for an artist, he joined the RTH Board of Governors. Even more surprisingly, he played an active part in the work of that board. In particular, he recounted the fact that most of his own music education had taken place while attending concerts and rehearsals of great orchestras and choirs. He pushed forward a plan that would provide free or low-cost tickets to students enrolled in the University of Toronto's Faculty of Music and its Conservatory, a program that came to be broadened to serve music students in other universities in Ontario. The program continues to this day — of enormous advantage to the young people planning a career in the performing arts and even more particularly, music studies leading to some other role in the cultural sector.

As he found himself a mature, experienced exponent of intelligent conducting, he was able to carry out professional development for conductors just reaching the ranks of beginners but ready to move on to higher levels of accomplishment. The role of trying to improve the capacity of a conductor is one that, for some, defies all efforts through usual educational techniques and procedures. It is a function that is so unique and personal and tied so completely to the individual's personal style that any effort to produce a common standard or methodology is perceived to be totally invalid.

Victor, fully aware of this perception and committed to the unique expression of every candidate, had been engaged in the teaching of conducting technique with fourth-year students at the University of Toronto for a decade and a half (and for another half-decade in Japan). In the early 1990s he met Dr. Harry Hurwitz, a psychologist and educator but most of all a lover of orchestral music. Just as Victor had experienced in his own efforts to qualify as a conductor, Hurwitz realized that to encourage professional development of more mature aspirants there had to be "hands on" opportunities for conducting a "live" orchestra.

The cost of providing such an orchestra in North America was quite beyond the budgets of faculties and conservatories carrying out their normal functions of preparing students for a career in music and conducting it in particular. Hurwitz decided that he would make his contribution to the improvement of orchestral conducting by providing a program in a country where he could find instrumentalists at a price that would not destroy the financial viability of the process. However, in Czechoslovakia these musicians could be found and an orchestra could be created. In 1993, he met Victor Feldbrill and realized he had found just exactly the person who could bring experience and achievement to bear on the efforts of a group of young people from around the world interested in lifting their conducting performance to a higher level.

A particular focus was found in an area of activity to which Victor had already given his commitment — the preparation of choral directors to confront the challenge of orchestral conducting and to achieve the confidence and techniques the orchestral forces demanded in order to perform the great works for both choir and instrument ensembles that are to be found in their repertoires — or should be! Thus, for a few weeks most summers during the 1990s, it was off to Czechoslovakia (except for the summer of 1995 when Zelda's impending death meant that Victor was by her side). After the summer of 1993, during which he was working with students intending to conduct instrumentalists, he put his attention to the choral scene and its need for expertise in the area of providing effective leadership to instrumental musicians.

He found the students selected were quite impressive. (Half were from the Eastman School of Music in Rochester, New York.) The orchestra players were better than he expected. For them it was a job with no expectation beyond a modest stipend. It often meant a series of frustrating experiences with conductors who were totally unable to cope. However, Victor's idealism was infectious and the orchestra members became positively adulatory. Particularly, they reacted to his positive respect for their role as instrumentalists and his patience with his very inexperienced potential conductors. Victor found the weeks passing quickly, particularly when Zelda came with him to Opava, to a castle reputed to have been occupied by Beethoven while he was composing his Symphony no. 4.

The students were ecstatic in their praise. Peggy Dettweiler was in his workshop in the summer of 1993. She was a choral conductor anxious to be more proficient before an orchestra. She remembers the solid, practical advice: "Don't depend on body movement … keep it in the hands and arms and don't lean over the piano." But more important was the cautionary counsel on interpretation: "Don't make it overly sentimental." Since that time she has conducted virtually the entire mainstream of choral presentation, including *Messiah*, *Elijah*, the requiems of Brahms, Verdi, Rutter, Mozart, Fauré, and Duruflé, and many more recent contemporary works. Her appreciation remains manifest as her career expands.[11] Most of all, she remembers an excellent teacher and friend who dramatically improved her conducting performance.

Another student, Stella Sung, was a student in Victor's composer's workshop in Olomouc, Czechoslovakia. Her reaction to Victor's work was equally positive:

> I found his approach to be firm yet compassionate and understanding and patient ... an absolute and total professional, without a lot of "show" and fussiness which so many conductors are wont to do and be. His conducting technique is elegant and refined, and he was able to motivate the orchestra to new heights.[12]

Victor eventually overcame the need to confront music critics in the manner that had tended to strain his relationship with them in Winnipeg, but his treatment by them in Toronto became another reason for his determination to be free of any long-term commitment to a single orchestra in any particular community. Arts criticism during the twentieth century seems infected with a determination to demand much from the flood of new Canadian performers arriving on the country's stages. It was a part of a recognized historic tendency of colonials to think that if anyone stood out in Canada they should be recognized by the élite forces somewhere else, particularly in Britain and the United States.

Some arts critics were caught up in the mission of demanding often impossible performance from homegrown talent in the hope that this would drive them farther and higher. Often it discouraged and humiliated unnecessarily. It was inconceivable that these Canadian performers would just want to stay, sing, play, and act in second-rate colonial Canada. For such critics, the fact that Victor had turned down that direction in his desire to remain in his country of birth simply was an indication of his unwillingness to compete with the best. It is a blessing that during the twentieth century the Maureen Forresters, Glenn Goulds, Steven Staryks, and a host of others have thrilled people around the world and this wrong-headed approach has largely disappeared. But it took a long time, and many Canadian performers were victimized by the nature of these responses to their talents and qualities.[13]

The twentieth century was one of enormous violence. It was a century of mayhem in which death and disability more than ever targeted the innocent. It was a century of enormously more effective weaponry. However, it was also a century of invention and creativity that improved the health and living conditions of millions of people.

The making of music may seem a long distance from all the havoc that has erupted as the first decade of the twenty-first century comes to an end. But music and its making is the way that a culture expresses its qualities — both its strengths and its weaknesses.

Victor, over his long career revealed that leadership in music could be achieved in a context of respect and civilized behaviour. He recognized that it was important to emphasize Canadian music and he believed that it should be played by appropriately rehearsed and fairly rewarded musicians. He knew from his own life how much music could enhance the relationships between people, whether as individuals, as communities, or as nations. The obsession that Victor might have had with the present and its immediate triumphs were de-emphasized by his concern with the future of the next generation, of the children and youth who he felt had the need to listen and benefit from the performance of great music and to be involved in its performance.

These Feldbrill tendencies are the very attributes of a society that is environmentally responsible and socially sustainable, and must be celebrated. Little wonder that Victor can, today, look back with pride and a sense of achievement on a career that has counted in a land that seemed beyond hope in its cultural expression but a few decades ago.

It is not clear whether the pressures to save the planet and its inhabitants will indeed be responded to with sufficient commitment and humanitarian determination — but the nature and quality of Victor's work in the arts and culture of his native land will be a model for those who wish to make the arts a central influence rather than merely a reflection of the society that must be reconstructed and transformed. Can Victor Feldbrill's work and influence as a conductor and advocate, a purveyor of belief that synergy, decency, and civility can replace the values of the money-changer, the warmonger, the religious fanatic, and the terrorist make a difference? If so, then his career will have had an impact beyond anything we can imagine.

As an age of culture and peace replaces the centuries of economic competition and incivility, the struggle to create a decent future surrounded by music that matters and means something positive to a reflective and sensitive people will have proved Victor Feldbrill right.

NOTES

Preface

1. Even as this book was being completed, Victor was invited to an eightieth anniversary celebration in Ottawa of the initiation of the close relationship between Canada and Japan at which the Emperor and Empress of Japan were present. He was surprised and pleased that his work in that country in the late 1970s and 1980s was remembered and valued by Canada's diplomatic corps in both countries.

2. Being Canadian explains the significance of sharing a history and a sense of place. That identity leads to different interpretations of success and failure, thereby explaining a contrasting pattern of career development that would have occurred if he had been an orchestral conductor in Europe, Britain, or the United States. This phenomenon is well outlined in John Ralston Saul's

recent volume, *The Fair Country: Telling Truths About Canada* (Toronto: Viking Canada, 2008).

Chapter 1
1. Victor Feldbrill, Interview, September 26, 2005.
2. Morry Kernerman, Interview, May 30, 2006.

Chapter 2
1. Victor Feldbrill, Interview with author, October 3, 2005. Victor, the young concertmaster, took his responsibilities seriously, at one point ejecting a fellow student and musician from a choral rehearsal. This young man was Phil Givens, who was to become one of Harbord's illustrious alumnae, serving as the mayor of Toronto and gaining a reputation as one of the most active chief magistrates in the city's history. Both he and Victor attended a school reunion decades later at which Givens announced with some emotion that Maestro Victor Feldbrill had been the only person in his long public career who had ever thrown him out of a meeting. To which Victor retorted, "You're still just as mouthy."
2. Victor Feldbrill, Interview with author, October 21, 2005. *Ibid.* Through a career of more than a half-century, on podiums across Canada and overseas, Victor was the prime promoter and exponent of John Weinzweig's music. He was the inevitable person to give the eulogy at his funeral in 2006 and to conduct the ensemble at the celebration of his life and music a few months later.
3. Victor Feldbrill, Letter to Zelda Mann, August 15, 1940. Feldbrill fonds, 2005-031/006 [01], York University Archives, Toronto.
4. Concert review, *The Varsity*, February 26, 1943. Feldbrill fonds, 2005-031/015[01], York University Archives, Toronto.
5. Concert review, Augustus Bridle, *Toronto Daily Star*, February 26, 1943, Feldbrill fonds, York University Archives, 2005-031/015, Toronto. A month later, Bridle commented on Victor's conducting that he exhibited "a certain elegant dignity, evident knowledge of the orchestra ensemble and high rhythmic vivacity that marked an exhibition quite worthy of a much older conductor." *Ibid.*, concert review, *Toronto Daily Star*, March 31, 1943, Feldbrill fonds, 2005-031/015.[01], York University Archives, Toronto.
6. Concert review, *Toronto Globe*, February 26, 1943. Feldbrill fonds, 2005-031/015 [01], York University Archives, Toronto. The *Globe*'s major critic, Hector Charlesworth, commented a month later on Victor's performance of the annual Gilbert and Sullivan: "He conducted with aplomb and distinction … he has a fine beat and inherent rhythmical aptitudes and seems destined to do admirable things." *Ibid.*, *Toronto Globe*, March 31, 1943, Toronto.

7. Francis Ireland, Letter to Victor Feldbrill, October 6, 1943. Feldbrill fonds, 2005-031/013 [06], York University Archives, Toronto. Ireland could be quite dismissive of conductors for whom she had little respect. André Kostelanitz had the nerve to do the César Franck's Symphony when her favourite conductor, Ettore Mazzoleni, had performed it the previous season. Her assessment of the incumbent conductor of the UTSO was that he "had been a nuisance." She promised that although she was leaving the employ of the SAC she would pass on her high regard for Victor to her successor in the post, as well as the information that he was now conducting his *Navy Show* orchestral string colleagues while working with Sir Adrian Boult. (Frances Ireland, Letter to Victor Feldbrill, March 13, 1945. Feldbrill fonds, 2005-031/013 [06], York University Archives, Toronto.)

8. Victor Feldbrill, Interview, October 25, 2005. These were difficult times for the Prom Orchestra. Reginald Stewart, though a fine conductor, had engaged himself in ongoing confrontation with members of the orchestra and more important with Ernest Johnson, its manager. Finally, Johnson fired Stewart for insubordination and for behaviour toward members of the orchestra that was quite unacceptable.

9. Victor Feldbrill, Letter to Zelda Mann, July 8, 1940. Feldbrill fonds, 2005-031/006 [01], York University Archives, Toronto.

10. Victor Feldbrill, Letter to Zelda Mann, August 22, 1940. Feldbrill fonds, 2005-031/006 [01], York University Archives, Toronto.

11. Victor Feldbrill, Letter to Zelda Mann, July 31, 1941, Feldbrill fonds, 2005-031/006 [31], York University Archives, Toronto.

Chapter 3

1. Victor Feldbrill, Letter to Zelda Mann, March 3, 1944. Feldbrill fonds, 2005-031/007 [04], York University Archives, Toronto.

2. Victor Feldbrill, Letter to Zelda Mann, February 15, 1945, including Beverley Baxter's copied review of *Meet the Navy*. Feldbrill fonds, 2005-031/007 [10], York University Archives, Toronto.

Chapter 4

1. Victor Feldbrill, Letter to Zelda Mann, July 23, 1944. Feldbrill fonds, 2005-031/007 [02], York University Archives, Toronto.

2. *Ibid.*

3. Victor Feldbrill. Letter to Zelda Mann, January 18, 1945. Feldbrill fonds, 2000-031/007 [10], York University Archives, Toronto.

4. Victor Feldbrill, Letter to Zelda Mann, October 22, 1944. Feldbrill fonds, 2005-031/007 [08], York University Archives, Toronto.

5. Victor Feldbrill, Letter to Zelda Mann, October 24, 1944. Feldbrill fonds, 2005-031/007[08], York University Archives, Toronto.

6. Victor Feldbrill, Letter to Zelda Mann, October 29, 1944. Feldbrill fonds, 2005-031/007 [08], York University Archives, Toronto.

7. Victor Feldbrill, Letter to Zelda Mann, November 18, 1944. Feldbrill fonds, 2005-031/007 [9], York University Archives, Toronto.

8. Victor Feldbrill, Interview with author, December 2, 2005.

9. Victor Feldbrill, Letter to Zelda Mann, November 14, 1944. Feldbrill fonds, 2005-031/007 [9], York University Archives, Toronto.

10. *Ibid.*

11. Victor Feldbrill, Letter to Zelda Mann, November 16, 1944. Feldbrill fonds, 2005-031/007 [9], York University Archives, Toronto.

12. Victor Feldbrill, Letter to Zelda Mann, January 22, 1945. Feldbrill fonds, 2005-031/007 [10], York University Archives, Toronto.

13. Victor Feldbrill, Letter to Zelda Mann, January 18, 1945. Mr. Stein was fascinated with the Canadian seaman who had such an interest in music. He questioned Victor on his attitude toward "the moderns," who turned out to be in his mind the composers Sibelius and Stravinsky.

14. Victor Feldbrill, Letter to Zelda Mann, February 5, 1945, Feldbrill fonds, 2005-031/007 [10], York University Archives, Toronto.

15. Victor Feldbrill, Letter to Zelda Mann, February 15, 1945. Feldbrill fonds, 2005-031/007 [10], York University Archives, Toronto.

16. Victor Feldbrill, Letter to Zelda Mann, January 19, 1945. Feldbrill fonds, 2005-031/007 [10], York University Archives, Toronto.

17. Victor Feldbrill, Letter to Zelda Mann, February 9, 1945. Feldbrill fonds, 2005-031/007 [11], York University Archives, Toronto.

Chapter 5

1. Victor Feldbrill, Letter to Zelda Mann, April 24, 1944. Feldbrill fonds, 2005-031/008 [02], York University Archives, Toronto.

2. Victor Feldbrill, Letter to Zelda Mann, April 7, 1945. Feldbrill fonds, 2005-031/008 [02], York University Archives, Toronto.

3. Victor Feldbrill, Letter to Zelda Mann, July 16, 1945. Feldbrill fonds, 2005-031/008 [2], York University Archives, Toronto.

4. Victor Feldbrill, Letter to Zelda Mann, July 29, 1945. Feldbrill fonds, 2005-031/008 [2], York University Archives, Toronto.

5. Victor Feldbrill, Letter to Zelda Mann, August 29, 1945. Feldbrill fonds, 2005-031/008 [2], York University Archives, Toronto.

6. *Ibid.*

7. Victor Feldbrill, Letter to Zelda Mann, October 22, 1945. Feldbrill fonds,

2005-031/008 [03], York University Archives, Toronto.

8. Victor Feldbrill, Letter to Zelda Mann, October 14, 1945. Feldbrill fonds, 2005-031/008 [03], York University Archives, Toronto. In the midst of his final lessons, Howells penned a thoughtful assessment that Victor copied to Zelda a few days later: "You know, Victor, we English are a strange race — we very rarely show our emotions — if we don't like a person, we usually put him off with some excuse or other and have nothing more to do with him. On the other hand, if we take a liking to persons we associate with them but never become particularly warm. But you seem to have that capacity to move us — a thing that very rarely happens — I really can't get over how beautifully you handle Adrian [Boult] — and do you realize you are one of the few people to see Beecham without having some rude and sarcastic remark thrown at him by that gentleman. You, Victor, definitely have a way about you and I'm glad to see it." Victor Feldbrill, Letter to Zelda Mann, October 19, 1945. Feldbrill fonds, 2005-031/008 [03], York University Archives, Toronto.

9. Victor Feldbrill, Letter to Zelda Mann, October 21, 1945. Feldbrill fonds, 2005-008/231 [03], York University Archives, Toronto.

10. Victor Feldbrill, Letter to Zelda Mann, November 10, 1945. Feldbrill fonds, 2005-031/008 [03], York University Archives, Toronto.

11. *Ibid.*

12. Victor Feldbrill, Letter to Zelda Mann, December 10, 1945. Feldbrill fonds, 2005-031/008 [03], York University Archives, Toronto.

13. Victor Feldbrill, Letter to Zelda Mann, November 9, 1945. Feldbrill fonds, 2005-031/008 [03], York University Archives, Toronto.

14. *Ibid.*

Chapter 6

1. Zelda Mann, Letter to Victor Feldbrill, July 3, 1941. Feldbrill fonds, 2005-031/010 [06], York University Archives, Toronto.

2. Zelda Mann, Letter to Victor Feldbrill, June 27, 1941. Feldbrill fonds, 2005-031/010 [08], York University Archives, Toronto. Victor came to expect such warmth but as she became more mature, her expressions of intimacy became more reserved. When in 1944, Victor complained about the "coldness" of her letters, she responded, "I'm not good at writing down my emotions." Yet virtually every letter spoke of her feeling of isolation and abandonment during the last years of the Second World War and her desire to commit herself to a splendid marriage and a glorious family life.

3. Zelda Mann, Letter to Victor Feldbrill, August 4, 1941. Feldbrill fonds, 2005-0321/010 [06], York University Archives, Toronto.

4. Zelda Mann, Letter to Victor Feldbrill, November 10, 1943. Feldbrill fonds,

2005-031/011 [03], York University Archives, Toronto.

5. Zelda Mann, Letter to Victor Feldbrill, April 14, 1944. Feldbrill fonds, 2005-031/011 [04], York University Archives, Toronto.

6. Zelda Mann, Letter to Victor Feldbrill, April 19, 1944. Feldbrill fonds, 2005-031/011 [04], York University Archives, Toronto.

7. Zelda Mann, Letter to Victor Feldbrill, June 13, 1944. Feldbrill fonds, 2005-031/011 [05], York University Archives, Toronto. I am indebted to Rabbi Arthur Bielfeld, who explained to me what Zelda fully realized — that Judaism is not a "faith community" but can be described more accurately as a family enriched by an intimate spiritual relationship. Thus the term "family" describes this religious commitment more correctly than any definition emphasizing a narrow belief system. My appreciation is owed to this friend and mentor.

8. Zelda Mann, Letter to Victor Feldbrill, October 10, 1944. Feldbrill fonds, 2005-031/011 [08], York University Archives, Toronto.

9. Zelda Mann, Letter to Victor Feldbrill, August 23, 1944. Feldbrill fonds, 2005-031/012 [07], York University Archives, Toronto.

10. Zelda Mann, Letter to Victor Feldbrill, May 28, 1944. Feldbrill fonds, 2005-031/011 [03], York University Archives, Toronto.

11. Zelda Mann, Letter to Victor Feldbrill, August 4, 1944, Feldbrill fonds, 2005-031/011 [06], York University Archives, Toronto.

12. Zelda Mann, Letter to Victor Feldbrill, July 17, 1945. Feldbrill fonds, 2005-031/012 [07], York University Archives, Toronto.

13. Zelda Mann, Letter to Victor Feldbrill, October 3, 1943. Feldbrill fonds, 2005-031/009 [12], York University Archives, Toronto.

14. Zelda Mann, Letter to Victor Feldbrill, December 27, 1944. Feldbrill fonds, 2005-031/011 [10], York University Archives, Toronto.

15. Zelda, like many Ontarians, were led to give up on the CCF as a viable political party, particularly as the federal election held weeks later brought similarly disappointing results. Years later, in the 1970s, in the process of writing his autobiography, David Lewis, a leading twentieth-century figure in the CCF and the major architect of its successor, the NDP, had the opportunity of considering "The Gestapo Affair." He read many of the documents unavailable to the commission, many of which indicated that in fact there was indisputable evidence of an illicit activity on the part of the Ontario Provincial Police known to George Drew, and that a whitewash by the investigating commission had occurred. David Lewis, *The Good Fight* (Toronto: Macmillan of Canada, 1981), 261–87.

16. Zelda Mann, Letter to Victor Feldbrill June 5, 1945. Feldbrill fonds, 2005-031/012 [05], York University Archives, Toronto.

Chapter 7

1. Reviews, Rose Macdonald, Augustus Bridle, n/d. Feldbrill fonds, 2005-031/015, Scrapbooks I, York University Archives, Toronto.

2. Review, Douglas Valleau. Feldbrill fonds, 2005-031/015, Scrapbooks I, York University Archives, Toronto.

3. Augustus Bridle, review. Victor Feldbrill fonds, 2005-031/15, Scrapbooks I, York University Archives, Toronto.

4. Rose Macdonald, review. Feldbrill fonds, 2005-031/015, Scrapbooks I, York University Archives, Toronto.

5. Review, *The Varsity*. Feldbrill fonds, 2005-031/015, Scrapbooks I, York University Archives, Toronto.

6. Victor Feldbrill, Email to author dated February 3, 2009, re: the Terence Gibbs "audition."

7. William Krehm, review on radio station CJBC, n/d, copy to be found in Feldbrill fonds, 2005-031/015, Scrapbooks I, York University Archives, Toronto.

Chapter 8

1. Victor Feldbrill, Letter to Zelda Feldbrill, July 2, 1947. Feldbrill fonds, 2005-031/008 [5], York University Archives, Toronto.

2. Victor Feldbrill, Letter to Zelda Feldbrill, July 4, 1947. Feldbrill fonds, 2005-031/008 [5], York University Archives, Toronto. The author and his spouse had the experience of singing under Robert Shaw's baton some forty years after Victor's interaction and he was still as articulate and still wore the same "sloppy, drooping shirt."

   Later in the festival, Victor met Shaw's mentor at Julliard, Julius Herford, for a private discussion. As he told Zelda, "He's a philosopher and one that does not talk down — but discusses with you." Victor was obviously in the process of discovering the kind of conductor he wanted to be and his assessment of Herford was that "he left a very profound impression with me." At the end of the discussion, Herford concluded by giving Victor the highest compliment: "I wish we had more students with your type of mind here [in America]. As a matter of fact I wish I could have you as a student at Julliard." Victor Feldbrill, Letter to Zelda Feldbrill, July 19, 1947. Feldbrill fonds, 2005-031/008 [5], York University Archives, Toronto.

3. *Ibid.*

4. Victor Feldbrill, Letter to Zelda Feldbrill, July 31, 1947. Feldbrill fonds, 2005-031/008 [05], York University Archives, Toronto.

5. Victor Feldbrill, Letter to Zelda Feldbrill, August 1, 1949. Feldbrill fonds, 2005-031/081 [06], York University Archives, Toronto.

6. Victor Feldbrill, Letter to Zelda Feldbrill, August 11, 1949. Feldbrill fonds, 2005-031/008 [06], York University Archives, Toronto.

7. Victor Feldbrill, Letter to Zelda Mann, June 18, 1956. Feldbrill fonds, 2005-031/008 [08], York University Archives, Toronto.

8. Victor Feldbrill, Letter to Zelda Mann, July11, 1956. Feldbrill fonds, 2005-031/008 [08], York University Archives, Toronto.

9. Victor Feldbrill, Letter to Zelda Mann, August 1, 1956. Feldbrill fonds, 2005-031/008 [08], Scrapbooks I, York University Archives, Toronto.

10. Victor Feldbrill, Interview, *CBC Times*, October 12–18, 1958, Vol. 11, No. 41, Winnipeg.

11. Victor Feldbrill, Interview with author, June 1, 2007.

Chapter 9

1. Ed Palmer, review (no publisher or date available). Feldbrill fonds, 2005-031/015, Scrapbooks I, York University Archives, Toronto.

2. George Kidd, review, *Toronto Telegram*, August 31, 1951. Feldbrill fonds, 2005-031/015, Scrapbooks I, York University Archives, Toronto.

3. Leo Smith, review, August 31, 1951. Feldbrill fonds, 2005-031/015. Scrapbooks I, York University Archives, Toronto. It was a particularly fortunate night for the Feldbrill family. There was a door prize given at that particular Prom Concert and Victor's father was the winner that night.

4. Victor Feldbrill, quoted in Don Anderson, *Tuning the Forks: A Celebration of the Winnipeg Symphony Orchestra* (Winnipeg: self-published, 2007), 22.

5. Janet Roy, Email to author, April 3, 2009.

6. George Kidd, review of pop concert, January 9, 1954. Feldbrill fonds, 2005-031/015, Scrapbooks I, York University Archives, Toronto.

7. John Kraglund, review, *Globe and Mail*, n/d. Feldbrill fonds, 2005-031/015 Scrapbooks II, York University Archives, Toronto.

8. Helen MacNamara, review of TSO pop concert, January 6. Feldbrill fonds, 2005-031/015. Scrapbooks II, York University Archives, Toronto.

9. Kenneth Winters, review of January 31 concert of the WSO, *Winnipeg Free Press*, February 1, 1957. Feldbrill fonds, 2005-031/015, Scrapbooks II, York University Archives, Toronto.

Chapter 10

1. Michael Olver, review, December 2, 1957. Feldbrill fonds, 2005-031/015, Scrapbooks I, York University Archives, Toronto.

2. John Kraglund, review, *Globe and Mail*, Toronto, December 22, 1957.

3. John Kraglund, review, *Globe and Mail*, Toronto, January 9, 1958.

4. Victor Feldbrill, article, *Winnipeg Free Press*, April 19, 1958, Feldbrill fonds,

2005-031/015, Scrapbooks III, York University Archives, Toronto.

5. Letter to WSO subscribers, April 17, 1958. Feldbrill fonds, 2005-031/015, Scrapbooks III, York University Archives, Toronto.

6. Victor Feldbrill, article, *Winnipeg Free Press*, April 19,1958. Feldbrill fonds, 2005-031/015, Scrapbooks III, York University Archives, Toronto.

7. Marie J.Duchesnaj, review, *Het Laatste Miews*, Brussels, July 2, 1958. Feldbrill fonds, 2005-031/015, Scrapbooks III, York University Archives, Toronto.

8. Review, *La Dernière Heure*, Brussels, July 2, 1958. Feldbrill fonds, 2005-031/015, Scrapbooks III, York University Archives, Toronto.

9. Review, *La Soir*, Brussels, July 2, 1958. Feldbrill fonds, 2005-031/015, Scrapbooks III, York University Archives, Toronto.

10. KennethWinters, review, *Winnipeg Free Press*, October 10, 1958.

11. S. Roy Maley, review, *Winnipeg Tribune*, October 10, 1958.

12. Kenneth Winters, *Winnipeg Free Press*, October 23, 1958.

13. S. Roy Maley, *Winnipeg Tribune*, October 23, 1958.

14. John Kraglund, review, *Globe and Mail*, Toronto, December 22, 1958.

Chapter 11

1. Victor Feldbrill, Interview with author, March 6, 2007.

2. Frank Rasky, article, *Toronto Sunday Star*, n/d. Feldbrill fonds, 2005-031/008, York University Archives, Toronto.

3. *Ibid.*

4. Aviva Koffman, Interview with author, January 10, 2007.

5. Kenneth Winters, review of special concert, *Winnipeg Free Press*, January 29, 1959.

6. Bill Richardson, Interview with author, December 18, 2007.

7. S. Roy Maley, review of April 2 concert, *Winnipeg Tribune*, April 3, 1959.

8. Kenneth Winters, Interview with author, December 16, 1959.

9. S. Roy Maley, review, *Winnipeg Tribune*, October 23, 1959.

10. Jeffrey Anderson, review, *Winnipeg Free Press*, November 26, 1959.

11. S. Roy Maley, concert review, *Winnipeg Tribune*, November 26, 1959.

12. *L'Événement-Journal/Le Soleil*, Quebec City, December 12, 1961.

13. Everett Helms, report on visit to Winnipeg concert, *Music America*, April 11, 1963. Feldbrill fonds, 2005-031/ 015, Scrapbooks V, York University Archives, Toronto.

14. *Ibid.*

15. *Ibid.*

16. Sir Ernest MacMillan, Letter to R.W. Richards, Chair, Board of the WSO, December 20, 1965. Feldbrill fonds, 2005-031/001[08], York University Archives, Toronto.

17. Hugh Davidson, Letter to R.W. Richards, Chair, Board of the WSO, December 9, 1965. Feldbrill fonds, 2005-031/001 [08], York University Archives, Toronto.

18. James Manishen, *Arts Encounters*, Interview with Victor Feldbrill, CBC Radio 2, March 28, 2004.

19. James Manishen, review of WSO concert, *Winnipeg Free Press*, March 27, 2004.

Chapter 12

1. Victor Feldbrill, Interview, March 6, 2006.

2. Kenneth Winters, review, *Winnipeg Free Press*, January 8, 1965.

3. Thus began a partnership of enormous respect on the part of both Victor and Lea Foli. Ultimately, Foli was approached by a major American orchestra to become its concertmaster. A very warm farewell note from Foli has survived (n/d): "I want you to know how much I have valued my association over the past years. You have given me an example to follow in your ability and determination to see the best in your musicians. Your sense of humour and courage on the podium also have not escaped me. To you I am deeply grateful!"

4. Kenneth Winters, review, *Winnipeg Free Press*, December 3, 1965.

5. Victor Feldbrill, "Report of the Winnipeg Symphony Orchestra Board of Directors from the Music Director," November 1965. Feldbrill fonds, 2005-031/001 [08], York University Archives, Toronto.

6. Leonard Isaacs, Letter to Board Chair R.W. Richards, n/d. Feldbrill fonds, 2005-031/001 [08], York University Archives, Toronto. In his memoir, *Five Lives in One*, Isaacs recounts his outrage. He had been a member of the board of the WSO but left when "Victor Feldbrill had been winkled out of the Conductorship by the machinations of a small but influential group of Board Members (this caused my temporary withdrawal from the Board since I felt I was being involved in something I regarded as professionally disreputable)." Leonard Isaacs, *Five Lives in One* (Hubbards, NS: Good Cheer Publishing, 1998), 147.

7. Eric McLean, review, *Le Devoir*, Montreal, February 4, 1963.

8. Press Release, WSO, May 4, 1966. Feldbrill fonds, 2005-031/001 [08], York University Archives, Toronto.

9. *Ibid.*

10. S. Roy Maley, review, *Winnipeg Tribune*, January 4, 1963.

11. S. Roy Maley, review, *Winnipeg Tribune*, April 23, 1965.

12. Victor Feldbrill, Interview with the author, March 6, 2006.

13. The WSO Farewell Concert program, the account of Victor Feldbrill's achievements. Feldbrill fonds, 2005-031/016 [08], Scrapbooks II, York University Archives, Toronto.

Chapter 13

1. Kenneth Winters, review, *Winnipeg Free Press*, October 22, 1963. Feldbrill fonds, 2005-031/016, Scrapbooks II, York University Archives, Toronto.

2. John Fraser, review, *Globe and Mail*, Toronto, October 8, 1964, Victor Feldbrill fonds, 2005-031/016, Scrapbooks II, York University Archives, Toronto.

3. Chester Duncan, CBC *Arts National*, November 2. Feldbrill fonds, 2005-031/016, Scrapbooks II, York University Archives, Toronto.

4. Ezra Schabas and Carl Morey, *Opera Viva — The Canadian Opera Company: The First Fifty Years* (Toronto: Dundurn Press, 2000) 85–86.

5. Trisha Baldwin, manager, Tafelmusik Baroque Orchestra, Interview with author, Toronto, December 15, 2007.

6. John Kraglund, review, *Globe and Mail*, Toronto, September 29, 1975.

7. William Littler, *Toronto Star*, September 29, 1975.

8. Victor Feldbrill, Letter to Zelda Feldbrill, October 19, 1958. Feldbrill fonds, 2005-031/009 [06], York University Archives, Toronto.

9. Victor Feldbrill, Letter to Zelda Feldbrill, October 20, 1968. Feldbrill fonds, 2005-031/009 [06], York University Archives, Toronto.

10. Victor Feldbrill, Letter to Zelda Feldbrill, October 30, 1968. Feldbrill fonds, 2005-031/009 [06], York University Archives, Toronto.

11. *Ibid.*, Victor Feldbrill, Letter to Zelda Feldbrill, October 3, 1968.

12. *Ibid.*, Victor Feldbrill, Letter to Zelda Feldbrill, November 8, 1968.

13. *Ibid.*, Victor Feldbrill, Letter to Zelda Feldbrill, November 13, 1968.

14. *Ibid.*, Alfred Knopf, quoted by Victor Feldbrill in letter to Zelda Feldbrill, November 15, 1968.

15. Victor Feldbrill, Letter to Zelda Feldbrill, April 18, 1968. Feldbrill fonds, 2005-013 /007 [07], York University Archives, Toronto.

16. *Ibid.*, Victor Feldbrill, Letter to Zelda Feldbrill, November 26, 1968.

17. *Ibid.*

18. Victor Feldbrill, Letter to Zelda Feldbrill, April 23, 1969. Feldbrill fonds, 2005-031/007 [08], York University Archives, Toronto.

19. William Littler, review, *Toronto Star*, October 23, 1970.

20. Lorna Betts, review (no publication indicated), September 20, 1971. Feldbrill fonds, 2005, 031/007 [07], York University Archives, Toronto.

21. Leon Major, Interview with author, January 28, 2009.

22. Lawrence Cherney, Interview with author, March 26, 2009.

Chapter 14

1. John Beckwith, review (no date or publication). Feldbrill fonds, 2005-031/015, Scrapbooks IV, York University Archives, Toronto.

2. Eric McLean, *Montreal Star*, January 2, 1962.

3. G. Gordon Lennox, *Ottawa Journal,* January 4, 1962.
4. George Kidd, *Toronto Star,* n/d. Feldbrill fonds, 2005-031/015, Scrapbooks IV, York University Archives, Toronto.
5. John Kraglund, *Globe and Mail.* Feldbrill fonds, 2005-031/015, Scrapbooks IV, York University Archives, Toronto.
6. Z.H. Lampert, review, *St. Catharines Standard,* n/d. Feldbrill fonds, 2005-031/015, Scrapbooks IV, York University Archives, Toronto.

Chapter 15
1. William Littler, article, *Toronto Daily Star,* April 23, 1970.
2. Professor Lee Willingham, Interview with author, October 29, 2008. A Willingham project at the Scarborough Board was that of bringing the best wind players together for a concert under a distinguished conductor. Though it was a band rather than an orchestra, Victor was selected by Willingham because of his reputation and the quality of repertoire he would choose. The concert was a resounding success and "the students loved him."
3. William Littler, "A Tribute to Feldbrill in Students Performance," *Toronto Daily Star,* n/d. Feldbrill fonds, 2005-031/017 [1], York University Archives, Toronto.
4. Ron Hambleton, review, *Toronto Daily Star,* October 27, 1974.
5. Trish Baldwin, Interview with author, November 2007.
6. Victor Feldbrill, Interview, September 14, 2006. The subject of this biography does not believe that anti-Semitic tendencies had any part in his being passed over as the conductor of the TSO. Others to whom the author spoke were not as positive. Toronto's anti-Semitism was not overt and obvious. Even in the 1930s there had been few Nazi-armbands and fascist salutes. There was no second riot in Christie Pits. The author can remember viewing signs in tourist areas that read GENTILES ONLY and NO JEWS ALLOWED. Social organizations and distinguished men's clubs were known to restrict their membership to non-Jewish members. There seemed to be a record of prejudice against Jewish leadership in corporations and arts organizations even when participation and support from this community was valued and celebrated.
7. Rosemary Hazelton, Ph.D., Interview with author, October 17, 2008.
8. Dr. Esther Cole, Interview with author, October 21, 2008. Zelda conscientiously attended the annual personnel meetings at which social workers could indicate their preference for the schools in which they might like to work. Zelda wanted to stay in the Park Street School (later renamed Nelson Mandela School). This was her mission.

Esther Cole and Zelda became close, both devoted to the larger interests of their respective professions. The former became president of both the Ontario Association of Psychological Services and the Canadian Association of School Psychologists, as well as the head of the Psychological Foundation of Canada. Zelda eschewed such involvement in professional organizations, recognizing her essential role in supporting Victor's career, and never losing her focus on the families of students she was seeking to assist.

9. *Ibid.*

Chapter 16

1. Review of Quebec Symphony Orchestra concert, December 12, 1961. Feldbrill fonds, 2005-031/ 015, Scrapbooks V, York University Archives, Toronto.
2. Frances Goltman, review of concert in Montreal's *Gazette*, July 17, 1963. Feldbrill fonds, 2005-031/010 [1], York University Archives, Toronto.
3. Joseph Siskind, review of NACO concert, *Ottawa Citizen*, April 19, 1990.
4. Victor Feldbrill, Interview with author, September 14, 2006.
5. *Ibid.* Years later Skazunetsky's son was to emigrate and eventually found himself in the string section of the TSO. He regaled his new colleagues with flattering stories of how his father and his colleagues had enjoyed Victor's visit to the Soviet Union in 1963.
6. *Ibid.* Victor also had as his "music that traveled well" for this particular visit: John Weinzweig's *Symphonic Ode*, Harry Freedman's *Images*, Harry Somers' *Passacaglia and Fugue*, and Pierre Mercure's *Kaleidoscope* were rehearsed and regularly performed.
7. Victor Feldbrill, Letter to Zelda Feldbrill, April 16, 1963. Feldbrill fonds, 2005-031/ 009 [01], York University Archives, Toronto.
8. Victor Feldbrill, Interview with author, September 14, 2006.
9. *Ibid.*
10. Victor Feldbrill, Letter to Zelda Feldbrill, April 24, 1963. Feldbrill fonds, 2005-031/009 [01], York University Archives, Toronto.
11. Victor Feldbrill, Letter to Zelda Feldbrill, May 5, 1963. Feldbrill fonds, 2005-031/009 [01], York University Archives, Toronto.
12. Victor Feldbrill, Letter to Zelda Feldbrill, December 20, 1966. Feldbrill fonds, 2005-001/009 [5], York University Archives, Toronto.
13. Victor Feldbrill, Letter to Zelda Feldbrill, December 23, 1966. Feldbrill fonds, 2005-001/009 [5], York University Archives, Toronto.

Chapter 17

1. Victor Feldbrill, Letter to Zelda Feldbrill, May 5, 1979. Feldbrill fonds, 2005-031/009 [14], York University Archives, Toronto.
2. Victor Feldbrill, Letter to Zelda Feldbrill, May 9. 1979. Feldbrill fonds, 2005-031/009 [14], York University Archives, Toronto.
3. *Ibid.*

4. Victor Feldbrill, Letter to Zelda Feldbrill, May 19, 1979. Feldbrill fonds, 2005-031/009 [14], York University Archives, Toronto.

5. Victor Feldbrill, Letter to Zelda Feldbrill, May 26, 1979. Feldbrill fonds, 2005-031/004 [14], York University Archives, Toronto.

6. Victor Feldbrill, Letter to Zelda Feldbrill, May 31, 1979. Feldbrill fonds, 2005-031/004 [14], York University Archives, Toronto.

7. *Ibid.*

8. Victor Feldbrill, Letter to Zelda Feldbrill, May 9, 1981. Feldbrill fonds, 2005-031/009 [15], York University Archives, Toronto.

9. Victor Feldbrill, Letter to Zelda Feldbrill, April 13, 1982. Feldbrill fonds, 2005-031/009 [16], York University Archives, Toronto.

10. Victor Feldbrill, Letter to Zelda Feldbrill, May 8, 1982. Feldbrill fonds, 2005-031/009 [16], York University Archives, Toronto.

Chapter 18

1. Victor Feldbrill, quoted in article, "A Canadian in Tokyo," *Globe and Mail*, September 7, 1981.

2. Victor Feldbrill, Interview with author, September 21, 2006.

3. R.P. Archambault, External Affairs Memorandum, June 12, 1979. Feldbrill fonds, 2005-031/031 [13], York University Archives, Toronto.

4. Ron Hambleton, review, *Toronto Daily Star*, April 5, 1982.

5. Arthur Kaptanis, review, *Globe and Mail*, April 5, 1982.

6. Victor Feldbrill, Letter to Zelda Feldbrill, May 17, 1982. Feldbrill fonds, 2005-031/009 [16], York University Archives, Toronto.

7. Victor Feldbrill, Letter to Zelda, June 18, 1982. Feldbrill fonds, 2005-031/009 [16], York University Archives, Toronto.

8. Victor Feldbrill, Letter to Zelda Feldbrill, May 23, 1982. Feldbrill fonds, 2005-031/009 [16], York University Archives, Toronto.

9. Victor Feldbrill, Letter to Zelda Feldbrill, September 15, 1982. Feldbrill fonds, 2005-031/009 [17], York University Archives, Toronto.

10. Victor Feldbrill, Letter to Zelda Feldbrill, September 9, 1982. Feldbrill fonds, 2005-031/009 [17], York University Archives, Toronto.

11. A.D. Gibson, "Canadian Maestro to Conduct the Ninth 8 Times in 6 Weeks," *Asaki Evening News*, December 20, 1983.

12. Rosalindah Orossa, review, *Manila Daily Express*, n.d. Feldbrill fonds, 2005-031/009 [17], York University Archives, Toronto.

13. Arthur Kaptanis, *The Canadian Composer*, Toronto, March 1984.

14. Arthur Kardonne, article, *Lifestyles* Magazine, Toronto, March 1984.

15. Ambassador Barry Connell Steers, on the bestowing of the Order of Canada, 1984. Feldbrill fonds, 2005-031/004 [5], York University Archives, Toronto.

16. Article in May 1985 issue of *Bravo*, the publication of Roy Thomson Hall. The names of the nominating committee were most impressive. As well as the chair, Nancy Westaway, there was prolific arts columnist Arnold Edinborough, honoured composer and choral musician Derek Holman (a legend as cultural and educational leader), the Honourable Pauline McGibbon, former lieutenant-governor of Ontario, and Geoff Butler, a notable arts administrator.

17. Arthur Kaptanis, review, *Globe and Mail*, Toronto, January 7, 1985.

18. Marcel Grilli, review, *The Japan Times*, June 6, 1982. Feldbrill fonds, 2005-031/005 [1], York University Archives, Toronto.

19. *Ibid.*

20. *Ibid.*

21. Ryuichi Shibato, review of April 1989 concert, *Ongahn no Tomo*. Feldbrill fonds, 2005-031/005 [1], York University Archives, Toronto.

22. M. Uno, review of Tokyo Philharmonic concert, September 1980. Feldbrill fonds, 2005-031/005 [1], York University Archives, Toronto. This critique of Victor's conducting leads one to realize that the most difficult element of his role in Japan to quantify is that of his instruction and mentoring of potential conductors. There are dozens of individuals conducting choirs and orchestras in schools, colleges, and universities whose skill and effective work can be traced back to Victor's teaching at Tokyo University.

There are even Japanese conductors who credit Victor with having much to do with their success on the international stage. One example will suffice. Kazushi Ono was a student of Victor's. He is now the principal conductor of Opera Lyon, a position he assumed in 2008 after six seasons as the musical director of the Royal Opera House of Belgium. His reputation as a conductor of new productions and old favourites and his commitment to world premieres of contemporary operas make him a leading figure in major opera houses around the world, including the Metropolitan Opera in New York. As well, he has appeared with some of the foremost orchestral ensembles, including the Leipzig Gewandhaus, the Israel Philharmonic, and the City of Birmingham Symphony Orchestra, as well as a host of major radio symphony orchestras.

When Victor's companion, Mae Bernstein, questioned Kazushi over dinner about what Victor's major contribution to his outstanding success had been, he responded with no hesitation. "It was Victor who began his conducting class with a simple statement. 'You have conducting technique in hand — I'm going to concentrate on the challenge of searching out the meaning of music and your commitment to the composer's creativity and inspiration.' I have never looked back since that moment," was Kazushi's analysis of his incredible career and Victor's role in the enhancement of it.

Chapter 19

1. Lorraine LePage, review, May 5, 1980, *St. Catharines Standard*. Feldbrill fonds, 2005-031/017, Scrapbooks I, York University Archives, Toronto.

2. Richard Newman, review, *London Free Press*, April 21, 1980.

3. Richard Newman, article, *London Free Press*, December 15, 1979.

4. There is no mystery behind the fact that the most respected and quoted experts in motivational leadership in the private sector, industrial and commercial, identify the reality of collective will that produces great music as the model for the so-called real world of business. There are few more comparable areas of creativity that demonstrate more dramatically the possibility of synergic relationships that simultaneously contain both collective direction and an individual sense of creative achievement. It was this balance that Victor brought to an orchestral world of fractured relationships leading to chaos and the silence that represented total failure.

5. Adrian Chamberlain, review, *Victoria Times-Colonist*, October 23, 1988.

6. *Ibid.*

7. Stephen Pedersen, "Conductor Feldbrill Shares Talent with Students," *Halifax Chronicle-Herald*, March 5, 1992. Feldbrill fonds, 2005-031/005 [1], York University Archives, Toronto.

8. Welmer Biernaan, review, *St. John's Record*, March 14, 1992.

9. Sara Kennedy, review of NACO concert, *Fredericton Daily Gleaner*, March 16, 1992.

10. Evelyn Greenberg, Email to author, March 4, 2009.

11. Evelyn Greenberg, Interview with author, March 3, 2009.

12. Hugh Fraser, article, *Hamilton Spectator*, October 24, 1990. Feldbrill fonds, 2005-031/019 [01], Scrapbooks I, York University Archive, Toronto.

13. Hugh Fraser, review of the *Messiah*, *Hamilton Spectator*, December 10, 1990. Feldbrill fonds, 2005-0321/019 [01], Scrapbooks I, York University Archives, Toronto.

14. Hugh Fraser, article, *Hamilton Spectator*, March 30, 1991.

15. Hugh Fraser, review, *Hamilton Spectator*, May 31, 1991. Feldbrill fonds, 2005-031/019 [01], Scrapbooks I, York University Archives, Toronto.

16. *Ibid.*, June 6, 1991[14].

17. Nancy Nelson, Interview with author, March 5, 2009.

18. Colleen Johnston, *Kitchener-Waterloo Record*, September 30, 1991.

19. Hugh Fraser, reviewer in the *Hamilton Spectator*, about a HPO performance of Brahms, was led to comment, "And I simply will not hear any more that Feldbrill is a 'dull' conductor. If Feldbrill is dull, then Brahms is dull … and we got pure Brahms."

20. Victor Feldbrill, Interview with the author, May 14, 2007.

21. *Ibid.* The 1990s brought a new genre of music to Victor's attention. A new venture had been launched in Toronto — the operetta performed by a professional company. The presence of a fine conductor was a major coup in securing the quality that was desired.

    Victor was quite aware of the contrasts in style and purpose behind the operetta and more serious forms of music theatre (no doubt reminding himself that his conducting had started in Harbord Collegiate auditorium with Gilbert and Sullivan). In this case he had to cope with Inire Kalman's *Countess Maritza*. It was a singular experience but not without recognition. Richard Ouzunian, the *Toronto Star* reviewer, accorded that "well-known Victor Feldbrill had led a secure orchestra with assurance ... this will be his first venture into the land of operetta and probably the last possible area of musical endeavour into which he hasn't ventured."

22. Ruth Budd, Interview with author, October 5, 2008.

Chapter 20

1. Walter and Emmy Homburger, note to Victor and Zelda Feldbrill. Feldbrill fonds, 2005- 031/018 [02], York University Archives, Toronto.
2. James Ehnes, Email to author, August 19, 2009.
3. Ann Cooper Gay, Interview with Ann and Errol Gay, December 5, 2008.
4. Lawrence Cherney, Interview, March 26, 2009. Victor has played an important role in making young people realize the contrast in the youth orchestra experience and that facing the professional orchestral musician. After an eruption of self-adulation by some youth players, he pointed out to them that they would have several full days to prepare a major work that the professional musicians as an ensemble must conquer in a few short hours. The reminder had a salutary impact on young players too soon convinced of their preparedness for professional work.
5. Victor and Lori Davies, Interview, April 3, 2009.
6. James Manishen, Interview, December 3, 2008.
7. Roxalana Roslak, Interview, May 6, 2009.
8. Gwen Thompson, Interview, May 6, 2009.
9. Johnny Cowell, Interview, May 2, 2009.
10. Stanley Solomon, Interview, April 8, 2009
11. Peggy Dettwiller, Email to author, January 25, 2009.
12. Stella Sung, Email to author, June 7, 2007. Stella Sung is professor of music in the University of Central Florida's Centre for Research and Education in Arts, Technology and Entertainment, and is an American composer of national and international stature. She has received awards from the National Endowment of the Arts and the American Society of Authors, Composers,

and Publishers. In her response she could not restrain herself from stating unequivocally that Victor "is really a wonderful person, musician, friend, mentor and much beloved by so many. I know that he has done so much to further the work of Canadian composers especially, and this is quite amazing ... they should be thankful that they had someone like Victor who was willing to take chances to further the art form."

13. In place of the judgmental element that tends to dominate in competitions for young musicians, Victor's legacy tends in the direction of encouragement. This fact is revealed in the number of awards and scholarships for young people that have been established in his name. Since his time in Winnipeg, a Victor Feldbrill Trophy for the finest violin contestant has been awarded at the Manitoba Music Festival each year. His association with the Faculty of Music at the University of Toronto resulted in a scholarship for fine string players and, as well, a conducting fellowship. The volunteers of the TSO have given a Victor Feldbrill Piano Competition Award for the best performance of a Canadian work. In the 1990s, the University of Toronto Symphony Youth Orchestra established the Victor Scholarship. The fund to support its work was initiated by Victor himself who took no fee for the conducting of the concert at which the award was established.

INDEX

Adaskin, Murray, 163
Agostini, Lucio, 166
Aitken, Robert, 238, 384
Alexander, Andrea, 274
Alexander, Honorable Lincoln, 387
Ancerl, Karel, 299–300, 328
Anderson, Jeffrey, 208, 210, 257
Anderson, Judy, 291
Anti-Semitism, 17–18, 36–38, 59, 97–98, 300, 321, 416
Applebaum, Lou, 39, 49, 211, 277, 315, 362–63, 374, 384

Archer, Violet, 163

Babiak, Elsie, 48
Baldwin, Trish, 253–54, 296
Bales, Gerald, 215
Barbirolli, John, 76, 78
Barker, Derek, 366
Barone, Joseph, 156
Baxter, Beverley, 72
Beaver, Martin, 371, 384
Beckwith, John, 209, 279, 294
Beer, Sydney, 85

Beecham, Sir Thomas, 76, 81, 85, 106, 107–08, 194

Bell, Leslie, 47

Benny, Jack, 95

Benson, Eugene, 263

Berlin, Boris, 140

Bernardi, Mario, 362

Bernstein, Leonard, 151, 153, 240

Bernstein, Mae P., 198, 296, 379, 393

Bettes, Lorna, 263

Binder, A.J., 118

Böhm, Karl, 161–62

Boost, Wim, 97, 99, 262

Boult, Sir Adrian, 48, 78, 81–82, 105–07, 151, 240, 257, 311

Bourgeault, Pat, 205

Bradshaw, Richard, 262, 266

Brailowsky, Alexander, 214

Braithwaite, Warwick, 77–78

Braun, Russell, 384

Brethour, Eldon, 23, 31

Bridle, Augustus, 51, 137, 141

Brott, Boris, 368–70

Budd, Kevin, 378

Budd, Ruth, 376–79

Buhr, Glenn, 212

Cable, Howard, 49, 371–72

Callwood, June, 351

Canadian Broadcast Corporation (CBC), 29, 47, 49, 71, 86, 142–44, 145, 150, 157, 160, 163, 166–72, 176, 190, 193, 204, 211, 214–15, 219, 220, 237, 249, 254, 255, 266, 310, 311, 337, 338, 366, 379–80

Canadian Opera Company (COC), 139, 245, 250–52, 254, 262, 264–66, 277, 383, 393

CBC school broadcasts, 271, 310

CBC Symphony Orchestra (CBCSO), 150, 158, 166, 170, 176, 183, 322

CBC Winnipeg Orchestra, 168–69, 178, 185

Chalmers, Floyd, 386

Chalmers, Jean, 386

Chamberlain, Adrian, 360–61

Chappell, Dr. Stanley, 153

Cherney, Lawrence, 266, 396

China, 17, 348, 349, 355

Christopherson, Walter, 279

Ciamaga, Gus, 344

Cohen, Eileen (*see* Eileen Feldbrill)

Cold War, 104, 317, 326

Cole, Esther, 307–08

Concertgebouw, 101–02, 103, 131, 225

Conservatory Opera School, 132, 150, 249, 276

Coop, Jane, 375

Co-operative Commonwealth Federation (CCF), 124–26, 410

Copland, Aaron, 151, 153, 226, 240

Corbett, Ted, 118

Cowell, Johnny, 398

Cox, David, 158

Crum George, 140

Davidson, Hugh, 218

Davies, Robertson, 254

Davies, Victor, 397–98

Davis, Andrew, 304, 428, 385

Davis, Honorable William, 351

Day, Marie, 253

Dettweiler, Peggy, 401–02

Dolin, Samuel, 184

Domb, Daniel, 304

Donatell, Mark, 373

Douglas, Tommy, 124–25, 224

Downes, Edward, 263

Drainie, John, 271
Drew, Honorable George, 125–27
Duncan, Chester, 251

Ebert, Peter, 261
Eckhardt-Gramatté, Madame S.C., 228
Ehnes, James, 388
Elton, Jack, 52, 190
Endo, Professor Masahisa, 333, 353
Entrement, Phillippe, 216
Evans, Glynn, 375, 384

Faculty of Music, 50, 130, 175, 249, 283, 329, 383, 400
Fallis, Mary Lou, 45
Farnon, Robert, 93, 240
Feldbrill, Alex, 20
Feldbrill, Aviva, 162, 181, 197–98, 201, 257, 268, 282–84, 329, 336, 393
Feldbrill, Debbi, 148, 162, 181, 197–08, 257, 268, 282–84, 329, 393
Feldbrill (Cohen), Eileen, 117, 120, 170, 179–80, 256–57
Feldbrill (Lederman), Helen, 19, 21–25
Feldbrill, Irving, 11, 26
Feldbrill, Jack, 20
Feldbrill, Nathan, 19, 20, 21–25, 58
Feldbrill, Ruth, 23–24, 120, 180
Feldbrill (Feldman) Sam, 20
Feldbrill, Victor
    ancestry and birth, 16–21
    awards and distinctions, 236, 238, 256–57, 258, 268, 288, 331–32, 351–52, 368, 400, 419, 422
    career choices, 22, 54, 65, 66, 67, 75–76, 132, 135, 150, 157, 162–63, 165, 166, 176, 179, 181, 182, 236, 241, 246–48, 261, 270, 282–84, 286–87,
311–12, 337–39, 348, 392
    childhood, 21–33 *passim*, 37, 148
    collecting scores, 49, 79–81, 84, 94, 102, 153
    conducting style, 38, 67, 77, 139–40, 146–47, 163, 173, 193–95, 265, 274, 313, 321, 323, 351, 373, 397–98
    early education, 23, 25–27, 30, 31, 34, 35, 37
    fatherhood, 163, 202, 282–84, 393
    leadership, 39, 86, 144, 145, 161, 167, 168, 191, 193, 231, 247, 252, 273, 296, 298–99, 323–24, 328–30, 354, 364, 367, 403
    love of art, literature, and film, 45, 86, 101, 111–12, 113–14
    love of music, 28, 276, 325, 392, 398
    marriage, 45, 115, 117–18, 121, 127, 179
    opera, 107, 139, 153, 160–61, 176–77, 245–66 *passim*, 283, 310, 374–75
    radio career, 29, 49, 71, 100, 106, 123, 157–58, 160, 166–68, 172, 179, 190, 271, 310, 331, 337, 356, 419
    reaction to negative reviews, 210–11, 229, 291, 302
    relationship with Zelda, 22, 44–45, 53, 104–05, 110–15, 121, 124, 283, 338, 391–93
    religious life, 37–38, 100–01, 112–13, 117, 148, 394, 410
    retirement, 12, 296, 323, 379
    separation from family, 64, 70–71, 100–01, 109–10, 112, 117, 124, 157, 163, 180, 198, 263,

283–84, 312, 324–25, 336, 337–39, 348, 397

support of Canadian composers, 12, 136, 142, 172–73, 199, 211–13, 217, 238, 252, 257, 311, 322, 387

support of symphony players, 229–30

television career, 29, 215, 310, 337

tours and touring, 83–85, 178–79, 187, 190, 205, 210, 222–24, 231, 238–40, 245, 250, 281–82, 299, 302–04, 309–10, 316, 318–19, 321–26, 368

travel, 199, 241, 257–58, 275, 310–11, 312, 315–16, 342

violin, 10, 26–29, 31–32, 35, 49, 52–55, 62, 64, 67, 76, 78, 93, 113, 118, 131–37, 151, 153, 166, 201, 248, 265, 422

work with youth, 11, 46, 138, 149, 167, 177, 190, 204, 227, 236, 247, 268–73, 280, 282, 296–98, 302, 327, 332, 334, 341, 382, 395, 422

Feldbrill (Mann), Zelda, 43–47, 53–54, 68–69, 92, 99–101, 104, 107–08, 109–28, 130, 133, 148, 157, 179, 189, 198–200, 261–62, 282–83, 305–08, 312, 323–24, 329, 336–37, 342, 368, 390–93

Feldstein, Carol Ann, 377

Field (Feldbrill), Irving, 19

Findley, Timothy, 352

First World War, 17, 20, 48, 58, 76, 90, 97

Fleisher, Leon, 154

Flichman, Yuval, 389

Foli, Lea, 230, 250

Forrester, Maureen, 384

Frankenstein, Alfred, 212

Fraser, Hugh, 368, 370–72, 375–76

Fraser, John, 234, 250

Freedman, Harry, 294

Fukui, Professor Iwao, 330–31

Galway, James, 358

Gay, Ann Cooper, 395

Geiger-Torel, Hermann, 250, 266

Geldbloom, Gerald, 32

Gerbrecht, Jerold, 394

Gibbs, Terence, 143, 166

Gibson, A.D., 347

Glick, Srul Irving, 238–39, 389

Gold, Evelyn, 48

Goldovsky, Boris, 153

Goldschmidt, Nicholas, 132–33, 139, 249, 256, 274

Goltman, Frances, 316

Goodman, Hyman, 137, 174

Gould, Glenn, 140, 170, 201, 208, 215, 318

Greenberg, Evelyn, 367

Grilli, Marcel, 353–54

Gruber, Hans, 119, 132

Guy, Elizabeth Benson, 139

Hagen, Betty-Jean, 144, 195

Haig, Alistair, 40, 42

Hambleton, Ron, 292, 344

Hamburg, Klemi, 141

Hamilton Philharmonic Orchestra (HPO), 368, 369, 371, 374, 388–89, 394

Harnoy, Ofra, 389

Harris, Neil, 220

Hazelton, Rosemary, 307

Heinz, Sir Bernard, 314

Helms, Everett, 216–18

Herford, Julius, 194

Hersenhorn, Samuel, 166
Homburger, Walter, 268–69,293–94, 298–99, 303, 328, 339, 385–86, 388
Hough, Stephen, 356
Howells, Herbert, 82–83, 84, 86–87, 105, 240
Hunter, James, 135
Hurst, George, 140
Hurwitz, Dr. Harry, 400–01

Ireland, Francis, 52–53
Isaacs, Leonard, 236
Iseler, Elmer, 384–85
Iwasaki, Professor Yohzo, 330

Janis, Byron, 280
Japan, 11, 313, 327–39 *passim*, 340, 341–48, 350, 352, 353, 355, 405, 419
Jennings, Sarah, 300
Joachim, Eugen, 346
Johnston, Colleen, 374
Johnston, Ernest, 53
Joliffe, Mary, 352
Joliffe, Ted, 125
Jones, Alan, 330–31
Judaism, Jewish settlement in Canada, 10, 16–21, 23, 35, 36, 44–45, 58

Kahane, Geoffrey, 317
Kander, Gerhard, 154
Kaptanis, Arthur, 345, 349–50, 352
Kardone, Rick, 350–55
Kasemets, Udo, 209
Kaufman, Walter, 169, 178, 184
Kernerman, Morry, 32, 53, 135, 149
Kidd, George, 168, 171, 173, 175, 206–07, 281
King, Mackenzie, 68, 126

Knopf, Alfred, 261
Knowles, Stanley, 224
Kolomyjec, Joanne, 371
Kord, Kazimierz, 303
Koussevitzky, Serge, 151
Kraglund, John, 170–73, 175, 177, 183, 195, 207, 209, 214, 254, 265, 281, 291
Kraus, Greta, 383
Krehm, William, 144, 174, 176, 207
Kris, Wilbur, 155
Kuit, Sjert, 96

Lambert, Rex, 271
Lamon, Jeanne, 296
Lampert, Z.H., 281
Landry, Rosemary, 375, 384
Langford, Marion, 274
Languirand, Jacques, 253
Laufer, Murray, 253
Lawson, John, 399
Lechow, Ross, 67–68
Leinsdorf, Eric, 124
Lennox, G. Gordon, 280
Lepage, Lorraine, 357
Levinter, Molly, 48
Lismer, Arthur, 32
Littler, William, 254, 263, 287–88, 292, 298, 385
Lortie, Louis, 366–67, 385
Louis Riel (opera), 251–66 *passim*, 283, 296, 386, 395, 398
Lund, Alan, 63
Lund, Blanche, 63

Ma, YoYo, 358, 367, 384
Macdonald, Rose, 137, 142
MacMillan, Andrew, 139
MacMillan, Sir Ernest, 46–48, 51–52, 68–69, 126, 131–32, 137–78,

157, 189–90, 217–18

MacNamara, Helen, 178

Mair, John, 135

Maley, S. Roy, 179, 194–95, 203–04, 207–09, 213, 241–43

Major, Leon, 253, 264

Manishen, James, 219, 398

Manitoba Opera Association (MOA), 251

Mann, Zelda (*see* Zelda Feldbrill)

Mansouri, Lotfi, 266

Margison, Richard, 370

Marshall, Lois, 207, 384

Mazzoleni, Ettore, 46–48,131–32,141, 175, 249, 256, 407

McCarthy, Pearl, 173

McCarthyism, 390

McClintock, Ellis, 49

McCool, Brian, 40–43

McLean, Eric, 237, 279

Meet the Navy (or *The Navy Show*), 48, 57–72 *passim*, 73–76, 79–80, 83, 85–86, 90, 93–95, 99–101, 104, 108, 113, 115–16, 123, 134, 179, 248, 312

Meet the Navy (film), 64, 104–05, 107, 127

Menachovsky, Esther, 44–45, 130

Menachovsky, Morris, 44–45, 117–18, 130

Mengelberg, Maestro Willem, 101

Milkis, Yascha, 377

Mills, Jane, 290–91

Moderna, Bruno, 260

Monteux, Pierre, 154–56, 189

Moore, Mavor, 253, 374

Morrison, Mary, 139, 238

Moseivitch, Benno, 85

Moss, Earl, 135

Murphy, Ken, 363

National Youth Orchestra (NYO), 276, 279, 280–82, 294, 315, 328, 396, 398

Navy Show (see *Meet the Navy*)

Neel, Boyd, 190

Nelson, Nancy, 373

Nelsova, Zara, 384

New York Philharmonic, 71, 154, 216, 287, 353

Newman, Richard, 357

Newman, Sydney, 80

Nystedt, Knut, 136

Oistrahk, Igor, 320

Oliphant, Betty, 351

Olver, Michael, 183

Orff, Carl, 160

Orossa, Rosalindah, 348

Oxley, Mary, 135

Ozawa, Seiji, 384

Ozolins, Arthur, 384

Palmason, Pearl, 377

Palmer, Ed, 167

Parlow, Kathleen, 133–35

Parr, Patricia, 171

Pearson, Honorable Lester, 361–62

Pedersen, Stephen, 366

Pelletier, Honorable Gerard, 260

Pelletier, Wilfred, 278–79

Penderecki, Krzysztof, 333

Pentland, Barbara, 205, 210

Pépin, Clermont, 140

Perrin, Harvey, 30–31

Peters, Randolph, 254

Petersen, Len, 271

Peugnet, Jean, 78

Pinnock, Trevor, 367

Polio epidemic, 38

Pops (pops) concerts, 48, 138, 150,

165, 170, 173–77

Pratt, John, 63–64

Prévost, André, 352

Primrose, William, 68

Promenade Symphony Concerts, 29, 53, 54, 165, 168, 171, 173, 407, 412

Queen Elizabeth, 206

Quilico, Louis, 315

Rasky, Frank, 199

Read, Ernest, 105–08

Reaney, James, 266

Reeves, John, 166

Relyea, Gary, 370, 375, 384

Richards, R.W., 236

Richardson, Bill, 204

Ridout, Godfrey, 49, 386–87

Robbin, Catherine, 384

Rose, Leonard, 213, 250, 357

Rosevear, Robert, 383

Roslak, Roxalana, 398

Rowland, Jane, 183

Roy, Janet, 169

Roy, Louise, 139

Royal Conservatory of Music, the, 47, 50, 130, 131, 133, 136–37, 170, 175, 249, 383, 384, 400

Royal Conservatory Orchestra, 48, 54, 132, 141, 150, 165, 276

Royal Winnipeg Ballet, 207, 223

Russia (*see also* Soviet Union), 44, 55, 59, 73, 148, 224, 319, 322

Saunders, Val, 302

Schabas, Ezra, 255, 302

Schafer, Paul, 213

Scherman, Paul, 176

Schonberg, Harold, 254, 265

Searle, Humphrey, 255, 258

Second World War, 17–18, 42, 58, 73, 99, 109–10, 381

Shaw, Robert, 152–53

Shulman, Nora, 304

Shuster, Frank, 40

Siegel, Harvey, 32

Silverman, Robert, 371

Simmons, Mary, 214

Siskind, Joseph, 317

Sloan, John, 331, 336

Smith, Leo, 168

Solomon, Stanley, 377, 399

Somers, Harry, 136–37, 158, 170, 176, 245–46, 252, 254, 266, 331, 387

Southam, Hamilton, 361–64

Souverain, Pierre, 383

Soviet Union (*see also* Russia), 60, 91, 125, 185, 225, 241, 313, 318–26

Spivak, Eli, 30

Staryk, Steven, 384

Steel, Darrell, 378

Stein, Erwin, 84

Steinberg, Sigmund, 29, 133

Stern, Isaac, 234, 394–97

Stevens, Ruth, 393

Stone, Leonard David, 231

Stubbs, Janet, 384, 395

Sumberg, Harold, 352

Susskind, Walter, 157, 183, 277

Sweeney, Gordon, 304

Symonds, Norman, 177

Tedd, Emily, 23

Thompson, Gwen, 398

Thomson, Hugh, 172

Tokyo, 330–38, 342, 343–45, 350, 353

Toronto Conservatory of Music (*see* Royal Conservatory of Music)

Toronto Mendelssohn Choir, 46, 384, 389

Toronto Symphony Orchestra (TSO), 10, 46, 47, 52, 68, 82, 112, 132, 138, 144, 149, 157, 166, 190, 206, 209, 214, 223, 270, 273–74, 282–83, 289, 294, 295, 298–301, 303–04, 328, 329, 333, 338, 362, 377, 385–89

Toronto Symphony Orchestra Women's Committee, 46, 53, 110, 138

Toronto Symphony Youth Orchestra (TSYO), 293, 295, 298, 328–29, 390

Toscanini, Arturo, 71, 79–80

Tovey, Bramwell, 212

Turgeon, Bernard, 386

University of Toronto Symphony Orchestra (UTSO), 50, 52, 82, 119, 263, 283, 289, 291, 293, 344

Uno, M., 354, 419

Valleau, Douglas, 137

Van Beinum, Eduard, 102–03

Van Otterloo, Willem, 159–60

Vickers, Jon, 384

Vienna, 161, 163, 176, 199, 262

Vienna Philharmonic, 161, 332

Von Zallinger, Meinhard, 161–62, 177, 249, 260–61, 263

Waddington, Geoffrey, 166, 168, 189, 271

Walter, Arnold, 255

"The Ward," 10, 18, 21, 22

Wardrop, Pat, 148

Watson, Joan, 382–83

Wayne, Johnny, 40

Weinzweig, John, 39–41, 49, 50, 163, 184, 227, 294, 323, 383, 386

Weldon, George, 81,107

Westaway, James, 293, 304

Westaway, Nancy, 352, 394

Whitton, Donald, 136

Wild, Eric, 63, 168, 207

Williams, Margaret, 31

Willingham, Lee, 288–89

Wilson, Charles, 263

Winnipeg, 19, 44, 168, 178, 184, 185, 187, 188–89, 193, 200, 213–13, 216, 219–20, 222–24, 226, 231–32, 240, 244

Winnipeg Symphony Orchestra (WSO), 169, 170–71, 184–85, 189–96 *passim*, 202–210 *passim*, 213, 216–18, 222–23, 229–30, 233–35, 239, 243, 250, 270, 273, 302, 316

Winters, Kenneth, 179, 194–95, 203–04, 208, 210, 229, 233, 242, 250–51

Wodson, Edward, 39

Wordsworth, J.S., 224

Worthington, Peter, 189

Zafer, David, 390

ALSO BY WALTER PITMAN

Elmer Iseler

Choral Visionary

978-1-55002-815-7 $40.00

In a career that spanned five decades, Elmer Iseler proved himself pivotal to the development of choral music in Canada. After founding Canada's first professional choir in 1954, he became artistic director and conductor of the Toronto Mendelssohn Choir. In 1979 he established Canada's leading chamber choir, the Elmer Iseler Singers. He also enjoyed a long association with the Toronto Symphony Orchestra, conducting more than 150 performances of Handel's *Messiah* and premiering complex twentieth-century music.

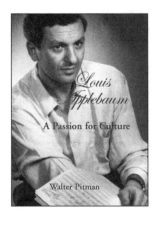

Louis Applebaum

A Passion for Culture

978-1-55002-398-5 $39.99

Canadian composer Louis Applebaum devoted his life to the cultural awakening of his native land, and this "magnificent obsession" drove him to become a founder of the Canadian League of Composers and the Canadian Music Centre. He was an instrumental figure in the early development of the National Film Board, the Stratford Festival, and the National Art Centre in Ottawa. For nearly half a century he composed music for the Stratford Festival, television, radio, and films. This illustrated biography explores the man who was beloved by his fellow artists and the icon to whom every Canadian, knowingly or not, is indebted.

Music Makers
The Lives of Harry Freedman and Mary Morrison
978-1-55002-589-7 $40.00

Music Makers examines and celebrates the extraordinary lives of composer Harry Freedman and his partner, soloist Mary Morrison. Harry, with roots in jazz and popular music, was a member of the Toronto Symphony Orchestra for twenty-five years. Canada's Composer of the Year in 1979, he has written an enormous repertoire that celebrates Canada and is sung and played around the world. After a stellar career in Canada as a popular singer and opera diva, Mary became an esteemed exponent of Canadian vocal works. She was a prestigious mentor and teacher of young Canadians, and received the League of Composers' Music Citation in 1968 and won Canada's major award as Opera Educator in 2002.

Available at your favourite bookseller.

 **DUNDURN PRESS**
www.dundurn.com

What did you think of this book?
Visit www.dundurn.com for reviews, videos, updates, and more!